UNHOLY ALLIANCE

UNHOLY ALLIANCE

A History of Nazi Involvement with the Occult

Second Edition

Peter Levenda

With a Foreword by Norman Mailer

CONTINUUM
New York • London

2002

The Continuum International Publishing Group Inc
370 Lexington Avenue, New York, NY 10017

The Continuum International Publishing Group Ltd
The Tower Building, 11 York Road, London SE1 7NX

Printed in the United States of America

Library of Congress Cataloging-in-Publication Data

Levenda, Peter.
   A history of nazi involvement with the occult / Peter Levenda ; with a
foreword by Norman Mailer.—2nd ed.
      p.   cm.
Includes bibliographical references and index.
   ISBN 0-8264-1409-5 (pbk.)
   1. National socialism and occultism.   2. Occultism—Germany—History.
   3. Germany—Politics and government—1933–1945.   4. Mythology,
Germanic.   5. Secret societies—Germany.   I. Title.
DD256.5 .L49   2002
133'.0943'09043—dc21

                                                            2002001447

To Rose and Vivica ("Alex"),
in lieu of the Citadel

Contents

Foreword to the Second Edition by Norman Mailer   1
Preface to the Second Edition   5
Introduction: At the Mountains of Madness   13

PART ONE   THE BY-PATHS TO CHAOS

One	Of Blood, Sex, and the Rune Magicians	29
Two	Volk Magic	55
Three	The Occult Messiah	80
Four	The Order of the Temple of the East: Sex, Spies, and Secret Societies	108
Five	Cult War 1934–1939	141

PART TWO   THE BLACK ORDER

Six	The Dangerous Element: The Ahnenerbe and the Cult of the SS	167
Seven	Lucifer's Quest for the Holy Grail	203
Eight	The Psychics Search: For Mussolini, the *Bismarck*, Assassins, and the Human Mind	225
Nine	Cult Counterstrike	240

PART THREE   WITCHES' SABBATH IN AMERICA

Ten	*Walpurgisnacht*, 1945	261
Eleven	Aftermath	280
Twelve	Is Chile Burning? The Overthrow of Allende, the Murder of Letelier, and the Role of Colonia Dignidad	309
Thirteen	Nazi Occultism Today	327

Epilogue: *Hasta La Vista,* Baby   354
Notes   367
Bibliography   389
Acknowledgments   399
Index   403

Foreword to the Second Edition

U*nholy Alliance* is a stimulating book to read for anyone interested in Nazism, magic, the penetralia of history, the cults of the occult, and the present agonizing anxiety of our lives. It is as if something larger than our educations, our sense of good and evil, our lives themselves, seems to be constricting our existence, and this anxiety illumines *Unholy Alliance* like a night-light in some recess of the wall down a very long corridor.

If magic is composed of a good many of those out-of-category forces that press against established religions, so magic can also be seen, in relation to technology at least, as the dark side of the moon. If a Creator exists in company with an opposite Presence (to be called Satan, for short), there is also the most lively possibility of a variety of major and minor angels, devils and demons, good spirits and evil, working away more or less invisibly in our lives.

For some, it is virtually a comfortable notion that magic is a practice that can exist, can even, to a small degree, be used, be manipulated (if often with real danger for the practitioner). For such men and women, the proposition is assured—magic most certainly does exist as a feasible process—even if the affirmative is obliged to appear in determinedly small letters when posed against technology: (How often can a curse be as effective as a bomb?)

Nonetheless, given the many centuries of anecdotal and much-skewed evidence on the subject, it is still not irrational to assume—even if one has never felt its effects oneself—to assume, yes—phenomena of a certain kind can be regarded as magical in those particular situations where magic offers the only rational explanation for events that are otherwise inexplicable. Indeed, this is probably the

1

common view. One explanation for the aggravated awe and misery that inhabited America in the days after the destruction of the Twin Towers was that the event was not only monstrous, but brilliantly effected in the face of all the factors that could have gone wrong for the conspirators. The uneasy and not-to-be-voiced hypothesis that now lived as a possibility in many a mind was that the success of the venture had been fortified by the collateral assistance of magic. Few happenings can be more terrifying to the modern psyche than the suggestion that magic is cooperating with technology. It is equal to saying that machines have a private psychology and large events, therefore, may be subject to Divine or Satanic intervention.

So let us at least assume that magic is often present as a salient element in the very scheme of things. Anyone who is offended by this need read no further. They will not be interested in *Unholy Alliance.* Its first virtue, after all, is in its assiduous detail, its close description of the events and ideas of the occultists who gathered around the Nazis as practitioners, fellow travelers, and in the case of Himmler and the SS, as dedicated acolytes, fortified cultists.

What augments the value of this work is the cold but understanding eye of the author. Since his knowledge of magic and magicians is intimate, one never questions whether he knows what he is writing about. Since he is also considerably disenchanted by the life practices of most of the magic workers, he is never taken in by assumptions of grandiosity or over-sweet New Age sentiments. He knows the fundamental flaw found in many occultists—it is the vice that brought them to magic in the first place—precisely their desire to obtain power over others without paying the price. The majority of occultists in these pages appear to be posted on the particular human spectrum that runs from impotence to greed. All too often, they are prone, as a crew, to sectarian war, all-out cheating, gluttony, slovenliness, ill will and betrayal. Exactly. They are, to repeat, at whatever level they find themselves, invariably looking for that gift of the gods—power that comes without the virtue of having been earned.

The irony, of course, is that most of them, in consequence, pay large prices in ill health, failure, isolation, addiction, deterioration of their larger possibilities, even personal doom. Goethe did not conceive of *Faust* for too little.

Peter Levenda captures this paradox. What he also gives us is a suggestion that cannot be ignored: The occultists on both sides in the Second World War (although most particularly Himmler and the Nazis) did have some real effect on its history, most certainly not enough to have changed the outcome, but enough to have altered motives and details we have been taking for granted. What comes through the pages of *Unholy Alliance* is the canny political sense Hitler possessed in relation to the separate uses of magic and magicians. Levenda's dispassionate treatment of charged evidence is managed (no small feat) in a way to enable us to recognize that Hitler almost certainly believed in magic, and also knew that such belief had to be concealed in the subtext of his speeches and endeavors. Open avowal could be equal to political suicide.

He was hell, therefore, on astrologers—and packed off many to concentration camps especially after Rudolf Hess' flight to England in 1941, did his best (and was successful) in decimating the gypsy population of Europe, sneered publicly at seers, psychic gurus, fortune-tellers, all the small fry of the occult movement. He saw them clearly as impediments to his own fortunes, negative baggage to his reputation. Yet Hitler gave his support to the man he made into the second most important Nazi in existence, Heinrich Himmler, an occultist of no small dimension.

It was as if Hitler lived within a particular Marxist notion. It was Engels' dictum that "Quantity changes quality." One potato is something you eat, a thousand potatoes are to be brought to market, and with a billion potatoes, corner the market. In parallel, a little magic practiced by a small magician can prove a folly or a personal enhancement, a larger involvement brings on the cannibalistic practices to be expected of a magicians' society, and a huge but camouflaged involvement, the Nazi movement itself, with its black-shirted Knight Templars of SS men, becomes an immense vehicle that will do its best to drive the world into a new religion, a new geography, a new mastery of the future.

All of this is in Levenda's book. It is an immense if obligatorily compressed thesis—the economies of publishing would never permit a one-thousand-page tome on this subject by a new author—and the potentially large virtues of the work suffer to a degree from over-compression—one feels the need to expand being held in much too close rein by the writer, but then, there are few daring and ambitious works that do not generate sizable flaws. Literature may be the most unforgiving of the goddesses!

In any event, I am delighted that *Unholy Alliance* is being republished because I have always found it a most provocative and valuable work on each of the three times I have read it, and have never come away without returning in my mind to the rich ore brought forth at the pit-head of virtually every page.

—NORMAN MAILER

Preface to the
Second Edition

In the years since 1995 when this book was first published, the author has had occasion to see some of his anxieties—predictions would be an overstatement—come to sad fruition.

The very ending of this book's final chapter, the quotation from Charles Manson that America's children were "coming right at you," came hideously to life with the Columbine High School massacre in 1999 in which children slaughtered their classmates with firearms. These same children had idolized the Nazis, and had selected Hitler's birthday—April 20—as the day to launch their sickening offensive.

In a note more harrowing than thrilling, author Stephen King reminded us in the *New York Times Magazine* of September 23, 2001, that the next phase of the Columbine children's crusade was to hijack an airliner and fly it into the World Trade Center in New York City.

Out of the guns of babes . . .

Religious fanaticism and mystical identification of the political body with the Godhead has led to increased terror attacks all over the world, most particularly of course the events of September 11, 2001. The ostensible reason behind this series of attacks was the removal of non-Muslim forces from the sacred soil of Saudi Arabia and the cessation of American support for Israel, both politico-religious goals reflective of intense mystical convictions.

In addition, we are just learning of the depth of the horror that has been taking place in the Balkan states—in Serbia, Croatia, Kosovo, and elsewhere—as the perpetrators of religious and ethnic cleansing and virtual genocide are brought to some form of justice at the Hague.

In Southeast Asia, the prime minister of a predominantly Muslim nation blamed the Asian economic crisis of 1997 on a Jewish conspiracy masterminded by George Soros.

In that same nation today, one can purchase reprints of Henry Ford's rabid anti-Semitic polemic, *The International Jew*, at newsstands everywhere. This particular edition, printed in South Africa, also includes the full text of the *Protocols of the Elders of Zion*.

In the immortal phrase of Yogi Berra, "it's déjà vu all over again."

Or in other words, and to paraphrase my own book, we are still fighting World War One.

On a somewhat happier note, Chilean government forces have raided Colonia Dignidad several times over the past few years in their efforts to arrest its notorious founder, former Luftwaffe pilot Paul Schäfer, and bring him to justice. As mentioned in both the Introduction and the final chapter of this book, I was the unwilling beneficiary of Schäfer's hospitality one Sunday morning in the Chilean winter of 1979. Schäfer has managed to evade capture, it is thought, by taking advantage of the elaborate tunnel system he had built under the Colony, a system designed in part by an American neo-Nazi and mastermind of the assassination of Orlando Letelier, Michael Vernon Townsley. (Ironically, Townsley's father was a Ford Motor employee in Santiago.)

Then, in the spring of 1999, I was invited to Germany for a taping of a television documentary on evil. The venue was the spiritual headquarters of Himmler's SS, the castle at Wewelsburg which is described at length in Chapter Six. I spent several pleasant days in the company of the film crew at our base in Paderborn, and made the acquaintance of a German filmmaker—Dr. Kerstin Stutterheim—whose documentary on Nazi occultism is essential viewing for anyone interested in the subject. *Faces of Evil* was aired on the TNT network during sweeps week in April, 2000 and included interviews with Marilyn Manson, FBI profiler John Douglas, author Poppy Z. Brite, and many other experts on evil and its forms in modern life, with voice-over narration by Malcolm MacDowell. I was honored to have been asked to participate, and even more thrilled when I realized that one of my culture heroes—from such films as *If, A Clockwork Orange*, and *O! Lucky Man*—was to be the film's narrator. It seemed like an embarrasment of riches.

Seven Years in Tibet opened in 1997, starring Brad Pitt as Heinrich Harrer, the German soldier who spent that length of time in Tibet during the Second World War and befriended the Dalai Lama, and is based on his memoir of the same title. What Harrer neglected to mention—to the surprise and shock of filmgoers—was that he was more than a mere soldier caught behind enemy lines: he was an SS officer of some standing and reputation. That the Dalai Lama would have befriended a Nazi gave everyone some cause for speculation. As in our *agon* over Watergate, we wanted to ask the Dalai Lama: what did he know and when did he know it? The SS's fascination with Tibet and the story of their official expedition to that country in 1938 is detailed at length in Chapter Six.

Pope John Paul II has begun a series of apologies for the actions of the Catholic Church over the past thousand years or so, actions that included war, murder, and persecution of minorities. These very public apologies are welcome, however late in coming. Some of these activities are covered in Chapter Eleven, where I discuss the efforts of some Catholic leaders to rescue Nazi war criminals from justice.

Magic and occultism have come back in vogue in America and in many other parts of the world. Not only the *X-Files*, but shows like *Charmed, Buffy the Vampire Slayer*, and *Sabrina, the Teenage Witch* can be seen on television stations in countries as remote from each other—in religious sentiment as well as geography—as the United Kingdom and Singapore, Venezuela and Hong Kong, Italy and Indonesia. *Harry Potter* became a record-breaker at the box office, just as it was being roundly condemned in some circles as encouraging children in the practices of magic and diverting them from the nervous embrace of organized religion.

Magic and politics. Since the biblical days of Saul and the Witch of Endor, political leaders have banned or spurned occultism only to secretly consult mediums, astrologers, and necromancers in times of stress. We need not look too far into the past to realize that this reaction is basic to our nature. One only has to think of President Reagan's astrologer to confront this combustible mixture of magic and politics in our own time. If we insist on looking at magic from the point of view of mainstream science—as an exploded system based on faulty hypotheses about the nature of reality—then we miss the point entirely, since the same could be said of religion as it could about some forms of art. Calling magic a "pseudo-science" is also setting up a straw man for burning at the stake. Magic does not pretend to be chemistry or physics. One might as well call Roman Catholicism, the paintings of Picasso, or the films of Marilyn Monroe pseudo-science, if one wishes to devalue them speedily and does not have the intellectual gifts to do so on their own terms. One might as well complain about the unnecessary complexity of Rube Goldberg machinery: confusing form with function is often a characteristic of the cultural critic as it is of the devout scientist, a case of wondering why roses are red and violets are blue. And as much as the scientist scoffs at magic, in equal terms does the politician, military commander, and terrorist mastermind employ magic as one of the weapons in a specialized arsenal of the arcane, alongside psychological warfare, disinformation, Vietnamization, and assassination. War is the ultimate proof of utility: if a weapon works, it stays in the arsenal. Magic has been part of the arsenal of politics and of war (the continuation, after all, of politics by other means) for millennia, alongside the club, the siege engine, gunpowder, advertising campaigns, and dirty tricks.

Far be it from this author, however, to wrestle with such complex issues in this limited space. He would rather give credit where it is due, and this he must do by the shovelful:

To Phil Tuckett of Bristlecone Films, Alan Brown, Brad Minerd, David Sharples, and the entire crew of *Faces of Evil*. There are no other people I would rather be with when the ghost of Heinrich Himmler looms over me in Germany. You made taping a documentary entertaining, stimulating, and a lot of fun.

To Dr. Kerstin Stutterheim, whose brilliant film on occult practices in Germany—*Mythos, Magie und Mord* (Myth, Magic and Murder)— should be seen by everyone who considers themselves an authority. Her encyclopedic knowledge of European film archives and the cultural context of both German occultism and Nazism is an invaluable resource.

To Michael Leach, whose gracious support and encouragement at critical stages was instrumental to this edition, as was that of Dr. Eugene Kennedy and Diane Higgins. Many thanks to you.

To Judith McNally, who believed in this book enough to become its informal advocate and guardian angel. Without Judith, this book would still be languishing in out-of-print limbo, unbaptized and un-saved.

To Frank Oveis, whose advice and suggestions have made this edition even better than the first.

To those other culture heroes who surprised the hell out of me by reading *Unholy Alliance* and contacting me with gracious praise:

To Jim Marrs, whose kind references in *Rule by Secrecy* made my day. To Jim Hougan, the investigative journalist I wanted to *be* after reading *Spooks,* and to Tracy Twyman of *Dagobert's Revenge* who put us together; and to Hans Janitschek.

To Whitley Strieber, with whom I once shared an agent, and whose personal quest somehow parallels my own; thanks for your kind correspondence, your unstinting support of *Unholy Alliance* and a very rewarding time on the Art Bell show, in spite of the potential difficulties of doing a live broadcast on a syndicated program when we were ten thousand miles—and a dozen time zones—apart.

To Norman Mailer. It is rare to find anyone in life who will go the extra mile for another based purely on principle, and with no reasonable expectation of reward. It is even more difficult when that person is a literary legend who is probably importuned at every corner by needy (or greedy) authors. There are really no words I can use to thank Norman Mailer (without a constant and compulsive rewrite that will never allow this book to make print) so I won't even try.

And finally to all the friends and fans of this book who must remain nameless; your E-mails, letters, reviews, and encouragement raised the energy necessary to get this done. Thank you all very much.

Southeast Asia
2002

That is the secret delight and security of hell, that it is not to be informed on, that it is protected from speech, that it just is, but cannot be public in the newspaper, be brought by any word to critical knowledge . . .

—THOMAS MANN

Introduction:
At the Mountains of
Madness

Four o'clock in the morning of an Andean winter found me shivering and alone on the streets of a small farming community in central Chile. It was profoundly dark, as only a poor village of sleeping farmers can be. But it was not silent.

From every side came the endless crowing of roosters and the unnerving howling of dogs like a sound track from hell.

There is something biblically ominous about a rooster crowing in the night and, when compounded by the braying of unseen hounds, one's composure is shaken into splintery fragments of old horror films. Monster movies, yes; and documentary films as well, for the twentieth century has given us a surfeit of both and it's sometimes hard to tell the difference between them. I remembered grainy scenes of goose-stepping soldiers, military vehicles groaning through the streets, civilians murdered in their homes. On television, when I was a child, it had been World War II in black and white. Today it was the Republic of Chile, in living color.

It was cold. I shivered. Under other circumstances I might have welcomed the blue-steel chill of anxiety as a tickle from the feather of Maat, the Egyptian goddess who measures the weight of the human soul against it. But there was, that night, even more at risk than the teasing promise of eternal life and the soul's weary passage through the gloomy domain of Anubis, the dog-faced God of Hell.

After all, there was more than hounds' teeth waiting for me in the dark.

The animals themselves were mysteriously invisible as I made my way on broken pavement past the shuttered windows of the town's bakery, grocery, stationery store; tiny buildings huddled together for warmth and succor beneath the bell tower of the village church. I supposed the dogs were tethered in yards and the roosters locked in coops behind the high, whitewashed stone and brick walls that lined the dismal streets. To the east behind me rose the Andes Mountains in all their brooding splendor, black against the black night sky. It was two days past the new moon, and the sky was full of stars.

There was menace in the air that winter. The papers had been full of stories about cells of resistance to Pinochet's fascist regime—the brave Miristas—being discovered by the army and wiped out with characteristic brutality. There was no police force in Chile; the army *was* the police. There was no Congress. The Army *was* the Congress. There were no courts. None were considered necessary. Even now, nearly six years after the violent and bloody overthrow of Allende's government, there was still martial law in the streets of Santiago. Only the evening before, I had to be certain to rush back to my hotel before curfew began as if I were a character in *Casablanca*. The Wehrmacht-style uniforms and goose step march of the Chilean soldiers did nothing to ameliorate the feeling that I was in a time warp, living in a German city sometime in 1939 instead of in a South American city in 1979. The recruiting posters for the army that depicted the Chilean officer's engraved dagger reminded me that I was in a country whose leader admired the SS. A nervous young man of perhaps eighteen in a greatcoat and Sam Browne belt, the distinctive helmet with the ear guards like something out of *Hogan's Heroes* pulled down over his forehead, had aimed his M-16 at me from the guardhouse of the military academy because I had tried to take his picture. The architecture of the academy itself was like something out of the wet dream of a Bavarian sadomasochist, but it was subdued when compared to the aggressively alpine motif of the Santiago Country Club.

And *La Moneda*—the Presidential Palace where Salvador Allende spent his final hours—was, like Chilean democracy, still in ruins.

So why had I gone deep into the South American interior—far from Santiago or indeed any other sizable city—to find myself un-armed and alone in the village square of Parral at four o'clock in the morning? If anything had happened to me there, no one would have known. There would have been no witnesses. No official reports. No body flown back to the United States for burial.

In fact, if things had gone just a bit more badly than they did, there would have been very little body left to send back.

I was in Parral, in central Chile, at the foot of the Andes Mountains that late June of 1979 because I was probing the heart of the Chilean darkness, a neo-Nazi encampment, cult and torture center known as Colonia Dignidad.

The Colony of Righteousness.

Mark my words, Bormann, I'm going to become very religious.[1]

—ADOLF HITLER

Like many people, I was shocked to learn of the Catholic Church's complicity in helping Nazi war criminals escape Europe and certain death at the hands of the Nuremberg Tribunals. The Church had provided them with visas and passports in false identities, an underground railroad out of Europe composed of monastery "safe houses" along the way, and—in some cases—religious costume: dressing up the various butchers and torturers in the robes of Catholic priests. That the Church would be involved in aiding and abetting these fugitives from justice was shocking enough; that they were helping some of the most rabid anti-Catholics the twentieth century had ever known was beyond comprehension. And the man in charge of this now infamous operation, called by various names *Caritas* or *Aktion Hudal,* was none other than the future Pope Paul VI.

These were some of the allegations made in a book by the bestselling author of *Patton* and *The Game of the Foxes:* Ladislas Farago. The book was called *Aftermath: Martin Bormann and the Fourth Reich.* With meticulous detail, Farago reported his search for *el gran fugitivo,* Martin Bormann—former Reichsleiter and Hitler's right-hand man— who, Farago claimed, had escaped to South America dressed as a priest. Farago even went so far as to claim that Bormann, using the name "Father Augustin," had *celebrated Mass* and performed at least one marriage ceremony in Argentina. Farago even had Bormann attending the funeral for former President Juan Perón, his alleged protector in Argentina.

The Nazi/South American connection is so well known it has become part of the folklore of World War II. Whether Bormann really made it to South America or died in Berlin in 1945 is still a matter for speculation. When Farago's book was published, there was a general reaction among establishment historians that he had been fooled and manipulated by unscrupulous Latin police departments and shadowy "informers" who had lied to him pathologically . . . and profitably. For some reason, it was anathema to believe that Bormann had escaped even though we knew Adolf Eichmann had made it to South America (where he was captured by the Israelis) and that Dr. Josef Mengele, the Angel of Death at Auschwitz, was in fact hiding in Brazil.

Heretofore a well-respected popular historian, Farago found himself attacked on all sides for daring to suggest—albeit with careful documentation—that Martin Bormann, the highest-ranking Nazi in the world after Hitler, had actually survived into the 1970s. Those of us who were familiar with the success of Simon Wiesenthal, among others, in hunting down Nazi war criminals through a labyrinthine maze of underground safe houses, secret societies, and foreign countries, were willing to at least credit Farago's *research*, which was as extensive, scrupulous, and thorough as one had come to expect of this Hungarian-born specialist in World War II history. But some of what he discussed seemed so outlandish that critics felt Farago was being had.

Like many others, I bought *Aftermath* and read it cover to cover in almost a single sitting. It was, after all, the height of Watergate paranoia those days, a time when anything was possible and when any criminal conspiracy by government leaders entirely credible. While his story read like any of the best political thrillers of the day, one statement in particular caught my eye. It concerned Bormann's living accommodations in Chile when he—according to Farago and to various Argentine and Chilean security officials—had to leave Argentina after the death of his friend, Juan Perón. It seemed he spent his time between a friend's estate outside Santiago and a small town south of the city. A town by the name of Parral:

> Located in the latter region is the weirdest Nazi encampment of the postwar world, housing a sect that combines Nazism and voodooism. Enormously rich from mysterious sources, it maintains a heavily forti-

fied *estancia* called Colonia Dignidad. It is virtually extraterritorial, enjoying privileges and immunities otherwise reserved only for diplomats. It was to the hacienda of Colonia Dignidad, called "El Lavadero," eighteen miles from Parral, camouflaged as a "cultural and welfare society," that Martin Bormann would move when, fatigued by his restless life in exile, he sought a place where he could be at peace.[2]

Nazism and voodooism? Weird encampment? Wealthy from mysterious sources? It sounded like something out of a Ludlum novel, and I began making arrangements to see it for myself.

Farago's book was published in 1974, the year after General Augusto Pinochet's overthrow of the Allende government in Chile, with its resulting dissolution of the Chilean Congress and the suspension of all civil liberties following the establishment of martial law. As the book by Thomas Hauser and later the Costa-Gavras film, *Missing,* made abundantly clear, Chilenos were not the only ones subject to arrest, interrogation, torture, and murder by government forces in Chile. Americans were also vulnerable. At least two American citizens were taken from their homes, tortured, and murdered in the days immediately following the coup.

Living in New York City, I was able to keep abreast of developments in Chile through a wide circle of emigrés and political refugees, some of whom were on government hit lists. Through them I was able to learn of the actual existence of Colonia Dignidad, although no one I spoke with knew very much more about it than was published in Farago's book. Chile was in turmoil; people were being rounded up and "disappeared" for years after the initial coup. It would be five years before I was able to venture into the Chilean hinterlands myself, but when I did I was to find that nothing there had changed. Nothing at all.

As I boarded the Lan Chile flight from Kennedy Airport in New York to Santiago, Chile, I was frisked for the first time in my life. My youthful, bearded appearance must have given the security people pause. Yet, a few minutes earlier a crew-cut, blond-haired American man in front of me had very kindly opened an aluminum carrying case and displayed his rifle with telescopic sight to the counter people prior to having it tagged for our flight.

The scene came back to me as I boarded the plane, knowing that at least one person—and an American at that—was taking a firearm with him, even if it was in the luggage compartment. So (I asked myself for the hundredth time that week) what was I doing traveling to that most frightening of potential destinations, a Third World military dictatorship?

Writing a book, as it turns out. A potentially soporific study of how religious and cult organizations have influenced political movements since the Middle Ages. The occult has rarely been a topic of serious study by professional historians; yet occultism and secret societies devoted to the occult have been known to wield a disproportionate influence over political events in many countries. While academic historians may agree that this has been the case in the past, no one seriously wants to entertain the notion that cults still function effectively—if somewhat haphazardly—in the present day. Because the basis for occult beliefs is often what historian James Webb has called "rejected knowledge,"[3] academics tend to reject occultists as history's sideshow freaks: gullible, wide-eyed, and crazed naifs floating in a twilight world of schizophrenia and paranoia. Whatever one thinks of the beliefs of the occultists—I thought—one must credit their basic courage and their unusually high levels of intelligence. Courage, because they have chosen to live outside the "system": of religion, of custom, of all those things with which society identifies itself and its members. Intelligence, because the occultists one comes across in the few histories available are generally well traveled, speak several foreign languages (including a few dead ones), and have done considerable reading in a variety of disciplines, both mainstream and underground. In effect, occultists share many traits in common with JFK conspiracy theorists; and, yes, paranoia *does* seem to be a prerequisite for membership in either community but then, as the late literary critic Anatole Broyard once remarked, "Paranoids are the only ones who notice things anymore."[4] I knew the occult was a major factor in the Nazi *Weltanschauung*, but this fact was being ignored both by most historians and by those people who considered themselves well read on twentieth century history.

As I write these lines, the Skinheads have become a menace both in America and in Europe and the rise of racist violence on both sides of the Atlantic seems to be taking social critics by surprise. No one seems able to understand what attraction the defeated Nazi Party holds for adolescent white males; certainly no one understands the dimensions of the potential threat to world peace a resurgence of Nazism has in store for us and for our children. To fill this gap—and to satisfy those smug critics of occult "histories" who insist that the evidence for a Nazi occult conspiracy is virtually nonexistent or at best irrelevant and trivial—I was busy developing a mass of source material that would show not only how the Nazi Party was essentially the product of a mystical and peculiarly occult vision, but that the weight of previous centuries of religio-political history would demonstrate just how pervasive is the relationship between politics and occult ideas.

So, to counteract the drowsy accumulation of dense references to forgotten fraternities and lunatic philosophies, Colonia Dignidad seemed like a natural: Nazis in hiding, weird voodooistic rites in the mountains, unlimited sources of income. It would be the crowning achievement of an otherwise dry, academic study of right-wing fanatics, fundamentalist Christian, Jewish, and Muslim sects, spiritual corruption and corporeal violence at all levels of society. Colonia Dignidad would represent relevant, up-to-date, man-on-the-scene research.

I had already spoken with Klan leaders and the members of several neo-Nazi organizations in the United States, most of whom were really pathetic groups of men who lived somewhere on the border of abused child and serial killer. I watched convicted Klansman Roy Frankhouser literally kick his mother down the stairs of his Reading, Pennsylvania, "church." I helped a Volkswagen van full of American Nazis find their way out of a small town when it turned out that none of the Master Race could read a road map. I stood on line at a McDonald's in New Jersey as a half-dozen crazed hypoglycemics, sporting outlandish black SS-type uniforms with red, white, and back double-thunderbolt armbands—the elite guard of James Madole's rabid National Renaissance Party—loaded up on Big Macs, fries, and shakes while I tried to appear as if I was traveling alone.

Now I was about to investigate the real thing. *Real* Nazis. Escaped war criminals. Pagan idolators. Screaming psychos in the Andean forests. Little did I know that at that very moment events were being put in motion ten thousand miles away that would have an effect on my activities in Chile and which would, in the final analysis, actually save my life.

Farago's book was roundly, even viciously, attacked. "It wasn't true. It couldn't be true. Bormann's body was found in Berlin, wasn't it? There were eyewitnesses who said that Bormann had been shot crossing a bridge, weren't there?" Therefore, the rest of the book had to be flawed. The troubling implication for me was that perhaps there was no Colonia Dignidad, or that the whole thing had been exaggerated beyond recognition. Perhaps Colonia Dignidad was nothing more than a community of old European immigrants, living out their lives growing the grapes from which the excellent Chilean wines are produced. Perhaps they were—as *Penthouse* editor Peter Bloch would later tell me to my astonishment—merely some unpleasant people who only happened to be German, and not Nazis-in-hiding.

Perhaps there was no Colonia Dignidad at all.

When I landed in Santiago I immediately tried to make reservations on a flight back to the States for the following week, but found that all seats were booked a month in advance. Nonetheless, I put my name on a waiting list and gave the airline the name of my hotel—the gravely misnomered Grand Palace, two floors of an office building in downtown Santiago. I phoned in every day and visited the ticket offices, but there were no seats, a situation that would soon change in an unexpected way.

I spent the first few days in Santiago seeing the sights, reheating my Spanish, and looking for a few of the locations identified in Farago's book as Nazi fronts. The house and gift shop of Mark Büchs was there, in the Providencia section on Calle San Pablo, just as Farago described it. Mark Büchs was a friend of Bormann, according to Farago, and a devoted Nazi. His gift shop was on the main street—with a large sign that said, simply, "Mark Büchs"—and I brazenly went inside and bought a small trinket. A souvenir, you might say, of my days of Nazi-hunting on a budget. Then, I followed Calle San Pablo down to the house at the cul-de-sac, which had several burly men standing around, doing nothing, staring at everything. There were two Mercedeses in the driveway; a nice touch.

I went back across the street from Mark Büchs's and took a few surreptitious photographs from behind a lamp post.

So far, none of this was earning me a Pulitzer. In the midst of all my Nazi-hunting paranoia, however, there was also sadness. After all, I was walking in the very footsteps of Pablo Neruda and Gabriela Mistral . . . for that country has given the world *two* Nobel Prize–winning poets. Chile had been the most literate country in the Western Hemisphere until the *coup d'état* that put Pinochet in power. Chile had also boasted the longest continuous democracy in South America. Unlike its neighbors, it had never succumbed to the peristaltic intervals of civil war and revolution that stereotype Latin governments in the eyes of most North Americans. Salvador Allende had been a democratically elected president who had also survived a confidence vote later in his administration. It would take a CIA-ITT–financed truckers' strike, punitive World Bank actions instigated by the United States, and a junta of Chilean military power—aided, abetted, and gleefully encouraged by the United States government under Nixon and Kissinger—to put an end to democracy in Chile for many years. And Pablo Neruda, Chile's most beloved poet, would die only days later; some say of a broken heart but the truth is much grimmer: his home was surrounded for five days by Pinochet's troops so that Neruda—gravely ill with cancer of the prostate—could not receive the vital medical attention he needed.

Later, a much-admired former Chilean statesman—Orlando Letelier—would be murdered in the streets of Washington, D.C., by agents of the Pinochet regime; victim of a conspiracy masterminded by an *American* assassin: a morally bankrupt psychopath and electronics freak who had designed the torture chambers of Colonia Dignidad.

In the end I managed to make arrangements to go to the tiny town of Parral, where the infamous Colonia was supposed to be located. I rode a very comfortable Pullman bus that took the Pan American Highway south through the village of San Fernando (a rest stop where I ate a cold hot dog on a stale bun: a local delicacy called *una vienésa,* a "Viennese") and then into the province of Linares. As we drove further south the sun began to set, and in the waning light at one stop I could see a small crowd of people—old men and a few women—in a poor, ramshackle village, huddling around a fire in an oil drum in the muddy dirt road that served as their Main Street. Small children, dressed in little more than rags, were coming from all directions carrying planks and odd lengths of lumber to feed the flames. It was as if they were tearing down their village, piece by piece, for warmth.

I arrived at Parral in the middle of the night. Other than the sounds of the howling dogs and crowing roosters, the streets were absolutely empty. There were no lights on in the homes, or around the square with its obligatory statue of Bernardo O'Higgins, the oddly nomenclatured Father of his Country. The Catholic church in the square was dark, its only illumination the deep red glow of the tabernacle lamp that affirmed the lonely presence of God somewhere in the mysterious heart of this remote village. In the distance, I could make out the train station and decided to walk in that direction and perhaps find someplace warm to sit until the sun came up.

June in Chile is the beginning of winter. It was quite cold, and I was getting hungry, but there was nothing for it but to wait until I could find someone to drive me out to the Colony. As I made my way down the deserted *calles* to the station, a bizarre figure from out of a Fellini film suddenly appeared in the dull wash of a streetlamp at the far end: a man, wrapped in a dark woolen poncho and wearing a beret, riding on a bicycle, and carrying a large greasy stick, with a mangy dog attached to his bike by means of a heavy chain.

He bade me stop and identify myself, claiming that he was the "night watchman" (*el vigilante*) for the town. He appeared old and grizzly, with a three-day growth of stubble, but he was the only human being abroad in the night and his dog looked vicious, so I dutifully handed him my passport.

"North American, huh? We've never seen a *norteamericano* down here before. Where are you from? Chicago?" He grinned at me in my trench coat, visions of Al Capone and bathtub gin dancing in his eyes.

"No. New York."

Almost as good.

"What are you doing here?"

"Waiting for a train."

At this, he laughed.

"A train? In the middle of Parral in the middle of the night? I don't think so. You had better tell me the truth."

As he was trying to find out what I was doing in his town, we were approached by two more men drawn by the sound of our voices.

These wore the uniforms—and carried the rifles—of the army, and my newfound friend made the introductions.

They also asked to see my passport, and they passed it among themselves, shifting their weapons from hand to hand as they did so. *Now* I was nervous. Would I be arrested? Would I be "disappeared" like my American predecessors? Would I be tortured first, then killed?

At that point, the night watchman, Señor Francisco Molinas, invited us all to his house for a drink.

The pickle jar of homemade *aquardiente* went around a few times, and I was observed drinking the stuff and eating a grape that had been marinated in that crystal-clear, overproof moonshine for what must have been more years than I was alive if the mule kick it gave me was any indication. The two soldiers leaned their rifles up against the wall of the one-room shack, warm in the heat of a smoky, wood-burning stove, and we all sat around talking.

I was well aware of my position, and I most certainly did not want to get drunk. I feigned shock at the tremendous alcoholic content of the moonshine, coughing and gasping, which brought smiles of approval from my companions along the order of "that gringo has never tasted really good, strong liquor before, not like we have in Chile." And eventually the topic of conversation turned to what exactly I was doing in their tiny town in the middle of a rural Chilean nowhere.

It was then that I realized I could not keep it a secret any longer. It was foolish to insist that I was simply waiting for a train, although that was the first thing that came to mind when I saw Mr. Molinas and his dog. I told them the truth, that I had come to Parral to seek Colonia Dignidad.

It was as if a cold wind had just gusted through the room straight from the snowy peaks of the Andes. My hosts sobered up immediately. It was their turn to be shocked, for it seemed as if they had truly not expected me to be there on so foolhardy a mission.

The troops warned me repeatedly not to go. That it was dangerous. That the people of *La Colonia* were hated and despised throughout the region. That they functioned as an independent state, completely separate from any local authority. That they operated a medical clinic that was free to the locals two days a week, but that it was a last resort for most Chileans because they did not trust the German doctors and especially not a particular German nurse with a sadistic gleam and brutal disposition. That they were all foreigners, not a Chileno among them. That they received checks for large sums of money that came in the mail from all over the world. Including the United States. That they were well armed. That if I went there, I would probably not return.

That they practiced strange rites in the forests on holidays that were unknown to the Christian calendar.

Whether it was the false courage of the *aguardiente* or the realization that I had come this far and wasn't about to return empty-handed, or the immortal confidence of a twenty-eight-year-old weekend warrior sitting around hobnobbing with armed soldiers in an alien land as if he belonged there . . . I decided that, as soon as the sun was up, I would go.

We parted amicably at dawn. The troops would not prevent me from going to the Colony. It was not against the law to go there, to voluntarily enter where many had tried to escape, only stupid. After the soldiers left, Señor Molinas introduced me to his young and beautiful wife and three children in a neighboring hut where they had been sleeping, wrapped in woolen blankets on the floor. Blinking in the light of a kerosene lantern, they stirred awake and smiled at me: a weird apparition in trench coat and camera. Molinas had to return to his mysterious occupation, and left me temporarily in the care of his brother, who insisted that I visit *his* house. Dawn was just breaking, and there was no transportation anyway, so I followed the shorter Sr. Molinas *hermano* to his home, whereupon he disappeared for a moment into another room.

Looking around, I could see that the people of Parral lived quite simply. There were religious pictures on one wall, and a heavily carved and painted wooden crucifix—that looked at least a hundred years old—on another. Finally, my host appeared and in his hand was a rifle.

It took me a moment to realize it wasn't pointed at me. He offered the rifle for my inspection—a surprisingly lightweight, bolt-action model of uncertain manufacture—and asked me if I wanted to go hunting with him and his friends. I swallowed, and then politely declined, saying that I had to go to *La Colonia*. He smiled a little ruefully and took a good, long look at me as if for the last time. He shook his head, and then my hand, and led me out the door and directed me back to the town square.

It still being deserted, I made my way on foot to a gas station on the highway outside of town that had a café, and I ate what I reasonably assumed could very well be my last meal, of steak and onions in an otherwise-deserted restaurant.

Then I returned to the square and, finding a cabdriver waiting around in front of the church—it was now Sunday morning and I could see preparations for Mass being made through the open doors—we agreed on a price and made for Colonia Dignidad with all haste.

In 1979, the Colony of Righteousness was reached by a dirt road off the Pan American Highway, south of Parral, that wound up and around a series of foothills of the Andes Mountains. At one point there is a fork in the road. A left turn will take you to a popular hot spring resort. The right road takes you past something called *La Colonia Italiana,* a poverty-stricken estate of starving burros and emaciated farmers, before you reach the higher ground and the main entrance to Colonia Dignidad. I thought it ironic that the German colony should be situated cheek by jowl with an Italian counterpart, as if the Axis powers had felt it necessary to reproduce themselves in microscopic form in this out-of-the-way section of South American forest.

But as we climbed higher into the mountains, passing a pair of *huasos* or Chilean gauchos on horseback, their Clint Eastwood hats and serapes making them seem like noble lords of the hills, I noticed a striking difference between Colonia Italiana and Colonia Dignidad. The latter smelled of money. The very forests—mostly dark and evergreen, like some kind of displaced Schwarzwald—seemed manicured. Finally, we crossed a small, decorative bridge and drove through an open gate to a parking area in front of a rustic wooden building that I guessed housed some sort of reception facility.

At this point my driver became very agitated. He urged me to take my photographs quickly so that we could get the hell out of there. I didn't need to be warned twice. I jumped out of the car and took perhaps ten or twelve shots in rapid succession, covering 360 degrees around me, elated that I had what were probably the only photos of Colonia Dignidad in honest (that is to say, civilian) captivity. It was then that I heard muffled conversation coming from behind the door of the wooden reception building, a building that I had thought was unoccupied. From the bursts of static that accompanied the voices, I knew that someone was talking on a radio. In German.

I ran back to the car and my driver hit the gas pedal . . . and then the brake in rapid succession. Before us, the gate we had driven through so brazenly only moments before closed electronically, and a car—a white Mercedes with venetian blinds in the rear window—appeared from nowhere to block our escape. All four car doors opened, and some of the largest human beings I have ever seen left the Mercedes and came over to surround our car. My driver's hands were frozen, white-knuckled, to the steering wheel, and he kept saying, over and over, "Oh, no. Oh, no." From every angle around us, more men appeared, some dressed in ersatz fatigues with Sam Browne belts and others in surgical blues. Visions of Mengele in his lab, or of the mad dentist in *Marathon Man*, fought for control of my heartbeat. All the men were running, panting, out of breath.

We had caught the Nazis with their pants down on a beautiful, sunny, Sunday morning . . . and now they had caught *us*.

I

THE BY-PATHS
TO CHAOS

The German soul has passages and galleries in it, there are caves, hiding-places, and dungeons therein; its disorder has much of the charm of the mysterious; the German is well acquainted with the by-paths to chaos.

—FRIEDRICH NIETZSCHE

⚡ 1 ⚡

Of Blood, Sex, and the Rune Magicians

Prologue: Christmas Day, 1907. A Castle in Upper Austria, on the Danube. Against a backdrop of snow-covered hills and ice-blue sky, church bells and Christmas carols, a flag is raised over Burg Werfenstein and, for the first time, the world sees a swastika banner fluttering in the breeze over Europe. Men dressed in white robes emblazoned with red crosses—Rune Magicians—raise their arms and voices in pagan chant to Buldur, the Sun God, Lord of the Winter Solstice.

The Order of the New Templars is proclaimed, while, only a few miles away, young Adolf Hitler has just buried his mother.

Most of us live in a world that is neatly organized around several basic principles. Like medieval serfs who lived secure in the knowledge that there was a God in heaven and a Satan in hell, that humanity was the battleground between these two forces, and that God was winning, we twentieth-century serfs bask in the comfort of a world that (we are told) is the product of purely scientific principles. Genesis has given way to *The Origin of Species* and the Big Bang. We have landed on the moon, rather than drawing it down with incantations and rites of witchcraft. We heal with lasers and sterilized instruments to a backbeat of the blips and beeps of electronic monitoring equipment; the fractured rhythms of the witch doctor's drums are but a faint echo of old fears and tainted memories.

Thus, we assume, all *sane* men and women are guided by scientific principles in their daily lives; and this is especially true, we sometimes like to think, of our politicians. What more prosaic a lot of people can there be but the House of Representatives or the House of Commons? A debate on the Senate floor—although televised in all its stultifying detail on something called C-SPAN—is rarely gripping; not quite the stuff of *Becket* or *Richard III*. There is little in the way of poetry or vision in American politics anymore, and that is largely because the Romantic ideals of our ancestors have been discredited with the passage of time. We are nations of laws, and these laws are constantly changing to reflect new "realities" created—not by philosophers or metaphysicians or theologians—but by scientists and technicians. The very fact that Americans can tune in their television sets and watch live coverage of a debate in the House over funding allocations for a program they've never heard of is somewhat comforting. It means, in fact, that the wheels of government grind on, in the open, with boring, peristaltic regularity, aided and abetted by scientific invention and technological achievement. A bureaucracy on Geritol.

While, outside on the streets, civilization is breaking down so fast Western society is on the verge of a catastrophe of major proportions.

A Communist might say the reasons for the decline of the Western way of life are purely economic and that the warring factions are economic classes struggling for dominance over the means of production.

But there are few Communists abroad in the land anymore; fewer still who could carry that argument with any conviction, no matter how reasonable it might seem today. After all, an L.A. street gang performing a drive-by shooting on rival gang members to enforce their control of the drug trade on some bleak city block seems hardly what Mao had in mind when he wrote "All power comes from the barrel of a gun," or what Marx and Engels meant by "Workingmen of all countries, unite!"

The polarity within which so much of the twentieth century was written—Communism and Fascism—has crumbled. The Soviet Union—Hitler's greatest enemy after the Jews—has fallen. The map of Europe has been redrawn, with a reunified Germany as its center-piece. Its capital is Berlin, once again.

Who had reason to celebrate the most when the Berlin Wall came down?

And who is celebrating now that the races have become, if anything, even more divided; when we read once again about a "Jewish-Masonic conspiracy" as the rationale for "ethnic cleansing"; when the potential for racial violence all over the world has escalated to heights unheard of thirty, forty years ago?

While science is humming along nicely *inside* our homes, just what the hell is happening *outside,* and why?

If we are honest with ourselves we know we can't answer all these questions with a few canned explanations about the decline of the nuclear family or the failure of the social welfare system. There is clearly something more going on here. Our politicians are not men of science; they never were. They live as dangerously close to the Beast Within as the rest of us; perhaps even more so. In the end, the difference between a seasoned politician and a gang-banger with a machine gun is very slight, a difference of style rather than substance. If that seems to be overstating the case, just ask anyone who lived in Berlin in 1919. Or in Munich in 1923. Or Vienna in 1938. Poland in 1941.

Santiago in 1973.

Or Sarajevo in 1994.

Ask anyone on the receiving end of Nazi occultism.

The epigraph from Thomas Mann at the beginning of this book is taken from *Doctor Faustus.* The author thought that both quotation and source were apt selections to christen this discussion. *Doctor Faustus,* after all, is a novel that takes place in Germany during the rise and fall of Hitler. Its title comes from a long German tradition of Doctors *Faustus:* magicians and occultists who have sold their souls to Satan in the next life for personal power and glory in this one. Thomas Mann himself lived to see his books burned in great bonfires throughout Germany in that impotent gesture by the Nazi government during the war of ideas that has characterized our century.

Even more apt, however, is Satan's own explanation for the "secret delight of hell": as Mann understands it, hell's delight is that it cannot be discussed or described, that "it is not to be informed on."

It is the author's intention, therefore, to steal some of hell's secret delight and security; to shine a light, however feebly or inexpertly, on that corner of history's basement few professional historians have dared to visit, and to show the reader *why*. We will trace the history of a cult so lethal no sensationalistic tales of satanic serial killers hacking women to death in suburban cellars can come close to matching the horror, or the evil; a cult that still exists to this day, its activities aided, abetted, and protected by a variety of the world's governments.

And to do that, we must begin with a scene of utter chaos; with the breakdown of civilization; with rooftop snipers and roving gangs with guns; with terror and madness; with mystical diagrams and pagan rituals in ruined castles; with a vision of hell itself.

We must begin with Munich in 1918.

Descent into Hell

The city is in turmoil. The Kaiser's republic has collapsed with the defeat of Germany in the First World War, and the whole country is up for grabs. It appears as if Germany is about to fall apart into the warring city-states from which it had been assembled nearly fifty years ago. The victorious Allies are demanding enormous concessions from Germany. The Russian Revolution has been in full swing for a year, and German soldiers returning from the front are being cajoled into helping midwife the same type of Communist regime amid the ashes of the Second Reich.

Kurt Eisner—an intellectual and a Jew, a defender of the League of Nations—takes the initiative and proclaims a Socialist Republic in Munich on the seventh of November, 1918. It looks as if there is going to be a Communist regime in Germany—or, at least, a Socialist one in Bavaria—after all. Hysteria grows among the nationalists, and with it despair that their nation is on the verge of realizing the dreams of Marx and Engels as codified in their famous Manifesto. Germans are bewildered, shocked . . . stunned into a kind of nervous stupefaction. They have lost the war, their country may be broken up once again into many separate bickering pieces, and there will soon be Communists calling the shots in Berlin and in the capital city of Bavaria: Munich.

Within forty-eight hours there is a meeting of the *Thule Gesellschaft.*
The Thule, a mystical society based in part on the theosophical writings of Guido von List and Lanz von Liebenfels—which is to say, an
amalgam of Eastern religion, theosophy, anti-Semitism, Grail romance, runic mystification, and Nordic paganism—meets every Saturday in spacious rooms at the elegant Four Seasons Hotel in Munich.
There are roughly 250 members of the Thule in Munich . . . and
over fifteen hundred in Bavaria. On that day, November 9, a bizarre
individual, an occultist, an initiate of the Eastern mysteries in Turkey
as well as of Freemasonry, and the leader and founder of the Thule—
the self-styled Baron Rudolf von Sebottendorff—makes an impas-
sioned plea to the assembled cultists for armed resistance to the Reds.
This plea eventually degenerates into a monologue on runes, German
racial theory, Nordic mythology, and other arcane lore. No matter.
Most of his listeners know what to expect. They are, in fact, members
of the supersecret, superracist, and superoccult "German Order Wal-
vater of the Holy Grail," or *Germanenorden,* which is using the name
Thule Gesellschaft—or Thule Society, a "literary-cultural society"—as
a cover to confuse Munich's fledgling Red Army, which is on the
lookout for right-wing extremists. Sebottendorff himself is Master of
the anti-Semitic *Germanenorden*'s Bavarian division under its leader
and founder, Hermann Pohl.

The Thule cultists—whose symbol is a long dagger superimposed
on a swastika—need no encouragement. They begin stockpiling weapons in secret supply dumps in and around Munich, anticipating a
counterstrike against the new Socialist Republic. They make alliances
with other nationalist groups, such as the Pan-Germans under editor
Julius Lehmann, the German School Bund, the Hammerbund . . .
and an organized resistance movement is born. All the mystical and
clandestine labors of the past twenty years involving a series of secret
and occult organizations with elaborate initiation ceremonies and
complex magical rituals, from the List Society's inner HAO (Higher
Armanen Order) to the Order of the New Templars, will soon culminate in a pitched battle in the streets of Munich between the neo-
pagan Thule Society and the "godless Communists."

FEBRUARY 21, 1919.   The idealistic but hapless Kurt Eisner—who
preceded political speeches with symphonic concerts—is assassinated

by a young count and would-be Thulist. The police descend upon Thule headquarters, looking for inflammatory leaflets and other evidence of Thule Society involvement in the plot. Was the notoriously anti-Semitic Thule Society somehow responsible for Eisner's assassination? Sebottendorff stonewalls, and threatens to instigate a pogrom if the police don't leave the Thule Society alone. The police comply.

APRIL 7, 1919.   A rebel Bavarian Soviet Republic is proclaimed in Munich as the legitimate minister-president of Bavaria flees north with his council to the town of Bamberg to prevent the Communists from taking over the government. The Thule organizes among the anti-Communist factions in Munich and Sebottendorff (together with his friend, the racist priest Bernhard Stempfle) begins conspiring with the "exiled" Bavarian government in Bamberg for a counterrevolt.

APRIL 13, 1919.   The Palm Sunday Putsch. An abortive attempt by the Thule Gesellschaft—with other anti-Communist groups—to take power in Munich. There is bloodshed. The Putsch fails. Munich explodes into anarchy. The Communists seize control of the city and begin taking hostages. The Red Army is on the march . . . and hunting for the Thule Gesellschaft.

APRIL 26, 1919.   Sebottendorff is away at Bamberg, busy organizing a *Freikorps* (Free Corps) assault on Communist headquarters, when a Red Army unit raids Thule Society offices and arrests its secretary, the Gräfin Hella von Westarp, and seizes the Thule membership lists. Six more Thulists are arrested at their homes, including the Prince von Thurn und Taxis, a well-connected aristocrat with blood relations among the crowned heads of Europe.

APRIL 30, 1919.   *Walpurgisnacht.* The High Holy Day of European Paganism and Witchcraft. The Red Army executes the captured Thulists and other hostages, shooting them against a wall in the courtyard of Luitpold High School.
   It is probably the worst mistake they could have made.

   The next day, an obituary appears in Sebottendorff's *Münchener Beobachter*—a newspaper which a year later becomes the official Nazi propaganda sheet, the *Völkischer Beobachter*—giving the names of the seven murdered cultists and laying the blame on the doorstep of the Red Army.[1] The citizens of Munich are finally outraged, shaken out of their lethargy. Thulists continue their well-organized campaign of agit-prop against the Communist regime. The people take to the streets.

The Free Corps—twenty thousand strong—marches on Munich under the command of General von Oven. For the first time in history, storm troopers—members of the Ehrhardt Free Corps Brigade—march beneath a swastika flag with swastikas painted on their helmets, singing a swastika hymn. As they enter the city, they find that the Thule has managed to organize a full-scale citizen rebellion against the Soviet government. They join forces.

When the dust settles on May 3, the Communists have been defeated in Munich, politically and militarily. Hundreds of people, including many innocent civilians, have been senselessly slaughtered in their streets and homes by the crusading "Whites" with the swastika banners. But there will be no Socialist or Communist government in Germany until after World War II, over twenty-five years later, and even then it will rule over only half of the country and will take its orders from Germany's most despised enemy, the Soviet Union.

But now, so soon after the victorious march of the Freikorps through the streets of Munich, the threat of a Soviet regime in the rest of Germany is still very real. Units of the navy are in mutiny, raising the red flag over Germany's battleships. France will march into the Ruhr valley, Germany's industrial heartland. But the spectacular success of the Freikorps has aroused the admiration of anti-Bolshevik forces all across Europe. In Riga, the newly formed Latvian Republic begs for Freikorps assistance to defend their country against the Bolsheviks and even the British support this decision. Hence, Freikorps units move to the defense of Latvia until the British themselves have to intervene to free Latvia from the death grip of these rabid proto-Nazi brigands.[2]

Even Germany's own right wing is divided into two camps: those in favor of restoring the monarchy and separating Bavaria from the rest of Germany, and those in favor of a unified Greater German Reich, without a monarch but with a leader, a leader with vision. A German messiah. A Führer. Where is that Führer to be found?

Unwittingly, the Thule Gesellschaft provides the answer. Meeting in the expensive Four Seasons Hotel, the leading industrialists and aristocracy of the city, along with a generous helping of local police and military officials, are designing a two-pronged strategy of political activism. The Thule Society will do the organizing, will make the right connections among the society figures, the wealthy capitalists, the intelligentsia. They will stockpile the weapons. They will organize units of the Free Corps, particularly the Ehrhardt Brigade (which will become an official unit of Germany's navy as the Ehrhardt Naval Brigade and, eventually, subsumed into Himmler's SS) and the Freikorps Oberland.

But another arm of the Thule has already begun recruiting—not among Munich's "beautiful people," the rich and the powerful—but among the working people, the lower- and middle-class citizens who have been hit hardest by the civil wars, the enormous rates of inflation, the chaos and confusion. There will be no overt involvement of the Thule Society in this group, which is to be called instead the German Workers Party and which will be led by a serious, humorless, railroad employee and locksmith named Anton Drexler. They will meet in a beer hall. Perhaps between the two groups—the Thule with its academics, nobles, and factory owners meeting at the Four Seasons, and the German Workers' Party with its rough-and-tumble factory workers meeting in beer halls—they will be able to form a united front against Communism, international Freemasonry, and world Jewry.

Within a year, this project of the Thule Gesellschaft will become the NSDAP: the National Socialist German Workers' Party. The Nazi Party. It will sport a swastika flag and a swastika armband, and its leader will be a war veteran, a corporal who had been sent by the German Army to spy on the organization: Adolf Hitler.

And by November, 1923, the tiny German Workers' Party will have grown to enormous proportions with many thousands of members, and will attempt to take over the country in the famous Beer Hall Putsch. The Putsch will fail, but Adolf Hitler the Führer will be born—not in a manger like the Son of God he often believed himself to be—but in a jail cell at Landsberg Prison.

What was the Thule Gesellschaft? What were cultists doing fighting Communists in the streets of Munich? What did they believe? How did it influence the Nazi Party?

A Philosophical Digression

The once-fashionable and still-controversial French philosopher Michel Foucault once described two major impulses in European culture and its dynamics of power.[3] The first of these he called "the blood." This impulse was directly related to old-fashioned concepts of political sovereignty. According to Foucault, the death penalty was important and indulged in heavily during this period because it represented the monarch's divinely given power to cause the death of enemies; i.e., to rob them of their blood. One pledged to defend a monarch to the last drop of one's blood. People became rulers owing to their consanguinity with the previous ruler (they shared the same blood, were of the same family). And, of course, although Foucault does not say it so baldly, an essential element of the dominant European religion, Christianity, is the idea of the redemption of humanity through the spilled (and sacred) blood of Christ.

This cultural conceit existed in the West well until the advent of the nineteenth century, at which time it was gradually replaced by the second of the two impulses, that of "sexuality." "Sanguinity" gave way to "sexuality" as political attitudes shifted from the importance of blood (and, hence, of the mystical value of death, the spilling of blood) to the importance of life itself: to the regulation of life's processes, the (selective) preservation of life, and the survival (or destruction) of entire populations. Power, therefore, was no longer a mystical quality of kingly blood—i.e., of an individual sovereign—but inherent in the control, manipulation, and interpretation of the sex act and its product. Power shifted—according to Foucault—from the *symbol* or sign of the blood toward the *object* of sex; Machiavelli moving down the talk show couch to make room for Freud, who will take it with him when he leaves.

The author has imposed this seeming digression on the reader because it so perfectly describes what will follow in the remainder of this book; we will be watching how these twin forces—blood and sex—came to be epitomized in the occult struggles, the mystical *agon*, of the Third Reich. Rather than remain an abstract philosophical problem, however, the themes of blood and sex become very real, very conspicuous in the writings, acts, and preoccupations of the magicians who gave birth to the Nazi Party and of those who carried out the gruesome policies of the SS. (Robert J. Lifton, who has written extensively on the psyches of the Nazi doctors, has also recognized this mystic obsession with "the blood" that characterized the Nazi phenomenon.[4]) The reader is asked to remember this brief encapsulation of Foucault's observations as we follow the argument down the last hundred-odd years since the birth of the German Theosophical movement and its illegitimate offspring, the sex-and-blood rune magicians List, Liebenfels, and Sebottendorff.

Before we get ahead of ourselves, however, let us begin where most Western twentieth-century occultism begins, with the birth of the Theosophical Society in New York City in 1875 and the subsequent occult revival that spread to England and the Continent with such powerful (and often dire) consequences.

Secret Chiefs, Secret Doctrines

Madame Helena Petrovna Blavatsky (1831–1891) was born in what is now Ukraine. She would be forty-four years old before creating the Society for which she is best remembered, but her most important achievements still lay ahead of her.

In 1877—two years after starting the Theosophical Society—she would publish *Isis Unveiled,* an energetic blend of Eastern religion and mysticism, European mythology and Egyptian occultism, whose rambunctious style would pave the way for her even more ambitious *The Secret Doctrine* in 1888. Some authors have written that the popularity of Blavatsky's writings in the late nineteenth century was evidence of an antipositivist reaction among the middle classes to the effect that science was having on religious belief.[5] In other words, science was going so far toward "proving" the errors of faith that the average person—suddenly up the existential creek without a paddle or a prayer book—embraced the quasi-scientific approach toward religion represented in *The Secret Doctrine.*

Darwin had published *The Origin of Species* in 1859 and this was followed by *The Descent of Man* in 1871; both books offered evolution as the means by which humans were created, as opposed to the Biblical account found in Genesis. The effect of the theory of evolution on religion was as great then as it is now; the controversy over Darwinism caused many people to question the existence of God, the possibility of redemption, life after death, etc. People were startled to discover that Biblical myths were at odds with scientific theories, and thus began to doubt everything they ever believed. They found themselves spiritually—and, perhaps, morally—adrift.

Blavatsky provided a much-appreciated antidote to Darwin even as she was brazenly appropriating (and reversing) his theory of evolution. As bizarre as her theories appear today, they were actually quite brilliant for her time, for they enabled intelligent and educated men and women to maintain deep spiritual beliefs while simultaneously acknowledging the inroads made by scientific research into areas previously considered beyond the domain of mere human knowledge. Blavatsky outlined a map of evolution that went far beyond Darwin to include vanished races from time immemorial through the present imperfect race of humans, and continuing on for races far into the future. Based on an idiosyncratic selection of various Asian scriptures—including a few she made up herself—*The Secret Doctrine*'s message would later be picked up by the German occultists, who welcomed the pseudoscientific prose of its author as the answer to a dream. The smug and condescending attitude of scientists and their devotees toward the "unscientific" had proved contagious among many in the newly created middle class, and mystics began to find themselves in the ridiculous position of having to satisfy the requirements of science in what are patently unscientific (we may say "nonscientific") pursuits. Modernism in general was seen as being largely an urban, sophisticated, intellectual (hence "Jewish") phenomenon, and this included science, technology, the Industrial Revolution, and capitalism. The only wholesome lifestyle was that of the peasant on his "land," and the naive beliefs of the people of the land, the *paganus* or pagans—with their sympathetic magic and worship of ancient gods in the form of such superstitious practices as fertility rites, the lighting of bonfires on particular days sacred to the old calendar, and the whole host of cultural traditions that can be discovered by consulting Frazier's *The Golden Bough*—were set up in opposition to "science," with its suspect lack of human warmth and its cold indifference to the "gods."

Science in its hubris was treading dangerously close to the territory claimed by religion (the origin of life, the creation of the universe, even the existence of God), and in order to get there it would have to dance a jig all over the occult "sciences." Science still smarted from the religious furors caused by Galileo and Copernicus; so rather than mount an all-out attack on God, it was a lot safer to conduct a rearguard action and go after the ghosts.

But then along came Blavatsky, who took new scientific attitudes *as they were popularly understood* and gave them a mystical twist. Taking her cue from Darwin, she popularized the notion of a *spiritual* struggle between various "races," and of the inherent superiority of the "Aryan" race, hypothetically the latest in the line of spiritual evolution. Blavatsky would borrow heavily from carefully chosen scientific authors in fields as diverse as archaeology and astronomy to bolster her arguments for the existence of Atlantis, extraterrestrial (or superterrestrial) life-forms, the creation of animals by humans (as opposed to the Darwinian line of succession), etc.

It should be remembered that Blavatsky's works—notably *Isis Unveiled* and *The Secret Doctrine*—appear to be the result of prodigious scholarship and were extremely convincing in their day. The rationale behind many later Nazi projects can be traced back—through the writings of von List, von Sebottendorff, and von Liebenfels—to ideas first popularized by Blavatsky. A caste system of races, the importance of ancient alphabets (notably the runes), the superiority of the Aryans (a white race with its origins in the Himalayas), an "initiated" version of astrology and astronomy, the cosmic truths coded within pagan myths . . . all of these and more can be found both in Blavatsky and in the Nazi Party itself, specifically in the ideology of its Dark Creature, the SS. It was, after all, Blavatsky who pointed out the supreme occult significance of the swastika.[6] And it was a follower of Blavatsky who was instrumental in introducing the *Protocols of the Elders of Zion* to a Western European community eager for a scapegoat.[7]

This is not to imply that Theosophy is inherently "fascist," or that Madame Blavatsky is somehow responsible for the horrors of Auschwitz. Although Blavatsky herself did not become *overtly* involved in political campaigning or intriguing, many of her followers and self-appointed devotees could not help but use their newfound faith as a springboard into the political arena. In this context it is interesting to note that Blavatsky's successor as president of the Theosophical Society—Annie Besant (1847–1933)—became an important figure in Indian politics during World War I and was the first woman elected to serve as president of the Indian National Congress. She served as mediator between various warring factions, and made the Theosophical Society (a magnet for intellectuals and Brahmin-class English-educated Indians at Theosophical Society headquarters in Adyar, outside of Madras) prominent in the Indian Nationalist Movement.[8] (Later, the Nazis would attempt to exploit the Indian Nationalist movement for their own ends, since India then was still under British control, making the Indian Nationalists and the National Socialists seem like natural allies.)[9]

The fascinating mixture of armchair archaeology, paleoastronomy, comparative religion, Asian scriptural sources, and European mythology that can be found in Blavatsky's writings was enough to cause a kind of explosion of consciousness among many women and men of her generation, including the scientists who would one day direct entire departments within the SS. Blavatsky's "creative" method of scholarship inspired admirers and imitators throughout the world, who considered the theories put forward in such books as *The Secret Doctrine* to be literally true, and who used her writings as the basis for further "research."

In a way, this was understandable. In ancient times, alchemists were the only chemists; as the centuries went by and science developed a philosophy and methodology of its own, the alchemists and chemists split off from each other and went their separate ways. So it was with the rest of academia. In the nineteenth century—bereft of a unified vision of humanity and cosmos, cosmos and God—it was no longer easy to be an expert in every field of science and philosophy; by the twentieth century, it would become impossible. The writings of people like Blavatsky and her spiritual descendants represent the last gasp of the "Renaissance Man" before science, medicine, the Industrial Revolution, and mechanized warfare made specialization a necessity and the medieval image of the all-powerful and all-knowing Magician a bitter-sweet memory.

German Initiates

The German Section of the Theosophical Society was founded in the town of Elberfeld on July 22, 1884. Blavatsky was staying there at the home of Marie Gebhard (1832–92), neé L'Estrange, a native of Dublin who married a well-to-do German and, moving to elegant surroundings in her new homeland, devoted her leisure time to a study of occultism and ritual magic. Frau Gebhard had corresponded regularly with the famous French magician and author of several popular books on magic, Eliphas Lévi (the Abbé Louis Constant).[10] She is known to have visited the Master at least once a year in Paris for ten years until his death in 1875 in order to receive personalized instruction in the occult arts. A room at her estate in Elberfeld was completely devoted to these pursuits, and it was there that the German Section of the TS was inaugurated with a Dr. Wilhelm Hübbe-Schleiden (1846–1916) as its first president.[11]

Although Hübbe-Schleiden would become well known as the publisher of the influential German occult magazine, *Die Sphinx,* prior to his occult career he was an outspoken supporter of German nationalism and colonialism. This is mentioned only to show how early on in the game occultism and political adventurism—specifically an elitist, racist adventurism—were linked. While not exactly a proponent of an early *Lebensraum* policy, Hübbe-Schleiden had once been the manager of an estate in West Africa and was at the time of his tenure as president of the Theosophical Society in Germany a senior civil servant with the Colonial Office, energetically promoting the expansion of Germany's colonies abroad.

In all fairness, however, it must be admitted that *Die Sphinx* was one of the first, and also more upscale, occult periodicals of its time. It catered to an intellectual audience and its contributors included scientists, philosophers, and other mainstream academics writing on a variety of topics, from the paranormal and psychical research, to archaeology and Christian mysticism. As such, it was firmly in the Theosophical camp, which required some sort of (one-sided) accommodation with mainstream science.

One man of science who would come to personify this uneasy truce was a Blavatsky enthusiast who became influential in the German movement. Dr. Franz Hartmann (1838–1912), the prolific author of a wide range of occult books, first studied medicine at the University of Munich. While spending seventeen years as an eye doctor (and sometime coroner) in the United States, he became interested in the Spiritualist movement and began reading Theosophical tracts. In 1883 he traveled to Theosophical Society headquarters in Adyar, India, to sit at the feet of the Masters, evidently impressing his hosts greatly. He was trusted so highly that, while Blavatsky was in Elberfeld helping jump-start the German Section, Hartmann was in Adyar as acting president of the Theosophical Society and remained in India until 1885.

Hartmann is of considerable interest to this investigation as it was he who helped create the *Ordo Templi Orientis,* a German occult society formed around the idea of sexual magic. Other illustrious members of the OTO will include another Theosophist, Dr. Rudolf Steiner, who will go on to form the Anthroposophical Society in 1912; Gerard Encausse, who—under the *nom de plume* of "Papus"—had written the first definitive text on the Tarot as a book of concealed illuminism;[12] and Aleister Crowley, whose A∴A∴, or *Argentum Astrum* ("Silver Star"), was founded in 1907, the same year as the Order of New Templars mentioned above. (The OTO will be discussed in greater detail in Chapter Four.)

Another personal friend of Mme. Blavatsky was Dr. William Wynn Westcott (1848–1925), another coroner and a Theosophist who founded the Hermetic Order of the Golden Dawn in England in 1888, the same year as *The Secret Doctrine* was published. Westcott claimed that the Golden Dawn was in reality the English branch of a *German* occult lodge, a claim that would later be proven a hoax and which is, for that very reason, highly suggestive; for why would anyone claim a *German* origin for their occult society when so many other cultures are much more consistent with popular mystical stereotypes, such as those of India or Egypt?

Whatever the reason, we have the Theosophical Society, the OTO, the Anthroposophical Society, and the Golden Dawn all intertwined in incestuous embrace. These are the organizations most familiar to a casual reader of occult histories, and we will come back to them later on, for they all bear directly on our story. For now, though, let us follow the careers of the German Theosophists to see where they will lead us.

Upon his return to Europe in 1885, Hartmann took up residence at a town near Salzburg, and the directorship of a *Lebensreform* sanatorium. *Lebensreform* (or "life reform") was a back-to-nature movement that espoused a wide range of "clean living" practices that would be the envy of any New Ager of today. Vegetarianism, abstention from alcohol and tobacco, homeopathy, and even nudism informed this movement, and Hartmann saw it as a vehicle for the more overtly mystical program of Theosophy.

Like most occultists who are inveterate "joiners" and collectors of paper dignities, Hartmann was not content to confine his spiritual search to the leadership available in the Theosophical movement or any other movement. Most Western occultism is long on text and short on practice (contrary to forms of occultism found in the East, which rely on strict discipline, rigorous mental and physical exercises, and the constant supervision of a teacher or "guru"), and occasionally a Western seeker—starved for genuine accomplishment—will accumulate vast quantities of initiations into wildly disparate organizations with awesome-sounding titles, hoping thereby to satisfy his ego if not his spirit. In this way, occultism becomes a hobby—rather like stamp-collecting, or bird-watching—but with the added benefit that the seeker elevates himself in his own eyes to stratospheric levels of arcane wisdom beyond the feeble understanding of mere mortals. That is, until the next occult order is formed and another—more formidable—initiation becomes available. (This phenomenon is by no means limited to occultists, of course; it is to be discovered among the highly elevated and multiply consecrated "bishops" of a wide variety of distaff Eastern Orthodox and Old Roman Catholic denominations, some of whom also become involved with occult secret societies, such as Theosophist Hugo Vollrath—mentioned below—who became "Bishop of Erfurt" under the jurisdiction of Metropolitan Abdul Bahai, head of the Gnostic Church of Haifa.)[13]

Thus Hartmann will become involved, in 1902, with one John Yarker whose Masonic order, the Ancient and Primitive Rite of Memphis and Mizraim, would claim many otherwise-sincere individuals as members. It would be from among the German leadership of this

organization that the future founders of the OTO—including Hartmann himself—would be selected. Hence, it is Franz Hartmann who
provides us with some excellent connections between the seemingly
apolitical Ordo Templi Orientis and the rest of the German occult
community, which was, more or less, aligned with either the *Lebensreform* movement or directly with the Pan-German, anti-Semitic movement which gave birth to Nazism. Thus Hartmann is the axle on
which this peculiar Wheel of Life will turn. Wherever we pick up the
thread of twentieth-century Western occultism and ritual magic, we
can follow it back along a trail that leads to Hartmann.

A few years later, Hartmann became involved with another *Lebensreform* community, this time at Ascona, in Switzerland, where we will
eventually find his associate and fellow OTO initiate Theodor Reuss
sitting out the First World War in 1917.

There Hartmann began his own journal, the *Lotusblüthen*, (*Lotus
Blossoms*) in 1892, which printed translations of many Theosophical
and related writings. *Lotusblüthen*'s logo included the ubiquitous swastika. Among Hartmann's many other publications were translations of
the *Bhagavad-Gita* (one of Himmler's favorite texts), and the *Dao De
Jing,* the sacred text of Taoism. It is a measure of Hartmann's popularity and reputation that some of his writings have been translated into
English and are available today under a variety of imprints.[14] Little of
what Hartmann wrote, however, could be said to fall under the OTO's
domain of "sex-magic."

Hartmann would eventually take on as a kind of disciple and aman-
uensis a young Theosophist, Hugo Vollrath (born 1877). In 1899,
Hartmann picked up this university student as a personal secretary
and the two would go on speaking tours together, trumping up business for the Theosophical Society. Vollrath, an intense young man
whose peculiar appearance dovetailed nicely with that of his mentor
(nicknamed "Dirty Franz" because of his slovenly deportment), eventually became involved with the Leipzig branch of the Society, and
soon found himself embroiled in one scandal after another. It quickly
became evident to the other members that Vollrath saw Theosophy as
a potential cash cow. He began a series of publishing ventures, introducing Theosophy and, later, astrology to the German-speaking public. The Theosophists complained about Vollrath's apparent lack of
sincerity to the General Secretary of the German Section of the Soci-

ety, who at that time was Dr. Rudolf Steiner. Steiner, a friend of Dr. Hartmann, had become involved with both Theosophy and the OTO only to eventually leave them both to found his own group, the Anthroposophical Society (which also exists to this day). In 1908, Steiner was forced to expel Vollrath from the German Section but the damage had already been done. The Theosophists had created a monster, and Vollrath would go on to become a Theosophical publisher to be reckoned with, providing a forum for the men who were laying the foundations of a New World Order.

An associate of Vollrath will be Johannes Baltzli, a Theosophist and the secretary of yet another mystical organization, the List Society.[15] Baltzli would contribute articles to Vollrath's new Theosophical magazine, *Prana,* and soon the bizarre ideas of racist and rune magician Guido von List would fill the pages of this otherwise-bland outlet previously devoted to the writings of Blavatsky, her successor Annie Besant, and wandering "Bishop" Leadbetter.[16] And, as if to emphasize how inextricable German occultism was with German racism, it is through his astrological journal, *Astrologische Rundschau,* that Vollrath has additional impact on our story, for in 1920 he turned it over to the editorial ministrations of no less a historic personage than the Baron Rudolf von Sebottendorff: mystic, Freemason, initiate of the Eastern mysteries, and now astrologer. The Baron needed a new career. After all, his last occult experiment—although an unqualified success in the political arena—had turned on him. He needed new pastures, and editing *Astrologische Rundschau* from the relative safety of Switzerland seemed just the ticket. Maybe there—with a completely new audience of adoring fans—he could forget about the Thule Gesellschaft.

And about Munich in 1919.

To hear most historians speak of the Thule Gesellschaft, one would think that it was a slight aberration, an anomaly that does not deserve close scrutiny. Oh, it is mentioned (almost in passing) in John Toland's *Adolf Hitler* and in works by Joachim Fest and other historians of the Nazi episode. Its founder, the same Rudolf Sebottendorff, wrote its story himself in a book he published in 1933, a book that was suppressed by the Nazis. But to understand the nature of neo-Nazism today it is necessary to investigate the origins of the Nazi Party itself much more thoroughly than has been done to date. For the Nazi Party was never merely a political party; it was always much more. Hitler himself warned his critics that if they understood National Socialism as a political party only, they were missing the point. Many observers have since agreed. Politics alone did not create such an engine of destruction, such a willing collaboration in mass murder of citizens from every walk of life. As Robert G. L. Waite says in his *The Psychopathic God: Adolf Hitler:*

> The hard historic fact about the genocide is that it was not caused by the exigencies of war, nor was it a political maneuver to cope with internal unrest and domestic conflict. These people were killed as the result of one of Hitler's ideas: the idea of a superior race and the need to exterminate what he considered to be the vermin that were attacking it.[17]

This was an "idea" that can be traced to Hitler's early, student days in Vienna and to the influence of racial tracts published by the leading occult, anti-Semitic lights of the day: Guido von List and Lanz von Liebenfels. And from there, directly to the occultist and Eastern initiate Rudolf von Sebottendorff and his brainchild, the Thule Gesellschaft. In this century, in Europe, racism had its roots in occultism. Racism is, after all, an expression of irrational fears (often, as we shall see, with sexual components) and the irrational often finds a home in the milieu of primordial, preconscious archetypes that is the environment of both religion and occultism. Racism and the occult were often found sharing the same magic circles in the early days of this century, and therewith hangs a tale.

The Protocols of the Elders of Zion

It has been the refusal of historians to view the Nazi Party as a religious—or at least a mystical—organization, a *cult,* that has contributed to so much confusion over the problem of neo-Nazism, "ethnic cleansing," the white supremacy movement, and the Skinheads.

Indeed, yet another Blavatsky protégé—during the time of Hartmann, Hübbe-Schleiden, and Vollrath—was the mysterious Yuliana Glinka, a Russian noblewoman who donated enormous sums of money to spiritualist mediums and their circles and who was instrumental in promoting that notorious forgery, the *Protocols of the Elders of Zion,* which, along with *Mein Kampf,* can be considered one of the sacred texts of Nazism and neo-Nazism. As Norman Cohn illustrates at some length in *Warrant for Genocide,*[18] the *Protocols* were largely the product of a conspiracy between the *Okhrana* (the Czarist secret police) and occult circles operating in Paris and St. Petersburg. Originally, this pamphlet was a smear against both the Jews *and* the Freemasons, and was probably created around 1895 to discredit enemies of the head of the Okhrana in Paris, one Rachkhovsky. It was the occultist Mme. Glinka who "leaked" the manuscript to the press (after first attempting to convince a journalist that she was able to speak to the dead!). The newspapers seized upon it in the heyday of the Dreyfus Affair and the first-ever Zionist Congress presided over by Theodor Herzl in 1897. Here was "documentary" evidence that the Jews, operating through the lodge network and secret rituals of the Masonic Society, were putting the final touches on their program of world domination. As is well known by now, the *Protocols* are a forgery, an old satire using an imaginary conversation between Machiavelli and Montesquieu to draw attention to the policies of Napoleon III; but at that time the authenticity of the *Protocols* was a matter of faith among some of the most influential political and intellectual leaders of Europe and would eventually become one of the sacred scriptures of Nazism.

Thus, this single most inflammatory and crucial document of the Third Reich had its origins in that strange twilight world where occultism and espionage meet, a world we will visit again and again in the course of this study. And it is important to realize that the Masonic Society was considered just as culpable as the Jews; that it was, in fact, a Jewish "front": for the Elders sign themselves as thirty-third degree Masons. The plot as described in the *Protocols* involves a schedule for world domination that was believed to be well on its way to full implementation. By taking over the reins of commerce and by fomenting world revolution, the Jewish-Masonic conspiracy against Christian monarchies was nearly successful. With the destruction of the Second Reich, the last bastion of Aryan supremacy was removed and victory virtually assured. Using the twin tools of Democracy and Communism, the Jewish-Masonic cult had emasculated the potentially troublesome populations of America and Russia. The rites of Judaism and Freemasonry would soon replace those of Jesus and Odin.

To the *völkisch* believers, their only hope of salvation was to be found—not in any revived Christian fundamentalism, for Christianity (as a Jewish creature, after all) was also suspect—but in the rediscovered faith of their fathers, the Odinist religion that had been stolen from them by the fire and sword of the Inquisition. The *Protocols* implied that the Jews had "infected" all governments, all commerce, all of the arts and media; everything was suspect. Only the pure faith of the Old Ones—abandoned for centuries and thus beyond reproach—could offer salvation.

The Rune Magicians

On the Continent there existed a gaggle of purely German nationalistic cults that were the result of this underground surge of neo-paganism. These cults were usually linked in some way with the more overtly political "Pan-German" movement, which sought to unite all the German-speaking peoples of Europe into a single, coherent nation. The "Pan-German" movement can be seen as analogous to those of the "Pan-African" or "Pan-Arab" variety, except that the latter are attempts to form unified fronts among individual nations for economic or political purposes, whereas the Pan-German movement envisioned a single, German national and racial entity that would abrogate or dissolve sovereign boundaries and unite the German speakers all over Europe wherever sizable numbers could be found.

In order to provide a solid philosophical or ethical framework for this peculiarly German lust for monolithic statehood, some sort of precedent was required to show that much of what is now Europe was actually once part of a greater German Reich, even if that Reich was in the remote—even prehistoric—past. If it could be proved that everything from the Ukraine to the Atlantic was at one time part of an ancient Teutonic Empire, then the German people would have historical justification for the acquisitive urges they were suddenly experiencing, as well as a seemingly rational excuse for the exercise of their right to bear arms against all and sundry. What was required, then, was the assistance of the twin sciences of archaeology and linguistics and where better do these two rational arts combine but in their bastard child, the runes?

The obsession with runes that was enjoyed by a certain minority of Germans at the turn of the last century has been discussed by other authors in other books, but usually as a kind of crank occupation not fit for serious academics. Before we go on to study the contributions to Nazi ideology by such famous rune promoters as Guido von List and Rudolf von Sebottendorff, it would behoove us to pause for a moment to observe to what extent this arcane lore was—and is—making its effect on traditional academia. After all, nothing devalues otherwise-useful information and research so much as to link it with the Nazis. So let us extricate the Black Order from the runes for a moment so that we can see what they are and why rune studies exerted the influence that they did.

Runes are simple alphabetic symbols. They owe their odd and distinctive shapes to the fact that they were designed to be carved on wood, stone, or metal, as opposed to written with a pen; thus, only straight lines are used to form the letters. The words formed by the runes that concern us are generally in some form of Nordic tongue, and thus belong to that class of things purely Teutonic, pre-Christian, and German. (At least, that is the Party line.) In the new, urban, middle-class world where a multiplicity of words, books, ideas, and philosophies seemed to contend in a violent thunderstorm of polysyllabic chatter, the clean simplicity and bare prose of the runes and their sagas stood (to the Pan-Germans, the anti-Semites, and the Aryan mystics) for a saner time, an honest time, when the questions were few and the answers as clear and natural as the light of the sun.

They are also tangible relics of an ancient legacy—landmarks of historic accomplishments. Unlike words printed or written on paper (a German proverb reminds us that "paper is patient"), runes were inscribed with earnest deliberation using iron implements on solid rock; serious messages from the past intended to survive the centuries. The effort required to carve these messages was quite different from the ease with which pen slides over paper; the implication being that whatever was written in runes was not the mindless static of superficial minds, chewing up the forests with self-absorbed monologues.

Further, if runic inscriptions could be found on stones buried or standing in such faraway places as Minsk or the Pyrenees, then the assumption was that Minsk and the Pyrenees were once German territories.

And, if the *sounds* represented by the runic symbols could be discerned in place names from other parts of Europe, then it followed that Germans had once colonized and settled in those places. This was much more convenient than actually finding runic petroglyphs *in situ,* for it meant that merely transliterating the name of a French town or a Russian river into appropriate runic words (which a clever runic scholar could do given virtually any cluster of native phonemes from China to Chile) was equivalent to proclaiming that town or river a domain of the once—and future—German Reich.

The alphabet was therefore abandoned for mystical purposes by the Pan-German cults in favor of the runes. What was the alphabet, after all, but some sort of Semitic invention? The runes, on the other hand, were the pure expression of people of German blood. If a rune were discovered carved into a stone found lying in a field in Tibet, for instance, it was simply further proof of Teutonic migration and domination. And once the swastika—a sacred symbol in many parts of the world that never knew a rune—was identified as a "rune," the Nazis were well on their way to proclaiming the entire globe German territory.

Although this concept seems a little farfetched, many academics of the day placed a great deal of importance on runic studies and on the use of runes to establish the extent of Nordic migrations. For instance, as late as 1932 and 1940 Hjalmar R. Holand was publishing his analyses of the famous Kensington Stone,[19] analyses that were later examined by some of the leading German rune experts in Nazi Germany, including Richard Hennig in the *Zeitschrift für Rassenkunde* (*Magazine of Race Science*) in 1937, Wolfgang Krause in an issue of *Germanien* (the official organ of the Ahnenerbe-SS: see Chapter Six) of the same year and Eilert Pastor in *Wacht am Osten,* also of 1937. If his analyses were determined to have merit, then the presence of Nordic peoples in America as far back as the fourteenth century (over a hundred years before Columbus) could be established, with rather sobering political ramifications considering Nazi policy regarding former Teutonic territories!

Briefly, the Kensington Stone is a slab carved with runic characters found on a farm in Minnesota in 1898. The runes describe an Indian massacre said to have taken place in the year 1362. While some scholars have considered the Stone to be a hoax, others disagree. Mr. Holand went even further, however, by suggesting that various Indian tribes may have intermarried with Nordic peoples at that time; a circumstance that would account for the presence of blue eyes and fair hair among the Mandan population, for example.[20] (Wouldn't this also, after all, explain how the swastika turns up in North America as a Native American symbol?) While Holand himself does not take all this to its illogical conclusion, it is clear that some in the Third Reich would have considered this just one more proof of ancient Teutonic expansion. More importantly, this work is not a Nazi propaganda tract or the crazed scribblings of a *völkisch* medium under the influence of peyote or Wotan. It is the sober offering of a college-educated American author of Scandinavian descent, representing his carefully considered contribution to the growing literature of rune studies.

Today, similar studies have been undertaken by American and European epigraphers and by the Diffusionists led by Harvard Professor Barry Fell.[21] These professional and amateur archaeologists have made substantial contributions to this neglected field, and labor to preserve from vandalism and neglect those ancient stone inscriptions wherever they might be found. Runic inscriptions *are* evidence of ancient voyages otherwise unrecorded, and refer to vast tracts of unexplored history for which few documents remain. They have also demonstrated sophisticated advances in astronomy and navigation that may require significant portions of world history to be rewritten.

Books and research like the foregoing provide the "missing link" between the fanciful and outlandish works by authors such as von List on the one hand, and the regular academic community that considers the rune scholars to be nothing more than a cabal of proto-Nazis on the other. It was too easy for an unwitting public to slide from the serious research of a Hjalmar Holand, for instance, to the "channeled" discoveries of a Guido von List.

The notion of a hidden science of runes was given heat by the writings of Blavatsky, in which the runes are discussed in connection with her peculiar racial theories.[22]

For example, if there truly is a caste system of races, and if the present Master Race is the Aryan, and if the Aryan is a blond-haired, blue-eyed Nordic race, then it stands to reason that the Germans are the Master Race. If runic symbols, such as the swastika, are evidence of a secret Aryan science of symbols, and if the ancient German (Teutonic) method of communication was this same runic system, and if runes can be discovered all over the known world, then (a) that is further evidence that the Germans are the Master Race and (b) it is also further evidence that Germans once ruled the entire world; from which it follows that Germany has a "legitimate" stake in such property. *Heute Deutschland, Morgen Die Welt.*

Even more importantly, the runes themselves have mystical as well as practical applications. They are not merely alphabetic symbols that identify their users as Aryans: within the construction of the individual runes themselves are certain potent designs—like printed electronic circuitry—that can connect one directly to God. Coded within their stark diagrams are secret formulae for achieving telepathic power, foretelling the future, and peering into the past: innate magical abilities that the Aryans—through inbreeding, neglect, and ruthless suppression by the Christian authorities—have lost. The remains of this occult science are to be found in an "initiated" interpretation of the runes and, in conjunction with an aggressive eugenics program, the careful application of rune magic will enable the Aryan race to walk once more with Odin, Frigga, and Thor in the sterile, frozen halls of Valhalla.

Thus the Aryans are not simply a superior race in a strictly Darwinian sense; they are also the Chosen People, divinely ordained supermen locked in cosmic combat with a race of subhuman beings—red, brown, black, yellow—under the command of the Jews, the Communists, and the Freemasons: worshipers all of the demon Jehovah. This satanic conspiracy has robbed the Aryan male of his manhood, has leeched from him his birthright, his mystical powers, the very land that once was his; it has enslaved him in chains made of debts to Jewish bankers, of twisted ideas of democracy and freedom learned from the Masons, under a dictatorship of the proletariat imposed by the Bolsheviks. The Aryan man is Samson, his beard shorn by a Semitic Delilah and his strength, his potency, utterly drained from him as he now strains helplessly against the wheel of commerce.

But then, how to explain the sad condition of this once and innately superior race? Divided, conquered, bereft of all its old territories, in enormous debt . . . what happened? And how to rectify the situation? For the answers to these questions, we must resort to the literature of the *völkisch* apologists, specifically to Guido von List and his student, the former Cistercian monk and darling of at least one modern "satanic" cult, Lanz von Liebenfels.

⚡ 2 ⚡

Volk Magic

There is no religion without magic any more than there is magic without at least a trace of religion. The notion of a supernature exists only for a humanity which attributes supernatural powers to itself and in return ascribes the powers of its superhumanity to nature.[1]

—CLAUDE LÉVI-STRAUSS

Return of the Teutons

In 1902, the Austrian novelist, poet, folk-historian, and philosopher Guido von List underwent cataract surgery. He was blind for almost a year. Like Hitler over fifteen years later—himself blinded by mustard gas during World War I—it was during this period of darkness that he received his greatest illumination. It was an experience that would transform his life, and that would later have an indirect effect on Hitler.

Guido von List (1848–1919) had begun his career as a nature worshiper and lover of ancient German folk myths and culture, a man who believed in the reunification of his native Austria with Germany, and who came to despise both Jews and Christians as alien forces in Europe who had robbed Germans of their spiritual and territorial birthrights. He wrote a series of romantic novels about the ancient

Teutons, and dreamed of reestablishing the ancient priesthood of Wotan, an organization he called the *Armanenschaft* either after the Teutonic warrior Arminius who defeated the Roman Legions under Varus at the Battle of Teutoburg Forest (A.D. 9), or after a qabalist bowdlerization of the name of one of the three Teutonic tribes mentioned by Tacitus in *Germania,* the Hermiones.

In 1875, the same year that Blavatsky founded her Theosophical Society in New York, List was invoking Baldur, the Teutonic Sun God, on a hilltop outside Vienna. In Baldur's honor, he buried eight wine bottles there in the shape of a swastika and pledged himself to the worship of the Old Ones, Baldur and Wotan being prominent among them. At this time, the *Armanenschaft*—the priesthood of the sun—was but a gleam in his Aryan eye.

He took up journalism when his family's fortunes went awry, and began daydreaming in print about the prehistoric Teutons, a hypothetically pure race free of the taint of spiritually retarded blood.

However, during his convalescence after cataract surgery at the age of fifty-four—dwelling in a temporary but nonetheless unnerving state of blindness—he understood that his main preoccupations of politics and race were but two halves of a single coin. Always interested in the past more than the present (what anthropologist Claude Lévi-Strauss, quoted above, might have interpreted as a morbid interest in death: an interest that is central to most, if not all, occultism as well as to the detective story), List had developed an intense fascination with the signs and symbols of heraldry as well as those of the proto-Aryan language he believed could be found in runes and ancient inscriptions. He was not alone in these ruminations. Like his contemporary, S. L. "MacGregor" Mathers (1854–1918) of the British secret society, the Golden Dawn, he had a desperate desire to represent himself as of noble blood (in Mathers's case, he saw himself as an heir to the old Scottish noble houses). He was joined in this obsession by his young colleague, Lanz von Liebenfels, who, like List, adopted the aristocratic "von" even though there was little evidence in either case that it was deserved. And all three of these men—List, Liebenfels, and Mathers— were set upon developing (or "rediscovering") a complete, internally consistent, quasi-qabalistic system of interpreting the world, each in his own way.

For Mathers, the story of the Golden Dawn requires a whole separate study and as this has already been done by several scholars, it will not be repeated here except as it bears upon our story.[2] However, let's point out at once that the names List and Liebenfels soon became synonymous with the Pan-Germanic *Völkisch* movement that eventually gave birth to the Nazi Party: they wanted to resurrect what they perceived to be the genuine Teutonic orders of knighthood and priesthood, a mission that included many occult and pagan teachings; at the same time, Mathers—who had military as well as aristocratic pretensions—was desirous of restoring the House of Stuart and once claimed to have rejected "politico-military" work solely on the grounds that it would have meant severing his connections with the Golden Dawn.[3] In fact, much of his correspondence during the late 1890s from Paris is concerned with just such matters. (His first published book was entitled *Practical Campaigning Instruction in Infantry Exercise,* a translation from a French original.) Curiously, one of his close friends in Paris was the German author Max Dauthendey (1857–1918) who wrote occult novels, among them the provocatively entitled *Die Frau von Thule* (1898).[4] The author has been unable to find any more concrete link between Mathers and his German counterparts, however, although the occult underground is always a "small world" and it would be highly likely that Mathers was at least aware of List and Liebenfels (possibly through some mutual Theosophical or Masonic link, via Hartmann for example). As we shall see, List adopted the Golden Dawn system of hierarchical and initiatory degrees so it is likely that he at least knew of Mathers even if Mathers did not know of List.

And just why it is that occultists yearn toward politics and titles of nobility, as well as to military campaigns and even espionage, is a problem quite beyond the scope of this book. Quite possibly, they have a perfectly understandable need to duplicate in society, i.e., in the "real world," what dignities and powers they have accumulated in the secret world of the occult Orders. After all, it's no particular satisfaction to a reasonably intelligent person if the only ones who know you are practically God are fellow cult members. In the eyes of society, you remain whatever you were when you began your spiritual Quest, or perhaps have become even less: considerably poorer, distracted in personality and appearance, abandoned by family and friends. This disparity between inner attainments and outer accomplishments can strain even the noblest of intentions. At any rate, the situation hasn't changed much in the last hundred years since Mathers strode about Paris in complete highland costume, Aleister Crowley called himself the Laird of Boleskine or dressed in the guise of a Russian nobleman or an Eastern potentate, and List and Liebenfels sported spurious heraldic emblems on their letterheads.

By the spring of 1903, List's thesis on the common origins of an Aryan language, runes, heraldic emblems, epigraphic and other inscriptions as evidence of a secret store of knowledge concerning the creation of the world has been written. Vaguely theosophical in nature—List had been quite familiar with the works of Mme. Blavatsky—his magnum opus also expounded on the occult significance of the swastika.[5]

Satan and Swastika

List had been fascinated with the swastika since his early youth, recognizing it as the Ur-symbol of the Teutonic (read "Ayran") peoples; a pagan sign equivalent in power and emotional meaning to the cross for Christians or the Star of David for Jews. He first pointed this out in a series of articles published about 1905–1908,[6] and thereafter this symbol began to take on more than just a cosmological or theosophical significance and would soon come to represent an entire body of ideas—both occult *and* political—that would eventually culminate in the formation of the Thule Gesellschaft nearly two decades later.

Called *hakenkreuz* (or "hooked cross") in German, the swastika is an ancient design, much revered in India and the Far East. The very word *swastika* is Sanskrit, formed of the words *su* and *asti* meaning "it is well" or "it is fortunate." The arms seem to spin around a central axis and, depending on the direction of the spin—clockwise or counterclockwise (deosil or widdershins)—the swastika in question is either male or female, yang or yin, positive or negative. In many Hindu and Buddhist paintings and Tibetan tangkas—as well as in temple architecture in China, Tibet, and India—the swastika appears in *both* forms as if to emphasize the necessity of the polarization of both forces. It has been asserted by some authors that a counterclockwise-turning swastika (the type eventually adopted as the symbol of the Nazi Party) is somehow a representation of Evil, but this would be unknown to the Eastern peoples who probably gave the world the swastika in the first place. As an example, a wooden statuette in the author's possession—purchased in 1991 at a curio shop in Shanghai—is of a kindly Kuan Yin, Goddess of Mercy, with a counterclockwise swastika carved on her breast.

Thus the swastika was not a Nazi invention, nor was its association with occultism solely a figment of Mme. Blavatsky's imagination. As early as 1869 the British astrologer "Zadkiel" (Richard James Morrison, 1795–1874) had already announced the formation of something called the Ancient Order of the Suastika;[7] the swastika symbol was also a common decoration for the covers of books by Rudyard Kipling . . .

. . . and in 1897 the young Adolf Hitler, attending school at the Benedictine Monastery at Lambach, would pass every day beneath an archway which bears the monastery's coat of arms cast in stone. Its most prominent feature is the swastika.

While an educated perspective on the swastika reveals the symbol as an ancient Eastern symbol of good fortune, words themselves have their own intrinsic power. Thus, when a German calls the swastika by the term *hakenkreuz* he is calling it a "hooked *cross*." To a German of the twentieth century (as for a German of the thirteenth century) the word *cross* has decidedly Christian overtones; a *hooked* cross therefore implies some deviation from, or modified form of, Christianity. In this way, the link between the inherently amoral swastika and questionable religious beliefs is made by way of the emotionally loaded term "hooked cross." When the various *völkisch* and German cultural societies began adopting the *hakenkreuz* as their emblem, then, they were just as conscious of its anti-Christian potential as they were of their own anti-Semitic intent. This was not paganism as a pure, Earth-Mother-worshiping cult (such as the modern Wicca phenomenon) but paganism as a movement set up in opposition to Judeo-Christianity as well as to Communism, Capitalism, and Democracy, which were all creatures of the Jewish-Masonic conspiracy. In the Listian mode, therefore, the swastika as *hakenkreuz* identifies the *völkisch*, Nazi movement as an ideological enemy not only of the prevailing *political* forces of the time but also of the majority *religions* of Western Europe. Whereas Communism set itself up in opposition to *all* religion, Nazism supported a pagan revival to *replace* the existing religions. It is perhaps this strategy *more than any other* that has allowed Nazism in various forms to survive its calamitous defeat in World War II and to continue to exert an influence over young people and old down the years into our present decade. Political systems come and go as they are useful or not; religions (in part because their immediate utility is not easily proven or disproven) can survive for centuries after their creation. After all, even Christianity itself survived hundreds of years of an underground existence before coming into its own.

The List Society

Although the Imperial Academy of Sciences in Vienna did not take List's occult researches seriously and rejected his thesis (as the Academy of Fine Arts in Vienna would later reject Hitler's applications), many other groups and individuals took him very seriously, indeed. A List Society was formed in 1907 to finance his work, and the roster of members and founders of this Society reads like an anti-Semitic *Who's Who* of early twentieth-century Austria and Germany. Clearly, the idea that there existed a "scientific" rationale for both racism and nationalism was very attractive to a certain element among the New Agers of the day, for science—the new religion—could thus be relied upon to provide moral support for a position that would otherwise seem either absurd or repugnant. The same motivation that prompted List, Liebenfels, and even Mathers to "prove" they had aristocratic blood also served to define the efforts of the *völkisch* supporters to prove that *German blood in general* was superior to that of the other races. And, in order to obtain an even greater degree of respectability, it was necessary to go deeply into the past in order to "discover" an aristocratic ancestor. For List personally, it was his great-grandfather who, he claimed, had been of gentle, if not noble, birth. For the *völkisch* movement in general, it was the mysterious race of Teutons from the mists of ancient European history who gave the German people— the *Volk*—their pedigree and excluded all other races.

It is difficult to give a perfect translation of the term *völkisch*. To an English ear, the term sounds suspiciously like "folkish" and, in a way, that is true if we do not make the otherwise-inevitable associations with "folk music," for instance, that somehow devalue the term "folk" for certain generations of Americans. For *völkisch* means not only "folkish" but also "national" or "popular" in the sense of "the People," similar to the Spanish concept of "*la Raza*"; especially in the context of the *völkisch* movement in Germany. This movement was nationalist in the extreme, for it extolled a perceived common heritage that was believed to go back over several (even hundreds of) millennia and which included everything from art to science, from medicine to communal living, from religion to magic. The German *völkisch* movement had all of these, and it was also inextricably linked to the *Lebensreform* (or "life reform") movement which sought to purify the German people by a whole program of "clean living" practices. (With the possible exception of nudism—although he was seriously attracted to paintings of nudes, and the more erotic the better[8]—Hitler incorporated all of these tenets into his own belief system. As is generally known, he was a vegetarian who did not smoke or drink; and he identified himself as the physical and spiritual incarnation of the *Volk* itself. As the virtually untranslatable Nazi-era slogan would tell us: *Ein Volk, Ein Reich, Ein Führer.* Perhaps: "One People, One Empire, One Leader.")

According to List, the German people—the *Volk*—could trace their spiritual ancestry by careful reading of the Edda, that compilation of Old Norse lore and legend from Iceland which became particularly sacred to Hitler. This belief was so pervasive that the Ahnenerbe-SS would later devote a whole category of its research to Icelandic studies in concert with its runic investigations, evidence of which can be found among the captured Nazi documents microfilmed in the National Archives.[9] (The enigmatic Grail scholar and SS officer Otto Rahn would even make a special pilgrimage to Iceland in search of the legendary Thule.)[10] The ancestral links to the past through Guido von List were thus kept intact until well after List's death in Berlin in 1919.

The style and nature of List's writings would be familiar to anyone who had read Blavatsky's *The Secret Doctrine* back-to-back with de Santillana's *Hamlet's Mill*. In fact, the latter could be said to represent (with abject and profuse apology to Professor de Santillana) Listian neo-Aryan philosophy taken to its logical conclusion: that the Edda, the runic poems and spells, the tree Yggdrasil, and all the Norse myths *do* represent a secret, sacred knowledge about the origins—not only of the Teutons or mythic Aryans—but of the entire human race, as these motifs are present everywhere and in many cultures from Africa to the Middle East to the Far East to the Western Hemisphere; except that, for Professor de Santillana, that origin lies not in a sunken hyperborean continent but in the stars.

(Some American Nazis actually became converts to this point of view, at least partially. The author is reminded of William Dudley Pelley, the leader of the fascist Silver Shirts organization of the 1930s, who eventually abandoned organized Nazism and went on to help found the "I AM" movement: a cult that believes in ongoing human contact with alien space creatures, and Soulcraft, a similar movement. To Pelley, the "Aryans" are descendants of an alien Master Race.)

Ultima Thule and the Secret Chiefs

The ancient homeland of the Aryan race was believed to be the legendary Thule: the northernmost point on earth, an entryway into a subterranean landscape peopled by giants. A kind of Teutonic Eden, Thule or Ultima Thule was the mythic origin of all "Aryans": an equally mythic white-skinned, blue-eyed, blond-haired race of wise giants who were once the masters of the Earth but who lost their birthright due to sexual liaisons with the irresistibly seductive members of inferior, subhuman, half-animal races.

It should be mentioned now that, according to science (and the dictionary), there is no such thing as an Aryan *race*. The term *Aryan* refers to a language group—what has been called the Indo-European language group—and not to a race of people. Obviously, speaking any of the Indo-European languages does not make one a member of the Indo-European "race." There is no such thing. Yet, this is exactly the type of reasoning that led the early "Aryan" promoters into one of the worst blunders of twentieth-century history.[11] They confused a language group with a race. They claimed that language was somehow a function of the blood. Indeed, the bulk of List's researches were based on interpretations of the ancient writing systems of the Celtic and Nordic peoples, the runes; i.e., they were etymological and linguistic studies, yet they steered him and his followers onto a disastrous course whereby the modern day residents of Germany and Austria were somehow the pure-blooded descendants of a master race of ancient Teutonic godlings, the *Ur-Volk*.

He was not alone in this, of course. The movement to isolate the German-speaking populations of Europe from all other "races" and to unite them into one cohesive national unit—the Pan-German movement—had begun much earlier, and there were many anti-Semitic political parties and discussion groups abroad in the land in the 1880s, a full fifty years before Hitler came to power. Some groups formed around academic types who claimed to have proved their racial theories based on linguistic research—such as List—and others on physical characteristics such as skull size or eye color (factors which would later figure so prominently in the membership requirements for the *Germanenorden*, later in SS racial identification programs and in experiments carried out at the death camps). During the same era of the Indian wars in the American West—which were quite reasonably understood by the Nazis as a federal (and therefore legal) program of genocide against the Native Americans in pursuit of a Yankee *Lebensraum* policy—Germans and Austrians were plotting its equivalent in the extermination of the Jews and, it is said, actually taking their lead from the blatantly racist American war on the Native American tribes.[12]

Unfortunately for the anti-Semites, the difficulty of forming an entire political party around the single issue of anti-Semitism made it necessary to continue the offensive by other means. Magazines, pamphlets, and books were written and widely disseminated on the subject of the heroic, blond-haired, blue-eyed Aryan peoples fighting the dark-skinned Semitic, Mediterranean, and African hordes. The pornography of anti-Semitism would eventually take the form of future Nazi *Gauleiter* Julius Streicher's obscene broadsides against everything from miscegenation to psychoanalysis. But a constant theme of this subculture was the rape and murder of beautiful blond women by the bearded, crazed, dark-haired mongrel races. Psychoanalysts would understand it as a theme of blatant sexual insecurity and, indeed, the anti-Semitic journalists and "academics" would constantly and openly rail against the sexual prowess of the inferior peoples and of how the Semites—through various means, but especially including the fledgling "Jewish" science of psychoanalysis—had nearly succeeded in emasculating the Aryan male![13]

(One may jump a few generations to Los Angeles in 1969, and ponder the murder of Sharon Tate—a beautiful, blond actress who was nine months pregnant—by a band of "mongrels"; one may match the famous photos of the day of Charles Manson to the caricatures of the crazed, bearded Mongrel murderers of the anti-Semite's dark fantasies; one may scan the interviews and transcripts of the case, and discover that a proposed motivation for the killings was to instigate a race war between whites and blacks; one may then reasonably jump to the present day and wonder about the conversion of neo-Nazis and members of the Aryan Brotherhood to Manson's "cause," and of Manson's adoption of the swastika as his "emblem." This is a problem we will deal with in a later chapter, but for now it is important to realize that this type of thinking is by no means alien to our times or to our culture.)

At one point the Aryan homeland, Thule, was actually believed to be in Iceland, for Iceland is also the repository of the most ancient Teutonic legends extant: the Edda. Nazi apologists and racial theorists pored over the Edda endlessly, looking for clues as to their own origins, the appropriate pagan rituals to perform to appease and summon the gods, and for justification for their political and racial theories. Prehistoric Nordic sites all over Scandinavia and Europe were investigated, and no stone was left unturned. Literally. There are pages and pages of documents and photographs of megaliths, dolmens, and standing stones from all over Europe, and their interpretation by Nazi academics, in the files of captured German documents in the archives of Germany and America.[14]

Thule was a siren song to these early German occultists. It was a pagan Eden; not a Semitic, Judeo-Christian paradise in the sweltering deserts or marshes of Iraq, but a cool Nordic landscape of virgin snows and evergreen trees in the far north. A place not of warm sensuality and Mediterranean seductiveness, but of a cold, uncompromising purity. Similar to today's romantic notion that the human race somehow originated in the stars—that the stars are our "home"—Thule was "home" to the Pan-Germanists and to the lonely, alienated, impoverished, and disenfranchised anti-Semites and *völkisch* sympathizers . . . and just as inaccessible. Further, just as today's romantics believe in our extraterrestrial origins and in continuing contact with beings from other planets (our forebears?), the *völkisch* romantics of List's day believed in continuing contact with the Supermen. It was a theme that vibrated subliminally throughout a lot of anti-Semitic literature and in more open form among their British counterparts in the Golden Dawn, who posited a race of "Secret Chiefs": superhuman beings who, they said, live secretly among us, and in the Theosophical Society, which held that Hidden Masters (the Great *White* Brotherhood) were guiding the world's destiny. Among the *völkisch* cults it was believed that—as soon as the Germans had purified the planet of the pollution of the inferior races—these Hidden Masters, these Supermen from Thule, would make themselves known, and the link which had been lost between Man and God would be forged anew.[15]

This is not quite as absurd as it seems at first glance, since a constant theme in much Jewish and Christian eschatology is that of the coming of a Messiah who will purify the world and destroy the "not-chosen." This Messiah always seems to be a rather militaristic being, whether the armed Deliverer of the Zealots and other pious Jews who await the New Jerusalem, or the Messiah of the Book of Revelation—the Apocalypse—who will lay waste with fire and sword in a global, if not galactic, conflagration. The German version is not so far afield from these cherished beliefs of the Judeo-Christian fundamentalists, but is based on racial qualifications (and thus is beyond the realm of personal choice and ethical behavior) rather than on individual moral or spiritual worthiness.

The tradition of Hidden Masters is not restricted to occult Aryanism, of course. Some Muslims believe in the "Hidden Imam," an Ismaili concept similar to the "Secret Chief" idea of the Golden Dawn. The Strict Observance Masonic society of eighteenth-century Germany also claimed a tradition of Secret Masters, and there is the tradition of the Nine Unknown Men of India, secret Masters of the world's various sciences who invisibly guide the fortunes of the human race. That Himmler believed in this idea is revealed by his masseur, Felix Kersten, who—in his memoirs—quotes the Reichsführer-SS on just this point with regard to the Freemasons.[16]

And then, of course, we find ourselves back on familiar ground with the ancient legend of Agartha—or Arktogäa—the subterranean kingdom of an alien race buried deep within the Himalayas or somewhere in the far North (at any rate, in the appropriately Nordic frozen wastes), another Aryan "Thule." Years before H. G. Wells described a similar race of beings in his novel *The Time Machine,* the English author and Rosicrucian Bulwer-Lytton (1802–73) was writing of a subterranean master race in his celebrated novel, *Vril.* All of this is mentioned only to show that these concepts of secret master race and subterranean kingdoms are not peculiar to German or even Nordic legend and myth, and certainly not to Nazi ideology, but form part of a global tradition that may have some basis in reality; a basis that is now dimmed by the passage of too many millennia to place it clearly and authoritatively into a modern perspective. The *völkisch* theorists were merely drawing on a bank of myth and tradition familiar the world over, and sculpting from selected pieces a cosmological worldview that placed the German-speaking peoples at the top of a pyramid of power.

Lanz von Liebenfels and the Templar Revival

The eccentric ideas of Guido von List were carried to another extreme by his young follower, Jörg Lanz von Liebenfels (1874–1954), who created the Order of the New Templars as a secret society bent on reviving the chivalric brotherhood of knights, but in an aggressively Teutonic—and anti-Semitic—format. While List's sympathies were clearly already pagan and anti-Christian, von Liebenfels sought to restore a non-Christian, Teutonic Grail Order to its rightful place in the world. He used those of List's racial and linguistic theories he found most appealing; but it should be remembered that von Liebenfels was a Cistercian monk who abandoned his vows but who never, in his heart, abandoned the Church . . . at least, not his idealized, medieval version of it. While von Liebenfels had no sympathy for the Catholic Church as such—for its *beliefs*—he had unbounded admiration for its pomp and ceremony, its elaborate ritual. He managed to combine this fascination with stately ceremony with a peculiar understanding of the Templar Order. To von Liebenfels, the Templars were an Aryan brotherhood dedicated to the establishment of a greater Germany and to the purification of the race. The Grail, in his estimation, was symbolic of the pure German blood.

Even modern historians of the Grail legends disagree on the meaning of the term "Grail." To a linguist, the phrase *Sangraal* or *Saint Graal* ("Holy Grail") may simply be a pun on *Sang Real* or "Royal Blood." Indeed, the British research team of Baigent, Leigh, and Lincoln offer just such a theory in their best-selling *Holy Blood, Holy Grail*;[17] except that for these gentlemen the Holy Blood is not that of an Aryan super race, but the very blood of Christ himself, preserved in a dynastic lineage kept secret for two thousand years and protected by a secret society with the unfortunate name of Priory of Zion, a title which, combined with mysterious purpose, has perhaps too many resonances to those fictional Elders and their famous *Protocols*.

The ambivalence of men like List and Liebenfels toward the Christ figure is revealing. Hitler himself would later insist that Christ couldn't possibly have been Jewish.[18] For all their hatred of Christianity and Judaism, many Nazis and anti-Semites were loath to throw the Baby out with the bathwater. That may have been simple pragmatism in the land of Luther; but it also may have been evidence of deep uncertainty over ingrained concepts like heaven and hell, retribution and salvation. As the title character in the movie version of *The Man in the Glass Booth* tells us, a Christian is "a nervous Jew with an insurance policy."[19] To turn one's back completely on Christ may have seemed unsettling to these Supermen. A serious exception to this would be, of course, Heinrich Himmler whose unabashed paganism we shall discuss in a later chapter.

This hearkening back to a glorious German past was what united List and Liebenfels, although in many other ways their paths diverged. It was von Liebenfels's notorious magazine, *Ostara*, that so attracted Hitler in the latter's early days as an impoverished artist in Vienna, and we now know that Hitler—so inflamed by the wild occult, racial, and anti-Semitic theories he found in *Ostara*—actually paid an unannounced visit to the editor's offices and came face-to-face with Liebenfels himself.[20] This information comes from an interview with von Liebenfels after the war, when he was struggling with the de-Nazification process and would have had no ulterior motive in describing this meeting since the revelation of a personal relationship with Hitler could conceivably only hurt him.

Who was Lanz von Liebenfels, and how did he manage such an emotional impact on young Hitler?

If all one had to go on were back copies of *Ostara,* we would have to say that he was a cross between Pat Buchanan and Henry Lee Lucas, with a little Jimmy Swaggart thrown in to provide the Biblical and sexual references. Actually, von Liebenfels was a bit more complicated than that.

His Order of the New Templars was an occult lodge that met at a ruined castle high on a cliff over the Danube—the eerie Burg Werfenstein in Upper Austria, a few miles upriver from Hitler's childhood home—among other sites. The members wore white, surplice-style robes emblazoned with the red cross of the Templars, a cross that von Liebenfels believed was formed of two, superimposed and counterrotating, swastikas. At the same time, another such lodge was operating in Germany: the *Ordo Templi Orientis* (Order of the Eastern Temple), which had nothing to do with Liebenfels's ONT but everything to do with Aleister Crowley as we shall see in a later chapter.

Von Liebenfels—in *Ostara* and in other publications, such as his weirdly entitled *Theozoologie oder die Kunde von den Sodoms-Aefflingen und dem Götter-Elektron* (1905), which we may translate as "Theozoology, or the Science of the Sodom-Apelings and the Electron of the Gods"—prescribed sterilization and castration for inferior races and, of course, denounced miscegenation owing to its pollution of the pure-blooded German *Volk.* He also sounded a theme that was to occupy all other racist ideologues, including Hitler, and that was the forced submission of women to Aryan men. To the Nazis and their ideological predecessors, feminism was an evil on the same level as Freemasonry, international Jewry, and Bolshevism. In fact, the Nazis believed feminism (like Bolshevism) to be a creation of international Jewry for the express purpose of finishing off the Aryan race. The irony has come full circle, of course, for the term "feminazis" has become a staple of Rush Limbaugh–style, talk radio agit-prop.

But von Liebenfels did not stop at sweeping political indictments. He included occult biology in his repertoire, with a concentration on the pineal and pituitary glands. He believed—as did Blavatsky and as do many current mystics and theosophists—that a space between these glands in the hypothalamus of the brain was formerly a supercharged area that gave Aryans the twin powers of telepathy and omniscience: the third Eye; but that—because of the pollution of Aryan blood with that of members of the inferior races—these two glands had so atrophied that the Aryan people had lost their psychic abilities. This is a somewhat liberal borrowing from the teachings of legitimate Eastern adepts who train their devotees in methods of awakening this innate potential (regardless of their racial background).

According to von Liebenfels, however, the solution to the problem of the incipient physical and spiritual degeneration of the Aryan race was not hatha yoga or Transcendental Meditation but the creation of a new priesthood of the Holy Grail; a new Knights Templar of the German Blood (for that was, according to von Liebenfels, what the Grail represented). As for the inferior races? They were to be deported; or incinerated as a sacrifice to God; or simply used as slave labor.

All of these proposals—from Knights Templar to slave labor, from Holy Grail to crematoria—were to be accepted, incorporated, and expanded upon by Adolf Hitler personally, and by the Third Reich as official policy. It was also von Liebenfels who proposed that the finest specimens of Aryan males should mate indiscriminately with the finest specimens of Aryan females in specially controlled and tightly monitored villages in order to create the super race.[21] This would, of course, be a cause taken up by Himmler's *Lebensborn* organization to which every SS officer was expected to belong.

Lanz von Liebenfels and his mentor Guido von List can be viewed as archetypal Social Darwinists and the Third Reich as Social Darwinism carried to its logical conclusion. Similar to the rationale behind the race eugenics programs in the United States (which also influenced American immigration policies, both of which the Nazis regarded with admiration and approval), it was an ideology of the survival of the fittest, and the enslavement and destruction of the weakest, from Jews to women, from the mentally and physically handicapped to the aged, from Slavs and Gypsies to Communists. Gradually, the distinction between race and ideology became so blurred that the Soviets were viewed as race enemies as much as political enemies. This explains the ferocity with which Russian Communists were slaughtered by roving bands of Einsatzgruppen during the war, notably under such racist ideologues as Dr. Franz Six and onetime Theosophist Otto Ohlendorf. To support this program, they enlisted the aid of history, of romance, of legend, and of the occult significance of alphabets, geometry, ancient architecture, ritual magic . . . and the Knights Templar.

During the early twentieth century in Europe, the romance and lure of the Knights Templar myth was strong. The original Order of the Knights of the Temple had been destroyed by an agreement between the king of France (Phillipe le Bel) and Pope Clement V in the fourteenth century. Their leader at the time, Grandmaster Jacques de Molay, was burned at the stake in A.D. 1314 and the Order's assets seized all over Europe (primarily in France). One reason for all this bloodshed and chaos was the fact that the Order had become notoriously wealthy by loaning money to the king . . . so much money that the king now had no hope of repaying it. The official reasons given by Church and State for the suppression of the Templars were much different, however, and it is the mystery of this Order that has given rise to so many myths and legends, and which has contributed to the creation of several occult societies in the twentieth century. The works of Louis Charpentier in France[22] and Michael Baigent, Richard Leigh, and Henry Lincoln in Great Britain[23] may be consulted for a more detailed discussion of pop Templar literature, but for now all we need to know is that the Templars were believed to be the heirs of a mystical tradition of which Lanz von Liebenfels considered himself the modern incarnation.

Created by the mystical philosopher St. Bernard of Clairvaux—and therefore corresponding to von Liebenfels's own Cistercian background—the Templars were originally nine Knights who abandoned all they owned and ventured off to the Holy Land to "protect pilgrims" who were on their way to the various Catholic shrines. How nine recently impoverished men were expected to accomplish this mission—especially while there were already large, fully funded knightly organizations in Palestine doing just that—was never explained. However, about the year A.D. 1118 they found themselves bivouacked at the site of King Solomon's Temple in Jerusalem and spent their days there in relative obscurity—nine knights in charge of the entire Temple site—until their return to France ten years later, no pilgrims having been especially protected.

The legend states that these nine men returned with something important. Something discovered in the ruins of the Temple. Whatever it was, it made the Templars unbelievably rich and powerful virtually overnight. They began building cathedrals all over France and—according to the legend—not a single Templar-built cathedral (and this includes the famous Chartres Cathedral) contained a crucifix anywhere as part of its original design. The author should point out to any non-Catholics that a *crucifix* is, strictly speaking, a representation of Christ crucified on a cross. The Templar buildings *did* contain crosses; they simply omitted depicting the crucified body of Christ on them. This was seen as evidence that the Templars did not believe in the crucifixion and by extension did not believe in the resurrection of Christ after death; that, in fact, the Templars had somehow ceased being Christians entirely and become heretics, or worse.

What did the Templars find in Jerusalem that exerted such a profound if pernicious effect? Some say the Templars had located the Holy Grail itself. Others, that the Templars had found the Ark of the Covenant with its famous contents: the stone tablets on which the Ten Commandments were inscribed, and the magical Rod of Aaron.[24] Whatever it was, it revealed a secret so shattering that a thousand years of Christian teachings lay helpless in the face of it.

And whatever it was, it could not protect the Templars indefinitely. The Crusades proved to be a catastrophic series of campaigns for Church and State and eventually the Holy Land was "lost" to the Muslims. At home, the Church was worried about the wealth and influence of the Templars and suspicious about their onetime cozy relationship with the Saracens: Muslim warriors with whom the Templars might have exchanged "initiations." Then there were the rumors that the Templar initiation itself included a ceremony in which the postulant would trample upon a cross; or in which obeisance was paid to an idol called Baphomet (a suspiciously Arabic-sounding name). There were even rumors that homosexuality was being practiced on a wide scale among the knights—a charge that would later be brought in the twentieth century against Ernst Röhm and many other SA men as an excuse for *their* destruction.

These rumors—including some "eyewitness" testimony—were used as evidence in an Inquisition against the Templars; the Order was destroyed; and whatever members managed to escape the bonfires of the Church wound up in Germany, Portugal, and, it is theorized, in Scotland.

Oddly enough, during the eighteenth century the Templar legend enjoyed a kind of revival during the development of speculative Freemasonry. Templar degrees were added, and a tradition grew up around them that the Freemasons had been somehow Templars in disguise, heirs to the same mystical tradition surrounding the Temple of Solomon. This is odd because the Nazis would later persecute Freemasonry and arrest many of its members even though the Nazi Party itself was heir to the Order of the New Templars created by its early theoretician and Hitler mentor, Lanz von Liebenfels, and in fact borrowed its swastika emblem. As we shall see, Liebenfels himself and other Templar organizations were also persecuted, notable among them the *Ordo Templi Orientis* or OTO of Theodor Reuss, Karl Germer, Franz Hartmann, and Aleister Crowley.

Thule Gesellschaft

Many followers of List and Liebenfels were not satisfied with the metaphysical, meditational, essentially passive and academic nature of the List Society and the Order of New Templars. While they devoured *Ostara* and similar publications—and professed to read the longer, more complex books of both List and Liebenfels—they found themselves inflamed by their wild rhetoric and the countless attacks on Jews, Freemasons, Jesuits, Bolsheviks, and Capitalists. It was no longer enough to perform pagan rituals at the summer solstice or to decode a particularly interesting series of runes found on a rock or described in a forgotten book.

If the theories and proposals of List and Liebenfels were right—if a war was, in fact, taking place between the forces of Light and Darkness and the fate of the entire human race was at stake—then why wasn't someone doing something about it? Why wasn't there a program in place to weed out the Jews and other *Minderwertigen:* "beings of inferior value"? Where were the Germans of pure Ayran blood? Why weren't they taking charge in the political arena? And why weren't all German peoples united in a single great Reich?

To that end, and following the lead of a wealthy if small-time industrialist by the name of Theodor Fritsch—whose publishing hobby included an inflammatory anti-Semitic periodical, the *Hammer,* and one of the first German editions of the *Protocols of the Elders of Zion*[25]—several members of the List Society and the ONT formed their own, ultrasecret and ultra-right-wing society, the *Germanenorden* (or "German Order") in concert with a more overt propaganda effort called the *Reichshammerbund* based loosely on the anti-Semitic diatribes to be found in Fritsch's *Hammer* magazine.

The *Germanenorden* had an impressive series of initiatory rituals, replete with knights in shining armor, wise kings, mystical bards, and forest nymphs. The desire of the founders was to implement a Masonic-style program of secrecy, initiation, and mutual cooperation to counter the imagined conspiracy of Jews and Freemasons with their secret meetings and hidden agendas. What the *Germanenorden* became was, essentially, an anti-Masonry: a Masonic-style society devoted to the eradication of Freemasonry itself; an anti-Judaism: a mutual help and support network based on racial principles (one had to prove one's Aryan heritage by providing birth certificates going back several generations) that was committed to the destruction of the Jews. (As offbeat as this all sounds today, the *Germanenorden* would be spiritually reborn decades after the war as the Italo-Argentine P-2 Society, which we will discuss later).

The *Germanenorden* was formally established—along with the *Reichshammerbund*—in May of 1912 at the home of Fritsch.[26] Things went along fine for a while until World War I broke out and many *Germanenorden* members found themselves called to the front. At that time, the Order began to weaken and split into schismatic factions until the arrival on the scene of Baron Rudolf von Sebottendorff.

Sebottendorff had an exotic past. Initiated into a Masonic society in Egypt and communicant with a variety of secret societies in the Middle East and Turkey—for whom he fought in the Balkan War of 1912—Sebottendorff was another self-styled aristocrat in the tradition of List, Liebenfels, Mathers, and Crowley. Born Adam Alfred Rudolf Glauer to a locomotive driver on November 9, 1875, young Rudolf would take to sea at the age of twenty-two. After some misadventures in Australia, he fetched up in Alexandria in 1900, visited the pyramids at Giza and witnessed the rites of the Dervishes. Later in Constantinople he learned Turkish from a Muslim imam and worked for a Sufi initiate at a town near Bursa, becoming initiated into Freemasonry there in 1901.

Although he returned to Germany for a short while, he would find himself back in Turkey in 1908, studying Islamic alchemy, mysticism, and the practices of a Dervish sect with Janissary lineage known as the Baktashi. It is said that he founded his own mystical lodge in Constantinople in 1910, eventually winding up back in Germany in 1913.

During the war, Sebottendorff made contact with the head of the *Germanenorden*, Hermann Pohl, with whom he shared a fascination with Nordic runes and Eastern mysticism. Pohl enlisted his aid as a recruiter for the Order in Bavaria and Sebottendorff became a very successful promoter during 1917, even going so far as to publish his own Order magazine, called *Runen* (*Runes*) in 1918. By the end of 1917, Sebottendorff was admitted to the exalted rank of Master of the Order's Bavarian section.

It should be recognized from the above that Sebottendorff's interest in the *Germanenorden* was obviously of a strongly occultist nature. His background was that of a mystic and Orientalist (as Arabists then were called); his contact with Pohl was made on the basis of rune symbolism and other arcane lore. Although he served in the Turkish Army, he managed to avoid conscription into the German Army because he claimed Turkish citizenship. Therefore, we do not see Sebottendorff as a fanatic German nationalist or political activist first; rather, he comes upon his politics somewhat later in the game.

By 1918, the *Germanenorden* in Bavaria had grown to over fifteen hundred members—an astonishing rate of growth particularly considering the number of able-bodied men who were fighting World War I at the time. In need of space, Sebottendorff would rent rooms at the upscale Four Seasons Hotel in Munich. These rooms would eventually become known as the meeting place for the Thule Gesellschaft. The Thule Society was originally conceived as a cover identity for the *Germanenorden* which, at this time, was becoming identified with the type of right-wing extremism and virulent anti-Semitism that the various German republican and socialist groups were seeking to weed out and destroy. In short, the *Germanenorden*—another magic-oriented, occult

society with its secret initiation rituals patterned after Masonic ceremony and its Theosophical-style philosophy encompassing everything
from Eastern mysticism to runic lore to a rabid, pseudoscientific racism—was considered a subversive organization and a threat to society.
The Thule Society, while ostensibly a "literary-cultural group," had as
its emblem the famous swastika superimposed on a dagger. The Thule
Society front fooled no one, probably—certainly not its members,
who, in the beginning were all *Germanenorden* initiates, and which
included the Justice Minister Franz Gürtner (who would retain that
title in the Third Reich), Ernst Pohner, the police chief of Munich,
and various titled aristocrats.[27]

Sebottendorff enlisted the aid of young ex-soldier and art student
Walter Nauhaus. Another occultist and a follower of Guido von List,
Nauhaus joined the *Germanenorden* in Berlin in 1916 and in 1918
made contact with Sebottendorff (the Order's Bavarian master) after
moving to Munich. The two magicians decided to divide the responsi-
bilities of attracting new recruits to the cult by having Nauhaus devote
himself to university-age prospects. Nauhaus was about twenty-six
years old at the time.

The membership restrictions of the *Germanenorden*/Thule Gesellschaft make those of the New York Athletic Club or any typical American "whites only" golfing *gesellschaft* pale by comparison (no pun
intended). Aside from proving one's purity of Aryan blood as far back
as the Thirty Years' War, there were physical examinations that had to
be passed (measurement of skull, foot; color of hair, eyes; etc.). In
addition, the deformed or simply *unattractive* were also refused admittance. Those uncertain of where they stood in relation to these
draconian requirements were advised to refer to past issues of von
Liebenfels's *Ostara*.

It was directly due to this screening out of potential members that
the minister-president of Bavaria's first Socialist government—the
oddly *sympatico* Kurt Eisner—was assassinated, thus precipitating a
national crisis. The assassin, a young count, was refused admittance to
the Thule Society because he had Jewish blood. Angry at the rejection,
and consumed by a desire to prove his pro-German *bona fides,* he shot
and killed Herr Eisner while the latter was actually on his way to quit
his post, letter of resignation in hand.

What happened next is detailed in the pages that begin Chapter One. The young art student and occultist Walter Nauhaus was one of the seven Thulists captured, and later murdered, by the Red Army during the debacle of April 30, 1919. Munich was "liberated" from the Reds in May and Sebottendorff—stinging from charges he had let the Order down and was indirectly responsible for the deaths of the seven Thulists by failing to conceal the membership lists—officially resigned from the *Germanenorden*/Thule Society organization in June of that year and devoted the following years to a serious study of the stars. The *Germanenorden* continued to operate until well into the 1920s and actually carried out several political assassinations—including that of Matthias Erzberger,[28] one of the signatories of the Armistice and hence a "November criminal"—making the name *Germanenorden* synonymous with political terrorism as well as occult conspiracy. As for the Thule Society itself, there is documentary evidence in the diaries of Thule member Johannes Hering to show that it lasted at least until 1923, the year of Hitler's Beer Hall Putsch.[29]

Its foremost creation, however, took place while Sebottendorff was still in charge in Munich, and that was the formation of the "workers' society" arm of the Order. Heretofore, the *Germanenorden* and the Thule Society were virtually the exclusive domain of the wealthy, educated, and prominent among Bavarian society. There was no room for the lower-middle-class elements who were hurting the most from the effects of war, revolution, and inflation. The enemies of the *Germanenorden,* the Communists and Socialists, *were* actively recruiting among these elements, however, poisoning them against their aristocratic leaders and promising them a heaven on earth, a "workers' paradise." The monarchists and industrialists understood the need to counter this threat, or else their population base—a given for a thousand years of royal rule over the peasant populations of Europe—would wither and die. The arcane occult theories and snarled academic prose that characterized the meetings and publications of the *Germanenorden,* the Thule, the List Society, and the Order of New Templars was not likely to be easily understood—or warmly embraced—by the largely Christian masses. The Thule, it was recognized, was an elite society, attractive only to those who had done the reading; to those who could afford the initiations and the leisure time to devote to occult studies;

and to those who had already abandoned their traditional Christian faith or who were on the verge of doing so.

Thus, in order completely to unify the German population in opposition to the threat of Bolshevism and international Jewry, Sebottendorff formed a workers' circle with a few handpicked men, among them Anton Drexler. This group did *not* meet at the fancy Four Seasons Hotel but at a tavern, and was called the German Workers' Party, the *Deutsche Arbeiterpartei* or DAP, a consciously Socialist-sounding title. It was this group that Hitler was sent to spy on in September, 1919, and which, five months later, became the National Socialist German Workers' Party, the NSDAP or Nazi Party.

As we shall see in more detail in Chapter Five, Rudolf von Sebottendorff would eventually return to Germany in the 1930s with a mission to revitalize his old Order, calling upon his former colleagues and even reissuing his old magazine, *Runen.* He wrote a book—*Before Hitler Came*—describing the early history of the Thule Gesellschaft and the Nazi Party, showing how the occultists had virtually created both the Party and Hitler. This book—consulted with appropriate caution—has become invaluable to researchers tracing the lineage of many of the principal actors and organizations in this drama and in providing a time line against which the history of the Nazi Party can be established.

However, his revelations aroused the ire of the Party—and particularly of Hitler, who would take steps to ensure that no one who knew of his early days would be around to talk about them. Sebottendorff was thrown into a camp for a while, and then released to make his way to Turkey, where he worked for German Intelligence as a perfectly useless agent until the war ended. (The degree of his ineptitude as a spy may be judged by the fact that Schellenberg, chief of SS Foreign Intelligence, never mentions the illustrious Sebottendorff in his memoirs even though he wrote at some length about his visit to the Nazi intelligence apparatus in Turkey.) The new Thule Gesellschaft never got off the ground, and died aborning, divided by petty squabbles among its members (including an acrimonious attack on Franz Dannehl) and increasingly under pressure from the Nazis to disband. But the damage had already been done, many years before.

It should be pointed out that there is a great deal of controversy over the early days and connections of the DAP with the Thule Society. Some historians insist that there was no direct connection between them—although many DAP members were also Thulists, such as Franz Dannehl, Karl Harrer, and Friedrich Krohn (who designed the swastika flag for Hitler), and although the adoption of the swastika as Party symbol is a virtual admission of the link between the List, Liebenfels, and Sebottendorff groups and the DAP and NSDAP. Indeed, during the "troubles" of 1918 when the German revolution was in full swing with the collapse of the Second Reich, Pan-German groups were shut down all over Germany with the exception of the Thule Society (which was, we remember, purely a "literary-cultural" society); and its premises at the Four Seasons Hotel were used as a meeting place—and sometime hiding place—for such notables as Rudolf Hess and Alfred Rosenberg, not to mention the poet Dietrich Eckart who was the Doctor Frankenstein to Hitler's Monster. (It was only Eckart's fast talking and fancy footwork that kept him and Rosenberg alive when the Red Army began arresting—and shooting—Thulists.) So, while we cannot show a document stating that the DAP and NSDAP were subsidiaries of the Thule Gesellschaft or the *Germanenorden,* the author believes it is safe to say that the DAP (and, by extension, the Nazi Party) was originally a creature of both the Thule Society and Sebottendorff (as claimed by Sebottendorff and as admitted by Toland),[30] and, certainly, the wildest, most extreme aims of the Thule Society would all eventually become official policy of the Third Reich, while its purely metaphysical and occult characteristics were adopted wholeheartedly by the SS.

Between them, Guido von List—an elderly man in flowing beard and quasi-Renaissance attire—and Lanz von Liebenfels (a younger, clean-shaven, somewhat more imposing sort photographed in the ritual vestments of his Order) created the atmosphere of "rational" anti-Semitism in Vienna that was based on suspect scholarship in a number of fields, from etymology and linguistics to anthropology, astronomy and astrology, archaeology, and the occult. Sebottendorff, with his initiations into Eastern cults and his background in Middle Eastern mysticism and Freemasonry, personified the Aryan Mystic. As an aristocrat, a proven man of action who fought with Turkish forces in the Balkan War, and with his political connections and his activism at the time of the 1919 Putsch, he showed what a serious occultist could accomplish with a few hundred men and a stockpile of weapons. Sebottendorff was an ideal figure, a perfect combination of mystic and militarist, an echo of the times when kings were initiates, and when priests raised armies.

Although he was held responsible by the Thule for the murder of the seven hostages held by the Red Army by allowing the Thule membership lists to fall into enemy hands, it was Sebottendorff who had tirelessly organized—first for the *Germanenorden,* of which he was a Master, and then for the Thule Gesellschaft, which he founded—and who had created an armed cult and sophisticated intelligence apparatus in the midst of pre-Weimar Munich. His Society had received such distinguished guests as Alfred Rosenberg, Dietrich Eckart, and Rudolf Hess. His Society had created the German Workers' Party, from which the Nazi Party would be born. And his Society bestowed the single most important symbol of the Third Reich upon the fledgling Nazis: the occult sign of the swastika, inherited from Liebenfels, Hitler's early mentor. Sebottendorff and the Thule Society were both ultimately and directly responsible for the collapse of the Soviet regime in Bavaria, both from force of arms and from force of ideas.

And it was an amazing time, no matter who was responsible; for an occult organization—a secret society based on Theosophical, runic, and magical concepts (a kind of redneck Golden Dawn with guns)—had fought an armed conflict in the streets of Munich against the purely political forces of a Soviet state . . . and won. Today, this would be considered the stuff of science fiction or, at worst, sword and sorcery fantasy. But in Munich, in 1919, it was reality.

SS 3 SS

The Occult Messiah

. . . this idea of himself as the German Messiah was the source of his personal power. It enabled him to become the ruler of eighty million people—and in the space of twelve short years to leave his ineradicable mark on history.[1]

—SCHELLENBERG

hat Hitler was fascinated by the occult is proven: the Berchtesgaden library, discovered in a mine after the war, contained many volumes on occultism.[2] His small collection of books as a student contained works on mythology and a collection of von Liebenfels's racist-occult magazine, *Ostara*,[3] and he even visited with the Templar Master (as seen in Chapter Two). Friends of his from the early days recall long conversations on occult themes—everything from reincarnation to yoga to paganism and magic[4]—and his later biographers, such as Sir Allan Bullock, record Hitler's familiarity with occult topics in the days prior to the Second World War.[5]

That Hitler ever actually belonged to an occult lodge has never been proven and, in fact, probably never will be. While Hitler appreciated the "scholarship" he discovered in the occult magazines and books he devoured, he never took a particular liking to the type of people who composed occult lodges. The occultists who were members of his inner circle—such as Hess, Rosenberg, Gutberlet, and Eckart—lived on the periphery of the Thule and *Germanenorden* lodges; while Eckart and Rosenberg may have been members of the Thule, it is clear to the author that they would have been exploiting that membership for their own, hidden, agenda. The leadership and influence of men like Sebottendorff was strong, and it is doubtful whether Hitler would have willingly accepted a role subservient to an occult (or political) master. History has shown that no occult order can survive two masters.

Hitler was an activist. Almost any action was better than sitting around a room in a robe and meditating on Thor. Hitler was a pacer. He couldn't sit still for long. And he was a demagogue, almost from the beginning. He had to lead; and if he couldn't lead, he would absent himself from the action and the conversation altogether. Hitler was a paranoid, and the occult holds special attractions for the paranoid. But Hitler as cultist? As a black-robed, ritual-performing, invocation-chanting priest of Satan? Probably not.

But Hitler as tool of other cultists?

Probably so.[6]

The basic details of Hitler's life story are so well known, and so well documented in other sources, that to repeat them here would cheat the reader who is, after all, looking for the occult angle to the mystery of the Third Reich. Let us concentrate then on those aspects of Hitler's life that reveal occult interests and involvements, all the while remembering what has been said here before: that there is no evidence that Hitler ever actually joined an occult society *per se,* but that the evidence for his fascination with occult themes and subjects is extensive and that a great portion of the program of the Third Reich concerning race, Jews, Freemasons, genetic engineering, etc., was the veritable platform of the *völkisch* and Pan-German occult lodges carried out in actual practice, a platform Hitler inherited from Liebenfels, Rosenberg, and Eckart during his early days in Vienna and Munich. Indeed, his major argument with the occult lodges was only *that they had been unable to carry out their programs in the real world.* Hitler, in a sense, had mastered himself and the "real world" to an extent that men like Mathers and even Crowley had not, but wished to. That is—not satisfied with phony titles and the accumulation of pedigrees and initiations that typified the fin de siècle occultist—he was able to take his occult beliefs and enact them on the world stage to a degree undreamed of by mainstream occult philosophers. In that sense, then, he *was* a tool of the occultists. More, he was their Creature.

Hitler was born on April 20, 1889, to an Austrian civil servant in the town of Braunau-am-Inn, a locale said to be famous at the time for its large proportion of native mediums.[7] It is even claimed that Hitler shared the same wet nurse as two famous "channelers" of the day: Rudi and Willy Schneider.[8] That Hitler himself might have been a medium was a contention made by a great many of his personal friends and other observers, who described the Führer in terms ranging from "hypnotic" to "demoniacally possessed" to the "Prince of Darkness" himself.[9] As this is a rather subjective judgment, for which no proof is available, let us pass over it in silence as there will be ample opportunity to examine the occult influences on Hitler's life from a variety of other sources.

Instead, we will begin with Hitler's childhood schooling at Lambach Monastery, from 1897 to 1899, under the guidance of Catholic monks. It is so indicative of the atmosphere in which the Nazi Party would later take root in Germany and Austria that, as mentioned earlier, the coat of arms of this monastery is a swastika before which Hitler would pass every school day and which even now adorns the chapel where Hitler would attend choir practice, and in several other places, and which was even visible from his apartment window.

Hitler (like Heinrich Himmler, Dr. Mengele, Joseph Goebbels, Klaus Barbie, and so many other prominent Nazis) was born and reared a Roman Catholic, a fact that is often forgotten.[10] His mother was devout, his father rather less so; and it is important to recognize that Hitler never got along well with his father but idolized his mother.

Like all good Catholic children of a certain age, Hitler was confirmed in the Church. The Roman Catholic Confirmation ceremony is one in which young Catholics reaffirm the sacrament of Baptism: that is, with their own voice they confirm their acceptance of the vows made for them by their godparents when they were infants. They officially reject "Satan, and all his pomps, and all his works," in a ceremony which evidently left the young Hitler either totally unimpressed or strangely tense, for he was distracted and restless that whole afternoon until some neighborhood children came by and invited him to a game of cowboys and Indians, which he joined with unbridled enthusiasm. We may wonder at what point Hitler lost his interest in the Church or, indeed, if he ever had any interest to lose. Many Christian organizations enthusiastically supported Hitler in the early years of his dictatorship, choosing not to believe that the virulently anti-Christian stance of his neo-pagan Nazi Party was sincere. They were accompanied in their folly by many Jewish people and organizations which could not accept that the anti-Semitism of the Party was anything more than a cheap political ploy.

Germany, of course, was the birthplace of the Lutheran Reformation, the last stronghold of the Holy Roman Empire and a country of Christians of whatever persuasion. Germany was also the country of *Walpurgisnacht,* that famous pagan festival celebrated on April 30 every year, traditionally at the top of Mount Brocken in the Harz Mountains, where the Witches' Sabbath supposedly takes place. Germany was also the scene of what we might call "Christian revisionism," an attempt to describe the resurrection of Christ as a myth perpetrated by his disciples: a thesis promulgated by Professor Reimarus of Hamburg in the eighteenth century, who insisted that Jesus was nothing more than a Jewish rebel, and that his body had been stolen from his tomb by his followers. Eventually, German scholarship would prove that the Gospels were written much later than anyone had previously realized, a position represented by no less than the esteemed Biblical commentator and professor of the University of Marburg, Rudolf Bultmann who, in his *Jesus and the Word*— published before Hitler came to power—came to the conclusion that the life of Jesus was virtually unknowable.[11] Thus we have a land where scientific research and religious fervor meet; a country that will occasionally engage in an almost masochistic turning-inward upon itself and its cherished ideals, devouring its own children in the process.

We have a nation where fierce religious beliefs live cheek by jowl with fierce religious dissent; a land where Lutherans and Catholics, Christians and pagans, each lay claim to the country's psyche. The Holy Inquisition was founded there in 1231 in response to the Cathar threat to the Holy See; yet Germany was also the birthplace of Rosicrucianism, the core documents of that movement—the *Fama Fraternitatis* and the *Confessio*—having been published there in 1614 and

1615. The infamous bugaboo of right-wing conspiracy buffs—the *Illuminaten Orden,* the dread Illuminati of Adam Weishaupt—began in Ingolstadt, Bavaria, in 1776 (the birthplace of Ernst Röhm and once the home of Heinrich Himmler and now of BMW, Ingolstadt is also well known as the city where the fictional Dr. Frankenstein created his Monster). And Germany became the country where the Anthroposophical Society of Rudolf Steiner was founded less than 150 years later, an organization that was banned and persecuted by the Nazis resulting in Steiner's own untimely death in 1925.

So it was perhaps inevitable that the type of occultism which would develop on such fertile soil would be the syncretist type represented by List and Liebenfels: an anti-Papist neo-Templarism mixed with Teutonic mythology and anti-Semitism, blended in a mind-boggling metaphysical stew and spiced with a fanatic desire to prove the undiluted "purity" of the blood. It also comes as no surprise that the ultimate British secret society of that era—the Golden Dawn—was traditionally said to have originated, not on that "blessed isle," but in Germany itself with the forged "cypher manuscript" of a nonexistent Fraülein A. Sprengel in Stuttgart. It was somehow important to the Chiefs of the Golden Dawn—Dr. William Wynn Westcott, MacGregor Mathers, and Dr. William R. Woodman—to demonstrate a *German* origin for their Society, even though later scholarship has shown that the forged documents were in a grammatically poor, error-ridden German. So why not a British or a Celtic origin? Or French or Italian, for that matter? Or Middle Eastern? Mathers's command of Latin was good enough to enable him to perform the first ever English translation of the *Sefer ha-Zohar,* the central text of Jewish Qabalism, from the Latin version by Knorr von Rosenroth, a translation still in use today.[12] Indeed, Qabalism is a major element of the Golden Dawn system of initiation. So why strain for a *German* origin for the Golden Dawn when Mathers could have forged an ancient Latin pedigree from anywhere else in Europe or the Middle East much more easily?

Because the late nineteenth century occult revival was taking place—not in England or France or anywhere else on the Continent—but in Germany itself: the land of the first Rosicrucians, the Teutonic Knights, Paracelsus, Johannes Trithemius, the notorious *Vehmgericht* (the secret tribunal to exact vigilante justice that was revived in Nazi Germany),[13] and other famous figures of medieval mysticism, both real and mythical. And it was from Germany, after all, that Aleister Crowley's most famous import originated, one still in existence today: the *Ordo Templi Orientis,* or OTO.

We have noted how Hitler was influenced by the writings of *völkisch* occultists like Liebenfels. This had happened at a time in his life when everything around him was falling apart. In 1907, his beloved mother died in an excruciating manner: diagnosed with breast cancer, she submitted to the painful application of iodoform to her chest. This was a method by which—it was believed—the acidlike characteristics of iodoform would literally burn out the cancerous cells. She succumbed, however, on December 21, dying in the light of a Christmas tree near her bed. (Four days later, Lanz von Liebenfels would raise his swastika flag over Burg Werfenstein, not far from the Hitler home in Upper Austria.)

That this experience would have figuratively burned itself into her son and thereby affect his psyche in profound and disturbing ways— particularly in relation to women and, possibly, to Jews (his mother's doctor was Jewish)—has already been discussed at length by other authors;[14] we may take a little license here ourselves, though, and call to mind another man whose early experience of the barbaric medical treatment of his mother would also affect him profoundly: Peter Ilich Tchaikovsky, the Russian composer, who at the age of fourteen watched his mother die at the hands of doctors who were trying to cure her from cholera by submerging her body in boiling water. In Tchaikovsky's case, he managed to channel a great deal of this traumatic episode into his music (while suffering from an ambiguous sexual identity in the process). In Hitler's case, there is similar evidence that his mother's gruesome death may have affected his sex life but, being rejected as an artist—his first career choice—no less than three times, he abandoned the humanities for politics and thereby came to vent his anger and frustration on the whole world. It has been said that Hitler's problem in terms of art was his inability to draw the human body; perhaps, then, his inability to purge himself of the trauma of watching his mother die in such a horrible fashion on the eve of the winter solstice.

Thus orphaned, estranged from most of his family, impoverished, continually rejected in his quest for acceptance at the Academy of Fine

Arts in Vienna, sleeping in men's dorms and living on the dole, this lover of grand opera—reduced to prostituting what he believed was his great artistic talent by painting picture postcards for tourists—was prime material for the paranoid screeds of the German and Austrian occultists. In another age, or another country, Hitler might have blamed his gross misfortunes on a plague of evil spirits and sought the assistance of an exorcist or witch doctor. Instead, the perfectly scientific-sounding jargon he found in *Ostara* provided him with another— equally occult and nefarious—enemy: an evil *race* whose very *blood,* and cells, and genes were slowly possessing and *dispossessing* the entire German people. Hitler would not have to burn sacrifices at the altars of pagan gods to obtain release from his demonic possession; he would only have to build the crematoria. Authors like Liebenfels took the racial theories of Blavatsky—with her innumerable root-races and her pyramiding evolutionary scheme—and mixed them with the programs of Social Darwinists and crank eugenicists, and took the resulting mixture to a logical conclusion: exterminate the subhumans and so avoid polluting the gene pool with their recessive traits.

Hitler was not *completely* credulous: that is, he did not surrender his entire life to a blind acceptance of occult beliefs; otherwise, he would have spent his remaining years sitting around séance tables and invoking spirit guides like many of his contemporaries, in Europe and America. Instead, Hitler was nothing if not pragmatic, and not easily fooled by fake mediums and other occult charlatans. He sought real-world solutions to the problems posed by mystics such as Liebenfels. That is, he agreed with occult *theory* and seemed to take much of it as accepted fact; it was occult practice—particularly the occult practices taking place in his own environment of self-deluded albeit self-proclaimed magi and bishops and seers—that he couldn't stomach, although he loved to read about occultism and to discuss it with those of his friends who had done some of the same reading. In this, he was not so different from millions of other people who enjoy being entertained by tabloid tales of true occult rituals and occult crimes but who would never actually *perform* an occult ritual.

To Hitler, the occult was possibly a further refinement of the Roman Catholicism he was brought up with. According to Schellenberg and other Nazis around the Führer, Hitler did not believe in an afterlife or a personal god.[15] The author, however, submits that it lay there in the back of his mind like the faint buzz of a mosquito. He couldn't ignore it completely; as it was for Himmler, the concept of an afterlife was probably simultaneously real and threatening to him, but not something around which he would arrange his life. He paid attention to omens and prognostications from a variety of sources, and was not averse to having others work magic for him (as we shall see); but, like a Mafia don, he kept his hands clean of the actual bloodletting itself.

In the years before World War I and after the death of his mother, Hitler lived in poverty in Vienna. (This would make him a typical occultist, even today. As the congenial author of many respected histories of secret societies and occult personalities—Francis King—once remarked in the author's presence, "It seems to be a requirement of great and powerful magicians that they live on public assistance.") He eventually had his own space at a men's dormitory where—after having been deloused—he was given a small, clean room of his own and managed to buy some watercolors. He would paint scenes of churches and local landmarks, and a friend would hawk them on the streets for a cut of the proceeds. It was in Vienna and during these tough times that Hitler made the personal acquaintance of Lanz von Liebenfels at the latter's office, sometime in 1909. Liebenfels remembered that Hitler appeared so distraught and so impoverished that the New Templar himself gave Hitler free copies of *Ostara* and bus fare back home.[16] It would be von Liebenfels who would greet the ascension of Hitler to Germany's throne with tremendous enthusiasm as a sign of the great occult power that was sweeping through the world under the sign of the swastika (before he was silenced by that same regime after Anschluss in 1938).

Hitler was also fascinated by the opera, particularly Wagner (1813–1883). The four operas that compose the famous *Ring Cycle* were a favorite, of course, and *Parsifal, Lohengrin* . . . virtually all of Wagner's mythological and mystical work. One Wagnerian opera that stands out as an early favorite of Hitler's is a lesser-known and infrequently performed work called *Rienzi.* Hitler was captivated by this opera and took a childhood friend to see it several times. They had to stand during the performance since they could not afford seat tickets. It is an intriguing footnote to the story of the occult Reich that *Rienzi*'s libretto was based on an historical novel of medieval Rome by the celebrated English occultist and best-selling author Lord Bulwer-Lytton (1803–1873). Rienzi was a patriot who attempted to reform the Roman government, but who eventually failed and went to his death. Rienzi—whose real name was Niccolo Gabrini—was often called "the last of the Romans." As for Bulwer-Lytton, who is probably best known for his *The Last Days of Pompei,* he was the author of the popular occult novels *Zanoni* and *Vril: The Coming Race,* the latter having inspired the creation of a German secret society by the same name. (Bulwer-Lytton's name would also be lumped together with those of Byron, Moore, Shelley, Rousseau, George Sand, and Victor Hugo as a member of the "Satanic School" of literature: a trend of certain Romantic poets towards the anti-Christian, unconventional, and occasionally obscene in literature.)

It would be Wagner's peculiar vision of cosmology and world history—that finds its most perfect expression in *Parsifal,* with its moving, if peculiar, pagan spin on the Christ mythos—that would influence Hitler and an entire generation of Germans who were cutting their milk teeth on Teutonic mythology as German prehistory and on the writings of erstwhile Wagner devotee Friedrich Nietzsche (1844–1900), the philosopher who popularized the concept of the "superman." The heady combination of Nietzsche and Wagner provided an atmosphere in which strange pagan societies could develop among the otherwise fastidious members of polite society. Groups such as the Thule Society, the Edda Society, the List Society, the *Germanenorden,* and the Order of New Templars would include nobles, military officers, college professors, and wealthy industrialists among their ranks. It was also the influence of Wagner to which we can attribute that fascination for orders of knighthood, the quest for the *pagan* Grail, Teutonic gods, and blond-haired heroes that would eventually dominate the *Weltanschauung* of Hitler's most ardent supporter, Heinrich Himmler.

About the year 1911 Hitler made the acquaintance of one Josef Greiner—another resident of the men's hostel, an unemployed lamplighter—and they would spend hours discussing such arcane lore as astrology, religion, and the occult sciences.[17] According to Greiner in his published memoirs,[18] Hitler was fascinated by stories of yoga and the magical accomplishments of the Hindu fakirs. He read with enthusiasm the travel books of Swedish explorer Sven Hedin, who blazed trails through the Himalayas in search of Tibetan Shangri-las.[19]

But in 1913, defeated in his dream of becoming an artist and thereby redesigning the great public buildings of Vienna, Linz, and other Austrian cities, Hitler finally left his homeland for Germany, crossing over the border from Austria-Hungary on May 24 and arriving in Munich the next day.

A year and a month later, Archduke Ferdinand would be assassinated at Sarajevo by a member of a Serbian secret society called the Black Hand. In July 1914, Austria will declare war on Serbia. Three days later, on August 1, Germany will mobilize against Czarist Russia; on August 3, she will declare war against France; on August 16, Hitler will enlist with the 1st Bavarian Infantry Regiment. The young artist—broke, his artistic efforts constantly rejected, and living a humiliating life on charity—embraces war with glee.

If there is still any doubt about Hitler's enthusiasm for occult and *völkisch* themes, the following should put all objections to rest.

Obsessed by some of his occult ideas, Hitler wrote a poem in the autumn of 1915, while in the trenches. Reproduced in part in Toland's biography of Hitler,[20] it sings the praises of Wotan, the Teutonic Father God, and of runic letters, magic spells, and magic formulas. Had it been printed today in any of a dozen occult and New Age journals of the author's acquaintance, it would have raised few eyebrows so consistent is its theme of magic, mystery, and esoteric paganism.

Adolf Hitler is twenty-six years old; by the time the war ends in 1918, he will have been awarded the Iron Cross, First and Second Classes, and will have proven himself an exceptionally brave combat soldier.

But in October of 1918, he is blinded by a mustard gas attack in Belgium. He temporarily loses his sight, and is sent to the sanitorium at Pasewalk. The doctors, not familiar with this type of condition, believe it to be psychosomatic. While they may be wrong, he does eventually regain his sight, only to lose it again as word of Germany's surrender reaches his ears on Martin Luther's birthday: November 9, 1918. (On that same day, in Munich, Baron Sebottendorff would call

the Saturday meeting of the Thule Gesellschaft to order and his cultists would begin to forge identity papers, spy on the Reds, and stockpile weapons.)

Yet it is during Hitler's blindness that he receives a kind of mystical
enlightenment, like that experienced by Guido von List many years
before during his own temporary blindness (or like that of Saul,
blinded on the way to Damascus) for, from that point on, Adolf Hitler
has changed. He has been illumined, perhaps. Spoken—as the Golden
Dawn would have said—to his Holy Guardian Angel, his higher Self.
He has been blinded fighting the Allies in defense of his adopted country, Germany, only to regain his sight to witness Germany's capitula-
tion and the abdication of the Kaiser—whom the Allies had already
characterized as the Antichrist—and the resulting collapse of the
Reich.

After the successful overthrow of the Soviet Government by the
Free Corps under Thule Society leadership, the Thulists recognize that
they need to organize the workers into a coherent political party, else
the Communists will return with a vengeance. Sebottendorff has already formed the Political Workers' Circle out of his base at the rather
expensive and exclusive Four Seasons Hotel. From this Circle will be
spawned the German Workers' Party with rail worker and locksmith
Anton Drexler at its head. It is this Party that Hitler will infiltrate—on
the orders of a Captain Mayr, who reports to a clique of wealthy
industrialists and officers operating coincidentally (?) out of the Four
Seasons Hotel—in September of 1919.[21] Drexler will give him a small
pamphlet that he has authored containing explosive phrases like "National Socialism" and the rather sinister "New World Order." Hitler
is captivated by these concepts, and decides that his spying days are
over. Drexler is equally captivated by the brash and outspoken young
Austrian corporal, and urges him to join the Party.

Adolf Hitler becomes German Workers' Party member 555.

Later, perhaps for superstitious reasons, Hitler will annoy the Old
Guard by claiming that he was member number 7; this will be proven
wrong when it is revealed that the Party began its numbering system
at 500 in order to appear larger than it really was. (Hitler was actually
member number 7 of the executive committee of the Party, formed

later.) In a bizarre coincidence, the number 555 will come up again a little later as the numerological value of the word *Necronomicon,* a book of black magick that was first introduced to the Western world in a short story by H.P. Lovecraft entitled "The Hound" (1922). Lovecraft was also an anti Semite and an ethnophobe, as many of his writings and letters attest. During the years that Nazism rose to total power in Germany, Lovecraft was writing stories about an unnamable evil that could be conjured using the formulas of the *Necronomicon* and along the way introduced yet another "black book," the *Unaussprechlichen Kulten* ("Unspeakable Cults" or, alternatively, "Unpronounceable Cults"!) of the mythical German anthropologist von Junst. He wrote about the mysterious and abhorred practices of Asians and Arabs in his short story "The Horror of Red Hook" among other tales and—save for the rather high literary quality of his stories when compared to the articles of a von Liebenfels—their racist nature could have easily promised him publication in select copies of *Ostara.* While the actual nature and extent of Lovecraft's anti-Semitism and ethnophobia have become the subject of much debate, it is safe to say that many of his stories do not meet the criteria set down by our faithful watchdogs of the Politically Correct.

(To followers of Aleister Crowley, the number 555 is the qabalistic equivalent of an ancient Hebrew term meaning "Darkness," an appropriate connotation from a Jewish perspective of what Hitler represented. But then, of course, 555 is also the number used by Hollywood for nonexistent telephone exchanges in movie and television scripts; one may also dial 555-1212, preceded by an area code, to get the information operator for that area code. I leave it to qabalists more advanced or more creative than I to interpret these "synchronicities.")

Gradually, Hitler—carrying out his own, mysterious agenda spawned at the sanitorium in Pasewalk—begins to assume total control of the German Workers' Party (*Deutsche Arbeiterpartei* or DAP). He changes its name to National Socialist German Workers' Party or *Nazionalsocialistische Deutsche Arbeiterpartei* or NSDAP. He will also design its emblem with the help of a Thule Society member, the dentist Dr. Friedrich Krohn, and the swastika will become the official symbol of the new Nazi Party.

Still broke, Hitler lives in a tiny rented room in Munich. His book-case has a few, well-thumbed volumes, including the memoirs of a famous Swedish explorer, Sven Hedin, (already mentioned) whose principal destination has always been Asia with an emphasis on Tibet. Sven Hedin will later become deeply involved with the infamous Ah-nenerbe: a research organization within Himmler's SS which was responsible for some of the worst atrocities of the Reich.

Dietrich Eckart

Although hungry, poorly (some say, ridiculously) dressed, and uncom-fortable in high society, Hitler comes to the attention of one of Ger-many's most famous poets, the eccentric genius Dietrich Eckart (1868–1923). Eckart, encouraged by his friends in the Thule, went to hear him speak at DAP meetings and, like so many people after him, became entranced by the hypnotic, wild-eyed Austrian fanatic. He takes Hitler under his wing and introduces him to the elite of Munich society.

Dietrich Eckart was a drug addict who owned his own newspaper. Famous for his translation into German of *Peer Gynt,* Eckart was one of Munich's coffeehouse darlings, as well known for his biting wit and sarcasm as for his felicitous use of the German language in poetry and plays. He was also a former mental patient and a rabid anti-Semite. With a circulation of some thirty thousand, his newspaper—*Auf Gut Deutsch* ("In Good German")—ranks with the *Völkischer Beobachter* and *Ostara* as a racist sheet with intellectual pretensions. His protégé was none other than Alfred Rosenberg, the Baltic-born anti-Semite who is later to become one of the architects of official Nazi pagan policies. Eckart, Rosenberg, and, later, Rudolf Hess become Hitler's closest companions and coconspirators in the first years of the 1920s in Munich. It was Eckart who, on his deathbed after the failed Beer Hall Putsch of November 8–9, 1923, was widely quoted as saying "Hitler will dance, but it is I who plays the tune. . . . Do not mourn for me, for I will have influenced history more than any other German."[22]

Eckart—it will be no shock to learn—was an occultist. An intimate of the Thule Society, he was as well versed in its beliefs (and, hence, of those of the *Germanenorden*) as any other member. He was also an early admirer of the weird cosmological theories of Hans Hörbiger, and introduced them to his Austrian corporal. His cozy relationship with both Rosenberg and Hess would have provided fertile ground for any number of wide-reaching discussions on mystical subjects. It has even been claimed that Eckart and Hitler attended séances in which ghostly ectoplasmic forms were seen; but, alas, there is no evidence for this.[23]

There *is* evidence, however, that Eckart was approached by none other than the eminent occultist Rudolf Steiner himself. Steiner was interested in forming an alliance with Eckart as the latter was known to be a mystic and as Steiner had his own politico-mystical agenda. During the "troubles" of the spring of 1919, Steiner sought out Eckart in an attempt to get coverage for his "Threefold Commonwealth" idea in the pages of Eckart's *Auf gut Deutsch,* an attempt that was doomed to failure. Eckart considered himself a "Christian mystic" and spurned Steiner's advances as a result of the latter's membership in the OTO, attacking Steiner in articles published in his newspaper in July and December, 1919. According to Eckart, Steiner was a crazed sex magician and a member of the Jewish-Masonic conspiracy.[24]

An article, written by Alfred Rosenberg and published almost a year after Eckart's death, asserts that Eckart was steeped in the lore of ancient India and was as well versed in the mystical concepts of *Maya* and *Atman* as he was in the poetry of Goethe and the philosophy of Schopenhauer and Angelus Silesius. This is extremely relevant, for it shows that Eckart believed in the idea of Cosmic Consciousness *(Atman)* and in the concept that the visible, tangible world is illusion *(Maya).* The term "atman" has also been used, and abused, by a variety of occultists to mean a higher Self and to refer to the next stage in human evolution, which was, of course, virtually a strategic goal of the Nazis and a tenet of their basic beliefs. The eulogy also describes another crucial element of Nazi ideology, and that is the alleged usurpation by the Jews of Christianity; for Rosenberg mentions that the Jewish Jehovah is corrupting the "so-called Christian churches."[25] This is an essential part of the Nazi mythos that we will return to in a later chapter.

As for Eckart himself, most histories give him very little print space. His influence over Hitler is downplayed, perhaps owing to the fact that there is insufficient documentation of the type needed to expand upon their relationship. Yet, for the last three years of his life, Eckart was Hitler's constant companion and the man who helped propel him into the public spotlight. It was Eckart who first introduced Hitler to all the right people, to the wealthy and powerful movers and shakers of Bavaria. Eckart clearly groomed Hitler for the role he was later to play and spent those three years orchestrating his rise to power. It was Eckart who helped arrange financing for the nascent Nazi Party from European and American industrialists, including Henry Ford. And it was Eckart who, along with Rosenberg, accompanied Hitler to Upper Bavaria with fifteen hundred Storm Troopers to "liberate" the town of Coburg from the Reds in what was arguably Hitler's first real military victory.

Hitler's popularity and influence in Germany was growing at a speed that must have amazed Hitler himself, considering that only a few years earlier he had been cold and hungry, living on charity. But his anti-Communist, anti-Capitalist platform was winning him converts from all over Germany's political spectrum. The old guard—those members of Germany's defeated army that came home to find their nation unrecognizable, in shreds from the hundreds of wars taking place between dozens of private armies and political parties, and in absolute economic chaos—drank in Hitler's speeches like cool steins of draft in the very beer cellars where the Nazi Party met. And on February 24, 1920—at the meeting during which his Twenty-Five Point program for saving Germany was proclaimed, introduced by Marc Sesselmann (a Thulist and member of the DAP)—he told them what they wanted to hear: that the war was lost because of Capitalists, Communists, Freemasons, and the ever-present bugaboo, international Jewry, which was behind them all. That the Germans were enslaved by punitive interest payments. That swift and violent action was needed if Germany was to be snatched from the jaws of a satanic conspiracy. The speech was welcomed by thunderous applause from the approximately two thousand listeners, and the die of the Nazi Party was cast.

At this time the *Protocols of the Elders of Zion* was being widely disseminated, and raising alarms about a grand conspiracy of Jews and Freemasons bent on destroying Germany as they were at that moment destroying Russia. If Hitler were in power, his listeners believed, he would throw out all these undesirable elements—by force of arms, if necessary—and the country would be right again. Of course, subtract all the Capitalists, Communists, Freemasons, and Jews from the population (and eventually all the Christians) and one wonders who would remain.

Eine Arte Menschenopfer (A Kind of Human Sacrifice)

As Hitler was tramping around Germany, raising consciousness and gathering recruits, a secret organization within the Ehrhardt Freikorps Brigade was itching for revolution. They eventually carried out (on June 24, 1922) the most famous assassination of the era, one that is still remembered today by those who lived through it, as Americans remember where they were when Kennedy was killed.[26] The society was called Organization Consul and its members included Erwin Kern, Hermann Fischer, Ernst von Salomon, and Ernst-Werner Techow. Organization Consul was a terrorist cell within the Ehrhardt Brigade, dedicated to carrying out bombings and assassinations against leftist targets and "Versailles" politicians, i.e., the "November criminals" who were believed to have sold Germany down the river at the Armistice and later at the Versailles Peace Conference. While the Freikorps marched openly and provocatively through the streets, their brothers in Organization Consul stuck to the alleys.

Their target for June 1922 was none other than Walther Rathenau, foreign minister of the Weimar Republic. Rathenau's father had founded what later became AEG, Germany's version of General Electric, by purchasing Edison's patents on the electric light bulb. Rathenau himself, a sensitive, artistic soul who became enmeshed in high finance, industry, and politics almost against his will (he was a lover of poetry and music who had written volumes of aphorisms under a pseudonym) was Jewish. But that was not his only crime. He was also wealthy, admired, powerful, and a man with far-ranging vision. He had virtually single-handedly ensured that Germany would be able to wage a continuous war under the Kaiser by arranging to bring all of Germany's raw materials under centralized control in 1914. He had successfully negotiated the famous Treaty of Rapallo with the Soviet Union when France was frantically trying to isolate Germany from the European community after the war. He had written books describing the political and cultural situation in Germany with insight and wit. In short, he was a man of many accomplishments and, what is more, a sympathetic and elegant figure whom even the conspirators admitted "unites in himself everything in this age that is of value in thought, in honor, and in spirituality."[27]

So naturally these Freikorps thugs were committed to his destruction.

We might not be discussing Rathenau at this point were it not for a peculiar phenomenon surrounding his death that is referred to by historian Norman Cohn. Of course, the Freikorps (and particularly the Ehrhardt Brigade, as we have seen) was heavily influenced by *völkisch* and other Pan-German occultism. And it was the Ehrhardt Brigade, remember, that marched into Munich that May Day in 1919 wearing the swastika as their symbol and singing the *hakenkreuz* hymn.

But Rathenau was identified with the most legendary conspiracy of all time, and was numbered among its members in the crazed imaginations of desperate men. Walther Rathenau, they believed, was one of the *actual Elders of Zion.* His assassination would be a blow against the international Jewish/Masonic/Communist/Capitalist cabal to dominate the world. He *did* unite in himself all those qualities and values recognized by the Organization Consul itself, and thereby symbolized the success of the Zionist conspiracy.

Therefore, according to Cohn:

> . . . Rathenau was not simply assassinated as an Elder of Zion, he was offered up as a human sacrifice to the sun-god of ancient Germanic religion. The murder was timed to coincide with the summer solstice; and when the news was published, young Germans gathered on hilltops to celebrate simultaneously the turning of the year and the destruction of one who symbolized the powers of darkness.[28]

In later years, Ernst Röhm would deliver a eulogy at the graves of two of the assassins, saying that their spirit "is the spirit of the SS, Himmler's black soldiers."[29]

The human sacrifice of Walther Rathenau—timed to occur on a pagan holiday or "sabbath" that was observed by Nazi cultists throughout Germany—was the signal that the new Aryan faith was increasing in strength. It certainly must have seemed that way to Hitler.

The Liberation of Coburg

With Eckart and now Rosenberg at his side, Hitler strode all over Germany like an avenging angel on a budget, seeking out targets of opportunity. With him could be counted upon a contingent of six hundred oddly dressed former Free Korps men who had sworn an oath of loyalty to the cause, a kind of bodyguard that was now known as the dreaded SA, the *Sturmabteilung,* the brown-shirted Storm Troopers.

The SA at this time was dressed in a motley of uniforms, many with patched and mismatched clothing, but their unifying symbol, of course, was the swastika, which they wore as armbands and which they flew as black-red-white flags after a design approved by Hitler. They were also accompanied by a brass band that played rousing marches at every public meeting of the Nazi Party and, at the event scheduled for Coburg, even had a van full of beefy Bavarians in lederhosen and alpenstocks for a little local color . . . and brute force.

Hitler himself had presided over very little actual armed conflict up to this time, but was ready for battle when they reached the town of Coburg in Upper Bavaria on October 14, 1922, for a "German Day" celebration. This time, they were met with opposition in the form of a crowd of anti-Nazis of various persuasions who began by jeering and shouting epithets, calling the Nazis murderers and criminals, and who proceeded very shortly to throw rocks at the marching Storm Troopers.

Hitler gave a signal with his whip, and the Troopers fell upon the crowd with merry and reckless abandon. (Hitler had often pictured himself as Christ throwing the money-changers out of the Temple, and the whip was his favorite weapon at this time. Even Eckart was growing tired of it, and began to think that maybe his protégé was a trifle insane.) The hostile crowd was forced back, and the march continued, but the talk on the street was that the Communists had only fallen back to regroup and that a major confrontation would take place in twenty-four hours.

The following day, in spite of a call to all leftists to throw out the Nazis, Hitler—who anticipated a full-scale battle with an opposition numbering close to ten thousand, and whose own SA contingent (swollen with newly arriving members and converts) now numbered only fifteen hundred—found himself greeted instead with wild approval by the people of Coburg and surprisingly the rest of the day passed without conflict. Hitler—his friends the poet-mystic Eckart and the architect-mystic Rosenberg in tow—had actually *liberated* the town of Coburg.

And now they were ready for the rest of Germany.

The Combination of Stellar Influences

In a letter written to Hitler by a female admirer in Munich a little over a month before the famous Beer Hall Putsch of November 1923, the future leader of Germany was advised of certain astrological predictions made by Frau Elsbeth Ebertin, the dowager empress of an impressive line of German astrologers whose innovative techniques are still employed today in Europe and America. The author believes that this is the first time that the entire letter has been published in English translation:

MUNICH, 30 SEPTEMBER 1923

Highly honored Mr. Hitler,

Allow me, as an old member and a fanatical adherent of your movement, to point out to you a matter that would surely interest you. I have in front of me a work of an expert of scientific astrology who is famous and popular in all of Germany, E. Ebertin Publishers, 1914.

The following is an excerpt of the article in question. No name is given in the article, but it can only be *your* esteemed person who is referred to therein (Ebertin, p. 54).

"A fighter born on April 20, 1889, at whose birth the sun stood at 29° of Aries, might, by his all too daring actions, place himself in danger and possibly soon contribute to the impetus which will start the stone rolling.

"According to the stellar constellations the man must definitely be taken seriously and is destined for the role of a leader in future struggles.

"It almost seems as if he whom I have in mind has been chosen by fate, under this strong influence of Aries, to sacrifice himself for the German people and to bear everything courageously and bravely; even if it should be a matter of life and death; but at the least to give the impetus to a German liberation movement, which then will erupt quite suddenly in an elementary way.

"However, I don't want to preempt fate. Time will tell, but as things are going at the time of my writing they cannot continue!

"The German people can only come to itself again in the political and religious field through some spiritual leaders sent by God, namely by the agency of individuals who believe in God and have a cosmological sensitivity, and who are above party politics, several of whom I have discovered among April natives (that is to say only if the star constellations are favorable).

"Once the right point in time will have come, i.e., once the Versailles peace treaty will have proved to be impossible to fulfill and will have been overturned, then the stars—which are now still shining in hidden places—will beautifully appear as shining meteors, similar to the heavenly bodies which are now newly discovered or become visible . . ." etc. etc.

You must forgive me if I could not help but inform you of the foregoing.

Most respectfully,
Heil und Sig!
Most devotedly,
Maria Heiden, Munich[30]

This author felt it worthwhile to quote the entire text as it illustrates both the self-professed "fanatical" devotion of the letter writer as well as the political sentiments of Frau Ebertin at this time. Frau Heiden quoted the comments from Ebertin's own book of predictions, *Ein Blick in die Zukunft (A Glimpse into the Future)* for the year 1924, which was published in July of 1923. It was brought to Hitler's attention by a number of other admirers as well, and Frau Ebertin herself sent a copy of her book to the Nazi newspaper, *Völkischer Beobachter*

. . . but according to Ebertin her predictions only served to irritate the Führer.[31] Hitler was not one who was willing to believe that his fate was out of his hands and written in the indelible ink of the stars, at least not when he felt he had the future—and Germany's—in his grasp, as he did that September of 1923.

But it all came to an end with the failed Munich Beer Hall Putsch of November 1923. An ill-planned and poorly executed attempt to take over the Bavarian government by force resulted in a major setback for the Party. Hitler was arrested; Hess—who had escaped to Austria—was being sought by the authorities and would eventually surrender himself; and Dietrich Eckart—Hitler's mentor and protector and the man who midwifed the Nazi Party into prominence—died at Hitler's mountain retreat, Berchtesgaden, on December 26 of that year, his protégé in prison but his optimism unbounded. Eckart knew where Hitler was headed, because it was he who had pushed him in the right direction.

To rebut those who claim that Eckart's influence and effect on Hitler was not relevant, one merely has to indicate the memorial services that were held every year in his honor by the Nazi Party, including the lavish ceremony on December 26, 1933 (the year Hitler came to power); the monument put up over his grave in Berchtesgaden; the eulogies written for him by such important contemporaries as Rosenberg (who would later become enormously influential in the Third Reich); and the speeches made on the anniversary of his death by such men as Baldur von Schirach (the head of Hitler Youth). Hitler owed a great deal to Eckart, and the evidence left behind shows that he knew and understood that; after all, the final words of *Mein Kampf* show that Hitler's infamous memoir was dedicated to him.

A Mark, a Yen, a Buck, or a Pound . . .

Another contribution of Eckart, and one that is frequently missed even by occult historians, is his connection with Henry Ford.

Eckart was approached by agents of the American automobile manufacturer as early as 1920–1921. Ford was a notorious anti-Semite, and had actually written a book—*The International Jew*—which was enormously popular in Germany where a German-language version with the title *The Eternal Jew* was a best-seller. Hitler had read it before writing *Mein Kampf,* and some authors insist that whole sections of Hitler's memoir were lifted, practically verbatim, from Ford's book.[32] Hitler even had a picture of Ford hanging in his office at Party headquarters (the Brown House) and stacks of *The Eternal Jew* piled up on a desk outside along with other Nazi literature. (Consider the surreal nature of *that* image. Imagine ousted Ugandan dictator Idi Amin with a framed portrait of Lee Iacocca . . .) It is worthwhile to note that the German publisher of *The Eternal Jew* (as well as of an early German edition of the *Protocols of the Elders of Zion*) was none other than Theodor Fritsch, the man who founded the *Germanenorden* in 1912 for which the Thule Society served as a front. (See Chapter Two.)

The support of Henry Ford was vital to the survival of the Nazi Party in the early days, and one of Hitler's proudest achievements. He would award that quintessential American with the highest Nazi honor it was possible to bestow to a non-German, the Grand Cross of the Supreme Order of the German Eagle, in 1938. He was the first American and only the fourth person to be given the award. And why not? Even Baldur von Schirach would credit Henry Ford's writings for having converted him to anti-Semitism. An earlier recipient of the award was Benito Mussolini that same year.

Thus it was Eckart who handled some of these early cash contributions from Henry Ford, and Eckart who, among others, dealt directly with the Ford representatives in Germany. As we continue along in our catalogue of this century's most unspeakable evil we must pause now and again to fully appreciate the depths to which some honored American heroes—industrialists, after all, like Ford; scientists, engineers, and technicians—have sunk, and to resurrect these memories (no matter how painful or simply distasteful) for they are crucial to a full understanding of who we are and of how we came to this impasse. Eckart, the drug-addicted occultist, racist, anti-Semite, and borderline psychopath as Henry Ford's bag man and Hitler's Bebe Rebozo, is one of those traffic accidents of history that merit a few moments of silent contemplation.

Money, connections, ideology. Perhaps no single other human would come to exert that type of influence over Hitler until Hanussen, the psychic and astrologer who honed Hitler's public-speaking skills . . . and who performed occult rituals on Hitler's behalf. As Eckart's ghost piped an infernal melody from beyond the grave, Hitler would indeed dance; and in that *danse macabre* Hanussen would lead.

Hanussen

In the last days of 1932, Hitler was contemplating suicide.

Released from prison in 1924 after the Beer Hall Putsch got him a light sentence for what was, after all, high treason, his *Mein Kampf* a best-seller, and his Nazi Party back and stronger than ever, he nonetheless was losing ground in the Reichstag. Hindenberg—the much-respected and very popular president of the Republic—was not pleased with the rough-and-tumble crowd that seemed to compose Hitler's voting bloc, and various ministers were conspiring against Hitler to keep him out of government altogether.

In 1932, they were succeeding. Hitler was facing a crucial election. Members of the Nazi Party were in danger of defecting to other political organizations. His own trusted disciples were dividing the Party into warring factions that could not be controlled.

And on Halloween night—the pagan Sabbath of Samhain—his mistress Eva Braun shot herself.

Although Eva survived what the doctors would later characterize as a serious suicide attempt, Hitler himself knew he was politically dead. It appeared as if he had lost the will to fight, and he began to speak more and more of his own death. He entered the political campaign a distracted, depressed leader who seemed unable to hold his fractious Party together. They lost heavily in the Reichstag five days later—losing seats to the hated Communists—and the press began publishing the Party's obituary.

At this nadir of his career, he turned to an old friend whom he had met years earlier, in 1926, in Berlin. This was Erik Jan Hanussen, a famous astrologer and master of several occult disciplines who had—it was said—taught Hitler everything from the body language and gestures to use in public speaking to what friends and associates he should cultivate.

The Viennese Hanussen—whose real name was Herschel Steinschneider, the son of a Jewish vaudeville performer—began his career as what Americans call a "carny," doing odd jobs in a traveling circus, until he began his own newspaper and threatened to publish vile things in it about people he knew unless they paid up! This small-time blackmailer soon became interested in hypnosis and mediumship and published several books on the subject, eventually becoming the darling of the international socialite set, a man who never failed to entertain at parties but who also provided more serious assistance to those of his hosts who needed a horoscope drawn up or a spell cast. He dyed his hair blond to fit his new persona as a Danish aristocrat, and dived into the frantic, heady atmosphere of early 1930s Berlin competing with astrologers, clairvoyants, and mediums of every description. Although he had never cast Hitler's astrological chart before, now in the late days of 1932 with Hitler morose and on the verge of doing himself damage, Hanussen erected his natal and probably a transit or progressed chart and appeared before Hitler with an eerie prognosis.

Hanussen told his host that there were good times ahead, but that a few "obstacles" remained that had to be eliminated. The implication was oddly surreal. The "obstacles" were not actual people or circumstances. Instead, Hanussen claimed, Hitler was the victim of some sort of hex or magical spell.[33]

History has not recorded who might have been responsible for this, and it is possible that all Hanussen knew—or claimed—was that "evil occult influences" were around Hitler, causing him to lose his edge. We may fantasize about a lodge of German magicians, summoning angelic forces to thwart the attempts of Hitler and his Nazi Party to gain power in Germany. We may wonder if a witch or sorcerer—operating alone in some mountain fastness in the Obersalzberg, perhaps—was casting a spell against Hitler for something as relatively trivial as a broken promise or unrequited love, and thereby altering the course of European history forever. We will certainly never know the actual dimensions of this baneful influence around the Führer, but the outcome of Hanussen's meditations was nothing short of spectacular.

In order to rid himself of this evil spell, he said, one would have to go to Hitler's hometown. At the time of the full moon. At midnight. In a butcher's backyard.

And remove a mandrake from the ground.

Now a mandrake is the man-shaped root famous throughout European folklore for its occult and medicinal properties. According to some traditions, one had to stop one's ears with cloth or cotton before pulling the root from the earth, as it would emit a piercing scream that would shatter the eardrums. A dog was sometimes used to pull the root from the earth as the magician kept his hands clasped around his own ears. The resulting shriek—it is said—normally killed the dog.

The mandrake is also known for its powers as an aphrodisiac, and as an amulet of protection. We must assume that Hanussen was thinking of this last property in connection with Hitler. Also, the significance of the butcher's yard should not be ignored: such a place would have given the surrounding earth the peculiar quality of a veritable Teutonic orgy of blood, dismemberment, death, and pain, which would have been mystically absorbed by the root itself.

Hanussen decided to perform the necessary rituals himself and set off for Hitler's birthplace in Austria, returning on New Year's Day 1933 with the amuletic root and with a prediction: that Hitler's return to power would begin on January 30, a date roughly equivalent to the pagan Sabbath of Oimelc: one of the four "cross-quarter" days of the witches' calendar.

It seemed an outrageous prediction but—after a series of bizarre coincidences and half-baked conspiratorial machinations on the part of his opponents—Hitler went from washed-up political has-been to chancellor of Germany with dizzying speed in thirty days and, on January 30, 1933, he assumed power.

Hanussen's impossibly optimistic prediction came true to the day.

That was not the end of Hanussen's ability to predict the future, however, for on February 26 of that same year—during a séance held that evening at his own lavishly furnished "Palace of Occultism" on Lietzenburger Strasse and attended by Berlin's movers and shakers—he predicted that the Communists in Germany would attempt a revolution, signaled by the destruction (by fire) of an important government building.[34]

The next day, the Reichstag was in flames and Hitler had all the excuse he needed to go from chancellor of Germany to Führer of the Third Reich. European history had been changed forever, and once more the Society Seer was right on target. But, six weeks later in April of 1933, Hanussen would be dead; murdered in a forest outside Berlin by agent or agents unknown. There was speculation that Hitler ordered the execution since Hanussen "knew too much" or perhaps might even have had connections to the Communist Party (hence his accurate prediction of the Reichstag fire; some mediums and psychics—and Hanussen was no exception—are known to "enhance" their abilities by gathering intelligence on their clients ahead of time or by bugging the rooms in which séances are held, etc. In fairness, however, no amount of dirty tricks could have explained Hanussen's accurate prediction of Hitler's enormous success in January). Another version had it that Hanussen's murder enraged the Führer, and that he ordered the death sentence for its perpetrator, Karl Ernst, who was executed during the Röhm purge with a bewildered "Heil Hitler" on his lips.[35] Another story, that SA leader Count Wolf Heinrich von Helldorf had Ernst arrest and murder Hanussen because the count owed him money, is also current.[36] Hanussen was said to have thrown orgies at the count's Wannsee villa, where attractive young ladies—usually "actresses"—were thrown into hypnotic trances and made to mime orgasms. The count was a rather degenerate sort who went through money like *schnapps,* and wound up owing a great deal to Hanussen, who carried the count's markers with him wherever he went. Needless to say, the markers were never found (which either proves that the count killed Hanussen and removed the IOUs from the body, or that the story is completely fictitious and never happened; take your pick).

And then, of course, Hanussen's father *was* Jewish, which would have been reason enough to execute the inordinately influential seer. Unfortunately, we will never know what happened, for Hanussen died as he had lived: the Count St. Germain of Weimar and early Nazi Germany, a complete and compelling mystery.

The Master of the Sidereal Pendulum

Another occultist in Hitler's inner circle was the Thulist, astrologer, and pendulum expert Wilhelm Gutberlet (born 1870). Gutberlet first comes to the historian's attention as a shareholder in the *Völkischer Beobachter*, Sebottendorff's former newspaper. Franz Eher Verlag was a publishing company that Sebottendorff purchased in 1918 for about five thousand Reichsmarks (RM). It consisted of a newspaper, the *Münchener Beobachter*, that had ceased publication with the death of its founder in June. Sebottendorff picked it up and moved its offices to the Thule meeting rooms at the Four Seasons Hotel, turning it into an anti-Semitic organ that was eventually taken over—after a series of intervening ownerships by other parties—by the German Workers' Party after Sebottendorff left Munich. In 1920, Wilhelm Gutberlet owned shares worth 10,000 RM, or about 8.5 percent of the total value of the paper. It was renamed the *Völkischer Beobachter,* and as such became infamous as the propaganda machine of the Nazi Party.

As mentioned, Gutberlet was a Thulist. He was also one of Hitler's earliest followers. A medical doctor, he was present at the first meeting of the German Workers' Party that Hitler attended and had remained a close friend and confidant since then. In other words, since 1919.

Gutberlet virtually disappears from most official accounts of the Nazi Party until he reappears in Schellenberg's memoirs. Walter Schellenberg was chief of the Foreign Intelligence section of the SD (*Sicherheitsdienst* or Security Service), and survived the war to write about his experiences as spymaster in Europe. According to Schellenberg:

> Hitler's racial mania was one of his characteristic features. I discussed this several times with Dr. Gutbarlett [sic], a Munich physician who belonged to the intimate circle around Hitler. Gutbarlett believed in the "sidereal pendulum," an astrological contraption, and claimed that this had given him the power to sense at once the presence of any Jews or persons of partial Jewish ancestry, and to pick them out in any group of people. Hitler availed himself of Gutbarlett's mystic power and had many discussions with him on racial questions.[37]

Thus, in Gutberlet, we have an occultist, a Thulist, an astrologer, a racist, a pendulum expert, and a confidant of Hitler, all wrapped into one. The matter of the "sidereal pendulum" itself will come up in a later chapter, but for now we can agree that Gutberlet's influence over Hitler's thinking must have been profound, for the Führer himself constantly ridiculed the *völkisch* occult groups in his official speeches . . . while secretly soliciting their advice and counsel away from the prying eyes of both the press and the superstitious Christian public. And it is revealing to know that Gutberlet, the astrologer and mystic, was consulted by Hitler on *racial* matters as well as on mystical subjects, thus providing additional evidence—albeit circumstantial—that Hitler's racism was fueled by his occultism.

List, Liebenfels, Eckart, Hanussen, Gutberlet. These are only five of the many occultists whose influence surrounded the Führer from his early days as an art student to his last days as leader of a ruined nation. To complete the story, we have to investigate Haushofer, Hess, Himmler and many others for—as the Reich consolidated and became more powerful—other occult lodges in Germany were active and were seen to pose a threat to the new regime. While drawing upon some of the same traditions as the Order of New Templars, the *Germanenorden,* and the Thule Society—Eastern religions, weird rituals associated with astrology and mythology, sexual formulas for becoming powerful and casting spells—they had other associations which made them suspect.

⚡ **4** ⚡

The Order of the Temple of the East: Sex, Spies, and Secret Societies

Heydrich was informed about the smallest detail of Hitler's private life. He saw every diagnosis made by Hitler's doctors and knew of all his strange and abnormal pathological inclinations. . . . They showed that Hitler was so ruled by the daemonic forces driving him that he ceased to have thoughts of normal cohabitation with a woman. The ecstasies of power in every form were sufficient for him.[1]

—SCHELLENBERG

The Silly Season

The British sometimes call periods of chaos in which the unpredictable always seems to happen the "silly season." Certainly, the years between the two world wars constituted a Silly Season for Europe. In 1920, Aleister Crowley started his ill-fated occult commune in Cefalù, Sicily, at the same time that D.H. Lawrence's novel *Women in Love* was published. In October, 1922, as Hitler "marched" on Coburg, Mussolini and his black-shirted Fascists marched on Rome. (One of their first official acts will be to ban occult orders and secret societies.) On December 16, 1922, the partners in archaeology Howard Carter and Lord Carnarvon officially opened King Tut's tomb, thus instigating a worldwide fad of everything Egyptian and simultaneously giving birth to the legend of the Mummy's Curse. That same year, the *Necronomicon* made its sinister debut in the pages of *Weird Tales* magazine. A year later—inspired by Mussolini's success in Italy—Hitler will attempt his own putsch in Munich, and fail.

By the end of 1923, Hitler was stewing in Landsberg Prison, writing *Mein Kampf* with the help of his good friends Rudolf Hess and Fr. Bernhard Stempfle, and enjoying a little geopolitical input from Professor Karl Haushofer.

The Entourage

We will discuss Father Stempfle in more detail in Chapter Five, and Rudolf Hess's flight to England (and its occult ramifications) will be analyzed fully in Chapter Nine. But a few words about both Hess and Haushofer and their relationship to the Führer will do well here.

Rudolf Hess was an early confidant and friend of Hitler, one of his few coconspirators arrested after the Beer Hall Putsch in 1923. Hess acted as Hitler's secretary while they both served prison terms. It was Hess who transcribed Hitler's dreary memoir *Mein Kampf*. From all accounts, Hess was something of a puppy dog around men like Hitler and Haushofer: blindly loyal, eager for any scrap of attention or affection, and fanatically devoted to these personalities (to a greater degree than to the ideas they represented). But he adopted their ideologies as his own, and ran with them as far as he could. Hess was the type of man that Hitler seemed to enjoy most, for Hess would never disagree with him; rather, he lived for every word that fell from the Führer's mouth.

Once the Nazis gained power in Germany—nine years after the Putsch—Hess became Hitler's right-hand man, ahead of all other Nazis and next in line in succession to the Führer's throne. He was

one of the signers of the infamous Nuremberg Laws, which deprived
Jews of their German citizenship and which paved the way for the
Holocaust. Naive, credulous, and always ready for a new faith to believe in—as long as it didn't interfere with his love affair with the
Führer—Hess was easily influenced by a wide variety of astrologers
and occultists and read avidly anything having to do with Eastern
mysteries and the power of the mind. He had been an intimate of the
Thule Society along with Eckart and Rosenberg, and his wife was as
mystically inclined as he was. But in 1933 Hess found himself in a
position of great power in Germany; his easy access to Hitler made
him very popular with the wheelers and dealers in the Party, men with
their own (usually hidden) agendas.

Among the latter could be counted Professor Karl Haushofer and
his son, Albrecht. Hess had studied under Haushofer at the University
of Munich and had brought the geopolitician to Hitler's attention
while they were both serving time in Landsberg. Although there is still
a great deal of controversy over just who influenced whom with regard
to the Hess Affair, it is likely that the Haushofers had something to
do with Hess's flight to England and that astrological advice (as well
as what was essentially a conspiracy against the Führer) also played an
important role.

Hess had been a keen student of Haushofer (1869–1946), the in-
ventor of *Lebensraum,* at the University of Munich. Professor Haushofer, a general in the Kaiser's army who had spent considerable time
in the Far East as military attaché for the German government and
who could speak and write Japanese fluently, was believed to have
been initiated into some secret society or other in Asia. This story of
Haushofer's occult initiation has appeared several times, most notably
in *Le matin des magiciens* by Pauwels and Bergier,[2] and his surviving
son Heinz has denied it vigorously. However, some evidence *does* exist
that Haushofer had an abiding interest in astrology and even claimed
a certain degree of clairvoyance. It is certain that Haushofer eventually
came to wield considerable power in the Third Reich, through both
his *Deutsche Akademie* and the *Institut für Geopolitik* at the University
of Munich—a kind of think tank–cum–intelligence agency—of which
he was director. His early associations with influential Japanese busi-
nessmen and statesmen were crucial in forming the German-Japanese

alliance of World War II. He was also the first high-ranking Nazi to form important relationships with South American governments in anticipation of military and political action against the United States, relationships that would eventually be exploited by war criminals—and Nazi cultists—fleeing the reach of the Nuremberg prosecutors.

In Hess he found an adoring, fawning student and true believer (for whom he actually had rather little respect) and Hess wasted no time in bringing the professor to the attention of Hitler at Landsberg Prison, where the three of them discussed Haushofer's *Lebensraum* concept and other ideas concerning global politics.

Haushofer deserves an entire book to himself and, indeed, the amount of available documentation on his life and work is considerable, so we shall not go into it here. It is enough for our purposes to say that, until he dropped out of favor, Haushofer was Hitler's most valuable political and military adviser, responsible for many foreign policy coups. His *Deutsche Akademie* had branches all over the world—including the United States—where information on local geography, economics, politics, military preparedness, food supplies, industrial capability, cultural affairs, media influence, etc. was collected and analyzed by teams of well-paid professional scholars, engineers, meteorologists, historians, psychologists, agricultural specialists, and advisers in virtually every aspect of human life. Blended with all of this otherwise scientific information gathering was a heavy dose of astrology, mysticism, and occultism which caused Haushofer, geopolitics, and the German Academy to be ridiculed in the world press . . . even as many governments were trying to set up geopolitical institutes of their own.

But it is the *Lebensraum* policy for which Haushofer is generally known in the short histories of the war that can be found in any library. *Lebensraum*—literally "living room"—is the doctrine that gave Hitler the "right" to seek to expand the Reich as far as possible into neighboring countries, seizing the land and deporting (or exterminating) the local residents and replacing them with Germans. It was a doctrine that was adopted enthusiastically by the Japanese, who were Haushofer's close friends, and which gave them the ideological basis for their invasion of China, the Pacific, and Southeast Asia. *Lebensraum* was the simple statement of policy which said that a sovereign nation, to ensure the survival of its people, had a right to annex the territory of other sovereign nations to feed and house itself. Japan was certainly a nation that could appreciate this idea, crowded as it is on a set of rather small islands that is poor in natural resources and which has to import nearly everything it needs to survive. The *Lebensraum* concept was crucial to Haushofer's general theory of "geopolitics" and was embraced by Hitler in those early days in Landsberg Prison. After all, if an esteemed professor at the University of Munich, and a former statesman and military theoretician for the Kaiser at that, said Germany would be justified in expanding its national boundaries at the expense of other nations, it was tantamount to a seal of approval from the intelligentsia for Hitler's wilder ambitions.

If the patient reader remembers what was broached in Chapter One concerning the ideas of Michel Foucault, it may be perceived that Haushofer's concept of *Lebensraum* is a manifestation of the "sexuality" impulse as an implement of national policy. While wars of conquest were conducted in the old days for religious reasons, or for sheer glory, or to avenge an insult real or imagined, Haushofer put forward the idea of "living room" as a kind of *natural law* that transcended sovereign boundaries and national agendas: the necessary expansion of a human population into whatever space could be found to feed and house it. *Lebensraum* was not presented as a plan of mass murder or as a weapon of the will of an individual despot, but as the *natural* expression of the need of a *people* for "living room": i.e., for the survival of an entire nation or race. In that sense, *Lebensraum* was the twentieth-century "sexual" (to use Foucault's term) extension of Hitler's nineteenth-century "sanguine" Messiah-complex entailing human sacrifice. The twentieth century thus became the battleground of the "blood" versus "sex" ideologies, and when no means of accommodation could be found between the two impulses it was only natural that Haushofer—whose *Lebensraum* theory was a twisted version of the sex impulse—should later come to doubt Hitler and to actively plan to destroy him.

After the flight of Hess to England, Haushofer came under attack from the Führer. Blamed for a baleful influence over Hess that contributed to Hitler losing his right-hand man and close companion from the old days—his dear little *Hesserl*—Haushofer and his eldest son and colleague, Albrecht, rapidly fell out of favor with the Reich.

The Hess flight was seen as a debacle for Nazi Germany, causing all sorts of political problems for Hitler. He did not want Russia or Italy to think he was making a separate peace with England, and his secret plan for the Russian invasion (code-named Barbarossa) was known to Hess. If Barbarossa should be revealed to the English, all would be lost, for Hitler *was* double-dealing, but with the Soviet Union and not with England.

Hitler quickly issued statements characterizing Hess as a sick individual with a history of mental problems; a strategy that was not entirely successful, for the man in the street wondered why Hess had remained the second most powerful man in Germany for so long if he was insane? Hitler also ordered the suppression of all fortune-telling practices and establishments, including astrology, palm- and tea-reading, séances, and the like on the assumption that occultists had brainwashed Hess into committing this treasonous act. Everyone knew that Hess took astrology and the occult arts very seriously, so this seemed to be a logical step to take. This "occult conspiracy" angle would be thoughtfully examined by elements of British Intelligence, which would consider using Aleister Crowley as a tool in an occult counteroffensive. (See Chapter Nine.)

Many historians have pointed to this general ban on occultism as evidence that Hitler did not believe in the black arts. They also cite references against the *völkisch* secret societies in a few of his speeches as further proof that the Führer was—even if somewhat insane—not as crazy as the stargazers or demon-summoners. However, as anyone who has had anything at all to do with occult societies knows very well, the internecine warfare that takes place among occultists at every level of sophistication is furious, spiteful, and altogether nasty. The stories about Crowley's own "magical war" with his mentor, Mac-Gregor Mathers, are well known, as are many of the fights that took place between various French lodges of the nineteenth century (which can be consulted in Richard Cavendish's thoroughly enjoyable *The Black Arts*).[3] Occultists in general have no difficulty distancing themselves—with appropriate invective and astral curses—from other occultists with whom they disagree on philosophical grounds; and virtually every "serious occultist" that the author has ever encountered has had nothing but disdain for tea-leaf readers, palmists, and cut-rate astrologers. Thus, in light of the foregoing, the author finds no contradiction at all in Hitler's fascination with occultism on the one hand and his order to ban "popular" occult practices on the other.

While Professor Karl Haushofer was not arrested or otherwise physically abused, his son Albrecht Haushofer *was* arrested and taken to Gestapo Headquarters at 8 Prinz Albrechtstrasse, an address with a reputation as dire and forbidding to the Germans as Dzerzhinsky Square and the Lubyanka are to the Russians. There he was interrogated for days about his relationship to Hess and about how much advance knowledge he had concerning the flight. Albrecht survived this interrogation more or less intact, and was released. What Hitler and the Gestapo did not discover, however, was that Albrecht and his father had developed connections to the German Resistance movement against Hitler. This would all be tragically revealed a few years later when, after the failed July 1944 assassination plot against Hitler in which Albrecht was a coconspirator, Professor Haushofer himself was sent to Dachau, the concentration camp conveniently close (nine miles) to Munich where the Ahnenerbe-SS had some unusual interests. Son Albrecht was sent to prison, and later executed at the last minute on the streets of Berlin as the city was falling to the Red Army.

Upon the collapse of the Reich, Karl Haushofer was questioned by Allied investigators working for the Nuremberg Tribunal eager to learn of his relationship with Hess, a relationship to which Haushofer—mourning the execution of his eldest son—freely confessed. Before he could testify in open court against his old student and comrade, however, he committed suicide by taking arsenic.

The rest of Hitler's entourage included, of course, the pagan ideologue Alfred Rosenberg (whom Hitler made head of the Nazi Party *pro tem* during his residence in Landsberg). Rosenberg—a native Balt with an abiding hatred of Soviets, Jews, and Freemasons—had appeared one day at Dietrich Eckart's apartment in Munich and offered him his services as a "fighter against Judah." The two soon became inseparable and it is believed that it was Rosenberg who introduced Eckart to the *Protocols of the Elders of Zion*. Rosenberg agitated for the creation of a state religion based on Odinic paganism and Teutonic magic, and could be relied upon to appear at the meetings of every major Nordic, Teutonic, and Aryan society in Germany both before and after the Nazis' seizure of power. It was Rosenberg who ordered that Freemason temples in the Occupied Territories be looted by Einsatz commandos and their contents shipped back to him in Berlin, an order cheerfully carried out by Franz Six and Otto Ohlendorf, both men known for their abiding interest in cult activity. Rosenberg's close associate and fellow pagan, Richard Walther Darré—a native of Argentina—was made Agriculture Minister of the Third Reich but Darré's interest was less in animal husbandry and crop rotation than it was in the mystical doctrines of the runes and the Blood and Soil. We have covered runic mysticism already; the Blood and Soil doctrine is too tedious to examine thoroughly here but the reader can immediately grasp its essentials if it is understood that, if it had been left up to Darré, pure-blooded German peasants would have reverted to fornicating in the fields on *Walpurgisnacht* to ensure fertility of the crops.

The team of Rosenberg and Darré picked up in Nazi Germany where the team of Rosenberg and Eckart left off in Weimar. Rosenberg, with his impeccable credentials dating back to the early days of the formation of the Nazi Party and its baptism of blood in the Beer Hall Putsch, was a high-profile Reichsleiter with a blatantly pagan and anti-Christian philosophy, a philosophy which received wide coverage in the German press. Darré was there to support this platform and, if possible, to do him one better on occasion. Together, they ran around the nation drumming up support for an official state religion based on the worship of the Old Gods, a religion that included purifying the Aryan race of elements that were in the process of polluting it and diluting the strength of its Blood. To these True Believers, sex was at once fascinating and repellent; the danger of the Jews to the Aryan man and woman was their sensuality, their ability to seduce the pure-bloods away from their duty to procreate only blue-eyed Teutons. The Jew was the Serpent in the pagan Garden of Eden.

One pagan and occultist who was not bothered with sexuality, however, and who made it a cornerstone of his philosophy was the English magician and tabloid-crowned "Wickedest Man in the World" (this, in the age of Mussolini, Hitler, and Stalin!): Aleister Crowley. Crowley—whose life has been well and thoroughly discussed by a wide variety of authors, including himself—provides us some entrée into the German occult scene of the 1920s and 1930s. Indeed, at one point Crowley was actually roughed up by a roving Nazi SA gang in what is arguably the single documented instance of a good deed in the entire history of the Nazi Party: the Storm Troopers stopped Crowley from beating his girlfriend!

Crowley will take us to such important German sex cultists as Theodor Reuss, Karl Germer, Eugene Grosche, Heinrich Tränker, and Marthe Küntzel, not to forget the British Army officer Maj. Gen. C.F. Fuller, who was once a guest of Hitler himself at the latter's Berchtes-gaden retreat to celebrate the Führer's fiftieth birthday on April 20, 1939; Fuller—an anti-Semite and contributor to Oswald Moseley's *Fascist Quarterly,* a devoted Thelemite (that is to say, follower of Crowley's own religion) and an intimate of Crowley—was said to be the "only Englishman that Hitler actually liked."[4] Crowley will take us on a tour of Leipzig, Munich, and the province of Thuringia, where a secret convocation of German occultists was held in 1925 to deter-mine the future leadership of the *Ordo Templi Orientis,* the German sex-magic occult lodge that would eventually be suppressed by the Nazis, its members thrown into the camps.

So, in order to understand what the "subversive" German sex cults were doing, and why, we must start with Aleister Crowley and what he was up to in Germany in 1912.

The Great Beast

Crowley was born on October 12, 1875, in England, not far from the town of Stratford-on-Avon where Shakespeare was born and only a few weeks before Baron Sebottendorff's own birth near Dresden that November. Raised in an oppressively fundamentalist Christian envi-ronment, he came early on to regard himself as the Beast of the Apoca-lypse, the one branded with a 666 and with the Whore of Babylon for aid and comfort. He became an initiate of the Golden Dawn—that fabulously complex jewel of European occultism—on November 18, 1898.

The Golden Dawn had been created ten years earlier by the team of Mathers, Westcott, and Woodman. As we have seen, the official story had it that the Golden Dawn was a branch of an order that existed in Germany, and that a charter from the parent lodge had been granted to the Englishmen from a Fräulein Anna Sprengel of Stuttgart. At the time that Crowley was initiated into the Golden Dawn, that would have been accepted as truth and Crowley would probably have believed that he was indeed being initiated into what was the British section of a German secret society. Since then, the German origins of the Golden Dawn have been more or less demonstrated to be a hoax. It is quite likely that the entire ritual and initiatory structure of the Dawn was nothing less than the brilliant invention of Mathers himself, an invention for which, sadly, he could never claim credit since a major element in the attraction of occult societies rests on their having a long and distinguished—if covert and underground— pedigree.

Interestingly enough, the degree structure of the Golden Dawn was based on the famous Tree of Life symbol: a complex diagram of ten spheres connected by a total of twenty-two paths (each path representing a letter of the Hebrew alphabet) that can be consulted in any one of a variety of books on qabalism and Western occultism. This same Tree of Life diagram was used by the old Wotanist Guido von List to represent the hierarchical grace structure in his *own* ideal Ario-Germanic society and, like the Golden Dawn, he reserved the top three degrees as being inaccessible to the average human being. (Crowley, of course, would eventually assume all three after leaving the Golden Dawn and forming his own organization, the A∴A∴) It is entirely possible that List—writing about these ideas in 1911—had adopted this degree system from the Golden Dawn, which had put it to use as early as 1888 based on "Anna Sprengel's" instructions. If so, the only way in which List could have discovered this degree system was either through initiation into the Golden Dawn or from another initiate who (breaking his oath of secrecy) described it to him. That the unregenerate anti-Semite and godfather of the Nazi Party, Guido von List, might have been a Golden Dawn initiate is an amusing if unsettling proposition but, thankfully, there is no evidence for this. However, there was much communication taking place at this time between England and Germany involving such occult celebrities as Golden Dawn initiate Dr. R.W. Felkin (who was actually looking for Fräulein Sprengel in Germany), Dr. Hübbe-Schleiden (whom we met in Chapter One as the first president of the German branch of the Theosophical Society) and Dr. Rudolf Steiner (who was involved at this time with Franz Hartmann's Masonic lodges as well as with the OTO). Felkin, intent on forging links with legitimate Rosicrucian lodges and acting under mediumistic supervision of a discarnate Arab entity by the name of Ara Ben Shemesh, was desperately seeking Sprengel and hoped that either Hübbe-Schleiden or Rudolf Steiner could assist in that regard. Needless to say, the search came to naught, but the fact of these three occultists communicating and exchanging information on cult activities is provocative.[5]

Historian Nicholas Goodrick-Clarke opines that List got the idea of a Tree of Life initiatory system from the inescapable Dr. Hartmann, who possibly heard of it from the energetic Dr. Westcott. If so, we have the leaders of the *Armanenschaft* (List's name for his own secret society), the Golden Dawn, and the OTO exchanging details on their secret initiations. That List would have based his hierarchy on the patently *Jewish* Tree of Life and borrowed the concept from the Golden Dawn—by way of the OTO—would seem merely ironic to a layperson but positively frightening to an occultist, for what it implies about the relationship between the anti-Semitic List organizations and the ostensibly apolitical Golden Dawn and OTO lodges. In any event, List amended the qabalistic correspondences to suit himself and essentially developed his own—Aryan—version of the Golden Dawn initiatory system.[6]

Another element of the Golden Dawn which is relevant to our case is that the structure of many of its rituals, the peculiar language in which its invocations are made, and the odd designs of many of the magic seals and insignia are all based on a system of occult correspondences known as Enochian, and codified within the writings of Elizabethan mathematician, philosopher, and spy, Dr. John Dee.

Crowley would become so conversant with the "Enochian" language that he would translate medieval spirit conjurations into that tongue for use by his own cult members. Having its own alphabet and its own rules of grammar, its very existence is a technical impossibility: an artificially created language developed by one (or at most two) men in the sixteenth century, John Dee and his assistant Edward Kelley. According to their story, it was given to them by an angel who communicated the language, the alphabet, and all the magic squares, invocations, etc. by means of a laborious process that took months of "scrying" in the equivalent of a crystal ball. The massive amount of manuscript that resulted from these bizarre efforts has been largely ignored by historians of the Elizabethan period, or cited as evidence of Dee's emotional instability. In fact, the existence of these writings was used for many years to discredit Dee's genius altogether. (This is a pattern of thought that exists to this day: occult practices are evidence of either insanity, emotional instability, or simple credulousness.)

However, recent research into the Elizabethan period and particularly concerning Dee's relationship to Sir Francis Walsingham (1530?–1590), Queen Elizabeth's secretary of state, suggests that Dee was on a secret mission for the British government at the time of the angelic revelations (which took place in Prague). Further, as the pseudonymous historian Richard Deacon has pointed out,[7] the Angelic language itself may have been devised as a particularly effective code—based on the work of famed German cryptographer Johannes Trithemius (1462–1516)—for communication between Dee in Prague and Walsingham in England.

In other words, the entire basis of the famous occult order known as the Golden Dawn may well have had its origins in espionage work, from the coded language of Elizabethan spy and mystic John Dee to the "Cypher manuscript" of a nonexistent German lodge.

Some years later, following his various and several initiations into the Golden Dawn, Crowley found himself in position to help a lodge brother, Gerald Kelly. Kelly, a distinguished member and president of the Royal Academy, had a sister by the name of Rose, who was engaged to someone she did not wish to marry. Crowley rushed to the aid of Rose Kelly, and proposed that—in order to thwart the fiancé—she elope with Crowley himself. It was to be purely a marriage of convenience, of course, whose only purpose was to ensure that she would not have to marry the unfortunate gentleman who was pursuing her. She agreed. They eloped. Fell madly in love. Consummated the union. And went on a honeymoon.

This, much to the consternation of her brother Gerald.

The honeymoon took the blissful couple to Cairo in 1904, where the event was to take place that would change Crowley's life—and the lives of thousands of his followers down the years—forever, for Rose, who had never before evinced any signs of mediumistic powers, suddenly began to "channel" an alien entity who demanded to speak directly to Crowley. To be exact, she began receiving impressions that the Gods wanted to speak with Crowley on an urgent matter and, for verification, she led Crowley to an exhibit at the Cairo Museum which bore the fateful number, 666. Rose, not aware of her husband's personal identification with that number and the Great Beast it represents, was obviously in contact with divine forces, and Crowley took her impressions seriously.

For three days in April, 1904, Aleister Crowley communed with a spirit called Aiwaz, an entity that Crowley had claimed at times to have been the Devil—Shaitan—itself. Aiwaz communicated a scripture to Crowley in the voice of three Egyptian gods—Nuit, Hadit, and Ra-Hoor-Khuit—that became known as *The Book of the Law:* the gospel of the New Age, the Aeon of Horus.

Crowley himself has written that the book initially repelled him;[8] that he put it away and actually lost track of the manuscript for five years until one day he found it in an attic and reread it for the first time since 1904. At that point, he suddenly realized he was holding the key scripture of the next Aeon (a magickal age of two thousand years). While Hitler would eventually proclaim a Thousand Year Reich, Crowley was doing him a thousand years better.

The Book of the Law attacks most modern religions, from Judaism to Christianity to Islam to Buddhism, and thus would have been an interesting document to the inner circle of the Reich. It also proclaims—in a book written in 1904—"I am the Warrior Lord of the Forties,"[9] an eerily prescient prediction of the greatest military conflagration ever to hit the planet.

Crowley's occult career did not end with *The Book of the Law*. In due course he penned many hundreds of tracts, pamphlets, articles, and books, all on the theme of "Magick": spelled with a "k" to differentiate it from all other types. When it came to Magick, Crowley was a genius. His command of mythology, religion, philosophy, the arts, and foreign languages was (and remains) legendary. He was the English version of a Guido von List with at least one important distinction: Crowley had a sense of humor, and it is through this sense of humor that the full range of his intellectual brilliance shines. Whatever one thinks of Crowley as a human being or of Thelema—the cult he founded on the basis of *The Book of the Law*—one thing is certain: Crowley was an inspired and engaging author on the whole field of occultism.

Sex Magick

Crowley accepted initiations into a variety of occult lodges and societies in his time, and eventually picked up an initiation into something called the *Ordo Templi Orientis,* or the Order of the Eastern Temple. This was the brainchild of one Karl Kellner, a wealthy German Freemason of high rank in a rather distaff branch of Freemasonry (the Rite of Memphis and Mizraim of John Yarker), who claimed that he was instructed in the techniques of sex-magic by a Hindu adept and two Arab magi during his travels in the East. He introduced this concept to his associates, Theodor Reuss, Heinrich Klein, and the ubiquitous Dr. Franz Hartmann, all of whom were also high-ranking Masons in Yarker's sect.

"Sex-magic" is a loaded term with all sorts of connotations, and it is perhaps best that we discuss what Kellner—and later OTO initiates—meant by it. It is, quite simply, a method of sublimating sexual energy to the will of the magician in a variety of rituals, for a variety of purposes, using the sexual practice appropriate to the desired end. Thus, everything from the missionary position to sodomy to masturbation has a magical analogue and refers to a different quality of occult power. The choice of partner is also a matter for some concern, and the practice of sex-magic has become so refined by later initiates of the Order that even the specific days of a woman's menstrual cycle (for instance) each has its own occult correspondence. While this concept may seem somewhat scandalous to the casual reader, one should remember that a core doctrine of all occultism—from the highest qabala to the meanest sympathetic magic—is that of *correspondences.* In this doctrine, everything that exists in the "real" world has a counterpart in the astral world. Thus an object made of gold can be used to represent the sun, which is itself representative of a host of ideas (vitality, warmth, the Male principle, action, ego, etc.). On this is magic based.

Following that line of reasoning through, every conceivable sort of sex act must also have its analogue in the astral domain, where magic works its mysterious wonders.

Obviously, this dimension was hard to find in the generally available teachings of the Golden Dawn, the Freemasons, and other like organizations with their heavy emphasis on formal ritual alone. The sex magicians also used a great deal of ritual—much of it familiar to magicians of other disciplines—but with some version of the sex act as the central feature. Magic is, after all, about power; about directing energy and will to a given end. Sex is the natural companion to this doctrine of power, for it is arguably the most potent of all human experiences. Wed sex to magic and theoretically one would obtain a dynamo of vast occult potential.

In India, this combination was already well-known as a form of worship called "tantra": a Hindu religious practice in which members of both sexes would participate in various rituals (not all of them overtly sexual by any means) designed to invoke the gods and to imitate the union of the two forms of polar power in the universe, the male and female energies referred to in China as Yang and Yin, respectively, and in India as Shiva and Shakti.

Traditionally, there are two forms of tantric ritual: right-hand and left-hand. Right-hand tantric ritual is that which takes place when the female participant sits at the right hand of the male. In this instance, actual physical contact between the partners will not take place.

It is left-hand tantra that gets all the attention, however, because of the mistaken notion that it is somehow "evil." The term "left-hand path" has become synonymous in the West with black magic and with evil sorcerers who have sold their souls to the Devil: a manifestation of the superstition that left-handedness itself is a sign of aberration. However, "left-hand" tantric ritual is simply that in which the female participant sits at the left hand of the male in the ritual. In this case, physical contact takes place between the two partners but this in no way mandates sexual intercourse every time, in every rite.

Certainly, among some practitioners in the East, the left-hand tantric circle has become a sexual one and there is a small library of techniques, rituals, invocations, chants, etc. appropriate to this type of magic. But the point to be made here is that *all* tantra is inherently sexual in nature as it is concerned with the activities of both the male and female gods and goddesses and their relationship to each other in the eternal play of creation. Whether or not actual sexual intercourse takes place on the physical plane or not is a matter for tantric "engineers" to decide, depending on the path chosen and the means agreed to by all parties. In all cases, the sexual act is considered subordinate to the ultimate goal of spiritual liberation. It is a means to an end, and nothing more.

As we have seen, Hitler was (probably unconsciously) putting this same knowledge to good use. As Schellenberg pointed out in the quotation that begins this chapter, Hitler had so sublimated his sexual urges that he found relief in the rabid speeches he made to the assembled, adoring masses and had long ceased to be interested in normal sexual intercourse with women. On the other side, his speeches were so mesmerizing that even foreigners who spoke no German at all were captivated by Hitler's oratory. In other words, the magical, tantric technique worked. Hitler wanted power more than anything else and was willing to sacrifice friends and lovers to that end. He transformed his sexual desire into a tool for obtaining power . . . and became the leader of Germany (a country he wasn't even born in). Schellenberg—who is no fool—even credits the stories about Hitler's "powers of intuition and personal magnetism,"[10] in effect giving credence to what a medieval audience would have called Hitler's abilities as a sorcerer. A modern, twentieth-century occult audience would call Hitler a sex magician.

But to return to Crowley, in post-Victorian England this was racy stuff. Sex magic was certainly far and away from anything the Golden Dawn was teaching, and Crowley became intrigued by it all when Theodor Reuss—the Outer Head of the Order (OHO) of the OTO—visited Crowley in London in 1912 (during the height of a flurry of occult activity in Germany involving everything from the death of Theosophist *éminence grise* Franz Hartmann, warring Theosophical societies vying for members and recognition, and the creation, by Rudolf Steiner, of his Anthroposophical Society that same year, not to mention the founding of the *Germanenorden* that May) and accused him of revealing the core secret of the Order in a publication of Crowley's called the *Book of Lies*. Crowley, taken rather aback, replied that he could not reveal the secret of the OTO since he had not attained the appropriate degree in the Order and had therefore

never been told what the secret was. When Reuss pointed out a revealing phrase having to do with a "Magick Rood" and a "Mystic Rose,"
(elements which, in a Freudian sense, could be understood as representing the male and female genitals, respectively) Crowley had a flash
of satori and the two men came to a mutual understanding.

Crowley visited Berlin later in 1912 to obtain a charter making him
the head of the OTO for Great Britain and all of the English-speaking
peoples of the world, in the process choosing as his magickal name the
title of that infamous Templar statue: Baphomet.

He then descended upon the rituals of the OTO with relish, rewrit-
ing them to make them more overtly sexual and incorporating his own
newly minted religious ideas—which he called *Thelema* after the
Greek word for "Will" (shades of Leni Riefenstahl!)—into the liturgy.
It was as if a whole new world was opened up to him, for now he
could make his favorite pastime—sex—not only compatible with
magick but central to it. He began to see that the whole universe of
magick—the rituals, techniques, specialized language—was merely a
means of presenting sexual information in a coded form. With this
sudden illumination came a profusion of small articles on sex-magick
that were translated into German by Reuss's people and published
there for the first time. Until relatively recently, in fact, they had not
been available in English at all.[11] These treatises discuss the occult
methods to be employed during autoerotic, heterosexual, and homosexual sex acts, and concern everything from uniting with one's god
or goddess through masturbation or intercourse, to making talismans
for various purposes, and even using sex to achieve enlightenment.
These few booklets can stand as the West's answer to, and interpretation of, Hindu tantrism, particularly of the Kaula Shastra variety, with
a little distaff Sufism thrown in for good measure. Quite simply, we
are dealing with the subordination of the sex act to the Great Work
by the magician and mystic of every age. The Christian eremites who
suffered intense sexual fantasies in the desert as they strove to transform their desire for sex into a desire for God would have recognized
the singular purpose in these Crowleyan tracts while at the same time
abhorring the practices described. Crowley maintains that *every* sex act
of an Adept is a sacred act and should not be the result of a lascivious
appetite; the papal encyclical *Humanae Vitae* is in essential agreement
on this. Yet, while Crowley—and the members of the German occult

lodges who were following this regimen—believed that every sexual act was a magickal expression of the Will and had to be performed with procreation in sight, it is not the type of procreation the Church has in mind. Crowley's ideal children were magickal children, such as described in his entertaining and revealing novel, *Moonchild.*[12] Every magickal act—and this includes sex—has a purpose that must be established beforehand. With Crowley—as with the Pope—there is (officially) no sex for pleasure only.

This attitude of Crowley's has been underrepresented in the many books and articles written about him. Most authors view Crowley's description of his sexual antics as "magickal rites" with a huge amount of derision; yet, his diaries are full of just such occult annotations as he meticulously recorded hundreds of sexual acts that he performed along with a careful description of their occult purposes: whether they were to consecrate talismans, obtain information through divination, commune with a spirit or a god, or whatever. Crowley was at great pains to find a way to indulge a tremendous sexual appetite in a manner that was free of any hint of the "baser" nature of sex. In this, he may have been searching for a way to satisfy subconscious elements of his psyche that were linked to his fundamentalist Christian upbringing: a way of having one's cake of light and eating it, too.

Whatever the purpose, and however successful or not he may have been, Crowley's initiation into the *Ordo Templi Orientis* is the source of much of the literature by and about Crowley today. The discovery of the existence of a *sexual* occultism was all the fuse this brilliant if eccentric Englishman needed to detonate the volatile compound of his great intelligence mixed with a sincere—if outlandish—spirituality.

That there existed a higher form of sex, perhaps the application of the sex act, sexual positions, sexual fluids, and even sexual pleasure to spiritual goals like illumination and unity with Godhead, appealed to Crowley immensely for it made of sex a magickal laboratory wherein any experiment was justified if not actually demanded by the rigors of scientific method.

The occultists of the OTO had applied "the art of German engineering" to the sex act, taking it, in effect, out of the bedroom and into the lab. (One is irresistibly reminded of Tim Curry as Dr. Frankenfurter in the *Rocky Horror Picture Show*.) Of course, the use of sex in rituals was nothing new to Europe. The use of sexual rites to insure fertility of the crops was known thousands of years before the word "tantra" became a commonplace on European tongues; and the witches were accused by the Holy Inquisition of conducting sex orgies on the top of Mount Brocken. The Rites of Eleusis were almost certainly sexual in nature, and sex in general formed part of many ancient mystery religions in Europe, the Middle East, and Asia (to wit: the voluminous evidence available in Frazier's *The Golden Bough*).

It could be argued that the advent of Christianity changed all that with its bachelor God, its virgin Mother, its celibate priests and nuns, and its general hostility to sex of any kind. It is probably for this reason that we find no discussion of "sexual secrets" in Freemasonry, for example, and the sexual discussions around Rosicrucianism are almost always hidden behind the heavily veiled symbolic shorthand of the alchemists.

In short, the mystification of sex has always been with us; so has the mystification of eating and drinking (in the Mass, in various pagan festivals of harvest time) and the mystification of respiration (in the pranic exercises of the yogis, in the meditations of the Eastern Orthodox "Jesus Prayer," etc.); in other words, all the senses and most physical functions have been the subject of magical or mystical practices at one time or another and sex is no exception. In the modern Western world, however, with the sexual act pushed into the background by a fastidious Christianity and not discussed in polite company, it was inevitable that only the most outrageous occult societies would have fixated on sex as the key to all other magical rites and powers. Thus, the popular image of the satanic altar in the Black Mass as being a nude virgin or prostitute is apt: to be anti-Christian was to be pro sex.

The Politics of Sex

But how does one maintain an anti-Christian stance in an environment unremittingly pro-Christian? Either by going underground—as the occultists did and still do—or by going overboard. The German lodges—such as the OTO and the Brotherhood of Saturn—opted for the former, but the Nazis chose the "left-hand path."

Let us read the words of SS officer Otto Rahn, the reluctant Nazi and enthusiastic Grail-seeker, who defines the problem for us towards the end of his *Luzifers Hofgesind*:

Whereas Christianity is occupied above all with Man and condemns Nature as antidivine by abandoning it to the atheistic realms of science and technology, Paganism believed that nature was full of gods. All phenomena were words or actions attributed to Genies and Spirits. In this sense one must consider it more pious, more "religious," more "Christian" than Catholicism and Protestantism which both display a desire for domination and the imposition of an implacable Law, ideas which permeated Christianity more due to the influence of Rome and Judaism than due to the influence of Christ.[13]

(It should be noted that this view—in a book by an SS officer published in Germany with, it must be assumed, Nazi imprimatur—anticipated the controversial 1967 article by Lynn White in *Science* magazine,[14] which blamed Christianity for the world's ecological crisis by calling our "arrogance towards nature" the result of "Christian dogma.")

So, there we have the "overboard" solution. Simply claim that you are more pious, more "religious," and more "Christian" than the Church. Claim you have penetrated to the deepest mysteries of Christianity and that, in your opposition to the organized Church, you are only doing what Christ did to the money-changers in the Temple and would do today had he been around and was the one with the whip. For this is what Hitler believed, and what Himmler carried out.

For example, the *Lebensborn* organization of the SS—which every SS officer was obligated to join—put some of this into practice. It was inevitable that someone like Hitler, who had grown up reading the pornographic occult newsletters of von Liebenfels and, later, of Julius Streicher, would have agreed to the institution of a cult brothel for the propagation of the Aryan race. In this organization, women selected for their racial purity and adherence to the Teutonic ideal of womanhood in physical appearance as well as in spiritual composition were maintained for their impregnation by equally Aryan SS men.[15] The *Lebensborn* communities were, in a sense, farms where Aryan babies were bred like blue-eyed cattle. There was even a plan to do away with the whole idea of matrimony as it placed an undue burden on the Aryan race, whose mission was to colonize the entire world with perfect racial specimens. There were, after all, many more non-Aryans in the world than Aryans, and it would take time and manpower to exterminate them all. Besides, healthy Aryan stock was needed to cultivate the fields appropriated during the drive to the East mandated by Haushofer's *Lebensraum* policy. Although the *Lebensborn* concept was never openly discussed as an anti-*Christian* policy—and anyway the Nazis in general and the SS in particular were the repository of the *real* secrets of Christianity and were on the verge of obtaining the Holy Grail itself—it was generally understood that the Catholic Church would not approve. The christening or baptismal ceremonies which took place in the *Lebensborn* communities were pagan rites devised by Nazi occultists to replace those familiar to these husbandless Lutheran and Catholic mothers; thus there could be no doubt among even this, the most militarily uninvolved segment of Nazi Germany, that Nazism was paganism, and that Christianity was to be eventually replaced as surely as Judaism was on the list for immediate extinction.

In this, however, the Nazis were close to their sometime brothers in arms, the anti-religious Socialists, for does not the *Communist Manifesto* describe the desirability of putting an end to marriage and the nuclear family?[16] And if this goal were to be reached, what role does sexuality play in the new society?

For the occult lodges, this was not a problem. Marriage was, indeed, a bit *petit bourgeois* and destined for the junk heap of history but, in the meantime, sexuality was still a powerful occult tool, the manifestation in the visible world of the flow of energy in the unseen dimensions. Magicians had "magickal children" on those planes, and could even create familiars and homonculi—artificial humans—using these techniques, thereby rendering the institution of marriage as a means of ensuring the future of the race rather *outré*. Magicians already lived in the world the Nazis were trying to create. It was a vast one, with a multiplicity of dimensions in endless space, and to their credit they did not require the use of crematoria or mobile gas vans to pursue their particular *Lebensraum*.

We have taken all this space to discuss the official Nazi attitude to sex and marriage since it can be seen as an indirect result of ideas current in Germany for many years before Hitler came to power: ideas concerning sexuality that were ostensibly alien to pious, anti-Semitic Germany and its organized religion and which had to come from somewhere. Hitler, with his hit-and-miss street education in the pages of *Ostara* and at the feet of men like Eckart and Hanussen, took a very broad-minded view of sex. Indeed, he is said to have known about SA Leader Ernst Röhm's homosexuality for years and tolerated it . . . a rather astounding generosity for that man in that time and place. In fact, a great many SA men were homosexuals, which should give the nervous nellies in the Pentagon pause: for the Brownshirts—the dreaded Storm Troopers; the brawling, two-fisted beer hall fighters; the drunken, angry mob of volunteer militiamen who defeated Communism in Germany and who propelled Hitler to power—were the epitome of military machismo . . . and Röhm, their leader and queen, was the ultimate fighting man.

Crowley went to America during World War I after being rejected for military service by his own government (or so he claimed), and when Hitler was fighting the Allies as an enlisted man in the trenches of France and Belgium, writing Wotanist poetry full of magical symbolism, Crowley was writing pro-German propaganda for *The Fatherland*, a journal published in New York by one George Viereck, who had known Crowley slightly from years before.[17] Crowley needed a job, and agreed to take over as editor of *The Fatherland*. He claimed to be Irish, which would have made him a natural enemy of the English if true (which it wasn't). He even went so far as to row out to the Statue of Liberty one day and mime burning his British passport, an event that was duly recorded by no less an astute observer than the *New York Times*.[18]

Later, when confronted by all of this, he would claim that he was really working for the British cause since he had turned *The Fatherland* into something of a joke. *Reductio ad absurdum* was the technique he employed: in other words, his articles were so outlandish that the journal was reduced to absurdity, a caricature of serious political discussion, which would help the British cause much more than harm it. In one such article, for instance, he compared Kaiser Wilhelm II to Parsifal in search of the Grail, and claimed that the Celts were descended from the same race as Osiris and Isis.[19] In another, an article dated November, 1917, for a sister publication of *The Fatherland* called *The International*, he wrote that the world's press was responsible for the war and that the aftermath of the conflict could only bring about "bankruptcy, revolution, and famine," which was certainly true but did not require the special skills of a master magician to foresee.[20]

Incidentally, the above topics were quite in keeping with Listian sentiments and would have been familiar to any *völkisch* audience.

George Viereck himself is something of a minor legend. He is probably the same Viereck whom Freud mentions as a "journalist, politician, writer, quite a handsome fellow" who supplied him with some food during the terrible shortages in Vienna at the end of 1919.[21] The same George Sylvester Viereck interviewed Freud years later, in 1926, on the subject of anti-Semitism and included the interview in a collection entitled *Glimpses of the Great,* that was published in 1930.[22]

And it was certainly the same George Sylvester Viereck who was implicated in one of America's most famous spy cases of the *Second World War.* Viereck—who was the illegitimate grandson of the Kaiser—became an enthusiastic admirer of the Third Reich and essentially its chief publicist in America from his posh apartment on Manhattan's Riverside Drive. The Kaiser had a son in the Gestapo, and Viereck used this connection to get close to Himmler, whom he saw as a kindred spirit: a royalist who admired the old Teutonic kings and who wished for nothing so much as a restoration of the Hohenzollern monarchy. Himmler, with his mystical worship at the shrine of King Henry I, with whom he identified, seemed simpatico; a door into the corridors of power for the scheming journalist.

Crowley's German Case Officer

During the First World War, Viereck became implicated in a plot to sabotage American factories as early as 1915 (in other words, two years before America entered the war). This would have been about the time he encouraged Crowley to take over as editor of *The Fatherland.* A briefcase full of plans for espionage, sabotage, and the invasion of the United States had been left, forgotten, by one of Viereck's agents on the Sixth Avenue El in Manhattan in plain sight of an American secret agent who had been sent to follow them. He picked up the briefcase and blew the story wide open. Oddly, Viereck never spent a day in jail for his role in the elaborate plotting against his adopted country.

With the start of the Third Reich, Viereck oversaw an extensive pro-Hitler propaganda campaign and was central to Nazi efforts to generate support among German-Americans for the Hitler regime. Through his "Board of Trade for German-American Commerce" he was also able to provide an underground railroad for German agents fleeing South America when they became unmasked.

But by far the most sensational aspect of Viereck's career was the revelation that a United States Senator, Ernest Lundeen of Minnesota, was in his employ. On August 31, 1940—one step ahead of an FBI arrest—Lundeen took a flight from Washington, D.C. to his home state, ostensibly to confess all to his wife. He never made it. Lundeen, an FBI agent sent to tail him wherever he went, and eighteen other passengers died when their plane went down in a severe storm amid suspicions of Nazi sabotage.

Two days later, and Lundeen's wife Norma was in Washington, demanding possession of the "Viereck files." These files revealed the full extent of Lundeen's complicity in Viereck's massive propaganda campaign, even to the extent of using the senator's franking privileges to send Nazi literature through the mail without ever paying postage.

Money is always a problem in espionage campaigns, and Viereck's was no different. Although he was being handsomely paid for his services by the Nazi government, the expense of importing propaganda materials past the censors was daunting. It is reported that Viereck received additional funds from the fascist and pro-Nazi dictator Rafael Trujillo of the Dominican Republic. But, eventually, Viereck brought off the brilliant plan of using the government of the United States to do his propagandizing for him. He paid Senator Lundeen thousands of dollars at a time for the privilege of writing his speeches for him, speeches which were delivered in the Senate and printed in the *Congressional Record.*

Eventually, Viereck was arrested, tried, and convicted, and managed to serve only about a year or so in prison before having his sentence reduced; but his effectiveness as a Nazi agent was thereby diminished.[23] What is not known is the extent to which Crowley would have been able to provide information on Viereck to British Intelligence, or if he could have been used to infiltrate Viereck's circle in New York City. Quite possibly Crowley's cover had been "blown" by this time: that is, perhaps he really *was* working for American and British intelligence services during the Great War, as he claimed.

In a written defense of his actions, published in 1929, Crowley insisted that as soon as America entered the war in 1917, the US Department of Justice employed him as an agent-in-place at his *Fatherland* and *International* editorial offices.[24] The author has so far been unable to verify this, but other—unbiased—researchers claim that Crowley was, indeed, telling the truth (see Chapter Nine).

To British Intelligence, however, Crowley was officially just "a small-time traitor"[25] who had no connection with any British Government intelligence or counterintelligence operation taking place in America. Or anywhere else. But the fact that they even had an opinion to express indicates that someone in British Intelligence was keeping an eye on Crowley, as indeed they were. In 1916, apprised of his pro-German propaganda effort in New York, agents of the London Police raided OTO headquarters and confiscated Temple paraphernalia. Whether this was for the purpose of conducting an actual investigation into possible criminal activity or simply as a means of retaliation against Crowley, is not known. But this would not be the last time Crowley would come to the attention of the Intelligence services.

Appropriately enough, during his tenure as editor of both *The Fatherland* and *The International* Crowley's romantic interests revolved around several German women in New York. Perhaps the most famous to Crowley enthusiasts was the ghostly Leah Hirsig, the younger sister of the Swiss-German Alma Hirsig, who had attended one of Crowley's lectures on occultism in 1918 (and who would later become involved with Pierre Bernard, the founder of the Oom the Omnipotent love-cult). She eventually moved in with Crowley in his Greenwich Village studio and became his "Scarlet Woman" (a reference to the consort of the Great Beast of the Apocalypse and a title Crowley used for many of his female lovers). Leah eventually became pregnant and bore a child—Anne Leah—in February of 1920. Shortly thereafter, Crowley decided to set up an occult community in Italy, on the island of Sicily and near the village of Cefalù. This was to become the famous Abbey of Thelema, the object of so much attention by the world press and, eventually, by the government of Benito Mussolini.

The Occult Spies

While Crowley was writing German propaganda in New York, some of his colleagues in the German and British OTO lodges and the

Golden Dawn were employed in actual military work. His former brother-in-law and fellow Golden Dawn initiate, Gerald Kelly, was working as a British secret agent in Spain.[26] Karl Germer (whom we will meet at the great convocation of occult leaders in Thuringia in 1925) was probably a spy for the German secret service during the Great War, and was awarded the Iron Cross, First and Second class[27] (as was, it will be remembered, Adolf Hitler, except that Germer entered the army as an officer while Hitler was an enlisted man). Was Crowley, therefore, supplying information on Germer's activities to the British and American intelligence agencies? If so, that would seem to exonerate him of any claims of treason by his government, but it would also seem to make him a traitor to his own Order. Did Germer ever discover the extent to which Crowley might have been spying on him for the British? Or was there a "gentleman's agreement" between the two magicians that enabled them to act as "double agents" against each other without anyone doing the other any real harm?

Theodor Reuss—Kellner's successor as head of the Order when the latter died in 1905 "in mysterious circumstances"—was also a member of the German secret service, but not during World War I. During the height of that war he can be found living at the Ascona vegetarian community at Monté Verita in the Ticino province of Switzerland (where we found Franz Hartmann almost thirty years earlier), and which then became the headquarters of the OTO for a while.

Years previously, however, Reuss had infiltrated the fledgling Socialist movement in England, where he spied on the family of Karl Marx for German Intelligence.[28] He did this in the guise of an admirer of Marxism, and most of his intended victims were actually emigré Germans living in London. This would have been in the years immediately preceding the founding of the OTO by Kellner, which was supposed to have taken place in 1895. By that time, Mathers—cofounder of the Golden Dawn—had already moved to Paris with his wife, Mina Bergson, sister of the famous philosopher and onetime president of the Society for Psychical Research, Henry Bergson (1859–1941). From about this time until Mathers's death in 1918, there is a lot of speculation about the involvement of the Golden Dawn with everything weird and Continental from the Edelweiss Society (an anti-Semitic front group operating out of Sweden) to an occult group supposedly organized around Karl Haushofer and called variously (by various authors) the Lumen Club or Lumen Lodge or

Luminous Lodge of either Berlin or Vienna (possibly confused with the Lumenclub of Vienna, an organization founded by a follower of Liebenfels which promoted Nazi ideology in pre-Anschluss Austria). While the Golden Dawn certainly had the English-speaking world covered—with lodges from England to America to New Zealand— there is very little evidence for genuine Golden Dawn activity taking place anywhere else, with the exception of whatever Mathers was up to in Paris. After Mathers's death he would have been unable to continue strategizing with German and Scandinavian occult groups, at least on the physical plane. The Edelweiss Society was at its heyday in the 1920s, and the existence of something called the Luminous Lodge is debatable. While it would have been physically possible for Haushofer to have met Mathers when both were living on the Continent at the same time, there would have been no earthly reason to do so. Mathers was an impoverished occultist living in France; Haushofer, a respected professor of geopolitics at the University of Munich. The likelihood of their having met on common ground is virtually nil. While there is evidence that Haushofer was interested in astrology and related forms of mysticism, Mathers was not selling horoscopes or doing the medium circuit, unlike people such as Hanussen. If there was any connection at all between Mathers and the Golden Dawn on one side and German occult lodges on the other, it would have been through either Hartmann or Crowley and there we have the two, verifiable links.

However, once the Nazis began to crack down on the occult groups operating in Germany and the occupied territories, the Golden Dawn—under the German version of its name, *Hermetische Orden der Goldene Dämmerung*—was included on the list, along with Crowley's A∴A∴ and Reuss's OTO.[29] The Nazis were nothing if not thorough; thorough . . . and paranoid. The list of banned societies was probably compiled by one Dr. Gregor Schwartz-Bostunitsch, a self-proclaimed authority on occult societies who entertained a consuming hatred for Freemasonry, Theosophy, and Anthroposophy, and who once counted a youthful Adolf Eichmann among his pupils.

The Weida Conference

Established at the Abbey of Thelema at Cefalù, Sicily, after the war in the spring of 1920, Crowley found himself chronically short of funds and made several trips to Paris and London in an attempt to raise money and gather disciples for his commune. One of these disciples was the unfortunate Raoul Loveday, whose botching of an occult ritual (it is said) resulted in his tragic death. It was this incident involving Loveday—an Oxford undergrad, who arrived at Cefalù accompanied by his friend Betty May—that eventually closed down the abbey. Ms. May, appalled at the degenerate goings-on and general squalor of the abbey and distressed at the death of her friend, returned to England after the occult funeral and told some rather hair-raising stories to the London papers. The resulting furore in England (human sacrifice, cannibalism, satanic rites, etc.) soon spread to Italy, and the Fascists decided to deport Crowley.[30] He left Cefalù in May, 1923, never to return. (His followers stayed behind for a while, but they eventually abandoned the abbey and it fell into general oblivion until a visit one day by filmmaker Kenneth Anger many years later.)

Crowley wound up in North Africa with Leah, wondering what to do next. Their daughter had died shortly after their arrival in Cefalù in 1920, the second of Crowley's children (both daughters) to have died young. In the summer of 1925 the acting head of the OTO—one Heinrich Tränker—invited Crowley to Germany to decide the fate of the Order; that is, Tränker (who had initially opposed Reuss's decision to have Crowley succeed him as OHO) had had a vision in which he saw Crowley as the new head of the Order.[31] Most of the German initiates had opposed Crowley on at least two grounds: the imposition of his personality and personal religion on the rituals and general philosophy of the Order, and the fact that he was an Englishman and not a German like themselves. While there is no evidence to suggest that the OTO was a *völkisch* or Pan-German or neo-Teutonic society, this was still Germany, after all, and Germany in the grip of a political fever with Hitler out of jail and *Mein Kampf* on the best-seller lists.

Yet, OTO initiate Karl Germer ("Frater Uranus") was prevailed upon to provide the funds necessary to transport Crowley to Germany from France, where he had been staying with a small group of disciples, and the Great Beast himself arrived in Thuringia in June of 1925 for the conference that would decide the fate of the Order.

Unfortunately, Crowley had sent a copy of *The Book of the Law* ahead of him for the chiefs to digest. It was quickly translated into German by one Max Schneider and all was more or less acceptable until the infamous third chapter, which contains the diatribe against Christianity, Judaism, etc. aforementioned. At this point, there was a flap among the chiefs and even Herr Tränker of the mystical vision demurred.

Heinrich Tränker was a Leipzig bookseller specializing in occult works, who had his own occult imprint in the pre-World War I days.[32] Also attending the conference were two Theosophists, Otto Gebhardi and the elderly Marthe Küntzel, as well as Germer, Eugene Grosche, two others (members of Crowley's entourage), and Crowley himself. It was held in the small town of Weida, near Gera, which was then evidently the headquarters of the OTO with Tränker as its acting head, or OHO.

After several days of politicking, although Tränker came around to seeing *The Book of the Law* in a slightly more favorable light, he still wound up opposing Crowley's stewardship of the Order. Eugene Grosche ("Frater Saturnus"), accepted Crowley as an important occult teacher but not as the OHO. It was left to Karl Germer to accept Crowley completely and unconditionally, and thereby the OTO split into three warring factions: the largely German, anti-Crowley group under Tränker, the new Brotherhood of Saturn under Eugene Grosche, and the OTO under Crowley, with Germer as his financial sponsor and devoted disciple.

Tränker's OTO was concerned with working the sex-magic degrees as created and refined by Kellner and Reuss without, however, having to accept either the Law of Thelema or Aleister Crowley as the occult messiah. Crowley, it should be emphasized, was the perfectly legitimate head of the OTO for Great Britain and the English-speaking peoples, anointed as such by Reuss. The question of whether or not Crowley was actually the head of the entire Order is a debatable one, since Crowley claims that Reuss appointed him as his successor. If that were true, however, why then the conference in Thuringia? It seems there was at least some room to debate Crowley's position as international OHO, and Tränker—who had the vision that Crowley should be the head—reneged and removed his support during the conference. As Tränker was acting head of the Order, it can be assumed that he held such position legally and with the approval—not only of the other members—but of Crowley himself, if only up until the Weida Conference when the OTO began to splinter in typical occult fashion.

Although Crowley, for all practical intents and purposes, lost the bulk of his German constituency, he left Thuringia with some new friends, among them Karl Germer, who would become OHO upon Crowley's death, and Marthe Küntzel who accepted the Law of Thelema and its Bible, *The Book of the Law*. It would be Ms. Küntzel who would wind up caring for some of the fallout from Crowley's rituals, in the persons of Leah Hirsig and her new companion Norman Mudd, at Küntzel's residence in Germany, until Leah returned to the States and Mudd committed suicide in the waters of the English Channel in June, 1934, coincidentally at the time of the Röhm Purge taking place in Germany.[33]

And it would be Ms. Küntzel who, full of approval not only for Crowley but for another occult messiah, would claim that Adolf Hitler's views were virtually identical with those found in the *The Book of the Law*; Küntzel, interrogated by the Gestapo because of her connections to Theosophists, Thelemites, and Freemasons galore, remained a devoted Nazi and a devoted follower of Crowley to her dying day. It is interesting that she found no conflict of interest between the two. Karl Germer would even claim that the Führer was, quite probably, Crowley's Magickal Son.[34]

Of the third group to leave Thuringia that summer, we may say a little more than has been mentioned elsewhere, for Eugene Grosche's Brotherhood of Saturn also managed to survive the war and to continue its own version of the sex-magic that was taught in the secret councils of the Ordo Templi Orientis.

Grosche's system took the rather Masonic outlines of the OTO a step further and created a whole system of sex-magic based on astrology. This was not a horoscope magazine approach to selecting one's spouse based on sun signs, but rather a complex method of determining sexual positions and partners according to the purpose of the ritual and the actual location of the planets as determined by reference to a common ephemeris and table of houses.

For the curious, the most important astrological aspect (according to this cult) is the square; that is, when two planets are ninety degrees apart on the ecliptic as viewed from the earth. This is supposedly an aspect of great tension between the planets, and those planets specifically related to sexuality (Venus, Mars, Neptune, and the Moon according to the Brotherhood) are particularly powerful for this type of working. All heterosexual and homosexual couplings have been accounted for in this system, as well as the specific positions to be used according to either the natal horoscopes of the individuals involved or actual transits, or both. Conjunctions of the planets were also considered appropriate, but the squares seemed to dominate the sex-magic practices of this group.

While it would take too much space to discuss the theory behind all of this and would perhaps bore the reader not willing to wade through some of the rather surreal jargon of the modern occult movement, suffice it to say that the square aspect was believed to represent a gate, open into the hidden dimensions. In general Western astrology, a square is often considered an unlucky or "hard" aspect: one that represents obstacles to success or illness, accidents, losses of various types. The magicians of the Brotherhood of Saturn saw it, therefore, as a gate opening upon this world from the domain of daemons; and daemons were thought to be nothing more than powerful forces which—to the uninitiated—appeared fearsome and evil but which the initiate (with proper training and discipline) could tame to more productive ends.[35]

This mystification of the sex act among the German occult lodges was perfectly consistent with later Nazi fashions regarding sex and power. As Susan Sontag points out in her essay, "Fascinating Fascism":

> The fascist ideal is to transform sexual energy into a "spiritual" force, for the benefit of the community. The erotic (that is, women) is always present as a temptation, with the most admirable response being a heroic repression of the sexual impulse. . . . Fascist aesthetics is based on the containment of vital forces; movements are confined, held tight, held in.[36]

While no one would accuse Crowley of repressing his sexual impulses, the transformation of sexual energy into a spiritual force was—and remains—the goal of the Ordo Templi Orientis and the other German sex-magic lodges, as it was a personal practice of Hitler himself. The vital force was worshiped as tantamount to magical power and—with the precise instructions of Eugene Grosche and others for the timing of the moment of orgasm to coincide with the passage of some star or planet over a hypothetical point in space—we can say that this vital force was restricted in its flow, subject to the conscious direction (the will) of the magician. Like the Nazi art that Sontag brilliantly describes, the German art of sex-magic is also "both pruri ent and idealizing."[37] While the Office of the Holy Inquisition used guilt by association to equate sexuality with the practice of witchcraft and devil worship (because sexuality was already considered base and animalistic by the Church) and thereby confirmed the evil of lust as a creature of Satan, the German lodges acknowledged this relationship of sex with darkness, sex with demonic forces, but cynically manipulated it toward various personal ends. One might reasonably agree that the Nazi ideal was to sublimate the sexual urge for the "benefit of the community" as Sontag has pointed out; but the German sex magicians were not concerned with the community at all. Their goal was their own benefit, the entirely personal one of spiritual enlightenment and individual power.

Sex and spies. And secret societies. The great sex magicians—Crowley, Germer, and Reuss—were enthusiastically involved in all three pursuits at various times of their lives. All had worked for Germany's benefit, even though Crowley insisted that he worked as a spy for the US Department of Justice and would later work for MI5. All were leaders of the *Ordo Templi Orientis*, a German sex-magick occult lodge. And when, in 1922, Theodor Reuss suffered a stroke and had to step down as OHO of the Order, it was Crowley—fellow spy and sex magician—who rushed in to fill the space. And when Crowley died, it was Germer (veteran secret agent) who took over as OHO.

Crowley has claimed that Reuss appointed him his successor as OHO of the Order, but that ignores the tremendous flap that took place when a German translation of *The Book of the Law* was made available to lodge members in Germany. It can honestly be said that most OTO members in Germany at that time disapproved of Crowley's taking over the OTO. They objected to the way he rewrote their rituals to deify himself and to enshrine his new religion of Thelema in their lodge work. Many initiates defected . . . or, it can be said, the Crowley faction defected from the original OTO organization. In the late 1970s, the author received a communication from a traditional (that is to say, non-Crowleyan) OTO lodge operating out of Frankfurt; evidence, if slim, that an OTO continued to function that had not accepted Thelema and was still working the original grades.

In Germany.

⚡ 5 ⚡

Cult War 1934–1939

It was on a dreary night of November that I beheld the accomplishment of my toils.[1]

—VICTOR FRANKENSTEIN

itler came to power—as Hanussen predicted—on January 30, 1933, in the shadow of the ancient pagan feast of Oimelc. A more important, if less pagan date, is that of November 9; possibly a date selected with premeditation by the Occult Messiah—or else, arrived at without much contemplation at all, just a weird little wrinkle in history.

First, of course, comes Germany's most famous contribution to world religion: Martin Luther, for November 9 is his birthday.

But November 9 was also the birthday of the founder of the Thule Gesellschaft, the man who organized Munich into a full-scale rebellion against the Communists, and who synchronized the Bamberg government and its regular and irregular troops for the final assault on the Bavarian Soviet: Baron von Sebottendorff. It was also the day that the Second Reich collapsed with the abdication of the Kaiser. It was the day that Sebottendorff called the Thule/*Germanenorden* brethren to arms. It was the day Adolf Hitler lost his eyesight for the second time at the Pasewalk sanatorium.

And so it was the day of the Beer Hall Putsch of 1923, a day that Hitler commemorated forever after with speeches and festivities, and sanctified with the creation of the Blood Order: a society of those men who marched with him on that fateful day, and symbolized by the Nazi flag that they carried and with which all other Nazi flags were "blessed" by being touched with it in impressive ceremonials presided over by Hitler himself. It was the day of a failed assassination attempt in 1939 on Hitler's life at a meeting commemorating the Putsch. (Coincidentally, November 9, 1939, was also the date the trial of American Nazi and Bund leader Fritz Kuhn began in New York City, a trial that resulted in his conviction on various charges and his sentencing to Sing Sing.) And it was also the day of *Kristallnacht,* when roving Nazi gangs went on a rampage in 1938, smashing shop windows and destroying Jewish homes, businesses, and temples. If anyone in Hitler's Germany believed in numerology, they would have spent considerable time in analyzing this most pregnant of dates for the Third Reich.

As he bent to the task of solidifying his position as absolute dictator of Germany—using the Reichstag fire in February 1933 as the excuse for assuming virtually total control of the government while waiting for the president to die—Hitler also began ensuring that very little of his past would be revealed to the public by his friends from the old days in Vienna and Munich. The "November 9" days.

Dietrich Eckart was already dead; Eckart's disciple Alfred Rosenberg was safely on board with the Party, as was Rudolf Hess. Hanussen will be murdered in the woods near Berlin only weeks after the Reichstag fire.

And May 10, 1933, would witness a quintessentially barbaric act of the new German ruling party: the burning of *hundreds of thousands* of books that were considered dangerous to the regime. Significantly, these massive bonfires marked the first time the word "holocaust" was used by the Western press in association with the Nazis;[2] it would be eight years before the same word would be used to describe the mass extermination of the "non-Aryans." This first, frenzied auto-da-fé—which took place all over Germany, in thirty cities—symbolized all that was wrong with the Third Reich and all that is still wrong with its admirers on both sides of the Atlantic: the anti-intellectualism that is born, not of an educated disagreement with particular philosophical ideas, but from a primitive's fear of what it cannot comprehend.

And there was one book in particular that really attracted everyone's attention in the newly Nazified Reichstag.

The Return of the Baron

Just when everything seemed set to allow Hitler to stride onto the global political scene with a minimum of personal embarrassment and domestic opposition, who should reappear but the one man who had the most to do with setting that very stage—Baron Rudolf von Sebottendorff!

He was probably the last person Hitler wanted anyone to hear from, for Sebottendorff knew where all the bodies were buried. The self-styled Baron was proud of his participation in the early days of the Nazi Party and of his struggle to free Munich from Communist control in 1919. Although the Thule Gesellschaft had died a slow death, Sebottendorff was back to revive it.

And not only that. The Baron had written and published a book. Entitled *Bevor Hitler Kamm* ("Before Hitler Came"), it outlined the entire early history of the Thule Society and the first days of the Nazi Party.

Sebottendorff's whereabouts after the successful putsch against the Communists in Munich in 1919 are well known. He left active membership in the Thule Society because his brethren held him responsible for the deaths of the original Seven Thulists who were executed by the Reds. For several years, the Baron published a series of astrological works which were very well received, and in 1923 he made for Lugano in Switzerland. There he wrote another occult treatise, comparing subjects as diverse as alchemy, Rosicrucianism, and Sufism. This completed, in 1925 he made for his occult "alma mater": Turkey.

For a while, Sebottendorff managed to convince the Mexican government to accept him as their honorary consul in Istanbul. This enabled him to travel throughout Central America and the United States for several years, but he returned to Munich after Hitler came to power in 1933. Perhaps he thought he could obtain a position with the new Nazi government based on his credentials with the Thule Society. Whatever his motivations might have been, they didn't keep him out of jail.

At a time when the Führer was trying desperately to win world recognition of his stature as statesman and Chancellor of the Reich, here was the old Orientalist, Pan-German, and occultist Sebottendorff virtually giving the game away in black and white. Hitler would not have been able to survive having this book on the reading list of those heads of state with whom he was most anxious to negotiate. Also, revelation of his connections to a patently *occult* organization like the Thule Gesellschaft might have resulted in an erosion of support from the middle class and in the renewal of opposition from other political blocs within Germany and even within his own political party. (The mid-1930s was a time of great upheaval within the country as various Nazi factions tried to gain the upper hand in the government, result-ing in the famous Blood Purge of 1934 and the execution of SA leader Ernst Röhm and many others.)

And then there was the attempt to blackmail the Führer, which proved to be the last straw.

The Blackmail Plot

A typed letter dated September 15, 1933, on Thule Gesellschaft sta-tionery shows Sebottendorff inviting one "Professor Stempfle" to a Thule Society meeting that Saturday evening.[3] It can be seen from this note that the Thule Society had returned not only to Munich but to its old headquarters at the Four Seasons Hotel, and to its old schedule of Saturday meetings, as if nothing had happened in the last fourteen years.

Even more interesting, however, is the addressee. Quite possibly it is the same Bernhard Stempfle who was the Catholic priest who had edited an anti-Semitic newspaper in the old days before the Beer Hall Putsch. A friend and coconspirator of Baron Sebottendorff, he had helped design the framework for armed resistance to the Bavarian So-viet Republic in 1919 by the legitimate government in Bamberg. He was a guest of Hitler's at Obersalzberg after the latter's release from

Landsberg Prison, along with Hess and Hitler's indefatigable press secretary "Putzi" Hanfstaengl. This bizarre trio helped Hitler to complete
the first volume of *Mein Kampf* in the spring of 1925. (It would be
published in Munich on July 18 of that year.) Stempfle was included
for his editorial services, and it was probably this access to information
on the early days of Hitler—including Hitler's reminiscences about his
youth in Austria and Munich—that led to one of the most scandalous
episodes of the early days of Hitler's rule in Germany.

Stempfle was a friend not only of Sebottendorff but of a strange
little gentleman by the name of J.F.M. Rehse, who owned what was
probably the largest single collection of Nazi memorabilia in captivity.
Rehse collected every scrap of paper he could find concerning the
Nazis, Dietrich Eckart, the Thule Society, etc., and meticulously catalogued each item and stored them in boxes. He and the anti-Semitic
priest Stempfle were close friends.[4]

In 1929, Father Stempfle made an astonishing claim. He professed
to own a letter that Hitler had written—but never mailed—to the one
true love of his life, Geli Raubal. Ms. Raubal was Hitler's niece (a
daughter of his half sister, Angela) and the Führer was infatuated with
her, saying on at least one occasion that she was the only woman he
could ever conceive of marrying. According to Stempfle, Hitler had
written an alarming, sexually explicit letter to Ms. Raubal.

The nature of the sex being discussed in the letter was of a rather
debased type, involving both masochistic and what the psychologists
term "coprophilic" fantasies. Obviously, it would spell political and
personal disaster for Hitler if this scatological letter were ever made
public. It had probably been stuck in some forgotten corner of his
rented room in Munich, for it fell into the hands of his landlady's son
and from there into the possession—or so it was said—of Mr. Rehse.

The existence of the letter became known to Hitler, who sent the
Party's treasurer—a discreet and trustworthy aide by the name of
Franz X. Schwarz—to obtain it from Rehse. Stempfle saw this as a
means of insuring the existence of Rehse's invaluable "Archive," and
convinced Rehse to extort enough money from the Nazis to enable his
archival pursuits to continue. Although it was blackmail, pure and
simple, Hitler agreed to assume financial responsibility for the collection, and in return Father Stempfle gave the purloined letter to the
Party treasurer.

Geli Raubal, to whom the famous letter had been addressed, had eventually committed suicide in Hitler's Munich apartment in 1931, during Adolf's failed run for president of Germany. The reason is unknown. (Eva Braun would attempt suicide during his *next* campaign in 1932. It seems Hitler shared Aleister Crowley's abysmal track record with women. Several of Crowley's mistresses, wives, and Scarlet Women committed suicide or wound up in mental asylums. Six of Hitler's mistresses attempted suicide: at least three succeeded, four if you count Eva Braun's final attempt in Berlin in 1945.)

Rehse probably never had the Geli Raubal letter in his possession in the first place, for the integrity of the Rehse Collection remained intact and can be viewed today on microfilm at the Library of Congress (the originals were "returned" to the Bundesarchiv in Koblenz).

Father Stempfle, however, did his penance for the sin of blackmailing Adolf Hitler, for he was murdered—terminated with extreme unction—in the woods outside Munich during the famous Blood Purge of June, 1934. His assassin pumped three rounds into his heart.[5]

These were the types of people Sebottendorff was calling to his side in 1933. It's possible that the Baron knew of Stempfle's blackmail scheme regarding the Führer, but the author has been unable to find proof of this. In any case, Sebottendorff was a dangerous man with dangerous friends and an equally dangerous flair for publicity. He, like Stempfle and that other troublemaker, Röhm, had to be stopped.

After his brief attempt at reviving the Thule—possibly with even more occult trappings and arcane rituals than before—he was sent to prison early the following year and released soon after, thus managing to avoid the Blood Purge in June, which might have resulted in his going the way of piously prurient Father Stempfle. Instead, he found himself back in Turkey, where he managed to convince the local head of German Intelligence to take him on as a secret agent . . . yet another occultist-turned-spy.

He did not cover himself with glory in this position.

The end of the war would find the hapless Sebottendorff broke, disillusioned, and thoroughly depressed. All that he had worked for since the early days of National Socialism had come to nothing. His own party—that is, the party he had done so much to create—had seen fit to imprison him at the moment of its greatest triumph. And now Hitler was dead and the Reich was in smoking ruins.

Sebottendorff committed suicide by jumping into the Bosporus. The date was May 9, 1945.

Cult War

Meanwhile, Hitler was on the rampage against dissident factions in the Party. June, 1934, saw the Blood Purge take place in which the head of the SA, Ernst Röhm, a longtime comrade in arms, was arrested and executed and the SA effectively shorn of its previous position and power in the Party. Many other enemies of the Reich—real and imagined—were targeted for death that summer, and the bodies piled up. Among those who escaped the Führer's wrath were Himmler, Hess, Rosenberg, Haushofer, and the other cultists around the dictator.

The death of Röhm was seen by many to be the key event, giving Heinrich Himmler and his SS virtually unlimited power in Germany and, eventually, in the occupied territories as well. But in order to consolidate this power a number of other steps had to be taken. The opposition had to be crushed. Himmler, the guard dog of the new Reich, was told to round up the usual suspects.

As early as May 26, 1934 (and therefore a month before the Blood Purge of Röhm and other enemies), an order of the Reich War Minister (1 p 90 J (I a) Nr 2066/34) quite bluntly stated:

"I forbid any member of the Wehrmacht, including workers, employees, and officials, from membership in Freemason lodges and similar Organizations."[6]

This was followed by more explicit instructions on behalf of the Party, instructions that were updated and expanded every few months and then every other year or so. To understand the official opprobrium in which the Freemasons were held, it is only necessary to read that section of the law which lumps Freemasons in with violators of the "race laws."[7] Also, a certain special hatred was reserved for those Masons who had the temerity to advance to the III degree of the Craft. These men were forbidden from participating in any but the lowest forms of labor and, in many cases, were subject to penalization of various types, punishment, and even a term in the camps.

This obsession with Freemasonry did not begin with the Third Reich but was a by-product of the first wave of twentieth-century anti-Semitism that took place during the First World War with the publication of the *Protocols of the Elders of Zion,* which described a Judeo-Masonic conspiracy to take over the world. The Jews—thought to be operating through the Masonic lodges of Europe—were believed to be planning world conquest beginning with the collapse of the monarchies. They had already "succeeded" with the American and French revolutions and were now well on their way to complete success with the destruction of the Kaiser and of the Czars of Russia. The Masonic lodges were believed to be fronts for the Jewish world government that was forming; their secret initiations, handshakes, code words merely a continuation of politics by other means: a way of operating clandestinely in their host countries. This was taken quite seriously by a large segment of the otherwise well-educated population, including university professors, lawyers, doctors, etc. The revelation of the "Judeo-Masonic" conspiracy "is presented as a turning point in the spiritual history of mankind."[8] The Germans were finally able to identify who and what had destroyed their country, brought them into war, and made them lose the war: a cabal of Jews and Freemasons bent on world domination.

In fact, Adolf Eichmann's first job as an SS noncom in Berlin in 1934 (after preliminary training at Dachau) was as a clerk working with Professor Schwarz-Bostunitsch, an "expert" on Freemasonry who had once worked for the Czar of Russia and who then became the scientific director of the Information Section of the SS Security Service, the SD or *Sicherheitsdienst.*[9] (Schwarz-Bostunitsch had been the author of various anti-Masonic polemics in his time and was quite possibly the Reich's preeminent expert on everything from regular Freemasonry to Rudolf Steiner and his Anthroposophy to the various cults that comprised the list of banned organizations used by the Gestapo.) The future head of the Bureau for Jewish Affairs of the Reich's Security Headquarters (RSHA), who would be ultimately responsible for implementing the Final Solution, Eichmann first worked in Berlin maintaining a card catalogue of information on the Freemasons. Later, he was transferred to the Freemasonry Museum proper. This museum, directly under the authority of the SS, was visited ("inspected") two to three times a week by Himmler himself. It consisted of material confiscated from Masonic lodges all over the Reich, everything from aprons and ritual implements to seals, photographs, documents, etc. There was a room decorated as a St. John's Temple and another as a St. Andrew's Temple. Eichmann's desk was in the St. John's room, where he catalogued thousands of Masonic seals and medallions, until his transfer to the "Jews"—*Judenamt*—Department of the SD.

One may obtain a rather intimate glimpse of the ferocity with which the imagined threat of the Freemasons was fought by looking over the shoulders of the Reich officials responsible for keeping the souls of the German *völk* free from any taint of this ancient brotherhood. As an example, we have before us a letter on the stationery of the *Reichsbetriebsgemeinschaft Druck* (The Reich Printers Management Union) of the German Labor Front *(Die Deutsche Arbeitsfront)* dated May 17, 1935. It shows the head of that organization requesting confirmation from the Information Office of the German Labor Front that several employees—Messrs. Strowigk, Buchhorn, and Kickelhahn— were Masons and that one Max Fischer was a Christian Scientist.[10]

A reply from the head *(Amtsleiter)* of that office—dated May 21, 1935—shows that one of the gentlemen in question, the unfortunate Hans Strowigk, was indeed a Freemason, and furthermore gives the dates of his initiations into the three grades of the Golden Plough Lodge beginning in 1931 and culminating in January 1933, about four weeks before Hitler came to power.[11]

The actual wording is suggestive. Strowigk is described as "a distinct enemy of National Socialism" *(ausgesprochener Gegner des Nationalsozialisumus)* for having advanced the three basic degrees of Freemasonry!

As for Buchhorn and Kickelhahn, the *Amtsleiter* had no information, but requested birthplace, dates, etc. to enable him to more thoroughly research the files. This letter ends with a "Heil Hitler" and the stamp of the German Labor Front. One wonders if the young Eichmann had been responsible for maintaining the card files that ultimately branded Strowigk a "distinct enemy."

More evidence regarding the Reich's anti-Masonic drive is represented by a letter addressed to the office of the Reichsführer-SS in Berlin.[12] Dated February 25, 1935, it is from the Central Office of the German Labor Front and concerns a rule book of the St. John's Pyramid Lodge (possibly containing membership lists) that is being enclosed. According to the letter, it was obtained by one of their workers whose father had been a former member of the Lodge. Accompanying this letter in the file is another, dated April 1, 1935,[13] acknowledging receipt of the book and signed by an SS-Obersturmbannführer-SS (the equivalent of a lieutenant colonel in the U.S. Army) at the office of the Reichsführer-SS.

This is the type of material that would have wound up in Eichmann's Section and, indeed, the dates in all the above cases seem to match the time of Eichmann's employment at the Freemasonry Museum, for he was not transferred to the *Juden* Department until the latter half of 1935.

Among other evidence that has been collected and microfilmed on the same roll at the National Archives in Washington, D.C. is an inventory of confiscated Masonic temple furniture and ritual objects;[14] a clarification of SS regulations concerning the employment of former Freemasons in the Luftwaffe (in which those holding III degree are considered, of course, the worst offenders along with those holding any important office in the Lodge);[15] and much other material. Some of these communications are both to and from the Gestapo, the Secret Police organization of the Third Reich that was eventually subsumed into the SS, and are marked "*Geheim!*": Secret.

One of the major anti-Masonic personalities in Nazi Germany—aside from Schwarz-Bostunitsch—was Rosenberg himself. Convinced that the notorious forgery, the *Protocols of the Elders of Zion,* was authentic and supplied with all the paranoid literature of the day linking a clandestine Jewish government with the operation of the Masonic lodges (after all, the *Protocols* are signed by an Elder or Elders with the obviously Masonic title of "33 degrees"), Rosenberg was certain that the Masons were a genuine enemy to be feared. On the first of May 1941, Hermann Göring confirmed that official policy by instructing all units of the Wehrmacht in the Occupied Territories to support Rosenberg's *Einsatztab* in the seizure of Masonic ceremonial objects, books, and temple property, these items being considered cultural objects representative of anti-Nazi ideology. These would have wound up in the Freemasonry Museum, or in Rosenberg's personal possession.

The entire list of proscribed organizations can be found in the *Zugehörigkeit von Beamten zu Freimaurerlogen, anderen Logen oder logenöhnlichen Organizationen* (Membership in the Offices of Freemason Lodges, other Lodges, or Lodgelike Organizations of the Reich's Home Office of June 6, 1939 (II SB 2212/39-6190 a*)). A swift glance down the names of Section B, "Freemasonlodge-like Organizations", will show the Theosophical Society, the Anthroposophical Society, the Golden Dawn, the OTO, and the Brotherhood of Saturn, cheek by jowl with the Odd Fellows, the Ancient Order of Druids, Christian Science, and something called—in English—the Independent Order of Owls! While it might seem that the Nazis were simply banning *all* fraternities and sects, one should remember that this was considered the "anti-Freemasonry" law and that all of the above-mentioned groups were lumped together under the rubric "Mason-like Organizations." The real enemy was Freemasonry. The others were considered—at least on paper—to be fellow travelers.

This was cult war, pure and simple.

There Is a Specter Haunting Germany . . .

Why this persecution of the Masonic societies?

The Nazis were not alone in history in their fear of Freemasonry. The Masons have always been much maligned since their creation over two hundred years ago. There was even a Masonic "scare" in the United States in the mid-1800s when they were believed to be infiltrating every level of government and conspiring to rob Americans of their democracy. And there was another Masonic scare much more recently in Italy, involving the infamous P-2 Society and members of the Italian parliament.

The Masons are, of course, a secret society. That is, there is a set of ritual phrases and handshakes that identify Masons to one another and which represent initiatory steps taken behind the closed doors of the Masonic temple. There are secret rituals of an initiatory nature (though most, by now, have been published), and secret doctrines that form the rich and varied tradition of Masonic "lore."

And then there are the oaths.

These are blood oaths, taken with great solemnity, which guarantee that the initiate will not reveal any of the secrets of the lodge under pain of quite terrible punishment involving torture, dismemberment, and death. The existence of these oaths alone would be enough to attract the attention of the authorities, for the governments of most (if not all) nations really don't approve of their citizens having secrets. (The author is quite certain that, were he to take an oath to keep secret his late grandmother's recipe for poppy seed strudel, some government somewhere would find it necessary to beat it out of him.)

In a dictatorship, the citizens can have no secrets since possessing a secret means withholding something from the Führer and this is not consistent with the idea of a dictatorship. In Nazi Germany, the citizens took oaths of loyalty to the Reich and to the person of Adolf Hitler himself. How could a secret legally exist in such an atmosphere, where everything is the property of the Führer? Secrets held by members of the *polis* imply dissent, and dissent can only legally exist within some form of democracy.

The secret societies, on the other hand, relish their secret oaths because they instill in the new candidate a sense that something really important is hidden behind all the veils of the temple. This, of course, is not always true. Aleister Crowley once wryly pointed out that, after taking a similar, terrible oath upon entering the Golden Dawn, the secrets that were revealed to him were nothing more than the Hebrew alphabet!

More importantly—and more dangerously, in the eyes of the Reich—a secret makes its keeper an *individual.* The Indo-European ("Aryan") root for the word "secret" gives us related words, like "self" and "secede."[16] Keeping a secret is a means of separating oneself from society at large, of *seceding* from the group, the government, the Reich. In Nazi Germany, there was no "self"; the slogan *Ein Volk, Ein Reich, Ein Führer* told you that, even if the Nuremberg Rally of 1934 didn't.

Also, the Masons believe themselves to be in possession of secret *knowledge* concerning the creation of the cosmos and thus of the truth behind the world's religions. Outsiders, therefore, came to believe that the Masons had set themselves up as higher than the Church and independent of the local laws, marching to a beat consistent with these esoteric rhythms. Certainly, if the Masonic oaths were to be enforced to the letter it would mean that the Masons would be conducting their own trials based on their own laws and executing their own judgments against transgressors—in effect, by-passing all branches of civil (and especially religious) government and becoming a law unto themselves. For this reason, certainly, membership in the Society of Freemasons was forbidden by the Catholic Church: an organization which already had a history of superseding civil legislation. And, secret knowledge of an occult kind has its parallels in secret knowledge of a political kind. Men (and women) adept at keeping one kind of secret and living one kind of secret life might be equally adept at keeping and living the other.

In fact, the membership of some early Masonic lodges reflects the attraction the cult of secret handshakes and costumed rituals had for some of the most famous freethinkers and rebels in history. Several studies have been published on Mozart's life as a Mason; Goethe and George Washington (and Franklin Roosevelt, Hitler's bugaboo) were Masons. The infamous *Illuminaten Orden* of Adam Weishaupt—yet another frothy Bavarian confection of political conspiracy lightly folded into an Enlightenment attitude toward organized religion (and also on the Nazis' hit list of banned organizations)—infiltrated Masonic societies in Germany, France, and Switzerland with political intent. Masons in the eighteenth century were largely aristocrats, intellectuals, adventurers, and artists; by and large they were the influential persons of the societies in which they lived, not unlike the Thule Society of later years, which thrived in the heady atmosphere of wealthy industrialists, idealistic nobles, and the Prussian officer class.

Add to this the romantically styled history of Freemasonry, which traces its covert lineage back to King Solomon and later through the Knights Templar—that other much-maligned and much-abused fraternity of crypto-occultists—and one has a conspiracy theory that transcends centuries and the globe. A conspiracy theory isn't much fun unless it reaches wide and deep, and the Freemasons fit the bill.

Several books that helped frame Himmler's early view of world history—and therefore wound up influencing the entire scope of the SS—were popular studies of Freemasonry in the style of the more rabid conspiracy theory books of today. These included *World Freemasonry, World Revolution, World Republic (Weltfreimauerei, Weltrevolution, Weltrepublik)* by Friedrich Wichtl and *Freemasons and Anti-Masons in Struggle for World Mastery (Freimaurer und Gegenmaurer im Kampf um der Weltherschaft)* by Franz Haiser.[17] These were books spawned from the great controversy over the *Protocols* and were based, in part, on "revelations" contained within that forgery. From these books Himmler borrowed the concept of the Kshatriya warrior caste of "Aryan" India, a concept to be found in the writings of Blavatsky and other theosophical authors and which made its way into the *völkisch* and conspiracy literature popular at that time, and enthusiastically adopted it as his own. He drank in the paranoid fantasies of Wichtl, who exculpated the Germans for any responsibility in having started the war, and instead blamed it on the Jewish-Masonic syndicate which included Trotsky, no less, as well as Lenin and George V![18]

Although Himmler may have needed a new Aryan Secret Society, he did not need another Thule Society around to foment discord. The Nazis knew all too well how much power a secret society could wield in Germany. The Thule was, after all, a front for the *Germanenorden,* and that organization had been conducting high-level assassinations for years when it wasn't organizing resistance against the Communists. The Masons had a rather vast underground network by comparison, and the benefit of two hundred years of organized activity from Germany to the rest of Europe, the Americas, the Middle East, and even Asia. By comparison, the Freemasons made the Thule Society look like the kindergarten of secret societies, at least insofar as the prestige of antiquity and international membership was concerned. Besides, the rumors had it that Masons were responsible for every political upheaval from the American Revolution to the French Revolution to the Russian Revolution. (As early as 1919, Alfred Rosenberg's articles for the *Völkischer Beobachter* were full of references to a worldwide conspiracy of Jews, Bolsheviks, and Masons to take over the globe.)[19] To the Nazis the Masons were a well-organized, hierarchical society with members in virtually every nation on earth which had enthusiastically taken part in revolutions and armed conflicts everywhere. Worse, they were seen as staunch supporters of democracy, and the word "democracy" to the Nazis carried a distaste almost as bad as "Jew." In fact, democracy was believed to be the weapon of Jewish interests, created to keep the common man living in a fool's paradise of equality and brotherhood while the cynical, conniving Jew reached into the worker's pocket and took all his money.

Democracy. Freemasonry. Judaism. Secret societies. The Nazis were bent on removing all trace of any philosophical opposition to their cause, for they knew the power of ideas and—the quotation of Chairman Mao notwithstanding—it was far stronger than the power of a gun.

The Nazis were not simply a political party. As has been mentioned before, they were a *cult,* and as such had every trapping of the typical cult, from a spiritual Master to a brotherhood of identically clad disciples, secret rituals performed in remote castles, and a sign—a totem— that summed up their ideology as effectively as the Cross and the Star. The swastika is the single, most obvious, even *glaring* piece of evidence to support this view, and yet calling the Nazi Party nothing more than a cult on steroids has yet to become an accepted and legitimate point of view.

Yet, as with any typical cult, its chief enemies were other cults.

Karl Germer Speaks to an Angel

One of the cults on the list of banned "Freemason-like" organizations is the *Ordo Templi Orientis,* which appears under the German translation of its name: *Orientalischer Templer-Orden (OTO),* number 14 on the list. The author has so far been unable to discover what happened to specific members of the anti Crowley faction of the OTO that remained loyal to Tränker, but the Eugene Grosche branch (the Brotherhood of Saturn) is number 15 on the list. It's interesting to note, however, that something calling itself Thelema Verlag was still publishing Crowley material in Leipzig as late as 1937.

Karl Germer was Crowley's chief disciple in Germany at the time Hitler came to power. He and Marthe Küntzel were holding down the fort while Crowley—who had visited Germany again briefly in the spring of 1930—was busy drumming up support abroad for Thelema. Ms. Küntzel had grown so infatuated with Hitler as early as 1925 that she had sent him a copy of *The Book of the Law* in German translation. Crowley had told her that the first country to accept the Law would become master of the world and Ms. Küntzel was determined that it would be Germany.

Some years previous, Crowley had attracted the attention of Scotland Yard. There is a record of a meeting taking place between Crowley and one Colonel Carter of the Yard concerning Crowley's activities on the Continent. He had just been deported from France—a move that was recorded in the world press—for the authorities felt that Crowley was in fact a spy for Germany, and that the OTO was nothing more than either a front for a German spy ring or a blind with which to confuse the intelligence services. As it happens, the meeting with Colonel Carter went well and Crowley was not subject to any prosecution by the British government.

That same year (1929) Crowley had married a Nicaraguan citizen—Maria Theresa di Miramar—in Leipzig in a marriage of convenience so that his new Scarlet Woman could obtain a visa for England, but he soon tired of her there and returned to Berlin, taking up with a series of German women. One of these, the thirty-six-year-old Gertrude "Billy" Busch, was the woman the Brownshirts rescued in 1931 when Crowley was slapping her around on a street corner.[20] He had met her while standing bemused in front of a travel agency on Unter Den Linden and soon thereafter consecrated her as one of his Scarlet Women, much to the consternation of Frater Uranus. The storm troopers found Crowley beating her on the street, and—according to John Symonds—"trod Crowley's face into the gutter."[21] Whether this was simply wishful thinking on Mr. Symonds's part, we shall never know. One thing is for certain, however; at the same time as Crowley was engaged in this peculiar form of worship of his Scarlet Woman, Gertrude, he was spying on the German Communists for British Intelligence. Living with the notorious espionage agent and avowed Communist, Gerald Hamilton—the onetime companion of Sir Roger Casement—he was able to spy on him in return for fifty pounds sterling, courtesy of MI5.[22]

But in 1935, the cult war began in earnest and the Nazis banned the Freemasons and similar Lodges. This included the OTO and the Golden Dawn, and Karl Germer—who had occult connections everywhere and was a high-grade Mason himself—was finally arrested by the Gestapo in 1935 and thrown into solitary confinement at the Alexanderplatz prison.[23] Prior to 1935, he had been largely responsible for Crowley's many debts and a letter survives to Crowley from Germer's wife complaining about the sum of fifteen thousand American dollars that Crowley evidently frittered away on red wine and Scarlet Women.[24] Fifteen thousand dollars was an enormous sum of money in pre-WWII Germany. This kind of largesse from a ranking German Freemason and leader of the German OTO to an English occultist—if indeed the financial transactions were known to the Gestapo—would have made Germer's punishment particularly harsh. Further, Germer was a known associate of Eugene Grosche, whose Brotherhood of Saturn was also on the list, and of the elderly Marthe Küntzel, the erstwhile Theosophist (now an enthusiastic member of the OTO and follower of the accursed Englishman, Crowley) whose personal papers and Order documents were seized. From all this, the Gestapo must have thought that Karl Germer was Satan incarnate.

As it was, he spent several weeks in solitary confinement and was cruelly tortured. Once the Gestapo were through with him, he was shipped off for ten months as a reluctant guest of the SS at the Esterwegen concentration camp.[25]

What happened to Germer during that year of internment, torture, and unspeakable inhumanity can only be the subject of conjecture. He wrote a memoir of his time in the camps which has so far remained unpublished, but it is to the spiritual transformation of Germer that the author refers; for Karl Germer—Frater Uranus, to give his Order name—claimed that it was while at Esterwegen that he attained Knowledge and Conversation of his Holy Guardian Angel.

This is a technical term in the lexicon of twentieth-century ceremonial magic, and was used to denote a particular state of enlightenment in the Golden Dawn and in Crowley's expanded version of the Golden Dawn, the A∴A∴. In a way, it denotes conscious "contact" with one's higher Self except that the Self as understood by modern psychoanalysis is woefully short of what the occultists mean by it. Imagine that there is an aspect of one's personality which has already attained the ultimate spiritual apotheosis it is possible to attain, that the eternal element of one's self—that element beyond space and time—already sits at the right hand of God. Between one's self and one's Self there exists a chasm so wide that most people never even know a Self exists; yet, after much concentrated effort in that direction suddenly, and perhaps all too briefly, there is a moment when the self becomes conscious of the Self: the two meet in a lightning flash of absolute awareness in which it is safer to say that there is a "before" and an "after" rather than a "self" and a "Self."

If all this sounds like so much hyperbole, that is perhaps more due to the lack of a proper vocabulary in the English language to describe an event that lies beyond the scope of normal experience. The Golden Dawn—borrowing the term from a medieval grimoire (book of magician's rituals) called the *Sacred Book of Magic of Abra-Melin the Mage*— used the rather cumbersome title "Knowledge and Conversation of the Holy Guardian Angel" to represent that moment of awareness that comes only after much meditation and psychological preparedness through ritual. The Holy Guardian Angel is, of course, what a Jungian might—for lack of a better term—call the Higher Self.

While this event is spiritually momentous, it is not the ultimate goal of the magician. Once Knowledge and Conversation has occurred, it requires more work and concentration to achieve a gradual *union* of self and Self and there are more obstacles to be overcome and trials to be survived before this can take place. Knowledge and Conversation of the Holy Guardian Angel is no guarantee of immortality or enlightenment, but this phase—no matter what one calls it—must take place before higher states are reached.

The Masons and the OTO are similar societies in that they offer a series of grades of initiation in which certain "secrets" are imparted or revealed to the initiate. The basic number of grades in Freemasonry is three, although there exist as many as thirty-three degrees in American Freemasonry and there are certain illegitimate and distaff branches that add degrees with reckless abandon. The Masonic society that Germer belonged to—that of Memphis and Mizraim (also banned by the Nazis)—boasted as many as ninety-seven degrees. However, these organizations are not "teaching" Orders in the sense of the Golden Dawn curriculum, which was quite complex and which was designed gradually to bring a person to spiritual enlightenment through a series of initiatory rituals that were complemented by private ritual and academic study. The A∴A∴, however, was just such a "teaching" Order, as it followed the Golden Dawn grades with the addition of three degrees on top of the eight created by Mathers, et al. Germer's experience in the concentration camp at Esterwegen can be understood in that context, then, as he was also a member of Crowley's A∴A∴.

A word about Esterwegen: this camp was built in 1933, shortly after Dachau and in tandem with Sachsenhausen.[26] Its purpose was clearly the internment and punishment of the ideological opposition, from Communists to Church leaders, from Freemasons to Jews. The prisoners were beaten and tortured daily in the relatively spacious camps (relative to their condition by 1943), and within a rather liberal time schedule. These first years of the camps were the worst in many cases, for individuals were easily singled out for brutal and bestial behavior. Once the camps became crowded far beyond capacity, the ability of SS guards to inflict specific torture on each individual became reduced. (Instead, the great masses of prisoners were subjected to inhuman and nightmarish living conditions in which corpses were left to decay in the barracks for lack of space—or time—to bury them. Those who were selected for medical experimentation, however, experienced the worst the human mind could conceive. More often than not, these experiments were carried out under the auspices of the Ahnenerbe-SS, an organization we shall study in the following chapters.)

In order to preserve his sanity during his incarceration and torture, Germer recited to himself those of Crowley's writings he had memorized; a set of scripturelike texts entitled the *Holy Books* that Crowley had collated back in 1907 (the year Liebenfels raised the swastika flag over Burg Werfenstein, and the year the A∴A∴ was founded) and published about 1909. Naturally, these texts are to be understood in light of *The Book of the Law* and reflect Crowley's communication with his *own* Holy Guardian Angel, Aiwaz: the Being of whom Crowley was made aware those three April afternoons in Cairo in 1904.

One of the texts included in that collection—*Liber Liberi vel Lapis Lazuli*—is subtitled "These are the birth words of a master of the Temple," a fairly obvious reference to the spiritual transformation undergone by Germer, as a Master of the Temple is the degree attained by those who have just "crossed the Abyss," i.e., undergone what psychologists and poets alike refer to as the "dark night of the soul."

That Germer should have attained spiritual illumination in a concentration camp sounds at first blush to be entirely inappropriate. Yet, a study of the literature of spiritual processes would demonstrate that the terrible anxiety and stress of the camp—when accompanied by constant meditation and spiritual exercises—could very well have resulted in just such a satori-like episode.

Masonic initiation in the first degrees is concerned with simulating physical trials. A blindfolded candidate for initiation is bound and brought before a group of men at the point of a sword. These days, this can be understood by most people as a lot of mumbo jumbo and few candidates would take the ritual seriously. In the early days of Freemasonry, however, being bound and blindfolded and dragged before a mysterious council and made to swear an oath at the point of a sword would have been seen as serious business, indeed.

For Germer, being thrown into a concentration camp, tortured, and threatened with extinction provided him with a natural initiatic scenario. He is said to have recited Crowley's *Holy Books* to preserve his sanity; what actually took place, however, was a Zen-like self-initiation in which the unnatural stress of the situation was further complicated by constant meditation on a spiritual path, resulting in a psychic explosion; similar to what the Zen teachers call a "satori." Ironically, this took place under the eyes of the SS, a rival cult dedicated to the eradication of just such independent initiatory experiences as Germer's.

Shortly thereafter, Germer was surprisingly released from the camp and made his way to Belgium, from where he managed to keep an eye on what remained of the OTO in Germany and particularly on Thelema Verlag in Leipzig. He was arrested once again in Belgium and deported to France, spending another ten months in an internment camp, before finally emigrating to America in 1941, thus escaping certain extinction in the last years of the war.

So perhaps he had a Holy Guardian Angel, after all.

To Defy the Stars

Others were not so lucky. In the insanity that followed the flight of Rudolf Hess to England in May of 1941, regulations were drawn up to forbid the practice of astrology. As it was known that Hess had consulted frequently with astrologers, the casting of horoscopes suddenly became a matter of national security and it was considered best if all astrologers were thrown into the camps.

The role of astrology in the history of the Third Reich is fascinating in its own regard, and several books have been published that describe it in some detail.

One of the most fascinating of these—because told from a first person perspective—is that of Himmler's astrologer, Wilhelm Wulff, entitled *Zodiac and Swastika*.[27] In it, Wulff discusses the early days of post–World War I Germany and the gradual growth of the Nazi Party, leading up to the eventual ban of astrology by the government. This ban took place over a period of years, beginning with a formal law against the practice of astrology in the Greater Berlin area and gradually extending to the entire Reich. People who consulted astrologers could expect—it was believed—a visit by the Gestapo. Wulff himself wound up in Fuhlsbüttel concentration camp for four months of interrogation and hard labor in June, 1941 (one month after Hess's flight to England). His books, files, and card indexes were seized and later returned only after he met with the Reichsführer-SS, Himmler himself.

(An indication of how sophisticated the Gestapo had become on the occult is evidenced by the type of questions they asked Wulff, including whether or not he had ever cast mundane horoscopes. The term "mundane" horoscope refers to those cast not of individual persons, but of countries, political parties, and other groups of people.)

After the flight of Hess, of course, a scapegoat was necessary and the astrologers were the unlucky victims. Prior to May, 1941, however, the reason for the initial ban remains murky, even today. Certainly, many astrologers predicted a doomed future for Hitler and the Reich and this was bad propaganda that had to be stopped. Also, the practice of astrology implied access to a source of information that the Nazis could not control: the stars themselves. It was as if the old stories about God keeping a big book in which everyone's sins were recorded was literally true; a good astrologer could perhaps consult the stars and reveal the secret machinations of the Nazi leadership.

But another problem the Nazis had with astrology was perfectly consistent with their primary obsession: race. How could a horoscope not take into consideration the *race* of an individual, but only the time and place of birth? Was the horoscope of a Jew, therefore, the same as that of an Aryan? If so, this was a good (if somewhat bizarre) argument against the "inferior race" and "subhuman race" dogma of the Reich.

Also, astrology's origins were suspect.

The first Western astrologers might have been Semites, at least according to the state of archaeological knowledge at the time. In any event, astrology was seen to be inextricably linked with various Asian sources that seemed racially impure. Did the ancient Teutons practice astrology? Most probably these hunter-gatherer-warriors held only the most tenuous notion of the movements of the sun and moon. (This would later prove erroneous, as recourse to Professor de Santillana's *Hamlet's Mill* will verify.) But as far as dividing the ecliptic into twelve zodiacal signs and assigning values for signs, houses, angles, etc., this was considered just too non-Aryan for words. If nothing else, it was egalitarian—virtually democratic—and seemed to argue against the Cult of the Will that was so necessary to the self-image of the Reich.

Wulff's approach, however, gave the interested parties among the Nazi elite a way out. Wulff had studied Sanskrit in order to read the ancient astrological texts of India. The system of astrology he used was based on a rather different method of computing planetary positions and rulerships than is generally practiced in the West. This "Hindu" form is known as Sidereal astrology, and is based on the actual positions of the planets and luminaries as seen against the backdrop of the ecliptic rather than on the traditional positions used by the more common (in the West) Tropical astrology. Thus, Wulff's system was both more scientific (the *actual* positions of the planets) and "politically correct": it was based on an *Aryan* system of astrology as translated from that ultimate Aryan tongue, Sanskrit.

Wulff's arguments in favor of the practice of astrology within the Reich are interesting in themselves. Wulff claims the reason he wrote the book was to answer a description of him by historian Hugh Trevor-Roper in *The Last Days of Hitler,* in which he says that "Schellenberg found that in politics Wulff was sound."[28] (Schellenberg was Himmler's counterespionage chief, the head of *AMT* (section) VI of the SD.) Wulff, angered that he was being perceived as a good Nazi, answered by writing his version of the period (a version, by the way, in which Himmler's famed masseur, Felix Kersten, comes out looking like the perfect cad).

Wulff's response to Himmler's objection that astrology did not figure race into the equation is interesting. Himmler complained that any system which applied in equal measure to members of every race was ideologically opposed to Nazi racial doctrine. (This was actually the Party line; during the *Aktion Hess,* in which astrologers were arrested all over Germany, they were asked a specific question from a printed form concerning this very issue.) Wulff answered, "But in the astrological manuals of the Aryan Indians . . . constellations have been described which reflect the diversity of racial characteristics and which have found practical expression in the caste systems of ancient Indian cultural life."[29]

Excuse me?

Based on the above explanation alone, we can conclude that Wulff's politics were—if not sound, then—at least presented in such a way that no reasonable objection from one of the most despised racists in world history would have been possible. What Wulff described above and in his own words was essentially the blueprint for a Nazi astrology. What Wulff does not discuss in his autobiography is his membership in something called the "Swastika Circle" in Berlin circa 1920, a group which included Ernst Issberner-Haldane, the famous palmist. Wulff contributed to a magazine issued by the ardent New Templarist Herbert Reichstein (von Liebenfels's publisher) in company with such noted—and pro-Nazi—astrologers as Reinhold Ebertin.[30]

(We may also find reasons to object to the manner in which Wulff fought with Kersten. While Kersten seems, from Wulff's account, to have been an obnoxious and thoroughly objectionable human being who was interested in feathering his own nest more than in actually saving Jews—despite his seal of approval from the World Jewish Congress after the war—Wulff might have swallowed his disgust and worked with Kersten to save a few more prisoners from the gas chambers. Instead, Wulff saw through Kersten's program of self-promotion and self-enrichment at the expense of these same prisoners and decided to work instead "for the end of the war." This, from a man who attacked both Kersten and Himmler for living in a dreamworld and being too confident of their own capabilities!)

To be fair, Wulff was walking on thin ice. He had been released from a camp and could go easily once again into that dark night. His very life was at the mercy of the men he found himself working for. Whatever his personal ideology, Wulff eventually wound up calculating charts for the exclusive use of the Reichsführer-SS, Heinrich Himmler himself, right up to the very end of the war. He had a ringside seat at the Byzantine machinations of various SS leaders and their confidants (including Schellenberg and Kersten) to save themselves, save prisoners, and/or save as much of Germany as they could. Those

who don't believe that Himmler would be calling on Wulff the astrologer at every hour of the day and night—through bombing runs by
Allied planes, strafed convoys, the arrest of Göring, the negotiations
with Bernadotte and the World Jewish Congress, the onward Russian
advance—hysterical for advice on what to do on virtually every decision he had to make, have never known otherwise normal people in
desperate straits. The account is quite believable in most parts, and
bears a foreword to the English edition by Walter Lacqueur, not a
man known for his gullibility. Further, Schellenberg did give Wulff
the credit he was due and, in Trevor-Roper's account, verifies that
"Himmler seldom took any steps without first consulting his horoscope."[31] Wulff survived the war to befriend respected occult historian
Ellic Howe, and to write *Zodiac and Swastika,* his memoir of the war
years. We will come back to Wulff in Chapter Eight.

His colleagues, however, were not so lucky. Dr. Karl-Günther
Heimsoth was a well-known and popular astrologer in Berlin, and a
close friend and confidant of the old Nazi hand Gregor Strasser.
Heimsoth had written several letters to Ernst Röhm, while the latter
was in Bolivia training troops, dealing with issues such as astrology
and homosexuality;[32] these letters were used as evidence of the vile
nature of astrology (guilt by association) in a 1932 attempt to discredit
Röhm's SA. In a rehearsal for what would happen seven years later,
after the Hess flight, selected astrologers and "fortune-tellers" were
rounded up during the Röhm Purge using the official ban on the
practice of astrology in the Greater Berlin area as a pretext. Dr. Heimsoth—the gay astrologer—was one of those arrested, and executed that
year.

II

THE BLACK ORDER

I can most highly recommend the Gestapo to everyone.

—SIGMUND FREUD

SS **6** SS

The Dangerous Element: The Ahnenerbe and the Cult of the SS

The hierarchical organization and the initiation through symbolic rites, that is to say, without bothering the brain but by working on the imagination through magic and the symbols of a cult, all this is the dangerous element, and the element I have taken over.[1]

—ADOLF HITLER

While the Gestapo was busy mopping up cultic opposition to the Third Reich, from Freemasons to astrologers to Thelemites, Himmler was fully engaged in turning the SS into the *official* state cult, with all the "dangerous elements" that Hitler described in the above extract from his table talk concerning Freemasonry. In this chapter, we will not only review the history of this bizarre organization but we will also examine some documents of the Ahnenerbe: the Ancestral Heritage Research and Teaching Society which became incorporated entire into the SS. These documents have never before been published in the English language.

167

Background

The SS (initials that stand for *Schutzstaffel* or Guard Detachment) was originally intended to be Hitler's personal bodyguard. The early history of the Party was such that the SA, or Brownshirts, were really the first shock troops—"Storm Troopers"—of the Nazis: brutal enforcers and street gangs in uniform that intimidated the opposition and acted as a kind of private army for the Party (a type of Free Korps, such as that supported by the Thule; indeed the leader of the SA, Ernst Röhm, had been a Free Korps leader well known around Thule headquarters). As the SA grew in importance and size it became an actual threat to Hitler's complete control of the state apparatus. Elements within the Party wanted Röhm out of the way and presented Hitler with enough trumped-up evidence to warrant Röhm's arrest and speedy execution on June 30, 1934. On July 1 the entire SA was to go on a month's holiday to prove that they had no intention to overthrow the government; Hitler's advisers, however, counseled a preemptive first strike against the SA anyway. As we have seen, the bloodletting did not stop with Röhm but was extended to include a wide range of persons and organizations (both of the Left and the Right) deemed hostile to the totalitarian regime Hitler and his disciples had envisioned. It was not the first time, nor the last, that the existence of an alleged conspiracy was used as the excuse for wholesale slaughter.

Before this time, the SS functioned as a kind of elite corps of pure-blooded Aryan supermen. Himmler joined the SS when it was still a bodyguard unit with no more than about three hundred members and he marched with Hitler's men during the Beer Hall Putsch of 1923, carrying a flag. After he became the head of the SS in 1929, however, he began to reform it along lines that can only be described as cultic, while its membership rose from three hundred to fifty-two thousand by 1933. The very selection of the twin Sig rune as its emblem had its roots in the doctrines of List and Liebenfels. (German typewriters manufactured during the Nazi era included the twin Sig rune as one of their keys.) Even the graves of dead SS men were adorned—not with crosses or other more traditional tombstones—but with a German rune symbol (the "mensch" rune) made out of wood. This same rune was used on the cover of the articles of the *Lebensborn* society,[2] the "human stud farm" operation of the SS, thus making a curious statement about the life and death cycle as perceived by the official pagans of the Reich.

Once Röhm was out of the way, however, Himmler came to a position of even greater importance. Eventually even the Secret State Police—*Geheime Staatspolizei,* or Gestapo—came under his jurisdiction, making Himmler one of the most powerful men in Nazi Germany and second only to Hitler himself in authority and enjoying the fear which the black uniforms of his elite SS aroused in the populace.

While it is known that he consulted astrologers and was interested in various forms of alternative medicine, alternative science, and alternative religion, what is not generally known is the extent to which the Nazi government became committed to serious support of such practices. Nor is it generally understood just how thoroughly Himmler's eccentric ideas of race, ritual, and mysticism came to infuse the entire Nazi phenomenon, thus coalescing into one of the most dangerous cults in the world. Much of what has been written before on this subject is either unavailable in English or, worse, the stuff of such tabloid-style journalism that serious historians are forced to laugh it off as the result of wild imaginations and the woeful lack of "primary sources." We will attempt to rectify that situation as much as we can in the space allotted us, with constant reference to supporting documentation, beginning in this chapter with the strangest of all modern governmental agencies, the mysterious Ahnenerbe: The Ancestral Heritage Research and Teaching Organization.

A Personal Confrontation

As I was researching the Ahnenerbe in the files of the Captured German Documents Section of the National Archives, I heard the archivists discussing the current attitude of many Americans toward the Nazis. They were dismayed at the relative lack of sophistication among average Americans when it came to the Third Reich, lamenting the fact that most of us seem to get our information on world history from Hollywood.

"The point of view out there is that the Nazi Party was some kind of science fiction fantasy," grumbled one man. The others murmured assent.

I thought it was a remarkably perceptive statement coming from these overworked and highly intelligent custodians of one of the world's most important collections of twentieth-century knowledge, and the image stayed with me for a long time.

Science fiction. That is how many of us think of the war by now, filtered as it has been through the creative eyes of filmmakers and of the producers of popular television programs for a citizenry that gets most of its information from canned news shows and made-for-TV movies. It's almost as if the Holocaust were a sideshow, something not completely relevant to the tales of Darth Vader–like SS officers in their black uniforms, jackboots, and silver flashes. In fact, how much of the Holocaust ever appeared in such popular television programs as *Hogan's Heroes,* for instance, which certainly did not glorify Nazism but instead made it seem ridiculous? Certainly, the *Indiana Jones* trilogy goes a long way toward depicting the Nazis in that "fashion," a situation *Jones* producer Steven Spielberg has attempted to correct with his more recent *Schindler's List.*

Combing through the files, however, one comes away with a more complex emotional reaction. Of course, there is that perverse initial thrill when one comes across a swastika letterhead for the first time and realizes one is looking at the actual documents of the Third Reich. "My God," you say to yourself. "Here it is. I am looking at *history.*" You realize that you are suddenly a lot closer to the Third Reich than you ever were, and it is not an entirely comfortable feeling. It is as if the printed pages were the spoor of the Beast itself; as if, in reading the lines, you become aware that you are not entirely alone in the forest. H.P. Lovecraft, the brilliant if racist father of gothic horror, depicted the infamous *Necronomicon* in much the same way, hinting that merely to pronounce the barbarous words would be enough to summon unimaginable evil.

But then I spent many long hours of many long days in front of microfilm readers, poring over page after page of official SS documents, diaries, reports, and publications . . . and slowly realized that I was becoming numb with a mystifying sense of horror, a horror that was at least partly directed toward *myself.* For what I saw in those pages was the spoor of the *bureaucratic* Beast: thousands of pages of boring correspondence, red tape, thank-you notes, official forms, polite inquiries, expense reports. It was like the contents of the file cabinets of any large corporation; like the files of any of the large corporations I had worked for in my time. I *recognized* the kinds of people who kept those files; I recognized their concerns, their anxieties, their hopes, their fears. I began to *identify* with the authors and recipients of those letters, the keepers of those files, the meticulous fillers of those forms.

And then, almost surrealistically, among the thousands of pages that marched across the magnifying lens of the microfilm reader in blinding profusion, I would come across a single word, buried in a report, a letter, a requisition.

Dachau.

Auschwitz.

Konzentrationslager.

Concentration Camp.

And I would feel the breath go out of me. For I was looking at the records of people like me; people who were working for a large, bureaucratic organization; people who were thinkers, scholars, academics. Authors. People whose interests lay in the bizarre, the unusual, the philosophical, the psychological—the occult. People specializing in what occult historian James Webb calls "rejected knowledge."

The men of the Ahnenerbe-SS.

And as they filled out their forms, wrote their letters, and filed their reports, millions of human beings were being tortured and killed in horrible, unbelievable ways by their coworkers. What Hannah Arendt called "the banality of evil" never came home to me quite so strongly as during the days I sat before the microfilm screen as if it were a magic mirror into the past, and watched people like me make casual, passing references to the death camps.

Ancestor Worship

So, how to describe the Ahnenerbe?

Imagine that the evening adult education program of the New School for Social Research had suddenly become an independent government agency with a budget as big as the Defense Department, with Lyndon Larouche as president and, perhaps, Elizabeth Clare Prophet as the physics chairperson.

Or maybe the summer session at the University of California, Berkeley, had become militarized and all the students had immunity from prosecution for any crime they had committed, or would ever commit, and could conduct any form of independent study they liked as long as they wore their black uniforms with the silver death's head insignia at all times and swore an oath of personal loyalty to the dean.

Then one might have some idea of what the Ahnenerbe was, and of the type of people it first attracted to its ranks.

It was a humanities program. With guns.

Some traditionally trained historians might find levity a trifle out of place in a study of one of the most heinous "academic" and "research" institutions ever created in the twentieth century, but if anything combines both unimaginable horror and sadism with a pose of sophisticated scientific method as it was applied to some of the most ridiculous and unfounded "scientific" theories ever concocted, it was Himmler's dream agency, the Ahnenerbe-SS.

The roots of the Ahnenerbe are a tangled snarl of various special interests. Depending on the source consulted, it was either founded by Himmler and the Nazi "eternal pagan," ideologue Richard Walther Darré, in 1935,[3] or it had existed before that time as an independent institute and was only absorbed into the SS much later.[4]

Whatever source is considered the most reliable, one thing is certain: the Ahnenerbe was not founded as an SS unit. Something calling itself the Ahnenerbe Society ("an association for clan- and heraldry-research assistance, heredity science and race-cultivation") had existed as early as 1928.[5] But on the first of July, 1935, a "Deutsches Ahnenerbe Verein" was formally established in Berlin by Heinrich Himmler and Hermann Wirth, along with some associates of Darré.[6] According to documents available to the Nuremberg Tribunal, it was formally incorporated within the SS only on April 1, 1940, even though for years previously its leadership was largely composed of both honorary and career SS officers. Indeed, according to the available records it is obvious that Wolfram Sievers already held the position of *Reichsgeschäfts-führer,* or Reich's Manager, of the Ahnenerbe with a rank of Obersturmführer-SS by 1937[7] and had been associated with the Ahnenerbe as early as August of 1935.[8] So Sievers's insistence that it only became part of the SS in 1940 is disingenuous, to say the least.

In any event, the Ahnenerbe existed as an independent agency prior to its incorporation into the SS and may have had its earliest roots as a research bureau formed by a number of German intellectuals (and outright occultists, like the Atlantis buff Hermann Wirth) who had been inspired both by the works of the *völkisch* writers of previous years and by the exploits of a generation of romantic adventurers and amateur archaeologists and anthropologists, a generation that included Wolfram Sievers's defense witness Friederich Hielscher, and the internationally famous Swedish explorer Sven Hedin.

Hedin, a native of Stockholm, left Sweden in 1885 at the age of twenty on his first trip abroad, to Baku on the Caspian Sea. From that time on, Hedin managed to visit most of Asia from the Caucasus to the South China Sea, but with a special emphasis on Tibet. In 1925 (at the age of sixty) he published a memoir of his travels—*My Life as an Explorer*—which was very well received in Europe and America, as were other travel books he had written on Tibet and China. (As previously noted, at least one of these was in Hitler's small collection of books in his early, pre-Putsch Munich apartment.)[9] Hedin's tales of trekking through snow-choked Himalayan passes in search of fabled Asian cities while both camels and guides perished in grisly profusion along the route contributed to the general fascination the public had for anything to do with the mysterious East, a fascination due at least in part to the writings of Mme. Blavatsky and her followers in the Theosophical Society, who saw the East (and particularly India and Tibet) as the repository of arcane knowledge hidden from the rest of the world for centuries.

The Germans could not help but be charmed by Hedin's accounts of his adventures in Asia. In *My Life as an Explorer* he describes his discovery of the ancient Chinese city of Lou-lan in the Taklimakan Desert, and of the artifacts he uncovered there which included an ancient, swastika-decorated rug nearly two thousand years old along with some of the earliest examples in the world of writing on paper. What must have bothered at least some of his *völkisch* audience, however, was his statement that ". . . not a single one of our ancient Swedish runestones is older than the fragile wooden staffs and paper fragments that I found in Lou-lan."[10] Heresy!

(Hedin revisited Lou-lan in 1934, at the ripe age of sixty-nine. Now, in the years since the Chinese Revolution, the entire area has become a restricted military zone where atomic testing is carried out and Lou-lan is lost once more to the shifting desert sand.)

There is evidence to suggest that the Ahnenerbe itself was formed as a private institution by several friends and admirers of Sven Hedin, including Wolfram Sievers (who would later find justice at the Nuremberg Trials) and Dr. Friedrich Hielscher who, according to the records of the Nuremberg Trial of November 1946, had been responsible for recruiting Sievers into the Ahnenerbe.[11] In fact, there was a Sven Hedin Institute for Inner Asian Research in Munich that was part of the Ahnenerbe[12] and as late as 1942 Hedin himself (then about seventy-seven years old) was in friendly communication with such important Ahnenerbe personnel as Dr. Ernst Schäfer from his residence in Stockholm.[13] Moreover, on January 16, 1943, the Sven Hedin Institute for Inner Asian (i.e. Mongolian) Research and Expeditions was formally inaugurated in Munich with "great pomp," a ceremony at which Hedin was in attendance as he was awarded with an honorary doctorate for the occasion.[14]

It has even been claimed that Sven Hedin and Karl Haushofer were friends, a claim that is not completely unlikely as the two had spent considerable time in the Far East during the same period: Hedin as an explorer and sometime ambassador-at-large for the Swedish government, and Haushofer as military attaché for the Germans. Given Haushofer's excessive interest in political geography and his establishment of the *Deutsche Akademie* all over Asia (including China and India, Hedin's old stomping grounds), it would actually be odd if the two hadn't met. Later, as the Ahnenerbe was formally absorbed into the SS and made an official agency of the Reich, Hedin still maintained contact with all his old friends there even though, by 1942 and 1943, the Ahnenerbe was steeped in the blood of projects that would earn its director, Wolfram Sievers, the death sentence.

Indeed, by 1941 it was already clear that Haushofer's *Deutsche Akademie* and Sievers's Ahnenerbe were virtually parallel organizations. Letters and newspaper clippings from that period—including *Deutsche Akademie* correspondence seized after the war—show that Dr. Walther Wüst, who was the "Humanities" chairperson at the Ahnenerbe and, with Sievers, part of its ruling administration, was also acting president of the *Deutsche Akademie*.[15] As the Ahnenerbe was also at this time an agency of the SS, Professor Wüst—Rektor of the University of Munich and an expert on Sanskrit, the Aryan Ur-tongue—enjoyed the dubious distinction of the SS rank of *Oberführer,* or Brigadier. And both organizations had made their field trips to the one place on earth whose name has become an epithet . . . Dachau.[16]

The Middle Point of the World

Once Himmler was fully in control of the SS, he began its transformation into a pagan religious order. The headquarters for this cult was situated at the medieval castle of Wewelsburg, near the towns of Paderborn and Detmold in the German province of Westphalia, close by the site in the Teutoburg Forest where Arminius made his stand with its famous, Stonehenge-like stone monument known as Externsteine.

> Here the secret Chapter of the Order assembled once a year. Each member had his own armchair with an engraved silver nameplate, and each had to devote himself to a ritual of spiritual exercises aimed mainly at mental concentration.[17]

Contrary to the flashy show enjoyed by so many other Nazi leaders—such as the irrepressible Göring—Himmler kept his Order Castle extremely private. No one was allowed inside who was not expressly invited by Himmler himself; thus, only the Inner Twelve and occasionally a select general or two, a Reichsleiter, or some other official would be welcomed, but only at Himmler's convenience. Secrecy was the key element in the SS and most especially at Wewelsburg.

> The focal point of Wewelsburg, evidently owing much to the legend of King Arthur and the Knights of the Round Table, was a great dining hall with an oaken table to seat twelve picked from the senior Gruppenführers. The walls were to be adorned with their coats of arms; although a high proportion lacked these—as of course did Himmler himself—they were assisted in the drafting of designs by Professor Diebitsch and experts from Ahnenerbe.[18]

Underneath the dining hall with its Round Table in a sunken chamber was to be found the "realm of the dead": a circular room which contained a shallow stone well. In this well, the coat of arms of the deceased "Knight" of the Black Order was to be ceremoniously burned.[19]

Each of the Inner Circle of Twelve had his own room, decorated in accordance with one of the great ancestors of Aryan majesty. In Himmler's case, his room was designed to reflect his hero, King Henry the Fowler, a Saxon king responsible for the first German "Drive to the East." Although some writers have argued that Himmler saw himself as King Henry's reincarnation, there is also testimony that he admitted to speaking with the dead king's ghost at night. In any event, Himmler created the King Heinrich Memorial Institute in 1938 in Quedlinburg as yet another boondoggle, this one devoted to the revival of the king's spiritual legacy.

It was within the great dining hall with its Round Table that Himmler and his Inner Circle of Twelve Gruppenführers would engage in mystic communication with the realm of the dead Teutons and perform other spiritual exercises.[20]

During an investigation of the commander-in-chief of the (regular) German Army, General von Fritsch, for "serious moral offences" (a charge later found to be a mistake resulting from a similarity in name between the general and a cavalry officer), Foreign Intelligence Chief Walter Schellenberg observed Himmler and his "Round Table" involved in one of these "spiritual exercises":

> He assembled twelve of his most trusted SS leaders in a room next to the one in which von Fritsch was being questioned and ordered them all to concentrate their minds on exerting a suggestive influence over the General that would induce him to tell the truth. I happened to come into the room by accident, and to see these twelve SS leaders sitting in a circle, all sunk in deep and silent contemplation, was indeed a remarkable sight.[21]

SS men were discouraged from participating in Christian religious ceremonies of any kind and were actively encouraged to formally break with the Church. New religious ceremonies were developed to take the place of Christian ones; for instance, a winter solstice ceremony was designed to replace Christmas (starting in 1939 the word "Christmas" was forbidden to appear on any official SS document) and another ceremony for the summer solstice. Gifts were to be given at the summer solstice ceremony rather than at the winter solstice, and a special factory was established for the manufacture of appropriately Aryan *tschochkes*. (A possible, though by no means documented, cause for this switch of gift-giving to the summer solstice is the death of Hitler's mother on the winter solstice and all the grief and complex emotions this event represented for Hitler. It's understandable that Hitler—as the Führer and at least nominally in charge of the direction the new state religion would take—would have wanted to remove every vestige of "Christmas" from the pagan winter solstice festival. As a means of denying his grief? Or as an act of defiance against the god whose birth is celebrated on that day, a god who robbed Hitler of his beloved mother? It's worthwhile to note in this context that for a national "Day of the German Mother" Hitler chose his own mother's birthday.)

These ceremonies were replete with sacred fires, torchlit processions, and invocations of Teutonic deities, all performed by files of young, blond-haired, blue-eyed Aryan supermen, ceremonies that, according to my informants, had been revived in the Andean mountains (a site sacred to the Nazi Hörbigerians, of whom more later), at Colonia Dignidad in the 1960s and which were still being performed there as late as my trip in 1979.

(It is ironic that the establishment of Christmas on December 25 was itself an attempt of the Church to identify the birth of Jesus with the winter solstice ceremonies of the pagans since Christ was most probably not born in December at all; hence, all Himmler was doing was reinstating a holiday that the Christians themselves had usurped for their own purposes, as indeed the rune manuscript—quoted below—suggests. And so it goes.)

Weddings and "christenings" (especially at the *Lebensborn* communities) were replaced by pagan SS rituals,[22] and, gradually, the entire Christian liturgical rubric was in the process of being replaced by a completely pagan version. Even the Hitler Youth were not immune. A so-called "Nazi Primer" published during the war contains many examples of pagan ideology and anti-Christian sentiment designed for its youthful readership.[23]

Even the selection of Wewelsburg as the cult center was far from accidental. According to Teutonic legend, an apocalyptic battle would be fought in that area between the forces of East and West, and the Eastern hordes would be defeated by a mighty storm. Himmler—who highly valued such old German myths—evidently believed he would have a ringside seat at the conflagration that would consume his enemies.

Paderborn and Detmold were also important archaeological sites in the view of the Ahnenerbe, for they contained important relics of Germany's ancient glory. It was even bruited about that the Nordic World-Tree—Yggdrasil—had its roots in that region on the border of Westphalia and Lower Saxony and might still be located, perhaps at the Externsteine site.

A typescript copy of an article that appeared in a monthly called *Lower Saxony* in 1903/1904 was preserved in Ahnenerbe files. Devoted to this pagan cult center located in the same region as Wewelsburg, it refers to the summer solstice celebrations that took place there as late as the middle of the nineteenth century:[24]

[They are] like giants from a prehistoric world which, during the furious creation of the Earth, were placed there by God as eternal monuments . . . Many of our *Volk* are known to have preserved pagan beliefs and their rituals, and I remember that some sixty years ago, in my earliest childhood days . . . the custom was to undertake a long, continuous journey that lasted for whole days and which only ended on St. John's Day, to see those ancient "Holy Stones" and to celebrate there, with the sunrise, the Festival of the Summer Solstice . . .

Goethe says, "Nobody can overcome the impressions of his earliest childhood," and I have also, despite a long and costly journey, often since celebrated the summer solstice on those very stones.

The summer solstice festival, of course, was kept sacred by the Nazis and, as we have seen, was the occasion of the "human sacrifice" of Walther Rathenau. But to tie in this prehistoric monument to twentieth century Aryan mysticism, the author—one A.E. Müller—goes on to say:

Especially included for your consideration are the sculptures found on the reverse of the Externsteine on which were thus originally discovered the image of the tree Ydragsil [*sic*], the World-Ash, whose melancholy myth embraces the Origin, the Life, and the Death of the Earth and its generations.

Müller goes on to describe how images of a human couple seen within the form of the root of the World-Ash, Ydragsil (*sic*), and embraced by the Serpent, Nidhögur (the symbol of a devouring Death), were used by the Church to substantiate its own legend of the "Biblical-Babylonian legend of the first human couple, Adam and Eve, and their fall into sin as a result" of the Serpent. Müller complains that the essentially pagan iconography of the four Norns and associated images were co-opted by the Church into representing other Biblical stories and that the whole monument was exploited for the purposes of converting the pagan population of Lower Saxony to that Semitic interloper, Christianity.

Concerning the cultic significance of Paderborn itself, we may refer to a letter addressed to Wolfram Sievers by one Von Motz that is to be found in the Ahnenerbe files. Dated January 29, 1937—from Detmold no less—the author begins by referring to a recent issue of the official SS magazine, *Das Schwarze Korps*:

> I am sending to you now . . . six photographs with explanatory text. Maybe these can appear in one of the next issues of *Schwarze Korps* in order to show that it is to some extent a favored practice of the church on images of its saints and so forth to illustrate the defeat of adversaries by [having them] step on them.
>
> The referenced essay also mentioned that there are depictions of the serpent's head, as the symbol of original sin, being stepped on [by the saints].
>
> These depictions are quite uncommonly prevalent. It is always Mary who treads on original sin.
>
> Now these pictures appear to me particularly interesting because the serpent refers to an ancient symbol of Germanic belief. At the Battle of Hastings the flag of the Saxons shows a golden serpent on a blue field. . . .
>
> The Mary Statue at Paderborn was erected in the middle of the past century in the courtyard of the former Jesuit College. As professor Alois Fuchs related several times before in lectures concerning the Paderborn art monuments, the artist that created the Mary Statue must have been a Protestant. This is for me completely proven because the face in the moon-sickle in every case represents Luther.

It is well known that Rome and Judah, preferring thus to take advantage of their own victims, created victory monuments for them.[25]

These are motifs which we find throughout the *völkisch* and occult impulses in Nazism: that the serpent, which represents Satan to Christians, was considered a sacred symbol for the Aryans; and that "Rome and Judah" shamelessly exploited the suffering of their own people by depicting them as heroes or as vanquishers of evil through their agonies (thus reinforcing weak, non-Aryan suicidal tendencies among the oppressed populations of Europe).

In a related context, Himmler—in conversations with Schellenberg—also discussed such subjects as European witchcraft and the Holy Inquisition at length. Himmler evidently subscribed to the belief—made popular across the Channel by British anthropologist Margaret Murray in *The Witch Cult in Western Europe* (1921) and *The God of the Witches* (1933)—that the medieval witches burned at the stake by the Church were pagans; he particularly stressed the fact that "so much good German blood" was "stupidly destroyed" when thousands of German witches were murdered by the Inquisition.[26] If it seems odd to the reader that the man who ordered the destruction of millions of Jews and Gypsies would decry the mass murder of pagans by the Church, then he or she may be assured that they are in good company. Particularly as Himmler—like Lanz von Liebenfels before him—actively admired the organization, ritual, and mystique of the Church while denouncing its most cherished beliefs:

> The SS organization had been built up by Himmler on the principles of the Order of the Jesuits. The service statutes and spiritual exercises prescribed by Ignatius Loyola formed a pattern which Himmler assiduously tried to copy. Absolute obedience was the supreme rule; each and every order had to be accepted without question.[27]

One of the books recovered from the so-called Hitler Library at Berchtesgaden after the war comes under the heading of "pagan rituals," and deserves a brief mention here.

Of the some two thousand volumes that were recovered (and which are now stored in the Rare Book Room of the Library of Congress in Washington, D.C.) many were of the occult sciences. One in particular concerns us at the moment, and that is *Das Buch der Psalmen Deutsch: das Gebetbuch der Ariosophen Rassen-mystiker und Antisemiten.* This can be translated as *The Book of German Psalms: The Prayerbook of the Ariosophist Race-Mystics and Anti-Semites.* It was written by none other than our old friend, Lanz von Liebenfels, he of the Order of New Templars, and is nothing less than a hymnal of hate, a "prayer-book" that proudly calls itself "anti-Semite."

To give the reader an idea of what, typically, the Ahnenerbe thought valuable and worth salvaging in the spiritual legacy of the world, one only has to glance down the list of works cited in *Tod und Unsterblich-keit im Weltbild Indogermanischer Denker* (*Death and Immortality in the Indo-Germanic Thinker's Worldview*) coauthored by R. Schrötter and Ahnenerbe Kurator Walther Wüst and published in Berlin in 1938, bearing a foreword by Himmler.

This official Deutsches Ahnenerbe publication contains appropriate quotations from the Vedas, the Upanishads, and the Bhagavad-Gita but doesn't stop there. It goes on to include everyone from Homer, Socrates, Plato, Cicero, Seneca, Marcus Aurelius, and Empedocles to the Eddas, Meister Eckhardt (the darling of the Pan-German mystics), Jacob Böhme, one of Dietrich Eckart's favorite philosophers Angelus Silesius and Giordano Bruno (who was burned at the stake by the Inquisition for his heretical—mystical—views). The collection also contains selections from Omar Khayyám and that other Persian philosopher-poet Rumi. This amounts to nothing less than a Nazi "canon" of important and accepted texts, appropriate for meditational reflection by prospective SS recruits and the general public alike. Of course, neither the Old nor the New Testament appears in the above collection.

* * *

It was not enough for the Nazis to assume a pagan stance; they had to prove that it was historically justified. Himmler wanted nothing so much as to be able to prove to the world that his personal idiosyncrasies were the stuff of reality. In order to do this, he enlisted the help of an organization that, by its very name, was devoted to restoring the ancient knowledge of the Aryan forefathers to contemporary awe: the *Ahnenerbe Forschungs-und Lehrgemeinschaft:* the Ancestral Heritage Research and Teaching Society.

Himmler gave the Ahnenerbe official status within the Reich in 1935 (thus protecting it and its members from the spate of new laws that were designed to ban occult-related activity); in 1940 it became a formal division of the SS. With over fifty separate sections devoted to a wide range of scientific and pseudoscientific research, the Ahnenerbe became a boondoggle for Nazi scholars of every description. There was a Celtic Studies group within the Ahnenerbe; a group to study the Teutonic cult center Externsteine (near Wewelsberg), which as we have seen was believed to be the site of the famous World-Tree, Ydragsil or Yggdrasil; a group devoted to Icelandic research (as the Eddas were sacred to the Teuton myth, and since Iceland was considered to be the location of Thule itself); a group that was formed around Ernst Schäfer and his Tibet expeditions; a runic studies group; a "World Ice Theory" division; an archaeological research group that scoured the earth for evidence of Aryan presence in lands as remote from Germany as the Far East and South America (an idea possibly inspired by the writings of Blavatsky and by contemporary research "proving" that the Aryan Norsemen had discovered America hundreds of years before Columbus); the list goes on and on.[28]

In fact, it was just such a servant of the Ahnenerbe, SS-Obersturm-führer Otto Rahn, who credited the belief of some Nazis that even Latin America held promise as a land of the Aryans, a view sacred to contemporary Chilean author Miguel Serrano. In Rahn's book *Lucifer's Servants* he describes a Mexican legend concerning the mystical Thule:

In the wake of Columbus . . . the sails of Ferdinand Cortez crossed the seas. It was he who conquered the kingdom of the Aztecs and Mexico for the benefit of Spain. In an account that he sent to the imperial court one reads that the king of the Aztecs had bowed to the Emperor because he held [the Emperor] to be the same Lord of luminous beings and superior essence "from which had issued his own ancestors." Montezuma had also been about to permit Cortez to appropriate all the idols . . . that is until he, the king—imprisoned by the gold-hungry conquerors and mortally wounded by them—understood who they really were. He refused to allow them to treat his wounds and, energetically resisting the idea of converting to Christianity, wished for nothing more than death. And he did die, the victim of a frightful mistake. Cortez was the envoy of the Pope and the Catholic emperor and not at all of the

"White God" for whom [the king] and his people had been waiting so long. This White God was to have come from the ancient land of Tulla or Tullan (which, according to their beliefs, had once been "a country of the sun" but "where now ice reigned" and where "the sun had disappeared")—that is to say: from *Thule.* Rather than the servants of Lucifer, those whom they had greeted . . . were the representatives of that "ilk" which, shamelessly, dishonors the face of our mother the Earth with its filth and its horrors.[29]

That "ilk," of course, is the Catholic Church.

Ironically, it would be Rahn's organization that would most permanently be identified with dishonoring the face of the Earth with filth and horror; for it should be remembered that this was the same organization that commissioned the infamous medical experimentation taking place at Dachau and other camps; an agenda fully consistent with the Ahnenerbe's program of "scientific" research.

There has been no complete and comprehensive study of the Ahnenerbe in English so far, and we will not attempt to do so here. However, let us examine several of the separate sections of this eerie operation by studying the documents that were saved from destruction after the war. By doing so, we will find that the Ahnenerbe is really the best evidence we have that the SS was a fully constituted cult. If the SS was Himmler's pagan answer to the Jesuits—as has been suggested many times, and by the Nazis themselves—then the Ahnenerbe was a kind of seminary and teaching college for the future leaders of the Thousand Year Reich.

The Rune Scholars

Among the documents that comprise the Ahnenerbe collection at the National Archives is an undated manuscript that was evidently intended to accompany Himmler's most famous "Christmas" gift: the red clay candlestick that was to be burned on the night of the winter solstice by all faithful SS leaders.

There is no space here to quote the document completely, and indeed it was meant to accompany some ninety-three illustrations which have not survived with the document. However, parts of this interesting work are worthy of translation here as they represent nothing less than a complete introduction to the subject of runes, from the point of view of a Nazi scholar working for the Ahnenerbe-SS.

The document begins:

> The Reichsführer-SS has sent to all SS Leaders the beautiful Swedish peasant candlestick, fired in red clay, that stands here before us as a symbolical Christmas—or Yule—offering. It is a replica of a piece that is located in the collection of the Deutsche Ahnenerbe in Berlin which, on the other hand, is itself a replica of the original that was stored in the Staten Historik Museum in Stockholm and which came from Hallands Province.
>
> Such peasant candlesticks in fired clay in the shape of a tower we find not only in Sweden, in Scandinavia and in North Germania [sic] but likewise in South Germania here in Germany, for instance in West-phalia.

It is worthwhile to point out that the use of the word "Germania" refers to the ancient Teutonic kingdom and not to Germany proper, which is referred to as *Deutschland* in the original.

The anonymous author then goes on for thirty-five, single-spaced pages to describe not only the candlestick itself but the whole history of the runes, and does not resist taking a few potshots at Christianity in the process. Some of this will be incomprehensible to those not well versed in runic symbols, but a few paragraphs will give one a taste of the type of scholarship-cum-ideology that is the hallmark of Ahnen-erbe publications:

> Both the Germanic God-Runes and God-Names—*hagal* and *man, mensch*—become, at the Christianizing of the Rune Calendar, *Christus,* translated as the God-Son, which in the Germanic meaning is repre-sented as *hagal* for "the creators of the most ancient world," i.e., of Time and Space. This old German deity, *Tuisco* ("from God" or "from heaven descended") as well as *Tuisto* ("the Twofold Name") as the Roman Tacitus in the First Century relates in his book about Germania, comes from a word meaning "Earth Born."

The *hagal* rune had a life of its own, of course. It became the title of a runic magazine published by Rudolf John Gorsleben, a friend of

Dietrich Eckart and onetime lecturer at Thule Society headquarters in Munich and later managed by Werner von Bülow after Gorsleben's death in 1930. (Gorsleben had served during the First World War with a Turkish regiment in Arabia, and thus was probably on the receiving end of the Arab forces under that brilliant military strategist, T.E. Lawrence.) The *hagal* rune—which is really an asterisk—accumulated a wealth of mystical and magical associations under Gorsleben's "scholarship." It became the mother of all runes, as each of the individual runes could be discovered hidden within it. To Gorsleben, the *hagal* rune signified nothing less than a mystical diagram for attaining unity with God.[30] It is also owing to Gorsleben that we first encounter an occult tradition concerning crystals, something that is enjoying a rebirth among the New Agers of today.

Later, concerning a different rune we read:

> And a thousand years afterwards we discover this "Son of the All-Father and the Earth": *Thor* or *Donar* . . . He, the Born-Again, who overcomes the wintry power of darkness and death, rousing all life from the tombs once more, is represented as a figure with upraised arms. His rune therefore is the symbolic sign of the upraised arms, two- or three-pointed; the former, the two-pointed Ψ Υ Υ the rune *k*, Anglo-Saxon name *cen* or "Light", and the latter the Ψ Ψ three-pointed *m* rune, called "Man" (Old Nordic *madhr*, Anglo-Saxon *man*), and an Old Nordic peasant rune-song says of this rune that it "gladdens man and makes the earth increase."

The "All-Father" is, of course, a Teutonic pagan term for God. It may be remembered that Sebottendorff's secret Order was called the *Germanenorden* All-Father And The Holy Grail, and that Sebottendorff's Order publication was (under the influence of Gorsleben and other Aryan cultists) entitled *Runes*. Further along, we find a slanting attack on the Church:

> This is the legacy of the Celtic Old Ones, of the most supreme Heaven-Father and Earth-Mother, which depict the Year-Wheel and the Soul; the Aryan, Germanic ancestral legacy, the former Christmas when the Yule Candlestick—reaching to the Year-Wheel God—stands silent next to the Soul of the Earth Mother which, revolving, spins upward.

Now, in conclusion, it remains only to clarify a final symbol. Whence comes this "Soul" that belongs to the Earth-Mother which, according to the ancient Aryan myth becomes the Heaven-Son, the "Joy of Man"? What is the origin of those "Red Hearts" which later become prominent on images of the Virgin Mary, the Mother of the Son of God Jesus Christ whose festival the Roman Church only decided in the Fourth Century AD to celebrate on December 25th, the ancient Aryan Winter Solstice festival? . . . We must turn our gaze back to that Ur-time when our Nordic, peasant ancestors of the New Stone Age erected those mighty clan dolmens three to four millennia before Christ: the "Giants' Beds" of which only a few in north Germany have survived the irreverent vandalism and brutal profiteering of the past two centuries.

Much of the foregoing would find a respectable home in any New Age or pagan publication today. Much of it is familiar to students of mythology and the occult. But as we wind up the Odinist ferverino, we once again come crashing into a reminder of just who is writing this thesis, and why:

Long ago our ancestor, that noble Nordic wife and mother, guardian of her family and of the meaning of the Homeland, was sacred; she to whom one could go—Seeress and Race-Mother—in order to know what was fit and proper. "We bow in reverence before the image of the German mother," said our Reichsführer Heinrich Himmler on the last Reich's Peasantry Day in Goslar. And so a German doctor once recognized the most-sacred image of our ancestral legacy, Earth Mother and Race-Mother, the miracle of the love of the Nordic Mother-Soul: that the sacred and eternal Homeland is renewed from her womb, embracing life, as she preserves and protects unsullied the most sacred spiritual and mental values of Family and Race.

. . .

And Frigga, Isis, Mary are merely names,
Transient veils of the hallowed womb.

The stars, suns and men's souls . . .
No mortal lips can praise your Majesty enough.
O incline, Mother, your divine countenance
And guide us to our sweet home in the Eternal Light.
We but wish to stand in faithful watch on the soul
of the Homeland, on the Living Tree of our Race,
and by its Führer.[31]

One can see how these "lapsed Catholics" still needed their dose of saccharin-sweet sentiments and sloppy poetry to get them through the night. The difference was the projection of the Catholic Church—poisoned by the Jewish Satan, Jehovah, and corrupted from a pure, Aryan version of an ancient deity, Krist—as one aspect of the enemy against which they were finally rebelling. One could offer some armchair psychology on this point, that the repressive sexual, social, and moral environment of Roman Catholicism contributed to this tremendous backlash against anything Christian; that it was necessary to deny the basic tenets of Christianity in order to wreak unspeakable havoc on the Jews; and that there were enough Catholic priests and bishops around to accommodate the Nazis—sometimes eagerly—that the SS must have felt they were on the right track, anyway. But if Rome was not the spiritual homeland of the Race, where were the occult secrets really being kept?

The Iceland Project

As we have seen, the Nazis viewed Iceland as the last surviving link to their ancestral homeland, Thule. This was an inheritance from their Ascended Master, Sebottendorff, who understood Ultima Thula, the famous destination of Pytheas in the fourth century BC, to be identical to Iceland. For them, Thule corresponded to their own Atlantis myth; while the rest of the human race might have descended from monkeys, the Nazis were convinced that the Aryan race descended from heaven. (Hence that discussion of the *Mensch* and *Hagal* runes as symbolic of a "descent from heaven" of the *real* "Menschen," the Aryan Man.) They believed that the Icelandic *Eddas* contained secret keys to their own history, and that possibly more clues still existed on that tiny republic in the form of dolmens, ancient caves, and prehistoric monuments, etc.

To galvanize support for a pan-Nordic union against the subhumans, they arranged for the formation of something called the Nordic Gesellschaft, or Nordic Society: an organization headquartered in Lübeck that was a pet project of mystic race theorist Alfred Rosenberg, by now a Reichsleiter and member of Hitler's innermost circle. Year

after year Rosenberg would address this society composed of members
from Finland, Sweden, Norway, Denmark, and, of course, Iceland to
warn them of the immediate danger to the "white race" coming from
the East, and of the essential unity of the Nordic peoples—based on
race and mystic ancestry—demanded by the combined Soviet, Jewish,
and Masonic threat.

To get an idea of who attended such meetings and of what was
discussed, we only have to read an article in the official Nazi newspaper, *Völkischer Beobachter,* concerning one such event, attended by
both Rosenberg and Soil-Mystic Darré (a cofounder of the Ahnenerbe):

> The conclusion of the 5th Reichs-Convention of the Nordic Society in
> Lübeck gained special importance from a grand speech by Reichsleiter
> Alfred Rosenberg . . .
> . . . the first speaker, National Librarian Dr. Gudmundur Finbogason
> of Rekjavik, presented a lecture about Icelandic-German cooperation in
> the field of Nordic Science.
> Subsequently State Council Johann E. Mellye, the president of the
> Norwegian Peasantry Association, spoke concerning the Norwegian
> Peasant Movement. Protocol Secretary Carl Patric Ossbahr, Stockholm,
> then spoke concerning Sweden's North-European mission . . .
> Reichsleiter Alfred Rosenberg heartily greeted the German and
> Northern country participants and then began to speak . . .
> The Reichsleiter reminded us . . . of the grave military and revolu-
> tionary events taking place in the Far East, the Near East, and in Spain.
> If the Scandinavian north and the Baltic states have been spared to some
> extent from political earthquake tremors, such signifies no more than a
> temporary reassuring moment for these people and for Europe alto-
> gether, and is not to be understood as a sign that these people and these
> nations themselves are able to escape the larger problems forever. The
> struggle between Tradition in its various forms and another Breed com-
> ing forth for a New Era shall become everyone's destiny.
> "Germany stands since 1933," so the Reichsleiter drove home, "be-
> fore the question: whether historical survival has come to an end or if
> the gravity of these events directly constitutes the makings for a renais-
> sance.
> "After a great struggle within the soul of the German people the
> entire nation finally agrees about the personality of the Führer . . . In
> only a few years Adolf Hitler's Germany has reaped the harvest of an
> entire millennium.

"This historical fact is big enough to demand attention. It must naturally extend widely beyond political limits because German problems, the first of which are the immediate social-political ones, are also the problems of the remaining peoples. The evolution of the other nations might go more gradually since they are not under an immediate force of destiny; still these problems are also theirs.

"We all stand under the same European destiny, and must feel obliged to this common destiny, because finally the existence of the white man depends altogether upon the unity of the European continent! Unanimous must we oppose that terrible attempt by Moscow to destroy the world, that sea of blood into which already many people have dived!" (Strongest applause!)[32]

The Nordic Gesellschaft even made the ailing Dr. Alfred Ploetz—founder of the Institute for Race Hygiene and the Nazis' most prestigious (if rather reluctant) race theorist—an honorary member about a year before he died.[33] Thus were the worlds of "scientific racism" or Social Darwinist eugenics and mystical Nordic paganism and anthropology linked, and to them both the political agenda of the Third Reich, which involved not only *Lebensraum* and a "drive to the East" but also the extermination of the indigenous populations of the Eastern countries. That Rosenberg and Darré would both attend these meetings is significant, for these men were the premiere pagans in Hitler's inner circle. Where Himmler wished to surround himself with the trappings of a twentieth-century secret society based partly on the Jesuits, partly on the Masons, and partly on the Templars, Rosenberg and Darré eschewed secret societies and occult lodges for a more general, more popular state-organized pagan religion designed to replace Christianity forever. While Himmler shared these ideas to a large extent, he was not likely to be seen stumping town to town for state paganism. He wanted to conduct his rituals in secret, far from the prying eyes of the profane.

Thus, while Rosenberg and Darré were doing their best to create the illusion of a pan-Nordic community, Himmler was authorizing missions to Iceland—under Ahnenerbe auspices—to search for pagan relics.

Thus we read—in a document addressed to the Ahnenerbe from Dr. Bruno Schweizer at Detmold, dated March 10, 1938—of a proposed research trip to Iceland that summer:

Plan for an Iceland Research Journey

From year to year it becomes more difficult to meet living witnesses of Germanic cultural feelings and Germanic soul attitudes on the classical Icelandic soil uninfluenced by the overpowerful grasp of western civilization. In only a few years has the natural look of the country, which since the Ur-time has remained mostly untouched in stone and meadow, in desert and untamed mountain torrents, revealed its open countenance to man and has fundamentally changed from mountainsides and rock slabs to manicured lawns, nurseries and pasture grounds, almost as far from Reykjavik as the barren coast section, a feat accomplished by the hand of man; the city itself expands with almost American speed as roadways and bridges, power stations and factories emerge and the density of the traffic in Reykjavik corresponds with that of a European city.

. . . the people forget such ancient techniques as . . . the forge- and woodworker's art, the methods of grass- and milk-cultivation, spinning, weaving, dyeing; they forget the old legends and myths that were once narrated on long winter evenings, the songs and the art of the old verses; they lost the belief in a transcendent nature . . . Their innate Germanic sobriety becomes cold calculation; pure material interests then step to the foreground; the intelligentsia migrates to the capital and from there swiftly assimilates international tendencies. Genuine Germanic vigor in Iceland is also often transformed into speculation and not at all through real trade; excessive pride of homeland drives them to want to be 150% more modern and progressive than the rest of Europe. This then often permits the present-day Icelander to appear in an unfavorable light and thus can not usually avoid giving a good German visitor a bad first impression.

These situations determine our research plan.

Every year that we wait quietly means damage to a number of objects, and other objects become ruined for camera and film due to newfangled public buildings in the modern style. For the work in question only the summer is appropriate, that is, the months of June through August. Furthermore, one must reckon that occasionally several rainy days can occur, delaying thereby certain photographic work. The ship connections are such that it is perhaps only possible to go to and from the Continent once a week.

All this means a minimum period of from 5–6 weeks for the framework of the trip.

The possible tasks of an Iceland research trip with a cultural knowledge mission are greatly variegated. Therefore it remains for us to select

only the most immediate and most realizable. A variety of other tasks
. . . should be considered as additional assignments.

Thus the recording of human images (race-measurements) and the investigation of museum treasures are considered to be additional assignments.[34]
(My italics, P.L.)

The following year, Dr. Schweizer proposed the creation of an Icelandic-German dictionary to help those future Nazi "researchers" in their endeavors, and was joined in this concept by other men of science. It is not known just to what extent the Icelandic people welcomed this quiet invasion of German scholars bent on performing "race measurements" on their citizens, or photographing valuable museum pieces for possible later, ah, "acquisition." Surely, the SS would have considered anything Aryan in the Icelandic museums as fair game for export, objects for further study and for research into their Aryan forebears.

But Iceland—Ultima Thule—was not the only piece of real estate to which the Nazis associated a peculiar Aryan heritage. One of the most important was that sad and bleeding country that has not stopped hemorrhaging since the early days of the Second World War and whose destiny has become such a matter of international publicity and concern. We are speaking, of course, of Tibet.

The Tibet Expedition

At dinner [Himmler] talked to me on various scientific questions and told me about an expedition to Tibet.[35]

—SCHELLENBERG

One of the more controversial stories circulating about the occult activities and interests of the Third Reich concerns Tibet. Much is made of the Nazi-Tibet connection in Pauwels and Bergier's *Morning of the Magicians* (*Le matin des magiciens*), a sixties international bestseller whose sometimes outrageous claims of magical forces and sinister conspiracies overshadowed a more serious message that discovers in the occult underworld of the Third Reich the seeds of a spiritual crisis about to be born.

It was therefore with some skepticism that the author approached the vast microfilmed records of the Captured German Documents Section of the National Archives to see whether or not there was evidence for such a mysterious "connection," and was rewarded by the discovery that several complete rolls of microfilm—representing hundreds of pages of documents—record nothing but the efforts and adventures of the SS-Tibet Expedition led by that tireless promoter of Tibetology in all its forms, Dr. Ernst Schäfer of the Ahnenerbe.[36]

What is even more striking is that the records contain not only Schäfer's personal and official correspondence, his Tibet notebooks, and his personal SS file, but also clippings from German newspapers chronicling the "SS-Tibet Expedition" in all its glory.[37]

What is compelling in these records is the day-to-day story of Schäfer's struggle to get his various expeditions off the ground: searching for the funding, permissions, and support from the Nazi government that were not always forthcoming. It would seem that Schäfer's primary goal in trekking through the Himalayas was more scientific in nature—and hence of less immediate value—than the Reich leadership was willing to accommodate. After all, much of Schäfer's reporting has less to do with concerns of a military value than it does with the flora and fauna of this inaccessible land. Schäfer's academic credentials were in zoology and botany, with some courses in geology, geography, and ethnology. He seems to have been marching in Sven Hedin's footsteps and was indeed for a time the head of the Sven Hedin Institute, the organization based in Munich that also became a "Reichs Institute" and eventually a separate section of the Ahnenerbe-SS.[38] As mentioned earlier, the files also contain correspondence from Hedin to Schäfer as late as July 27, 1942, in which Hedin signs himself as *Ihr treu und aufrichtig ergebener* ("Your faithful and sincerely devoted . . .")[39] after forwarding greetings from his sister, to Schäfer's wife, and to the Kurator of the Ahnenerbe, Dr. Wüst. Schäfer's SS personnel file shows one trip to East and Central Tibet from 1934–1936 and another to Tibet (the official SS-Tibet Expedition referred to in the press) from April 1938 to August 1939 . . . in other words, during the period of the so-called "phony war" that predated the invasion of Poland in September of 1939.[40] Thus, we cannot rule out the hypothesis that Schäfer was involved in something more than butterfly gathering in this historic (and official) trek to the Himalayas at a time of great international crisis and global tensions. To be sure, Schäfer was not back in Germany two months before preparations were being made to organize a Tibetan–North Indian strike force to oust the British from their rule in India.[41]

Ernst Schäfer was born in Cologne (Köln) on March 14, 1910, the son of an important industrialist and director of the Phoenix Rubber Company, and attended school in Heidelberg and Göttingen before becoming part of a Tibet expedition organized by the Academy of Natural Sciences in Philadelphia in 1930, when Schäfer was only twenty years old. He then became a member of the American Brooke Dolan expedition to Siberia, China, and Tibet in 1931.[42]

In 1933, Hitler became chancellor of Germany and it appears as if Schäfer was one of the "March violets" who got on the Nazi bandwagon after Hitler consolidated his political power that spring. His membership number in the Nazi Party was 4690995, and his personnel record shows membership in the SS as beginning in the summer of 1933, rising in rank to Untersturmführer in 1936, Obersturmführer in 1937, Hauptsturmführer in 1938 and finally to Sturmbannführer in 1942. He had also been awarded the coveted *Totenkopfring*, or Death's Head Ring, which was the rune-inscribed piece of SS jewelry designed by *völkisch* occultist Karl Wiligut (described in the following chapter on Otto Rahn), and was a member of Himmler's Personal Staff (as was Wiligut). All of this is mentioned to demonstrate that Dr. Schäfer was nothing if not the ideal SS man, at least on paper. The orders raising him in rank were signed by Himmler, and his fiancée had to undergo the usual investigation of her racial background as the prospective spouse of an SS officer. (They were married—evidently with the blessing of the Reichsführer-SS—in December of 1939, and were busy dutifully producing Aryan offspring; three daughters by 1944.)

But as an academic, Schäfer's published works include—according to his SS dossier—*Berge, Buddhas und Bären* (*Mountains, Buddhas and Bears* oh my!), *Unbekanntes Tibet* (*Unknown Tibet*), and *Dach der Erde* (*Roof of the World*). Among his articles can be found this typical one in English: "Four New Birds from Tibet" in the 1937 *Proceedings of the Academy of Natural Sciences, Philadelphia*. So, Ernst Schäfer was also a scientist who published regularly in respected journals on his discoveries, and an explorer who emulated the master, Sven Hedin, by writing books about his travels in the mysterious East.

Thus, we have established that Dr. Schäfer was a man of many parts: one part SS officer and one part scholar, one part explorer and one part scientist: a Nazi Indiana Jones.

Schäfer was a career scientist who does not seem to have been interested only in the possible military potential of his travels in Tibet but kept meticulous notes on the religious and cultural practices of the Tibetans, from their various colorful lamaistic festivals to Tibetan attitudes toward marriage, rape, menstruation, childbirth, homosexuality (and even masturbation). For instance, in his account of Tibetan homosexuality he goes so far as to describe the various positions taken by older lamas with younger boys and then proceeds to inform his audience how homosexuality played a significant role in the higher politics of Tibet.[43]

One wonders how Schäfer was privy to such intimate detail of Tibetan sexual practices, and then comes across a report by SS-Obersturmführer and filmmaker Ernst Krause (who was part of the SS-Tibet Expedition of 1938–39) dutifully recording his personal observation of a fifteen-year-old Lachung girl masturbating on a bridge beam.[44] (It is not known whether Krause took advantage of this opportunity to film this particular episode, but the author was startled to discover that a collection of his film clips—silent, black and white—*have* survived and may be viewed at Tibet House in New York City in VHS cassette format; certainly this is one of the most intriguing video documents of the Third Reich.)

There are pages of such careful observation of the local people engaged in a variety of intimate acts that would otherwise have been performed privately had it not been for the ever-present and watchful eyes of the Master Race.

Happily, not all of Schäfer's observations were of the sexual habits of the Lachung and other Himalayan peoples, nor of the flora and fauna, as the following article from the Nazi *Völkischer Beobachter* of July 29, 1939, relates:

Dr. Ernst Schäfer, SS-Hauptsturmführer, has now completed the first German SS-Tibet Expedition with extraordinarily great success and will soon return to Germany with his guides. The participants of the expedition visited, as the first Germans, the capital of Tibet, Lhasa, the seat of the Dalai Lama, as well as Tibet's second-largest city, Shigatse, the capital of the Panchen Lama, and visited the huge monastery of Taschtimmps first visited in 1907 by Sven Hedin. By comparison, Sven Hedin's Trans-Himalaya's discoveries required several trips to accomplish. The harvest of the expedition regarding botanical and zoological collections is uncommonly rich and rare and of great value.[45]

And an article from *Der Neue Tag* dated July 21, 1939, is even more informative:[46]

Sacred Tibetan Scripture Acquired by the Dr. Schäfer-Expedition on Nine Animal Loads Across the High-Country

(SPECIAL) FRANKFURT—20 JULY   The Tibet Expedition of Dr. Ernst Schäfer, which during its expedition through Tibet stayed a long time in Lhasa and in the capital of the Panchen Lama, Shigatse, is presently on its return trip to Germany. Since the monsoons began unusually early, the return march of the expedition was hastened in order to secure the shipment of the precious collections. The expedition has singularly valuable scientific research results to inventory. In addition to outstanding accomplishments in the areas of geophysical and earth-magnetic research they succeeded in obtaining an extra rich ethnological collection including, along with cult objects, many articles and tools of daily life.

With the help of the regent of Lhasa it was Dr. Schäfer who also succeeded in obtaining the *Kangschur,* the extensive, 108-volume sacred script of the Tibetans, which required nine animal loads to transport. Also especially extensive are the zoological and botanical collections that the expedition has already shipped, in part, to Germany the remainder of which they will bring themselves. The zoological collection includes the total bird-fauna of the research area. Dr. Schäfer was also able, for the first time, to bag a Schapi, a hitherto unknown wild goat. About 50 live animals are on the way to Germany, while numerous other live animals are still with the expedition. An extensive herbarium of all existing plants is also on its way. Furthermore, valuable geographical and earth-historical accomplishments were made. Difficulties encountered due to political tensions with the English authorities were eliminated due to personal contact between Dr. Schäfer and members of the British authorities in Shangtse, so that the unimpeded return of the expedition out of Tibet with its valuable collections was guaranteed.

No further mention is made of the sacred scriptures, the *Kangschur*, which is the core document of Tibetan Buddhism, and I have been unable to discover what happened to it after the war, though (for reasons too complex to discuss here) I suspect it wound up in a museum in Vienna. (It is worthwhile noting that nowhere in the above-mentioned article does the term "SS" appear, or "Nazi." *Der Neue Tag* was a newspaper published in Prague, and the article was printed only two months before Blitzkrieg began. In an identical article published the following day in the *Hannoversches Tageblatt*—a German newspaper—the missing "SS" in "SS-Tibet Expedition" is faithfully restored.)

Sadly, a search of other articles from the same period do not reveal the disposition of the 108 volumes of sacred scripture.

An interesting aside to this story of the official SS expedition to Tibet is revealed by a list of the expedition members. They include one Dr. Bruno Beger, an anthropologist. Later, Dr. Beger would become better known as one of the scientists who—working for Professor Hirt of the Ahnenerbe—was involved in the collection of 115 human skeletons at Auschwitz for inclusion in a Nazi Anthropological Museum.[47] Assisted by one Dr. Fleischhacker, Beger selected the skeletons while their owners were still alive as Jewish, Polish, and Asiatic prisoners of the death camps. The "specimens" were then murdered at Natzweiler concentration camp in such a way as to avoid damaging the skeletal material and their bodies were shipped out for scientifically managed decomposition.

Beger's "mentor" according to interviews with other Nazi scientists was the same Dr. Ernst Schäfer,[48] and Beger even provided Schäfer with a collection of Asian skulls while he was collecting over a hundred "Jewish Commissar" skulls for the Berlin Institute. Another colleague of both Beger and Schäfer was the botanist, Dr. Vollmar Vareschi, whom we find at the Sven Hedin Institute in Munich when he isn't attending lectures with his friends on various pseudoscientific topics.[49]

Dr. Hirt himself was also involved in the notorious study of the effects of mustard gas on yet another 150 prisoners at Natzweiler.

Much has been made of this expedition, and elsewhere it has been suggested that the "earth-magnetic" and "geophysical" studies—undertaken in the inhospitable terrain of the Himalayas during a time of the greatest international crisis—were actually experiments conducted by order of the Reichsführer-SS himself; that is, that they were bizarre scientific attempts to prove the World Ice Theory, a theory which—had it been proven—would have provided the Third Reich with an invaluable weapon against its enemies.

The Hörbiger Doctrine

Among the intimidatingly vast accumulation of Ahnenerbe documents on microfilm at the Archives are manuscripts, journal articles, and newspaper clippings concerning the *Welt-Eis-Lehre* or *World Ice Theory* once popularized by Austrian engineer Hans Hörbiger,[50] a favorite of both Eckart and Hitler. Hörbiger's vision of a universe composed of spinning balls and particles of ice managed to account for every crank cosmological theory from Atlantis to Lemuria and obviously owed a great deal to Madame Blavatsky's idea that the Earth is far older than the geologists tell us it is, and that it once had multiple moons and —*natürlich!*—multiple root-races. Hörbiger's ideas were embraced by some South American occultists of the author's acquaintance who believe to this day Hörbiger's contention that the Andes Mountains were once the site of an advanced civilization since its peaks were the only land mass above sea level during one of the last great Ice Age "meltdowns" . . . about six thousand years ago! Indeed, the Chilean author and Nazi mystic Miguel Serano subscribes to similar theories.[51]

The details of the World Ice Theory are too tedious to go into here; suffice it to say that the concept of a universe composed of little more than ice crystals in various stages of formation and deformation corresponded neatly with *völkisch* instincts. After all, Nordic Man was a creature of the ice fields and thus the natural ancestor of the human race: the being most fit to rule in a universe composed entirely of snow. (Where Sartre will one day see Nothingness at the root of the chestnut tree and recoil in horror, Hörbiger saw only sleet, and rejoiced.) Did not the ancient Nordic legends refer to the land of ice at the top of the world, the Teutonic Atlantis or Ultima Thule, as the origin of all Life? And doesn't the very *whiteness* of ice and snow itself suggest certain, ah, racial characteristics consonant with the divine source of the universe?

It was probably no accident that Hörbiger counted among his closest friends Ottocar Prohaszka, the Catholic bishop who acted as ideologue for the fanatical Nazi Arrow Cross Party of Hungary.

The real value of the World Ice Theory to the Nazis—aside from the fact that it represented an *alternative,* underdog science, and the Nazis were always looking for alternatives—was its supposed utility in weather forecasting. The nation that could accurately predict the weather far into the future was obviously the nation with an edge in military strategy. One need only recall how weather patterns disrupted many Nazi campaigns—from the freak flood that destroyed much of Rommel's matériel in North Africa to the severe winter that blocked Nazi victory in Russia—to know how important it was for the Reich to have a corner on meteorology.

For instance, a publication entitled *Zur Welteismeteorologie* (*On World Ice Meteorology*) by a Dr. E. Dinies, published by the Reichs Office for Weather Service in Berlin in 1938, quotes from Hörbiger's "epic work" *Glazialkosmogonie* (*Glacial Cosmology*) and provides tables of data comparing ice temperature and air temperature for relative humidity values.

With some (perhaps unconscious?) irony, the editors of the Nazi student newspaper *Rhein-Mainische Studentenzeitung* summed up the problem best in their lead for a series of brief articles on the World Ice Theory. Dated June 1, 1938, the lead-in reads:

> Our time is rich in theories about the formation and structure of the world. Frequently these days such matters are dealt with by laymen. In our opinion only scientists and experts can successfully answer these kinds of questions. For instance, there has been a great deal of talk in recent years about the World Ice Theory. We have asked therefore a variety of scientists to tell us their position on the questions piling up concerning the World Ice Theory and we offer them now to the public.[52]

And the paper goes on to compare the theories of Hörbiger and his coauthor Fauth to those of Galileo!

In a manuscript authored by an anonymous SS-Obersturmführer, we note the same attempt to put the World Ice Theory into a purely "scientific" framework, with the same unselfconscious irony:

The Need and Format of a New Implementation of the World Ice Theory

As the Reichsführer-SS himself first spoke out in support of the Viennese engineer Hans Hörbiger's World Ice Theory, he offered, by way of substantiation, the following: "Hans Hörbiger's monument doesn't need to wait a hundred years before it is built, one can employ these ideas even today." Of course, the implementation of the World Ice Theory ordered by the Reichsführer-SS must be planned in accord with scientific methodology. Thus is the manner of working in the Administration for Scientific Research in the Ahnenerbe unambiguously set forth. At the same time, however, a change from the usual method of implementing the World Ice Theory has been decided upon as well:

A scientifically thorough study of the World Ice Theory, together with a proof of its veracity, should be preserved from false teachers. This is only what official science attempts to do itself.[53]

Do we note the presence of a slight inferiority complex? Or was there some internecine conflict over the manner in which the World Ice Theory was being handled by nonscientists within the Ahnenerbe? After all, the theory was a pet project of many occultists and believers in Atlantis, including one of the founders of the Ahnenerbe, Hermann Wirth. This document, dated December 9, 1937, might have been part of the ammunition used by a faction within the World Ice department of the Ahnenerbe (probably being led by that earnest soul, Dr. Scultetus, who wanted the occultists out of the World Ice department so that he could conduct appropriately "scientific" experiments proving its validity) that eventually convinced Himmler to put the theory to the test in the frozen wastes of the Himalayas, where variations in altitude, humidity, and temperature could be meticulously recorded with the same vivid intensity that Lachung sexual practices were observed and logged and the truth—or myth—of the World Ice Theory established at last.

Schäfer returned home from Tibet in the summer of 1939. By September, the world had changed forever. And on the summer solstice of 1941—a date sacred to the pagan calendar, to the cultists at Paderborn, Detmold, and Externsteine, and to the memory of the sacrificial lamb, Walter Rathenau—Hitler invaded the Soviet Union, thus ripping the veil from before the tabernacle of the Jewish-Masonic-Bolshevik cabal.

Only a month later, and he was *two hundred miles outside Moscow,* within easy striking distance of total victory in Russia.

And then—inexplicably, astoundingly—*he decided to wait.*

Historians will never agree on why Hitler chose this disastrous strategy. He sent crucial divisions to Leningrad and the Ukraine while the main army waited in position for two months before moving on Moscow. It bought the Soviets all the time they needed, for in October the snow—the politically correct, white, *white* snow—began to fall.

Six months later, the Nazis had lost over one million dead in the freezing wastelands outside Moscow. In summer uniforms, light boots, no winter clothing at all of any kind, the Germans lost more men to the ravages of winter than to Soviet machine guns. Out of the 162 divisions thrown against the Red Army, only eight were combat-ready in the spring of 1942. Why did Hitler wait?

Because the Hörbigerians—under the auspices of the Ahnenerbe's meteorological division—had predicted a mild winter.

The Knight, Death, and the Double

The SS-Tibet Expedition was not composed simply of a handful of academics who got caught up in the war, but of dedicated *Nazi* scientists with their own agenda; men who were constitutionally capable of using the "raw material" of the concentration camps for their own research, research which was designed to support the blatantly occult racial, anthropological, and archaeological theories of the Third Reich, specifically of Himmler's Black Order, the SS.

How could otherwise sane, scientifically trained professional men become involved in such gruesome and sadistic activity? Dr. Robert J. Lifton, who has spent twenty years studying the Nazi doctors, has suggested the psychological phenomenon known as "doubling,"[54] a kind of splitting apart of the personality to accommodate two types of reality, the normal and the obscene. It may be safe to say that this is also a phenomenon common to many people who become involved in the occult. It is usually necessary for serious occultists to conduct themselves appropriately in the "real world" while simultaneously maintaining privately held, complex belief systems that have little in common with the beliefs of those around them. This is much more than simply believing in a different religion or belonging to an unpopular political party. Frequently, the occultist is operating with a totally different set of moral and spiritual values, a set based on an alternative view of the world. The serious occultist of, say, Germany has much more in common with the occultist of New Orleans or Bangkok than the Roman Catholic has with the Lutheran of any country. It is for this reason that occultists are frequently reviled everywhere they are found, for their secret beliefs and practices are considered heinous and inimical to the well-being of the State.

In Nazi Germany, however, the State became an occult organization and the secret beliefs and practices of a select coven of deranged occultists became the official policy of the nation. Scientists, doctors, and professional people in every field found themselves "doubling" to the extent that what would be considered normal, civilized behavior in a healthy society had to be suppressed in favor of a fanatic belief in the purity of the race and the sacred mission of the Occult Messiah. Science was still expected to carry on, however, and scientists found themselves making their knowledge and method subservient to the New Religion.

This might have been a bit harder to swallow had it not been for the fact that social conditions and official policies in the rest of the world seemed to favor the Nazi programs. Eugenics policies in the United States were looked upon for confirmation of the Nazi eugenics programs; prestigious American financiers such as Henry Ford wholeheartedly supported—with cash donations—the Nazi Party from its infancy; the wholesale slaughter of the Native American population in the United States was a practical model for the Nazi *Lebensraum* program and particularly for the genocide of Jews, Gypsies, and other indigenous populations of Eastern Europe; the Catholic Church supported the Party's anti-Communist crusade; and the British, after all, gave us the world's first concentration camps.

Therefore, it became obscenely easy for an armchair academic to suddenly find himself (and this was, remember, an exclusively *male* environment) encouraged to go into the "field" as it were and collect human skulls by examining their living owners in advance. All for the sake of scientific research, of course. The cult had made it easy to suspend normal modes of conduct; as in any cult, the cult leadership

decides what is, and is not, moral. The cult leader is the sole inter-
preter of the sacred texts. Within the sex cults, for instance, the laws
and taboos pertaining to sexual morality in society at large were abro-
gated in favor of the occult version; adultery was no longer a crime, as
an example, and even so prestigious an occult ancestor as John Dee
was known to have swapped wives (albeit reluctantly) with his assistant, Edward Kelley, on the advice of an Angelic being.[55] The Judeo-
Christian injunctions against murder, fornication, and adultery were
similarly suspended under the leadership of David Koresh, for instance, at his commune near Waco, Texas. In that environment, previous marriages were effectively "annulled" by Koresh, who saw it as his
prerogative to sleep with the wives of the male members of the cult
and even with their underage daughters. The relevant point to be
made is that the cult allowed this activity; Koresh's moral universe was
reinforced by the acquiescence of his followers and became the only
real moral standard for the "chosen." In their view, the rest of the
world crawled blindly through a swamp of spiritual ignorance, victim
of conspiracies and evil, vested interests. The rest of the world was to
be feared, for it could not allow such a beautiful creation as the
(Branch Davidians, Temple of God, Nazi Party) to exist.

This is the famous *Führerprinzip* (Führer Principle) in action.

Perhaps, then it would be fitting to end this chapter with a quote
from a song composed by some concentration camp prisoners forced
to build Himmler's Grail Castle at Wewelsburg:

> *And the stones are hard, but our step is firm*
> *As we carry along the picks and the spades*
> *And in our hearts,*
> *In our hearts the sorrow;*
> *O Wewelsburg, I cannot forget you*
> *Because you are my fate . . .*
> *And whatever our future is,*
> *Nevertheless we say "yes" to life.*
> *Because soon a day will come*
> *And we will be free![56]*

By 1943, some 1,285 concentration camp inmates had gained their
freedom . . . and were buried in the red earth of Westphalia or burned
in the crematorium at Niederhagen.

SS 7 SS

Lucifer's Quest
for the Holy Grail

As long as I live I will think of Sabarthés, of Montségur, of the Grail castle, and of the Grail itself that may have been the treasure of the heretics spoken of in the Records of the Inquisition. *I haven't been fortunate enough, I admit, to discover it myself!*[1]

—SS-OBERSTURMFÜHRER OTTO RAHN

Probably one of the most outlandish—yet somehow oddly grand, strangely cosmic—endeavors of the Third Reich in general, and of the SS in particular, was Himmler's search for the Holy Grail. This was an actual program of the SS, a program which has since been immortalized in the first and third films of Steven Spielberg's *Indiana Jones* trilogy. The author is not aware of the degree to which Spielberg was cognizant of actual SS operations designed to acquire such legendary treasure, but there is enough fact in the fiction to warrant serious consideration in this chapter.

In order to understand what Himmler was up to, we will have to look at the climate surrounding the Ahnenerbe and at what many readers probably think of as being a purely *Christian* symbol: the Holy Grail. As we do so, we will come across a fascinating individual whom history has treated rather shabbily, the young SS officer and historian, Otto Rahn (1904–1939).

It was, after all, Otto Rahn who helped popularize the notion that the Grail was not the special property of the Catholic Church (should it actually exist, and should it ever be found). For Rahn, the Grail was an emblem set up in *opposition* to the established Church—indeed, was a *Luciferian* symbol—and for this the Nazis were grateful; for, if Rahn's conclusion was correct, it gave them a philosophical and historical edge over organized Christianity.

The Crusade against the Grail

Rahn's first published work, *Kreuzzug gegen den Graal (Crusade Against the Grail),* was devoted to a study of what is sometimes referred to as the Albigensian Crusade: a war that took place between the Roman Catholic Church and a Christian cult known alternatively as the Albigensians (after the town of Albi in southern France) or the Cathars: "the Pure." The Cathars were a type of fundamentalist Christian sect that enjoyed enormous popularity in thirteenth-century Europe, even among the nobility. They were opposed to the materialism of the Catholic Church and what they perceived to be the corruption of Christ's teachings by the Church. In many of their beliefs, they were closer to the Gnostics and Manichaeans than to Roman Catholics; indeed, there is a great deal of evidence to suggest that they might have been a Manichaean survival. Regardless of their actual origins, however, they began attracting converts in large numbers, particularly in France.

Their beliefs included the doctrine that Christ was pure spirit and had never inhabited a human—that is, a material—form; that the dead will not be resurrected in the body, since the body was made of matter, which the Cathars viewed as Satanic; that there were two forces in the universe, one of good and the other of evil; that procreation was evil, as it increased the amount of matter in the world and trapped souls within material forms.

That death was good, and not a time for mourning; that there was no particular reason why the bodies of the dead should be revered since the bodies were the evil part of the human constitution.

Naturally, they were branded as heretics by the Church and eventually Catholic armies were sent to destroy them under order of Pope Innocent III in 1209. It was from a Catholic commander—a Cistercian abbot, no less—surrounding a French town composed of both Cathar and Catholic civilians (men, women, and children) that we receive the immortal line: "Kill them all. God will recognize his own."

The belief of the Cathars—and of their close relatives, the Albigensians or Albigeois of the Languedoc region of France—that matter was essentially impure and evil, and that only spirit was pure and good is a patently Gnostic doctrine. The belief in two gods—one evil, the other good—is both Gnostic and Manichaean. Hence, it has been argued that the Cathars were an extension of a Middle Eastern sect of Manichees or of Gnostics in possession of a "secret tradition" concerning the life and death of Christ and the origins of Christianity. The Cathars claimed that the Bible (particularly the Old Testament) was full of references to an Evil God—Jehovah—even as they insisted that the Bible was either full of errors or had been interpreted incorrectly by generations of self-serving Roman Catholic theologians. (One should remember that in 1209 the Gutenberg press had not been invented and that Bibles were in scarce supply. Those that existed were in the dead tongues of Latin and Greek, and in the possession of the Church. The average person knew very little of what was in the Bible, except for what he or she was told by a priest.)

Another Cathar peculiarity is that—perhaps late in their tragic story—they legitimized a form of ritual suicide, called the *endura:* one simply starved oneself to death, or was poisoned, or was strangled or suffocated by the brethren. They also rejected most of the sacraments of the Church as so much superstitious nonsense. In their anti-Papal stance they were close to the rather more Calvinist Waldensians with whom they have been frequently—and erroneously—linked.

At dinner . . . he spoke of India and Indian philosophy. This led him to speak of a subject which was a hobbyhorse of his: in a lively manner he described to me the result of researches in German witch-craft trials. He said it was monstrous that thousands of witches had

*been burned during the Middle Ages. So much good German blood
had been stupidly destroyed. From this he began an attack on the
Catholic Church, and at the same time on Calvin; before I had
caught up with all this he was discussing the Spanish Inquisition and
the essential nature of primitive Christianity.*[2]

—SCHELLENBERG

These words from Foreign Intelligence Chief Walter Schellenberg's
memoirs concerning a meeting with Himmler in the Ukraine in the
summer of 1942 indicate just how interested the Reichsführer-SS was
in such philosophical and metaphysical questions, including early
Christianity, Calvinism, the Inquisition . . . even the witch trials, on
all of which Himmler considered himself something of an expert.

The Cathar ideology must have appealed to him and the other
Nazis in a profound way. After all, the very word "Cathar" means
"pure," and purity—particularly of the blood as the physical embodi-
ment of spiritual "goodness"—was an issue of prime importance to
the SS. The Cathars railed against the gross materialism of the
Church; the Nazis viewed themselves as inherently anti-Capitalist,
even though they were forced to deal with large industrial concerns in
order to obtain absolute power in Germany. (To Hitler and his followers, Capitalism was immoral and they equated it with the excesses of
the Jewish financiers that—they said—had brought the nation to ruin
during the First World War and the depression that followed.)

The Cathars, in denying the value of the Old Testament and in
attacking Jehovah as a kind of Satan, naturally seemed to be in perfect
agreement with Nazi ideology concerning the Jews and, as we shall see,
with the current incarnation of neo-Nazi ideologues in the Christian
Identity movement and in the Process Church of the Final Judgment.

Further, the Cathars were fanatics, willing to die for their cause;
sacrificing themselves to the Church's onslaught they enjoyed the
always enviable aura of spiritual underdogs. There was something
madly beautiful in the way they were immolated on the stakes of the
Inquisition, professing their faith and their hatred of Rome until the
very end. The Nazis could identify with the Cathars: with their overall
fanaticism, with their contempt for the way vital spiritual matters were
commercialized (polluted) by the Establishment, and with their pas-

sion for "purity." It is perhaps inevitable that the Cathars should have made a sacrament out of suicide, for they must have known that their Quest was doomed to failure from the start. They must have wished for death as a release from a corrupt and insensitive world; and it's entirely possible that, at the root of Nazism, lay a similar death wish. Hitler was surrounded by the suicides of his mistresses and contemplated it himself on at least one occasion before he actually pulled the trigger in Berlin in 1945. Himmler and other captured Nazi leaders killed themselves rather than permit the Allies to do the honors for them. Haushofer committed suicide. Even Sebottendorff plunged himself into the Bosporus. Perhaps the passionate desire of concentration camp survivors to see all Nazi war criminals executed for their crimes—even at this late date—represents an unconscious realization that suicide (like a natural death) is too good for the monsters of the Reich; that, like the Cathars whom they admired, the Nazis saw in suicide that consolation and release from the world of Satanic matter promised by this most cynical of Cathar sacraments.

For some reason, it became popular to assume that these same Cathars were in possession of a mysterious sacred object and that, on the eve of destruction of the last major Cathar opposition at the fortress of Montségur in southern France on March 14, 1244, some Cathars managed to escape with this object down the side of their mountain citadel (then under siege by Catholic troops). This sacred object has been identified by later generations of amateur historians as nothing less than the Holy Grail.[3]

Before the collapse of Montségur, as some (mostly French) authors have proposed, the Grail was in the possession of the infamous Order of the Knights Templar, the Order after which von Liebenfels and Kellner named their respective cults; the same Order that was created by St. Bernard of Clairvaux, the famous abbot of the Cistercian Order. Depending on whom one reads, the Templars were believed to have discovered either the Grail or the Ark of the Covenant (or both?) during their sojourn in Palestine at the site of Solomon's Temple. Several studies have been made of the Templar cathedrals—Chartres in particular—to prove that the Templars left a coded message in stone revealing that they brought a sacred object of great value back with them from the East, an object whose tremendous, otherworldly power enabled them to finance, design, and build a series of magnificent churches all over France in an amazingly short period of time. Indeed, the time line is suggestive for, according to an authoritative work on the subject by Henry Adams, during the space of one hundred years (from A.D. 1170 to A.D. 1270) the Church built eighty cathedrals in France and hundreds of other "cathedral-class" churches at an estimated cost of one billion in 1905 U.S. dollars.[4]

The pseudonymous author on alchemy and architecture, Fulcanelli, contributed to this idea of a Templar secret tradition in his *Le Mystère des Cathédrales,* first published in 1925. It has been translated into English and forms the core of yet another mystical tradition.[5]

Just why the Cathars should then have found themselves in possession of the Grail remains something of a mystery. Certainly there is a robust literature concerning the Grail—known as Grail Romances to the historians—that identify it as anything from a sacred stone that fell from the sky (the *lapis exilis* or *lapis ex coelis*) to the actual cup used by Jesus at the Last Supper and which was used to catch drops of his blood during the crucifixion. Indeed, Wolfram von Eschenbach's *Parzival* depicts the Grail as a *stone* and not as a cup; the older romance by Chrétien de Troyes depicts the Grail as a *cup* and not as a stone, and this image is perpetuated in Malory's *Le Morte d'Arthur.* As if to compromise on this controversy, one of the carved figures on the north door of Chartres Cathedral—that of the Old Testament High Priest Melchisedek—is shown holding a Cup from which the Stone rises.

And from time to time various objects have been found which their owners claimed to be the Grail but none of these have stood up to even cursory scrutiny.

Recently, the writing team of Walter Birks and R. A. Gilbert have conspired to put an end to all the speculation.[6] Birks served with the British Army in the Middle East during the war with the rank of major, prior to which he had been involved in esoteric and spiritualist circles in England; Gilbert is an historian of occultism, most notably of the Golden Dawn. Together, they denigrate the writings of Rahn as "tortuous reasoning and linguistic lunacy"[7] and the book by Baigent, Leigh, and Lincoln *(Holy Blood, Holy Grail)* as evidence of a "lunatic theory" supported by an "inchoate mass of irrelevancies."[8]

For Birks and Gilbert, the treasure of Montségur "never was": it was not the Grail, not a cache of Templar gold, not the bloodline of Jesus, but "the power to transmit the apostolic succession, the seed perhaps of a higher form of Christianity to be revealed when the world is ready to receive it."[9] They base this theory on Biblical exegesis, interpretations of the Dead Sea Scrolls, the writings of Josephus and others, and on what remains of Cathar ritual and theology. Birks was present at a Cathar research site at Ussat-les-Bains in the late 1930s (although too late to have met Rahn, who also researched and lived at the site) and was friendly with one Antonin Gadal, about whom more later. Birks himself states that it was during conversation with a member of the Nosairi sect in the Middle East that he realized the Cathar treasure was not a material Grail at all, but the "Light-filled vessel": i.e., a purely metaphorical image based on the cup of sacramental wine which the Nosairi use to drink "to the Light": an emblem of the true teaching of Christianity before it became confused and bowdlerized by the Evangelists and the various Councils. This is all involved with a Nosairi tradition of the "way of the Stars," that a human soul, after death, proceeds up a ladder of lights, of stars, to heaven. Birks was satisfied with that, and the doctrine of Light provided him with a great illumination (no pun intended); but we have come full circle, for the way of the Stars and the doctrine of the Light are amply represented by the myths of the Celts, the Nordic peoples, and many others in whom Rahn discovered the scattered fragments of a lost mystical tradition, and the "Light-filled vessel" may be an entirely appropriate reference to Rahn's rediscovered doctrine of Lucifer, the Light-Bearer.

SS-Obersturmführer *Parzival*

As mentioned, one of the most famous Grail romances is that composed by Wolfram von Eschenbach, entitled *Parzival*. It is this particular romance that has remained the authoritative word on the subject for many people, and which was the work that inspired Otto Rahn in his researches (and Richard Wagner in his famous opera by the same name).

Rahn was an impoverished scholar of history whose soul became inflamed by equal doses of Wagner and von Eschenbach in his youth.

The beneficiary of a classical education in both literature and philology, he spent five years traveling throughout Europe in search of myths, legends, and the records of heretical cults, all of which he believed would point to the existence of a native, crypto-pagan, Gnostic-type religion in Europe. Finding mythological and philological links between such varied phenomena as the troubadours, the Grail legends, European paganism, and the heretical sect known as the Cathars Rahn felt he had discovered evidence of an ancient German religious tradition that had been suppressed by the Church.

Identifying the pure knight Parzival as a Cathar or Cathar manqué, Rahn went on to write a history of the Cathar rebellion from the point of view of Grail Romance. Although this sounds like pure Guido von List or Lanz von Liebenfels, Rahn was a scholar of somewhat greater integrity who based his work on accepted primary sources (such as the records of the Inquisition, the poems and songs of the troubadours, and the medieval Grail legends) and on his own, on-the-scene research.

He arrived in the Languedoc region of France in 1931 and there met a gentleman well-known in Grail circles, Antonin Gadal.[10] Gadal maintained a private Cathar museum at the small town of Ussat-les-Bains, a tourist attraction and spa in the Pyrenees with an allegedly Cathar connection. He also had an extensive library on the subject of the Cathars and the Grail, from which Rahn probably derived much benefit. Gadal was a member of a society called *The Friends of Montségur and the Grail,* of which the noted historian René Nelli was vice president (it was Nelli who would translate Rahn's work into French).[11] The society—as its name implies—believed that a connection existed between the Cathar movement and the Grail Romances. This concept had been broached in 1906 by the popular French author Joséphin Péladan in *Le Secret des Troubadours.* Former Golden Dawn member Arthur Edward Waite had discounted the theory that the Grail legend had anything to do with either Cathars or Albigensians in a book published three years later *(The Hidden Church of the Holy Grail),* but then Waite was in a state of apostasy from the Golden Dawn as he had denied their occult rituals as essentially evil and replaced them with Christian versions, forming his own rather boring occult order in the process.

In May of 1932 Rahn decided to become an innkeeper to support his researches and invested in a local establishment at Ussat. By September he was bankrupt, and disappeared from France only to reappear shortly thereafter in Germany. By then, he had accumulated quite enough information to write his own book on the subject of the Cathars and the Grail, *Kreuzzug gegen den Graal,* which was published in 1933 and translated into French the following year as *Croisade contre le Graal (Crusade Against the Grail).*

Although the book did not earn Rahn a lot of money, it eventually came to the attention of no less an admirer than Heinrich Himmler.

According to one version of the story,[12] the Reichsführer-SS personally invited the author to meet him at his Prinz Albrechtstrasse headquarters in Berlin. There, he offered Rahn a commission in the SS and virtually unlimited resources for which Himmler expected Rahn to continue his research into the Grail legends, the Cathars, and related subjects of Aryan interest.

According to another version,[13] Rahn was a personal friend of *völkisch* "channeler" Karl Maria Wiligut—also known as SS-Oberführer Weisthor—a gentleman who had once been certified insane but who nonetheless claimed that he had perfect recall of the entire ancient history of the Teuton peoples going back over *200,000* years, a kind of ancient racial memory upon which he could call at any time. This was, of course, a very handy ability to possess and Himmler considered himself fortunate to have access to the services of a man who could fill in those great gaps of Teutonic history that result when a master race proves rather lax in developing a written language. Wiligut's ability was, he claimed, due to the fact that his family's lineage had been kept pure at every generation down the millennia from that time in the misty past when the gods of air and water mated in humid embrace to produce the milky Wiligut bloodline. Wiligut, another of Germany's rune scholars, clairvoyants, and Teutonic mystics, held salon-type meetings at his home on arcane Aryan topics at which Himmler *and* the young Otto Rahn were said to be frequent guests.

Wiligut insisted that Christianity was really a German invention; that Christ was really the ancient Teutonic god Baldur, who was crucified by a schismatic group of Wotan-worshiping thugs. Baldur, however, managed to escape to the Middle East and . . . and . . . well, the rest is New Testament. His remaining followers in Germany built a cult center sacred to their faith at the prehistoric site of Externsteine, which was to become the subject of much discussion and excavation by the Ahnenerbe. (See Chapter Six.)

Of course, like most other occult theory, Wiligut's cross-eyed thesis is based on a number of verifiable historical traditions that can be found in a careful reading of ancient texts, in this case of the Eddas and other Scandinavian and Gothic lore that predate the Christian conversion of these peoples by hundreds (and not hundreds of thousands) of years. Baldur, for instance, was a slain and resurrected god like many other agricultural deities of many other lands. The Norse Creation story is remarkably similar to that of ancient Sumeria, with the known universe created out of the corpse of another slain god. That Christianity adopted pagan ceremonies, cult centers, holidays, and myths is by now well known; in fact, it becomes increasingly difficult to identify just what a "pure" form of Christianity would look like. However, Wiligut's problem—and the problem of many amateur historians in his class—is that he took the myths and legends of the ancient European peoples and blended them together with theosophical and other newly coined mystical beliefs with little or no historical basis. The commonality of motifs in these various myths from widely divergent sources may best be explained by the type of research undertaken by MIT Professor de Santillana (as mentioned in a previous chapter) and others who see in these stories a coded form of astronomical observations. The relatively new sciences of epigraphy and paleoastronomy may answer many questions previously considered the domain of occultism.

Yet, on the basis of this and related historical fantasies, Wiligut was made the head of the Department of Prehistory at the Race and Settlement Office (RuSHA) of the SS, and eventually attained the exalted rank of SS-Brigadeführer, or Brigadier, on Himmler's Personal Staff. It was Wiligut who designed the *Schutzstaffel*'s special Death's Head (*totenkopf*) ring, a device replete with runic symbols including the inevitable swastika as well as those of Wiligut's *personal* armorial design. The latter detail implied that somehow Wiligut was, himself, the last and sole physical repository of glacially pure Teutonic blood; a claim that was the cornerstone of his philosophy and which gave him that unique unbroken memory which made him so valuable to those lesser mortals who could only prove their racial purity back to the year 1750 (as required of SS recruits) and whose race memory had therefore fallen victim to the ravages of ancient couplings with diseased and drooling subhumans, such as Hungarians.

It has been said that Rahn was introduced to Himmler by Wiligut himself, and that Himmler accepted the young scholar into the SS on Wiligut's personal recommendation. Wiligut then kept in constant touch with Rahn as the latter went about on his travels through France, Germany, and Iceland, hot on the very cold trail of the mysterious Cathar treasure he believed was the Grail. He communicated his findings to Wiligut periodically in letters that were to be shared with no one else but Himmler, so secret and so important were their contents. One wonders what these secrets were, for they are certainly not to be found in Rahn's second book, a work published under Nazi supervision. However, some letters from Rahn to Wiligut *have* survived,[14] marked "extremely confidential," dealing—for instance—with linguistic evidence of pagan sites concealed within modern German place names, and begging the Seer to communicate his findings with "the Reichsführer-SS only." As these letters are dated as early as 1935—and signed with a hearty "Heil Hitler!"—we can see that Rahn *was* intimate with the highest circles of the SS hierarchy by this time. Rahn's friend Paul Ladame, however, insists that when he ran into Rahn in July, 1936, on the Joachimstaler Strasse in Berlin, Rahn was resplendent in full SS uniform, bearing the flashes of the *Liebstandarte Adolf Hitler* and, when asked how he had come to be wearing such a thing, replied "My dear Paul, a man has to eat!"[15]

Whether or not Rahn was any kind of real Nazi, his two books do reveal, however, that he believed the Catholic Church had all but destroyed essential elements of a secret German religious tradition, a tradition whose persecution began with the Cathars in the thirteenth century and which ended, triumphantly, with the destruction of the Templar Order a hundred years later. The German tradition was not a Christian one in the generally accepted sense. Rather, it was a pagan religion whose elements were appropriated by the Church as a means of diluting it of its power: the Grail, the knightly Orders, the sacred Quest, and the eternal struggle between Light and Darkness. Except, for the Cathars as filtered through the meditations of Rahn, Light in this case was represented by—not Jesus or Jehovah—but by another spirit, the "Light-Bearer." To Rahn, this Entity represented the highest good. To Rahn (at least officially), the Nazi Reich in general—and the SS in particular—became the servitors of an ancient pagan cult whose god was known to the medieval Christians not as Jesus but as *Lucifer.*

Lucifer's Servants

As we saw in the preceding chapter, Himmler's personal agenda was to amass enough data—archaeological, historical, cultural, religious, and occult—to prove that the Aryan "race" was superior to all other races on earth and that the Germans were the inheritors of the Aryan bloodline. He also had to prove that, at some point in history, what are now the German peoples owned virtually all the real estate in Europe. This would not only seem to legitimize Hitler's Drive to the East, but might prove useful in establishing that the Germans had an historical right to do whatever they wanted with whatever inferior, mongrel races they found there.

Proving the existence of a hitherto unknown German religious tradition that predated Christianity and which was more in tune with the German *Volk* would go a long way toward propping up Himmler's other theories and give substance to the twin policies of Aryan racial superiority and German claim to the land. It would provide the necessary philosophical underpinning for an occult renaissance in Europe and prove stronger than the various Christian sects that had arbitrarily divided the race along ideological lines. A German spiritual tradition that transcended Christian history would provide a *blood religion* that could unit the racially pure peoples of Europe—Aryans in diaspora—and thus erase national boundaries and Christian sensitivities in one blow.

(To those readers of today who find this mission a trifle weird, might the author be permitted to remind them that no less a modern state than Israel was founded along pretty much the same lines? Jewish claims upon the territory are based upon religious scriptures, and citizenship in the State of Israel is limited to those who can *prove* they are Jews. One may remember the difficulty Ethiopian Jews had in emigrating to Israel. The author does not point this out in order to devalue Jewish claims upon the territory known as Palestine before 1948, but to illustrate a point: that great nations—and national agendas— are sometimes erected on such weak timber as a human-interpreted word of God or on the blood of the "Aryans." If it *could* have been proven that the so-called Aryan peoples were at one time in the distant past in control of vast amounts of European, American, and Asian real estate . . . so what?)

In this dubious endeavor, Himmler had two distinct sets of ideological opponents. First of all, there were the genuine scientists who disparaged such canonical Nazi claims as Aryan racial purity and the prevalence of an Aryan cult or proto-Christian society over all of Europe and Asia in the distant past. For these, Himmler hoped to provide concrete evidence that Aryans (and, hence, Germans) had established communities in such remote locales as Minsk in Russia, northern India, and Tibet. The *Deutsche Akademie* and later the Ahnenerbe were both heavily involved in the archaeological work necessary to buttress this argument.

His second opponent was the established Christian Church itself. Himmler's dream was to create, out of the SS, a new religion based on the pagan elements of what he perceived to be the original, Ur-Aryan religion of ancient India and Europe. However, many Germans were devout Christians. Hitler himself realized this, and knew that he had to play politics with them for as long as the churches held power and as long as the people felt they owed spiritual allegiance to the churches and what they represented. In this he was as cynical in his dealings with the Church as he was pragmatic with the Capitalists.

Himmler, on the other hand, wanted nothing so much as the destruction—not only of the organized Church—but of Christianity itself. And, with the assistance of Wiligut and other like-minded individuals, Himmler drew up new ceremonies and a new liturgical calendar to thoroughly replace Christian versions. He was dealing Judaism the death blow in the camps and with his roving bands of death squads, the *Einsatzgruppen,* under the command of such men as Theosophist and convicted war criminal Otto Ohlendorf and the notorious Dr. Six. The Church was next on the list. How better to capture the attention and imagination of the pious than to appropriate the Grail as a purely pagan and Aryan symbol, actually restoring to the Grail its original character and identity? The Grail figured prominently in European folklore as a powerful occult symbol, and was also the basis for a Wagnerian opera that was just as powerful, just as compelling. It was assumed that Wagner, an admitted anti-Semite who provided the sound track for the Third Reich, would not have wasted his time writing a Christian or Jewish propaganda tract. Therefore, Wagner's own take on the Grail must be consistent with rest of the Aryan operatic canon that included, of course, the *Ring Cycle.* It was all Aryan myth and, therefore, part of a single, continuous epic story.

Rahn's thesis went a long way to establishing just that. Based on research undertaken in the Languedoc region of southern France and especially at fabled Montségur, site of the Cathars' last stand, Rahn believed he had acquired enough evidence to repudiate any Christian claim to the Grail. The Grail of von Eschenbach and Richard Wagner was redeemed as the ultimate Aryan relic around which Himmler would build his pagan Temple. The castle at Wewelsburg, with its Round Table for himself and the members of his Inner Circle, would be the heart of a new metropolis; the chamber containing the Round Table and the crypt below it would be the *precise geographical center* of the new city, the Aryan Camelot, and of the New World itself. And what is King Arthur, a Round Table, and Camelot without a Grail?

Initially, Rahn did not seem to hold pro-Nazi ideas in the least. According to his friend, the French author Paul Ladame,[16] Rahn thought the Nazis faintly ridiculous. But he was starving. He could not turn down a lucrative offer of employment with Himmler, and so he eventually donned the black uniform of the SS and continued his researches better fed and more warmly (if somewhat ostentatiously) clothed.

He may not have had much of a choice in the matter, but it was a decision that nevertheless proved his downfall. As Himmler encountered more and more difficulty in finding hard evidence to prove his Aryan thesis, he became increasingly disillusioned with Rahn and his ilk. Finally, according to Ladame, he gave the frightened young scholar an ultimatum: he would finish his next book by October 31, 1936—the pagan festival of Samhain—and provide it to the Nazi editors for approval. Or else.

This, Rahn managed to do. According to one source, he was then sent to Dachau for the four months of scheduled military training required of all SS men (as was Adolf Eichmann at the same camp

Heft 1 16. Jahrgang

Berlin, 12. Lenzings 1933

Runen

ᛟ.ᛜ.ᚠ.

Zeitschrift für germanische Geistesoffenbarungen und Wissenschaften.

Merkblatt des Germanenordens ᚹᚨᛚᚠᚨᛏᛖᚱ

errichtet 20. Hornungs 1912

Nur Sonnenkindern raunen die Runen!

Runes: Journal for German Spiritual Revelations and Science

Ostara, magazine created by Jörg Lanz von Liebenfels

Unterzeichneter beantragt für sich (und seine Familie) die Aufnahme als Besucher der Thule Gesellschaft.

Ich versichere an Eidesstatt, daß ich nicht mit Juden oder Farbigen verwandt oder verschwägert bin.

Ich weiß, daß ich nach 6 Monaten die Aufnahme in die Gesellschaft beantragen kann.

Ich weiß, daß der Monatsbeitrag für mich und meine Familie 1 RM beträgt.

München, den

Unterschrift

Vorstehende Erklärung meines Mannes gilt auch für mich. Ich bin mit Juden weder verwandt noch verschwägert.

Unterschrift

Genaue Anschrift:

Kinder:

Verheiratet:

Application form to join the Thule Society, which includes the following declaration: "I swear under oath that I am neither related nor married to Jews or colored persons."

Newspaper memorial to Nazi "poet" Dietrich Eckart
on the tenth anniversary of his death

Montségure

Model of Weweslburg

Theatrical set for *Parsifal,* prototype for dining hall
with Round Table at Wewelsburg

Wewelsburg

Himmler and Hitler in Wewelsburg

SS-Tibet Expedition

Das Ahnenerbe

Berlin-Dahlem, am 23. Januar 1940
Pücklerstraße 16

S/Wo.
_____

Bitte in der Antwort das vorstehende Geschäftszeichen angeben
Zuschriften an einzelne Mitarbeiter verzögern die Bearbeitung

An

ᛋᛋ-Hauptsturmführer

Dr. Ernst S c h ä f e r

B e r l i n
- - - - - - - - - - - -
Hohenzollerndamm 36

Nachdem vom Präsidenten des "Ahnenerbes", Reichsführer ᛋᛋ
Heinrich Himmler, die Zusammenfassung Ihrer Forschungstä-
tigkeit in München - Salzburg in Übereinstimmung mit Ih-
ren eigenen Arbeitszielen angeordnet wurde und Sie zum
Abteilungsleiter in der Forschungs- und Lehrgemeinschaft
"Das Ahnenerbe" ernannt wurden, bitten wir Sie, nunmehr
zu veranlassen, dass die Ergebnisse Ihrer Forschungsrei-
sen bezw. Ihr Arbeitsmaterial entsprechend überführt
wird. Wegen der technischen Durchführung bezw. des
Transportes wollen Sie sich bitte zu gegebener Zeit
mit dem rechts Unterzeichneten in Verbindung setzen.

Der Kurator: Der Reichsgeschäftsführer:

ᛋᛋ-Obersturmbannführer   ᛋᛋ-Sturmbannführer

Reichshauptstelle: Berlin-Dahlem, Pücklerstraße 16. Fernruf 897721
Postscheck: Berlin 99001 · Bankverbindung: Bank der Deutschen Arbeit A. G., Berlin C 2 / Dresdner Bank, Depositenkasse 65, Berlin C 2

Letter from Heinrich Himmler, as president of "Ahnenerbe," appointing
Dr. Ernst Schäfer head of the Ancestral Heritage Research and Teaching Society.

Der Reichsführer der Schutzstaffeln der NSDAP.
Personal-Kanzlei

Fernsprecher:
Ortsleitung Sammel-Nummer 11 61 01

Postscheck-Konto:
National-Sozial. Deutsche Arbeiterpartei
Schutzstaffel" München 17535

Anschrift:
Reichsführer-SS
Personalkanzlei
Berlin SW 11
Prinz Albrecht-Straße 9

Abteilung: P 8 Ka/O.
Tgb. Nr.:
Betrifft:
Bezug:
Anlage:

Berlin, den 5. Dezember 1938

An den

SS-Obersturmführer
Dr. Ernst S c h ä f e r

Gangtok-Sikkim/Indien

Die SS-Personalkanzlei teilt Ihnen mit, dass der Reichsführer-SS
mit Wirkung vom 21. Dezember 1938 nachfolgende Beförderungen ver-
fügt hat:

Dr. Ernst Schäfer	SS-Nr. 138 803, Pers.Stab RF-SS
	zum SS-Hauptsturmführer
Beger, Bruno	SS-Nr. 263 712, Pers.Stab RF-SS
	zum SS-Obersturmführer
Krause, Ernst	SS-Nr. 293 712, Pers.Stab RF-SS
	zum SS-Obersturmführer
Wienert, Karl	SS-Nr. 288 240, Pers.Stab RF-SS
	zum SS-Obersturmführer
Geer, Edmund	SS-Nr. 31 384, Pers.Stab RF-SS
	zum SS-Obersturmführer.

H e i l   H i t l e r !
Der Chef der SS-Personalkanzlei

SS-Oberführer.

Letter promoting various members of the Tibet Expedition to higher rank in the
SS: Dr. Ernest Schäfer to Hauptsturmführer; the other four to Obersturmführer.

A winter solstice ceremony, filmed in Argentina in 1933 by the Auslands-Organisation (foreign division) of the Nazi Party. The film, entitled *Wintersonnenwende,* was directed by Gerhard Huttula.

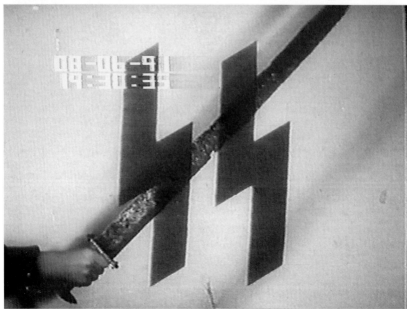

Stills from the SS film *Deutsche Vergangenheit wird lebendig*
(The German past is living), promoting German ancestral heritage.

several years earlier). That would have been sometime in the last half of 1937.[17]

He resigned his commission in the SS sometime after leaving Dachau.

Then, in 1939, at the age of thirty-five, he was dead.

The book that resulted from this relatively unknown Nazi project was entitled *Luzifers Hofgesind* or *Lucifer's Servants,* sometimes translated as *Lucifer's Court.*[18] It reads quite differently from Rahn's first book, which was at least sincere in its effort to portray a kind of occult underdog group of purists who held the secret of the ages in their hands if only the rest of us would pay attention. *Lucifer's Servants,* on the other hand, is at least partly a genuine Nazi propaganda tract and several passages make a good case for the worship of Lucifer, if one follows (and credits) Rahn's exegesis on several ancient sources including *Parzival* and the surviving texts of troubadors, Cathars, and even Persian mystics. Indeed, this idea of Lucifer as a benign or divine being was familiar and congenial to the "white light" Theosophists of the 1920s who, after all, entitled one of their official German publications *Luzifer.*

The following citations should adequately illustrate this claim (all translations by the author, all emphasis by Rahn):

> It was necessary, in effect, to be faithful to God until death, "and God will give to his servant the crown of eternal life," as it is written in the Bible. Having established that, for the Church of Rome—the sole repository of "Truth" in the eyes of its faithful—the troubadors were members of the servants of the Devil; having also established that they were faithful to the God of Love; and finally having established that they celebrated—as numerous examples have proved—the marvels of the crown of Lucifer, it is permitted to believe that they had faith in the existence of a *Luciferian crown of eternal life* (to speak Biblically). And if we follow this thought to its logical conclusion, we will say that, for them, *the God of Love was none other than Lucifer in person.*
>
> This hypothesis will become certain if we allow our thought to range more widely: the god *Amor* is the god of Spring, as is Apollon. . . . Apollon brought back the light of the Sun: he is a light-bearer, or "Lucifer." According to the *Apocalypse* of John, Apollyo-Apollon was equated with the Devil, and according to the belief of the Roman Church . . .

Lucifer is Satan. Consequently, the god of Spring *Apollon-Amor* is, according to the doctrine of the Church, *the Devil and Satan*.[19]

In a further ferverino on the subject of Lucifer, he writes in the
same chapter:

There is much more [Light] than in the houses of God—cathedrals and
churches—where Lucifer neither is able nor wishes to enter due to all
the somber, stained glass windows wherein are painted the Jewish
prophets and apostles, the Roman gods and saints. The forest, that, that
was free![20]

As the above two passages indicate, Rahn is using Biblical and Pa-
tristic writings to support his thesis that the Cathars and the troubadors were, in a sense, Devil worshipers . . . but only so far as they
worshiped pagan gods whom the *Church* had demonized. In an earlier
chapter Rahn notes that Esclarmonde, a famous Cathar saint, "one of
the noblest women of the Middle Ages" and heretic of the highest
rank, believed that Jehovah—the Old Testament God of the Jews—
was none other than Satan himself; that Christ never died on the cross
and that, therefore, his suffering and death do not redeem the lives or
souls of his followers. (This idea that Christ did not die on the cross is
one possible reason why Templar postulants were to trample a crucifix
underfoot during their initiation ceremony into the Order, and may
be the reason there were no crucifixes at Chartres.) "Cursed by the
Pope, detested by the King of France, she thought—until her dying
breath—of nothing other than the religious and political independence of her country."[21] These ideas—Jehovah the "god of the Jews"
as the real Satan, inherent falsehoods in the Gospel account of Christ's
life, and dying for the *religious* and *political* independence of the
state—all had a receptive audience among the scholars of the Ahnenerbe and of the SS in general, and still does among the racist and anti-
Semitic Christian Identity movement today. The Cathars had represented a *pure* form of Christianity that denied even large portions of
the Bible, and they were a political threat to the established Church;
certainly, Himmler could approve of this point of view married, as it
was, to the idea of a pagan Grail and of the Cathars as "guardians of
the Grail." Characterizing Jehovah as an evil demon tallied nicely with

the mass destruction of his followers in the camps, and made the extermination of the *race of Jehovah* an even greater *spiritual* necessity. Now they were no longer simply members of an inferior race that conspired to rob good Germans of their money, their pride, and their birthright; they were also the children of Satan.

Further, and perhaps even more importantly, as the Old Testament Jews were worshipers of Satan, then Christ could not possibly have been Jewish. Strip away the Jewish content of the New Testament and—relying on the Biblical "revisionist" scholarship of generations of genuine German academics who cast doubt on the validity of the Gospels themselves—you are well on your way to accepting Wiligut's thesis that Christ was Baldur, and a Teutonic Sun God!

The "Crusade against the Grail"—subject and title of Rahn's first book—was that undertaken by the Catholic Church during its vicious assault on Catharism, in which hundreds of thousands were brutally murdered. To Rahn, the Church was the Enemy both during the time of the Cathars in the thirteenth century and right up to the present day. Worse, it was the enemy of all that was pure, and noble, and good in the world, ideals represented by the Grail: centerpiece of *Parzival,* of Wagner's operas, of the *Morte d'Arthur,* and the entire Camelot mystique. The idea of the virgin knight, on a mystic quest throughout Europe for the Sacred Cup, must have appealed enormously to the young, virtually penniless scholar. Himmler referred to his SS men as the knights of a new Order, and one must wonder if Rahn felt—in his heart of hearts—somehow at home in his elegant black uniform with the silver runes, a new Teutonic Knight on the same sacred quest for the Grail. In his introduction to the French translation of *Luzifers Hofgesind (La Cour de Lucifer),* Paul Ladame insists that Rahn joined the SS because there was no option: Himmler offered him a salary, perks, and the freedom to conduct his own academic research unhindered. To refuse would have seemed like madness, and perhaps would have resulted in Rahn's eventual imprisonment anyway.

Other scholarship on the question provides a somewhat different perspective. Evidence from the Nazi side depicts Rahn as an enthusiastic Grail scholar, an admirer of Wiligut (a man who claimed that the Bible was a German creation; a man whom anyone in his or her right mind must have *known* was a lunatic), and an eager member of the SS.

At first glance this is consistent with Rahn's introduction to *Lucifer's Servants,* which ends with the proud and defiant claim "My ancestors were pagans. My forebears were heretics."[22] Yet, there is a mystery surrounding Rahn's sudden and unexplained *resignation* from the SS, a resignation that took place a little over a year after his leave from military service at Dachau.

He resigned his commission in February 1939.

He died less than a month later, on March 13 of that same year, supposedly from exposure while hiking in the mountains. This, from a seasoned traveler, and a trained survivalist (as all SS men were), at an altitude of less than 2,000 meters a week before spring! As Ladame puts it, "to die of cold the 13th of March at less than 2,000 meters, one needs a lot of patience, a strong will . . . and time . . . perhaps one or two weeks."[23]

Thus Ladame disputes the dating, insisting that his friend died in 1937, shortly after finishing *Lucifer's Servants.*[24] Ladame claims that Rahn was no Nazi, and no racist. He insists that the Nazi elements in *Lucifer's Servants* were not of Rahn's making or, if they were, they were inserted at the command or instigation of the SS. And, not surprisingly, Ladame implies that Rahn was murdered; executed by his former colleagues for reason, or reasons, unknown.

Unfortunately, there is some documentary evidence that Otto Rahn was alive and well at least as late as January 1938, when he gave a lecture—based on *Luzifers Hofgesind*—to the Dietrich Eckart Society at Dietrich Eckart House in Dortmund, in Westphalia . . . a lecture that was reported upon in the local newspaper. From the tone of the review, Rahn was in fine form that evening:

> The Albigensians were exterminated. 205 leading followers of Lucifer were burnt on a huge pyre by Dominicans in the South of France after a large-scale priestly Crusade in the name of Christian clemency. With fire and sword, the Lucifer doctrine of the Light-Bearer was persecuted along with its followers. The Albigensians are dead, but their spirit lives on and has an effect today through new devotion and rejuvenated enthusiasm. The Vicar of Christ could truly burn men; but he was mistaken if he believed that he burned along with them their spirit,

devotion and longing. This spirit became alive again before many men yesterday, powerfully and visibly, in Otto Rahn, a descendant of the old Troubadours.[25]

Could someone as intelligent as Rahn's published writings indicate he was, a scholar for whom medieval legend and lore came alive only through careful research and study, have willingly taken up with a character like Wiligut, who claimed that the Teutonic tribes had a verifiable history going back to the year 228,000 B.C. . . . when the Earth had an embarrassment of three suns? As much as one may wish to argue with the thesis of *Crusade against the Grail* or *Lucifer's Servants,* there is nothing of the raving mystagogue about Rahn. One likes to think that his period of obligatory military service at Dachau opened his eyes to the horror of the Reich, and that—in a final, doomed but proud gesture of dignity—he resigned his commission in the SS in outrage and disgust at the atrocities he may have witnessed at the death camp associated with the SS base there; and was then murdered for his insubordination a month later.

Then, too, the fact that both Wiligut and Rahn retired from the SS at the same time—*in the same month*—is suggestive of some collusion between the two mythologians: the one elderly and quite insane, the other young and quite intelligent. Rahn's exploits and the mystery surrounding his resignation and subsequent death have received a great deal of attention in European circles over the years, although they are little known in America. His unusual life story has led to considerable speculation that Rahn actually *did* discover something in his travels, and that since he seemed to confide in Wiligut they both had to be gotten out of the way to protect the secret. That, in fact, they "knew too much." Wiligut was kept under SS lock and key for some time until the end of the war, and died in 1946; he was eighty years old and, with his background of mental illness, hardly a serious threat to the Reichsführer-SS. Rahn, on the other hand, was a bit more of a liability and—so the theory goes—he had to be killed.

Either that, or Himmler decided to can them both at the same time when reports of Wiligut's earlier hospitalization for mental illness became common knowledge within the SS. But why would news of Wiligut's infirmity have jeopardized Rahn's career?

There is an intriguing note in the definitive study of Wewelsburg by Prof. Dr. Karl Hüser[26] to the effect that Rahn was kicked out of the SS because of his homosexuality. Himmler had a rabid dislike of homosexuals, and through the auspices of Nazi psychiatrists at the Göring Institute tried to have several SS men "cured" of this "malady."[27] Many homosexuals, of course, wound up in concentration camps themselves. Although that was probably not an option with an SS man as relatively well known as Rahn, he was possibly looking at some sort of reprisal in the future, either professionally or in some other way. Unfortunately, we shall never know.

One final possibility—though there is no evidence to support it—is that Rahn himself was the first of the SS men to take refuge in that sad Cathar rite, allowed only to the privileged few, the Perfect; that, in the mountain snows above Kufstein, *and on the anniversary of the destruction of Montségur,* the miserable scholar exchanged the secret of the long-sought-after Grail for that other treasure of the Cathars: the consolation of a noble death.

Holy Blood, Holy Grail

If the Cathars and troubadors—heirs of a Gnostic tradition in Europe, possibly brought over from the Middle East from whence the Templars had brought their own mysterious rites—were crypto-pagans as Rahn believed, and if the set piece of their mythology was the Holy Grail, then it follows that the Grail is not a *Christian* symbol at all but a purely pagan one. And if the Grail is a pagan ikon, then the Nazis— overt pagans as they were—saw in the Grail a sacred instrument of divine power that they could use for their own ends. As the inheritors of the pagan traditions in Europe (at least in their own eyes) the Grail belonged to them. After all, were they not the spiritual descendants of the Teutonic Knights, a chivalric Order that pressed Germany on in a Drive to the East centuries before Hitler's invasion of Russia? Were they not the people of the Runes? The people of the Pure Blood?

Messrs. Baigent, Leigh, and Lincoln might have been more correct than they realized when they entitled their famous book *Holy Blood, Holy Grail.* For them, the Grail was in reality the bloodline of Jesus Christ, preserved down through the millennia and safeguarded by yet another secret society, the Priory of Zion, which the authors link to an underground tradition of Freemasonry and Templarism spanning the centuries and which finds its modern manifestation in the Knights of Malta, Italy's P-2, and other such groups.

Part of the problem lies in the term "holy grail," and in the word "grail" itself. Messrs. Baigent et. al. consider that the term *sangreal* as found in *Le Morte d'Arthur* and other Grail Romances is really composed of two words: *sang* and *real,* that is, *blood* and *royal.* (The term *sangreal* is usually interpreted to mean *san greal,* "holy grail.") It is an attractive theory and to an extent linguistically satisfying since no two authorities can agree on where the term "grail" comes from and what it means. By denying that such a word really has any meaning at all—that it is merely the result of misunderstanding the syllable break in *sangreal*—we have neatly solved the problem of the Holy Grail by revealing its true nature as Royal Blood. After all, the Grail makes its appearance to Parzival alongside a lance that is dripping blood onto the floor. This scene is presented wordlessly, without comment, as if in a dream. Was the intention of the author to communicate the fact that *sangreal* really does indicate "royal blood"? This would have pleased the Nazis enormously if the story had been current at the time, for the Nazis were nothing if not Blood enthusiasts after the Foucault model introduced in Chapter One, and—if they could have somehow linked the concept of "royal blood" with a Teutonic Christ and the Aryan race—they would have had the basis for a new religious synthesis that could have brought together all acceptable Christians and pure-blooded Aryans in one, big, happy (if rather inbred) family.

By claiming the Grail as their own the Nazis rob Christianity of a huge chunk of its popular mythology. The chalice a Catholic priest raises during the Mass becomes a pagan cauldron; the mystery of the Blood of Christ becomes a hollow echo of pagan sacrifice. Appropriation of the Grail symbolism then becomes an assault on Christian faith itself; at least, on the popular faith of the *lumpenproletariat* of Europe, from the Pyrenees to the Alps to the Caucasus.

That the Grail *was* originally a pagan symbol is today virtually beyond debate; that it was appropriated by romantic elements within the Christian world (as was much pagan iconography) is certain. However, had Himmler succeeded in producing an actual "Grail" during the war, the effect on the Christian populations of Europe might have been traumatic. Depending on the spin, it would have signaled either the divine mission of the Nazi Party as true inheritors of the ultimate representation of occult power . . . or the need for a holy war against the black-clad SS, the satanic monsters who had "stolen" God's sacred Cup from the righteous.

As it is, history records no such discovery of the Grail by the Nazis, or by anyone else. Birks and Gilbert claim that there is no evidence that Nazi hierarchs had any interest at all in the Cathars or in Mont-ségur.[28] Yet, Himmler *had* enlisted the talents of a young Grail scholar in a search for the perfect centerpiece for his secret cult headquarters at Wewelsburg, and put his favorite prehistorian, SS-Brigadier Karl Wiligut, in charge of the project. Whether Cathar or Templar, sacred stone or golden cup, finding the Holy Grail was certainly a dream of Himmler's; his Wewelsburg center was beyond any doubt a reverent shrine to the legend of the Round Table. If he eventually gave up on the search, one imagines he did so only with the greatest reluctance.

A final word on Montségur—this time by Sabine Baring-Gould, an author who wrote extensively on history and travel at the turn of the century—is in order, for it shows how Rahn's feelings were shared by a great many people on both sides of the Channel:

> The treasures of the Albigenses . . . have never been recovered; but the true treasure, for which they fought and for which they died, the emancipation of the human soul from the fetters of slavery in which it had been bound by Rome, has been won by nearly all Europe.[29]

⚡ **8** ⚡

The Psychics Search:
For Mussolini, the
Bismarck, Assassins, and
the Human Mind

M ost of what the Ahnenerbe undertook had very little application in the real world other than for propaganda purposes. If they could prove—through their archaeological researches—that the "Aryans" had conquered everything east of the Rhine to the Chinese border, it would have at least justified (in their own minds) their military aggression against most of the world. If they could prove "Aryan" racial superiority through their anthropological experiments at Dachau, that would justify (again, to their own minds) their extermination of the "subhumans." And, if they could come away from the savage medical experimentation in the camps with a coherent scientific study of the effects of various drugs, of freezing and rapid thawing, etc. on humans, then they could justify to themselves the unbelievable sadism of their doctors, such as Sigmund Rascher.

Occasionally, Hitler had to receive verification from his colleagues that the expense of such organizations as the Ahnenerbe-SS was justified. Himmler was under a great deal of pressure to show positive results. After all, he was spending a lot of money on his SS fantasies, including the fabulous shrine at Wewelsburg, which seemed to have no identifiable military purpose. Of course, he was also raising his Waffen-SS as a worthy competitor of the Wehrmacht (the regular German Army) and indeed these elite troops were distinguishing themselves in combat as well-trained, well-motivated, death-defying fanatics. But such competition gave rise to jealousy and suspicion on the part of the old-time generals who had fought Germany's battles with distinction in previous conflicts. And, when the Ahnenerbe's archaeological digs began coming up empty, Himmler was hard-pressed to demonstrate actual value in other areas.

In September 1943 he had his chance.

The Pendulum Solution

When Hitler received word of the imprisonment of Mussolini by the Fascist Council on orders of the king on July 25, 1943, he was understandably distraught. On a personal level, although his political platform did not agree completely with Italian fascism, Hitler still saw Il Duce as something of a spiritual mentor. More importantly, Mussolini was an ally. He had been replaced by Marshal Pietro Badoglio, who at that moment was negotiating with the Allies for Italy's surrender. Only two weeks earlier, Allied forces composed of both British and American units had landed in Sicily and were meeting with less-than-enthusiastic resistance from Italian troops. This crisis caused the implosion at the emergency meeting of the Fascist Grand Council (which had not even met since 1939), resulting in a demand for the restoration of the monarchy under King Victor Emmanuel III; in essence requiring Mussolini's resignation as leader of the armed forces. This was enough to alarm the Führer, but in early September Allied forces had crossed from Sicily onto mainland Italy . . . and Badoglio rushed to sign an armistice with the Western powers. Italy—bereft of Mussolini's leadership—had been handed over to the Allies. Germany had been betrayed.

No matter what, Mussolini had to be rescued and Fascism once more restored to its rightful place in Rome.

But there was a problem. No one knew where Mussolini was being held.

According to Walter Schellenberg, head of the Foreign Intelligence Division (AMT VI) of the RSHA (*Reichsicherheitshauptamt* or Reich's Main Security Office) in his published memoirs,[1] he had no idea where Mussolini had been taken after his arrest by the Carabinieri. The RSHA was an organization created by the notorious Reinhard Heydrich in September 1939 to combine the various secret police agencies (the Gestapo, the SIPO, and the *Sicherheitsdienst des RFSS* or SD) into a single, monolithic police organization under Himmler's control.

According to Schellenberg, Hitler had given orders to find and rescue Mussolini as early as the beginning of August. However, Schellenberg was at a loss as to where Il Duce was being held. And he was already in hot water with the Führer for suggesting that Hitler withdraw German troops to a position on the wrong side of the Po River to aid Badoglio in his efforts to "neutralize" Italy. Hitler considered such reasoning defeatist, and wanted Schellenberg arrested and thrown into prison (at best) or executed for treason (at worst).

Himmler (who prized Schellenberg's abilities very highly and who would come to rely upon him extensively in the last days of the war) managed to run interference, and promised Hitler instead that his intelligence service would find Mussolini. Thus, both Himmler and Schellenberg were extremely motivated in their search for Mussolini, and were willing to try anything.

Schellenberg, though, "had not the faintest inkling of where he was." To go on in his words:

> Therefore, Himmler summoned some of the practitioners of the "occult sciences" arrested after the flight of Hess to Great Britain, and had them closeted in a Wannsee country house. These quacks were given orders to find out the whereabouts of Mussolini.[2]

The "quacks" were quite expensive, demanding the very best in food, wine, and cigars, all of which were paid for by Schellenberg's department. Imagine the scene for a moment, and savor it if you will: people who had been arrested and thrown into the death camps in

1941 were now, in 1943, summoned to the aid of the Reichsführer-
SS, Heinrich Himmler himself, on a mission of great importance to
the Reich. A hairbreadth away from being sent back to the camps if
they failed and possibly being tortured and killed as the very "quacks"
Schellenberg said they were, they instead settled in quite comfortably
and ordered the best of everything: like prisoners on death row requesting their last meal. It was either a mark of incredible audacity or
an indication as to how far gone these individuals were that they were
able to maintain their composure under these terrifying circumstances
and go so far as to make the Foreign Intelligence Service foot a hefty
entertainment bill for their "services." And a hefty bill it must have
been, for it has been the author's experience from direct observation
that occultists in general have tremendous appetites.

For a while it must have been touch-and-go at the country house,
and the anxiety levels of both SS officers and psychics alike must have
risen to previously unrecorded heights. After all, finding Mussolini was
a top priority of the Führer himself. He was counting on the Italian
leader's help in forming a new Fascist government and holding the
line in Italy against the inexorable Allied advance. Moreover, there was
danger on other fronts—notably in the Balkans—of the Italian Army
simply surrendering *en masse* and leaving vast territories to the like of
Marshal Tito of Yugoslavia. Thus, finding Mussolini was no sideshow.

And the outlook for locating Il Duce using psychic powers didn't
seem too optimistic at first. Even Himmler must have doubted the
wisdom of employing his former prisoners in this ultrasensitive intelligence mission.

> Nevertheless, a "Master of the Sidereal Pendulum" succeeded at last in
> locating Mussolini on an island west of Naples. To do this seer justice,
> it must be recorded that at the time Mussolini had no apparent contact
> with the outside world. It was, in fact, the island of Ponza to which he
> had been transferred at first.[3]

In other words, the "Master of the Sidereal Pendulum" had successfully located the most famous Italian prisoner of the twentieth century
. . . and with no more than a decent meal, a few drinks, a good smoke,
and a pendulum swinging over a map of Italy.

It will be remembered that one of Hitler's closest friends was the
"Master of the Sidereal Pendulum" Dr. Gutberlet. Whether or not it

was this same "Master" who worked on the Mussolini problem is not revealed. Yet, Schellenberg's use of the same phrase to describe both men is provocative, if only coincidental.

At the same time, astrologer Wilhelm Wulff was summoned to the office of Arthur Nebe, the head of the Kriminalpolizei and an SS-Obergruppenführer who was also charged with finding Mussolini. According to Wulff's own account,[4] he drew up a Hindu astrological chart and pinpointed Mussolini's location on the same island of Ponza, which had been identified by the "Master of the Sidereal Pendulum." Wulff's success with this and other projects for Nebe led to the Gestapo releasing all of his previously confiscated books and most of his papers,[5] and marked the beginning of his short career as Nazi astrologer working directly for Nebe, Schellenberg, and, eventually, Himmler.

As for Mussolini, he was later taken to a hotel on the top of the Gran Sasso (in the Abruzzi), where he was spectacularly rescued by German commandos and glider pilots under the command of Austrian-born Luftwaffe officer Otto Skorzeny. Skorzeny will figure later in our account in a somewhat more sinister context, but for now let us examine the pendulum swingers a while longer.

The Naval Research Institute

Schellenberg's psychics were not the first pendulum specialists to be employed in an intelligence capacity by the Reich. Earlier, a mysterious department of the German Navy used just such a technique in an effort to locate Allied warships in the Atlantic Ocean.

The best account we have of this agency—referred to rather cryptically by some authors as the Naval Research Institute—is from Wulff's memoir, *Zodiac and Swastika*,[6] in which he reports that he was recommended as a scientific research assistant by his friend, Dr. Wilhelm Hartmann, a Nuremberg astrologer and director of the *astronomical* observatory there in 1929,[7] who was obviously in the good graces of the Nazi regime. Wulff at this time had been recently released from Fuhlsbüttel prison and had been working for a pharmaceutical company.

He had never heard of the institute to which he was now assigned in Berlin, and learned to his astonishment that the navy was engaged in paranormal research of the most extreme variety:

> All intellectual, natural, and supernatural sources of power—from modern technology to medieval black magic, and from the teachings of Pythagoras to the Faustian pentagram incantation—were to be exploited in the interests of final victory.[8]

The man in charge of the top-secret institute was Captain Hans A. Roeder of the German Navy. His "crew" on this astral voyage was composed of specialists in every field from astronomy and astrology to ballistics and spiritualism. The top priority of this motley accumulation of psychics and scientists was the location of enemy ships.

Before the days of satellites and AWACS, there was no reliable method for determining the location of enemy convoys beyond actually seeing them (by which time it was usually too late to do anything about it). Radar and sonar were good only for quite limited ranges. If a system could be developed that would pinpoint the location of battleships, destroyers, cruisers, and supply vessels hundreds if not thousands of nautical miles away, then absolute dominion over the sea could be virtually assured. U-boats could be sent directly to the spot on the map where the enemy convoys had been located and the offending vessels sunk without wandering about for weeks in the open sea looking for targets of opportunity, wasting precious time and fuel.

The navy came up with the idea of using pendulum experts after an experience with an elderly architect by the name of Ludwig Straniak, whose home was in Salzburg. Straniak—a master builder who was also an occultist and author of at least one book on the subject, *The Eighth Force of Nature*—claimed the ability to locate anything with his pendulum, and said that if he were shown a photograph of a ship, he could locate it on a map. The navy decided to give him a try, and Straniak was shown photographs of two of Germany's proudest vessels: the *Bismarck* and the *Prinz Eugen*. Naturally, these were ships whose precise location would have been considered a top military secret for the "unsinkable" *Bismarck* especially was the pride and hope of the whole country. A juggernaut of armed nautical might, the *Bismarck* was the flagship of the new German Navy put to sea in 1941.

Its destruction had become an obsession of the British Admiralty. They would play hide-and-seek with it for weeks in a desperate attempt to sink it once and for all.

Straniak studied the photos of both ships, and then held a small device on a string over a map. A pendulum in this instance can be virtually any small object—like a crystal, a metal weight, a glass bauble, even a paper clip or a nail—tied to a string and allowed to dangle over a map or a chart of numbers and letters (much like a planchette on a Ouija board). Subtle forces are believed to move the pendulum in various directions depending on the question being asked or the information sought. In this case, the pendulum was suspended over a map of the world's oceans and Straniak would slowly pass it back and forth until either the pendulum began to move on its own accord or until Straniak felt a stirring—a weight slightly in excess of the normal force of gravity and possibly pulling in a different direction—and then the position of the pendulum over the precise coordinates of the map would be noted at that time.

Astonishingly, Straniak did what the British Navy could not. He identified the exact location of both ships.

One can easily imagine the consternation of Naval Intelligence officers when it was learned that a man with a string and a weight could sit in a Berlin office building and locate their most prized warship without benefit of advanced electronics or a network of spies. *And it meant that the British, too, might possibly have someone like Straniak working for them,* pinpointing the exact location of their ships and transmitting that information to the submarine fleet. Indeed, the huge losses suffered by the German Navy due to the success of the British Admiralty in locating their ships and U-boats led many to assume an "occult" explanation. (They would not realize until the end of the war that the Brits had cracked the German code system.)

Straniak's success actually irritated some people in Berlin, who—perhaps suspecting some sort of hoax or weird series of multiple coincidences—demanded that Straniak be tested thoroughly to determine the extent of his gift. In one of these tests, a piece of metal was placed on a sheet of paper for a few seconds and then removed. Straniak was then brought into the room and asked to identify the spot on the paper where the small metal object had rested.

The results were consistent. Straniak could identify the precise spot, even when he was not allowed into the room to see the actual sheet of paper used but had to use the same size paper in a different room.

Straniak's odd ability was evidence that there exists in nature a force that science has yet to recognize. As usual, this aggravates scientists. So, men of science were summoned to Berlin to devise even more strenuous tests for Straniak and the pressure on the old man became too much. Straniak began to fail these tests miserably, and then to fall ill. It would be awhile—until the 1943 search for Mussolini—before the pendulum swingers could cover themselves in glory again.

Zen and the Art of Memory

At about this time, astrologer Wilhelm Wulff was brought to Berlin, but on a rather different mission. Wulff's other speciality—beyond Hindu astrology and his own preferred vocation, sculpture—was Asian religion and mysticism, including Hinduism and Buddhism. According to Wulff the Japanese had just captured Hong Kong, and in the process demonstrated to the world their suicidal fanaticism. This would have been in late December 1941 . . . that is, only six months or so after the Hess flight to Great Britain and the roundup of astrologers and occultists that took place, but Wulff puts his internship at the Institute at March 1942, six months after his release from prison.[9]

The Japanese troops had thrown themselves bodily into the attack on well-fortified positions in Hong Kong, anticipating the much-vaunted "human wave" tactic of the Chinese Communists. Japanese soldiers would block the firing apertures of pillboxes and other fortifications with their own bodies. They would rush, screaming, into strongly held positions and fall by the thousands and still not give up the charge. Clearly, the Wehrmacht could use a few divisions of men like that and it was Wulff's job—as a specialist in Asian religion and mysticism—to come up with a proposal on how best to instill such a complete and utter disregard for one's own safety into the common German soldier.[10]

Sadly, we do not have any more information at our disposal on these proposals. We don't know if Wulff completed them, or if the

Wehrmacht eventually made use of them if he did. One thing is certain, of course, and that is that the first SS divisions put into actual combat were models of just this type of "complete and utter disregard" for their own safety. They rushed into extremely dangerous situations and came out victorious. The Wehrmacht had to grudgingly admit their prowess and courage.

The incident at the Naval Research Institute concerning Asian psychological techniques modified for German purposes takes us into another realm of psychic warfare, one that has persisted to this day. As in World War II, the impetus for developing a means of psychologically conditioning combat troops began with a threat from the East. Five years after the end of the war, another one broke out in Korea. This time, American soldiers were returning home from brief periods of captivity in Korea and Manchuria having undergone complete personality changes. The term "brainwashing" became the watchword of a generation of military men, intelligence officers, novelists, and filmmakers, who saw a whole world of terror and unseen saboteurs in the idea of men who could control human behavior—Svengali-like—from afar. As usual, the credit for the invention of this technique was given to unknown masters in the mysterious East.

But brainwashing was more than simply a method for turning liberty-loving American troops into diehard Communists; it comprised the entire field of behavior modification, including the implanting of false memories and the retrieval of true ones. It also concerned the programming of the perfect assassin: one who would kill without regard for his personal safety . . . and then forget who had programmed him to kill, and why.[11]

To these sinister ends an entire menu of devices and theories were employed, from hypnosis to hallucinogens. And the first to experiment with drugs as a means of altering human behavior were the Nazis.

As revealed by statements in Wolfram Sievers's diaries and by other records and Nuremberg testimony concerning medical experimentation at Dachau,[12] the Ahnenerbe was actively involved in a program of experimentation on unwitting prisoners with the use of mescaline. Under SS-Sturmbannführer Dr. Kurt Plötner and an inmate-assistant, Walter Neff,[13] drinks given to concentration camp prisoners were spiked with mescaline and the prisoners observed for signs of altered human behavior.

This experimentation continued right up to the end of the war. An entry in Sievers's official Ahnenerbe diary for February 1945 shows that discussions were being held with SS-Hauptsturmführer August Hirt concerning the use of both mescaline and canabinol by the *Soviets,* and this being coordinated with RSHA Amt VI, in other words, with Schellenberg's own Foreign Intelligence Section. The actual entry reads:

> 14. Drugs for various purposes / for coordination with RSHA, Amt VI, SS-Stubaf. Lassig reference Hirt in connection Soviets employment Caucasian rue (Steppenraute?) with Mescaline (synthetic manufacture) and Canabinol.[14]

It is doubtful that either the Soviets or the Nazis were experimenting or using mescaline for purely medicinal purposes. Hirt, of course, was one of those involved—with Bruno Beger, Oswald Pohl, and Rudolf Brandt—in "anthropological research" carried out at Auschwitz, in which the skulls of POWs and concentration camp inmates were measured in order to develop a standard against which various grades of human and subhuman skull structure could be compared. Sievers's diary for 1943 is full of references to this work being carried out under Ahnenerbe jurisdiction at Auschwitz.

Also being studied—and this, by the notorious Dr. Rascher—was the possible application of Hennyon root extract as a cure for cancer.[15] Rascher also developed his own styptic formula,[16] and one may well wonder just how this particular type of research—the development of an agent to stop bleeding under battlefield conditions—was carried out. One can be forgiven for doubting that the notorious sadist Rascher (whose thirst for other people's pain was exceeded only by that of his wife) used self-inflicted wounds as test samples. In fact, as Nuremberg testimony would eventually reveal, living prisoners were shot at close range to simulate battlefield conditions and the styptic formula then applied to see if it would work.

During this same time, the OSS would not consider falling behind its enemies in mind-control research. A "truth drug" committee under the direction of Dr. Winfred Overholser at St. Elizabeth's Hospital in Washington, D.C.:

. . . tried and rejected mescaline, several barbituates, and scopolamine. Then, during the spring of 1943, the committee decided that *cannabis indica*—or marijuana—showed the most promise, and it started a testing program in cooperation with the Manhattan Project . . .[17]

These are the words of John Marks, who went a long way toward exposing the origins of CIA mind-control research in the bloody laboratories of Dachau in his book *The Search for the "Manchurian Candidate."* And, lest we rest comfortably in the assumption that *our* people were not as ruthless as the Nazis, Marks goes on to record that:

Wherever their extreme experiments went, the CIA sponsors picked for subjects their own equivalents of the Nazis' Jews and gypsies: mental patients, prostitutes, foreigners, drug addicts, and prisoners, often from minority groups.[18]

After the liberation of Dachau, US investigating teams read through the Ahnenerbe and Luftwaffe files on the concentration camp experiments, looking for anything that might be useful in a military application. Marks goes on to note that "None of the German mind-control research was ever made public."[19] Other than the hints of it we can discover in Sievers's diary and similar memoranda, that pretty much remains the situation today. A glimpse, however, into the techniques employed by the Nazis might be had from a look at the famous 1939 attempt on the Führer's life by a possibly psychotic individual named Elser who planted a bomb in a wooden pillar which went off just a few minutes too late to do the world any good.

The Beer Cellar Bombing

Himmler himself was not unaware of the progress of the mind experiments and took an avid interest in their outcome. At the time of the attempt on Hitler's life known as the Beer Cellar Explosion of November 8, 1939, Himmler ordered the suspect—the Swabian engineer Georg Elser—subjected to injections of a "truth serum" called pervitin and, eventually, interrogations by four hypnotists.[20] Thus, even as early as November 1939, Himmler's Black Order was aggressively employing drugs and hypnosis in intelligence matters.

Hitler had just finished giving his usual November 8 speech in honor of the failed Beer Hall Putsch of 1923 and had left the building when a bomb went off right where the Führer had been standing. Oddly enough, Hitler had finished his speech a few minutes *early* as if he were aware of the threat. Anyone familiar with Hitler's speaking knew that he rarely, if ever, cut a speech short. In this instance, his change of habit saved his life—just another instance of his famous intuition at work.

A suspect—Georg Elser—was picked up and the interrogations began. Historians still disagree as to whom Elser was working for, if anyone. Nazis on the scene, such as Walter Schellenberg, tended toward the view that Elser was a psychotic who worked alone and who had planned the assassination attempt for a year before carrying it out. Others were not so sure, and Hitler was determined to show that he had been the intended victim of a conspiracy.

The bombing had the effect of making everyone paranoid. Many Nazi officials agreed with Hitler and feared that Elser had not acted alone in the attempt, but had been conspiring with either a Communist cell, an Allied hit team, or even with an internal cabal of anti-Hitler Nazis. Himmler was certain that two British officers, Best and Stevens—recently arrested by Schellenberg—were Elser's handlers even though Schellenberg knew it wasn't possible. Arthur Nebe, the Nazis' chief Criminal Investigator, had to endure Himmler's other fear that a left-wing Nazi such as Otto Strasser might have been responsible. Himmler—in need of confirmation from *some* source if his own Criminal Investigation people could come up with nothing more substantial than a "crazed, lone assassin"—even went so far as to enlist the aid of a trance medium to scour the aether looking for signs that the dreaded Strasser was to blame.

A further side effect of the Elser bombing was the prediction—by the brilliant if eccentric Swiss astrologer Karl Ernst Krafft (1900–1945)—of an attempt on the Führer's life that very day. Krafft had tried to warn the Nazis of the possibility, but his report was filed and forgotten.

Krafft's contact within the RSHA (the Reich Security Service) was Dr. Heinrich Fesel (1890–1958), an amateur astrologer and yet another student of Sanskrit, who had been recruited by Schellenberg. Fesel worked for AMT VII of the RSHA, the "Ideological Research" Division that handled occultism, Freemasonry, and cults. From 1941–1945, this division had been under the leadership of one Dr. Franz Alfred Six,[21] a scholarly SS-Brigadeführer who earlier became prominent as the leader of the *Vorkommando Moskau:* a death squad that roamed occupied Russia, murdering hundreds of civilians, dissidents, and Jews in 1941. Six joined the SD in April of 1935 when he was only twenty-six years old; in 1939 he became head of AMT II of the RSHA. A year later, Heydrich named him his future representative in Great Britain after the hypothetically successful Nazi invasion of the British Isles. In other words, Dr. Six would have been largely responsible for a program of "ethnic cleansing" in England had the Nazis managed to invade and occupy that country.

Prior to his involvement with the SS, Six had been the dean of the faculty of the University of Berlin, and a professor of law and political science; "one of the most distinguished professors of his generation."[22] He joined the Nazi Party in 1930, long before Hitler came to power.

Dr. Six served about four years of a twenty-year sentence for war crimes after the war before returning to work for the "Special Forces" section of the Gehlen Organization (the spy cabal of ex-Nazis used by the American CIA for anti-Soviet intelligence work) together with longtime Rosenberg friend Dr. Michael Achmeteli and Dr. Emil Augsburg, a Standartenführer with Adolf Eichmann's notorious S-4 department in charge of the "Jewish problem." It is said that Himmler created the bizarre occult research division of the RSHA—AMT VII—specifically for Six, so pleased as he was by Six's enthusiasm for hunting down the enemies of the Reich in Russia during the summer of 1941 at Smolensk.[23]

In 1961, Six was still at large and this time working as an agent for the Porsche automobile company.

Six's former subordinate, Adolf Eichmann, standing trial for war crimes in Israel, had worked for Daimler-Benz, Porsche's competitor. Six—one of the most eager murderers of Jews in the Reich—very kindly showed up in Jerusalem as Eichmann's defense witness.

(As of this writing the scholarly and satanic Dr. Six is still at large and will probably never serve more than those four years in prison long ago for the war crimes he committed with such enthusiasm.)

When the attempt on Hitler had actually taken place, Krafft began pestering the Nazis and calling their attention to his prediction. This was a mortal error, for eventually Krafft ended his days as a guest of the SS and would die in a concentration camp. He was one of many astrologers who came under official suspicion after the flight of Rudolf Hess to Scotland, and wound up arrested and packed off to the camps, even though in Krafft's case he had previously been on Fesel's payroll at AMT VII of the RSHA.

The "affaire Krafft" has been described in great detail by occult historian Ellic Howe in *Urania's Children*,[24] but the salient points should be briefly mentioned here as an indication of the extent to which the Reich used occultists, astrologers, clairvoyants, etc. in a climate of total war.

Although Krafft's peculiar character made him a difficult person to work with, his brilliance seemed to make him, at times, indispensable. He is typical of that type of genius for whom no science has yet been invented; i.e., imagine Einstein having been born in an age when mathematics was virtually unknown. Or Mozart, a child prodigy in music, born to a family of cavemen. That Krafft was a genius is probably without doubt; that he was forced to find an outlet for his genius in such areas as astrology is probably more an indication that whatever Krafft was born for had not yet been invented than evidence that Krafft was somehow congenitally neurotic or paranoid, or intellectually impaired.

A few months after his prediction about the Hitler assassination attempt came true, Krafft was hired by the SS—supposedly under contract to Dr. Goebbels, the Nazi propaganda chief—to compose a translation of Nostradamus's famous prophetic quatrains in such a way that the medieval French seer would seem to be predicting a Nazi victory in the Second World War.

This was obviously to be used in a propaganda effort against the Allies, and at first the task was undertaken with gusto. After a while, though, Krafft experienced pangs of conscience at distorting the message of the ancient astrologer and struggled to make his version an acceptable vision of the original. It should be mentioned that Krafft was an enthusiastic Nazi and sincerely believed that Nostradamus had predicted the Second World War and various German victories.

Eventually, in December of 1940, Krafft's version of the Nostradamus prophecies was published in a limited edition of 299 copies, but it was not enough to save him from the camps. On June 12, 1941—a month after the flight of Hess—he was arrested by AMT IV of the RSHA: the notorious Gestapo. This time, even his highly placed friends in the Party—including the Nazi Governor-General of Poland, Hans Frank—could not help him. Frank himself had attended the meeting with Hitler and Bormann in which it was decided to blame the flight of Hess on the astrologers.

Karl Ernst Krafft—the astrologer who accurately predicted the Beer Cellar Bombing—joined that other famous Hitler seer, Hanussen, in a bitter, undeserved fate, for he died on the way to Buchenwald from Oranienberg concentration camp on January 8, 1945.

ᛋᛋ 9 ᛋᛋ

Cult Counterstrike

It might be assumed from the preceding chapters that the cultic elements of the Second World War were all on the side of the Nazis. This was not the case, as we will attempt to show in this chapter. Several rather famous officers of the British intelligence services were involved in a campaign to anticipate or even counteract the activities of the German cults and their grim reincarnations in the Ahnenerbe-SS, Goebbels's Propaganda Ministry Department AMO (Astrology, Metapsychology, Occultism), the Naval Research Institute, and AMT VII of the SD.

This does not imply that the Allies were taking occultism seriously. They did recognize, however, that the *Nazis* were taking it seriously and for a while it was incumbent upon British Intelligence to discover as much as they could about the various occult sciences adopted by the Nazis in general and the SS in particular. Once they realized that Himmler was listening to his astrologers, they knew that a few good astrologers working for the British could tell them what Himmler's astrologers were telling him.

That there is a certain level of internal consistency in astrology was taken for granted; that is, a Sun-Mars square affecting the first and fourth houses of someone's natal chart—an event that could be identified by simply referring to an ephemeris and a table of houses, astrological tools which are pretty much identical no matter what country one is working in—could be interpreted similarly by both the British astrologers and the Germans; or, at the very least, a British astrologer

240

familiar with the methods employed by his German counterpart would be able to predict with reasonable success what the German astrologer was telling Hitler, Hess, or Himmler. The fact that such planets were in alignment at all was something of which every astrologer anywhere would be aware, and could thus be used in such a way by a capable propagandist to insinuate the success or failure of a military enterprise.

And when the Nazis banned the German occult lodges, they provided the Allies with a useful tool to use against them. The occult lodges had an underground network throughout Europe—replete with coded phrases, secret hand signals, and the like—that could be exploited by the intelligence agencies and it was to this end that secret agents like future novelists Dennis Wheatley and Ian Fleming toyed with the idea of using Aleister Crowley's connections in Germany (and among the secret societies of Europe and America) against the Third Reich.

Crowley Redux

The British War Office had a long memory.

During the Great War it was well known that Aleister Crowley had written pro-German propaganda from a safe berth in New York City. Crowley's protestations that he was really working on behalf of Allied Intelligence interests—from the British Secret Service to the American Justice Department—*seemed* to have fallen on deaf ears back in Great Britain, where Crowley was officially characterized as a "small time traitor" by the former British naval attaché in Washington, Sir Guy Gaunt. However, Crowley's services to MI5 during the period between the wars proved reliable enough, and there is some evidence that he might actually have been telling the truth about his World War I experience in New York. According to at least one researcher,[1] the Americans admitted that Crowley actually *was* working as their intelligence agent while editing *The Fatherland* and *The International,* just as Crowley himself had always insisted. Whatever one cared to believe about Crowley's loyalty and motives, however, by 1941 the situation had changed dramatically.

Hess had been seduced into flying to Great Britain in what was probably one of the greatest intelligence coups of the war thus far (a coup that was badly bungled by the British when it actually occurred, for they did not make the political hay out of it that they could have). But who actually did the seducing? Nazi astrologers who advised Hess in all sincerity to undertake his doomed "peace mission"? A German resistance movement, of which Karl and Albrecht Haushofer were members, feeding Hess false information concerning their connections with sympathetic British nobility?

Or was it another cabal entirely?

While the whole story of the Hess flight may never be known, there is enough evidence to suggest that the occult circle around Hess might have been infiltrated by astrologers working for MI5.

And that's where Aleister Crowley comes in, as one of MI5's oddest—but potentially most useful—secret agents.

In the first place, most of Crowley's cronies on the Continent were being rounded up and sent to the camps. All the occult lodges were banned, from the Golden Dawn to the Masonic Societies to the OTO, and this was especially true after the Hess affair. Ceremonial magicians with outrageous titles of astral eminence were being shoved unceremoniously into Esterwegen and Dachau. Crowley's many German mistresses had probably wound up in similar circumstances (those who had not committed suicide or found themselves in mental asylums beforehand), either as social misfits, "useless eaters" (a term that covered every variety of the physically and mentally handicapped), or simply as guilty by association with Baphomet himself.

But the leadership of the Third Reich was replete with deranged mystics, even after the lodges had been shut and the camps swollen with the presence of Freemasons, Thelemites, Theosophists, Odd Fellows, and Swedenborgians. Some occultists were actually being freed to work for the Nazi cause (as described in the previous chapter). And, interestingly enough, Crowley's old partner-in-propaganda, George Viereck, was still operating his pro-German apparatus in New York City, this time with a decidedly Nazi agenda. Viereck had actually grown somewhat well-to-do on the constant flow of funds coming his way from Party sources in Germany, funds that were paying for his adroit hand at propaganda and disinformation.

Was there a chance that Crowley's connections and knowledge of the occult scene—particularly in Germany, but also in the United States—could be used in a constructive way to aid the Allied cause?

The Devil Rides Out

Dennis Wheatley is the well-known author of dozens of novels as well as a few nonfiction books. It is said that even Hermann Göring was a Wheatley fan, and a Nazi spy in London once communicated to Berlin that Wheatley would make an excellent *Gauleiter* for northwest London after a Nazi invasion![2] In the United States he is perhaps best known for his occult novels of which three—*The Devil Rides Out, To the Devil a Daughter,* and *The Satanist*—stand out as more "hardcore" than the others. These books introduced modern ceremonial magic to Wheatley's audience and combined elements of Thelema—Crowley's cult—with those of some Eastern religious practices and the more staid Golden Dawn rituals and Theosophical beliefs in a hodgepodge of cultures that proved nonetheless exciting to that portion of the market that thrills to tales of Satan worship and secret, worldwide societies that mix sexual initiations with military adventurism (an "Allied" version of the Nazi Bolshevik-Jew-Freemason conspiracy theory). Needless to say, the Thelemites and Satanists both come out looking pretty much the same: lewd black magicians with terrible body odor who live in fear of arousing the displeasure of Lucifuge Rofocale, the British Foreign Office, or some other Demon.

Oddly enough, Wheatley is one of the very few occult novelists who actually met the Beast himself. According to his own account—published in *The Devil and All His Works*—he found Crowley a wonderful conversationalist and had him to dinner several times.[3] In another place in the same book—a nonfiction summary of occult practices and beliefs with an emphasis on the seamier side—he mentions casually that he worked with Churchill's own Joint Planning Staff during the war in a basement under Whitehall.[4] What he neglects to mention (for fear of arousing the wrath of Lucifuge Rofocale? or of being prosecuted under the Official Secrets Act?) is that, laboring in an intelligence capacity along with that "other" spook novelist, Ian Fleming, he actually once considered using the services of Aleister Crowley around the time of the Hess flight.

This was not so strange as it might seem. In the first place, of course, it was well known that Hess was mystically inclined and deeply involved with astrology. The German resistance movement knew that the Haushofers had secretly turned against the Führer, and that the Haushofers were also—if only peripherally—involved in occult practices; indeed, it was an open secret that Albrecht Haushofer was something of an astrologer himself, or at any rate an educated layman.[5] Who better to debrief Hess the Egyptian-born mystic than another mystic, one with strong ties to the German occult movement: Aleister Crowley himself?

Further, it was probably no secret at all to American and British intelligence officials that deep within the United States' own rocket program—and thus engaged in a highly classified race against the Nazi scientists at Peenemünde—lurked another Thelemite and member of Crowley's OTO, the brilliant engineer Jack Parsons.

Parsons was involved in rocket fuel research, principally of the "solid-fuel" variety, and therefore his work was vital to the war effort and to the subsequent space program. A charter member of Cal-Tech and the Jet Propulsion Laboratory, Parsons is probably the only known occultist—and certainly the only Thelemite—who has a crater on the Moon (dark side) named after him.

Although this is not the space to go into the Parsons story in detail, some information is necessary to show the extent to which Crowley's organization was involved in magick and the war effort on the side of the Allies and on both sides of the Atlantic.

In 1939, Jack Parsons became involved with Crowley's OTO through the Agapé Lodge of California, then being run by one W. T. Smith, who had been a Thelemite since 1915 via the Vancouver Lodge under Charles Stansfeld Jones ("Frater Parzival"), an accountant and a very early member of the OTO from the first days of Crowley's rulership of the Order's English-speaking world community. In 1942—a significant year as we shall see—Crowley removed Smith from leadership of the Agapé Lodge and installed Parsons as its chief.

The Agapé Lodge was run from Parsons's home in Pasadena, where rituals were held daily and from where Parsons would collect membership dues, etc. and forward them to Karl Germer on the East Coast, who would send them on to Crowley in London. In other words, this OTO Lodge was being run more or less openly during the war by a man—magickal name "Frater 210"—simultaneously involved in critical work for the war effort, under the spiritual guidance of a former concentration camp inmate who corresponded regularly with a man accused of being a former German spy, now living in London!

Parsons joined the Guggenheim Aeronautical Laboratory, California Institute of Technology (GALCIT) in 1936, working for Frank J. Malina and Theodore von Karman at Pasadena on various problems related to rocket propellants.[6] Once America entered World War II, the need for discovering a reliable solid propellant became crucial, particularly if the Navy was to develop JATO (Jet Assisted Take-Off) aircraft.

Try as they might, the GALCIT people could not come up with a workable formula. The fuels they developed had a tendency to deteriorate after only a few days, making them impossible to transport and store aboard ship. All the different types of black powder fuels were tested and scrapped.

Finally, it was Jack Parsons who came up with the solution that enabled America to enter the rocket-propelled aircraft race. In 1942—the year he became head of the Agapé Lodge and moved its headquarters into his home—he decided to abandon the black powder concept altogether and came up with a solution that could only have come from someone with a working knowledge of the arcane lore of alchemy and magic: Greek fire.[7]

To this day, no one really knows how he intuited the switch from black powder to asphalt and potassium perchlorate. But it worked, and was GALCIT's first breakthrough of the war. The solid propellant designed and formulated by Jack Parsons became widely used by the US Navy in 1944 and 1945 with great success.[8]

Parsons himself, however, became the subject of what might have been a Federal investigation into his occult activities during the war. In April 1945—the month the war ended in Europe—he became involved with one "Frater H," who proved a disastrous companion for Frater 210. Claiming he was working either for Naval Intelligence or the FBI or even, oddly, LAPD—depending on the source you believe, if any—Frater H succeeded in virtually destroying Parsons's life and his grip on reality. Performing various rituals of sex-magick and angelic invocations with Frater H, Parsons believed he had contacted some of the same higher powers with which Crowley had conversed

in Cairo in 1904; he even went so far as to communicate these beliefs
to the Great Beast himself, without going into details, pledged as he
was to a pact of secrecy with these alien beings. Crowley rightly assumed that Parsons was being made a victim of some sort of confidence trick just as the mysterious Frater H was absconding with
money from a joint account he held with Parsons and wound up actually marrying Parsons's girlfriend.

By 1948, Parsons had declared himself the Antichrist. By 1952,
Parsons—now known as "Belarion Armiluss Al Dajjal Antichrist"—
would drop a vial of fulminate of mercury at his home laboratory
and with the resulting explosion one of the more brilliant—if terribly
sad—figures in contemporary occultism would be dead at the age of
thirty-eight. Upon hearing of her son's death, his mother committed
suicide the same day.

"Frater H"—the man who was most responsible for leading Parsons
into madness by (among other things) stealing his money and his girlfriend—was none other than science fiction author and Scientology
creator L. Ron Hubbard.

In addition to people like Parsons in America, Crowley's contacts
throughout Europe were numerous and they involved a wide range of
people from society-type spiritualists who dabbled in ritual magic to
coffeehouse intellectuals and artists of various persuasions to the lowest
rungs of civilization. His utility to MI5 during his Berlin days, when
he spied on German Communists, was not forgotten. Further, he had
been cultivated by Dennis Wheatley, who found the occult fascinating
and who eventually—according to Anthony Masters—became a low-
level initiate in what must have been one of Crowley's own magickal
lodges, the A∴A∴ or the OTO.[9] The ostensible reason for this was to
study magic under the Master, so that he could lend an air of veri-
similitude to his occult novels. Anyone interested in seeing how much
Wheatley absorbed merely has to pick up any of the three above-
mentioned books and study them carefully. The reader will find
Crowley's A∴A∴ degree structure used and many of the incantations
and rituals (in appropriately abridged forms) shamelessly exploited for
dramatic effect.

Crowley was introduced to Wheatley by the journalist Tom Driberg, who would later become a Labour MP and who for years served

as an MI5 spy inside the Communist Party of Great Britain.[10] (Driberg, referred to as "Z" in Wheatley's book, joined the Communists and dutifully reported back to MI5 until being discovered by British spymaster and Soviet mole Anthony Blunt, who had him kicked out of the Party.) While Wheatley admits he found Crowley fascinating, he did not feel the Great Beast merited the degree of awe and fear that his followers and detractors, respectively, accorded him. It was Driberg who was quick to point out that Crowley did, indeed, possess marvelous occult powers but, alas, that the ritual in Paris had all but killed him.

This story—which became one of Wheatley's favorite tales and which is repeated in several of his books—has Crowley invoking the Great God Pan in the upstairs room of a hotel on the Left Bank along with the assistance of his "son," the pseudonymous MacAleister. Evidently the ritual (like the proverbial surgical operation) was a success, but the assistant died. Crowley himself—according to this tale— spent four months in a mental asylum after being found completely naked and curled up in fetal position in a corner, gibbering. Needless to say, this story does not appear in any of the official biographies of Crowley but it's a great story, nevertheless.

(It should be pointed out that John Symonds—whose biography of Crowley, *The Great Beast,* was published in 1951—refers to Mr. Driberg's loan of Crowley's diaries on his acknowledgments page without giving us a clue as to how Mr. Driberg—Wheatley's "Z," Member of Parliament, and British secret agent—managed to be in possession of them in the first place, so soon after Crowley's death in 1947.[11] Was the story about the Paris evocation of Pan contained within those very pages?)

Wheatley—who was friendly with many of the twentieth century's most famous occultists, including the reincarnationist Joan Grant and the author Rollo Ahmed (whom he may have once tried to recruit into MI5)[12]—also had an abiding interest in crime and detection. It was in this connection that he happened to meet one of the most famous names in the history of British intelligence, Maxwell Knight.

Knight was the prototype for Ian Fleming's character, "M": the Intelligence chief whom we always see in the movies giving Sean Connery or Roger Moore his dangerous, "license to kill" assignment. What is not generally known is that "M" was also introduced to Aleister Crowley—by Dennis Wheatley—and was actually quite friendly with the Magus.

Wheatley had met Knight at a party and the two hit it off right away. Knight wanted to get a book published, and Wheatley helped him to publicize it. What they eventually realized is that they also shared an interest in the occult.

Wheatley invited Knight to dinner at his home when he knew Crowley would be there, and the three of them became quite friendly. Wheatley and Knight approached Crowley on the subject of *magick* (Crowley's version, spelled with a "k" to distinguish it from both legerdemain and from other, lesser, forms of magic), and Crowley agreed to take them on as students. This has got to be one of the most startling, if amusing, situations imaginable; for here is Maxwell Knight— "M" after all—accepting a kind of occult initiation from Aleister Crowley and becoming his pupil![13] Himmler was obsessed by the idea that British Intelligence was being run by the Rosicrucian Order and that occult adepts were in charge of MI5 (a view still held today by such political eccentrics as Lyndon LaRouche). How would he have reacted had he known that the formidable Maxwell Knight, head of Department B5(b), the countersubversion section of MI5, was a disciple of Aleister Crowley himself? And that Dennis Wheatley—he of the occult novels favored by Göring—was also a student of Crowley's and simultaneously working for Churchill's Joint Planning Staff?

Oh, how the black candles would have burned that night!

Particularly if Himmler had also been told that yet *another* British secret agent—this time James Bond novelist Ian Fleming of the Department of Naval Intelligence—was plotting to bring Reichsleiter Rudolf Hess to England on an occult pretext involving . . . Aleister Crowley.

As this story is told in several places by respected historians of the British Secret Service,[14] and thus has the seal of authenticity, it is worth repeating here for the benefit of those not normally involved in such research.

It is generally agreed among the various sources that the outlandish idea of capturing Rudolf Hess—a man largely viewed as Hitler's second-in-command at the time—began with Ian Fleming. Fleming, who had been a banker before the war, wound up at the Department of Naval Intelligence in what was essentially a desk job. Hungering for more dramatic employment and realizing he would not get it at DNI, he turned instead to Knight, who had a reputation for being something of a maverick (and who had, more importantly, a direct line to Churchill through yet another mutual friend of Wheatley and Knight, Desmond Morton). Basically, the idea was this:

There had been a rather subversive organization in Great Britain known as The Link. The Link was ostensibly an Anglo-German "cultural society" once under the auspices of a Sir Barry Domville, who had also once been Director of Naval Intelligence from 1927 to 1930, but who had since been interned because of his pro-Nazi sentiments and connections. The Link had been under Knight's surveillance in the 1930s and then dissolved when enough evidence was found implicating it in espionage activities and the like.

Fleming—whiling away his time behind a desk at DNI—had been reading the files on Domville and an idea occurred to him.

He thought that if the Nazis could be made to believe that The Link was still in existence, they could use it as bait for the Nazi leadership. The point was to convince the Nazis that The Link had influence sufficient to overthrow the Churchill government and thereby to install a more pliable British government, one which would gladly negotiate a separate peace with Hitler.

But whom among the Nazi leadership was naive enough to fall for the story?

Rudolf Hess had always been something of an Anglophile and it was known through intelligence sources—probably by way of the Haushofers and their Resistance circle—that he was anxious for peace with England so that Germany could concentrate on defeating Russia, the "real enemy." Hess also had a reputation for being something of a gullible sort who surrounded himself with mystics and stargazers.

It was but a short leap from there to realizing that Knight's friend and occult mentor, Aleister Crowley, would be quite useful in such a context. Also, it is possible that Fleming—poring through the DNI files as he was—had come across Sir Guy Gaunt's World War I records on Crowley. Gaunt, it will be remembered, was Britain's naval attaché in Washington during that war, and therefore DNI's man in America. He also ran an effective espionage campaign in the States that kept an eye on pro-German activities, and was even running agents inside the Austrian Embassy. Gaunt had succeeded in arranging the capture of an important German saboteur—Captain Franz Rintelen von Kleist, who was responsible for several explosions at US arms factories—and eventually retired to Tangier with the rank of admiral. When Crowley's hostile biographer, John Symonds, wrote to Gaunt concerning Crowley, it was Gaunt who agreed with Symonds that Crowley was just a "small time traitor."[15] Gaunt had kept Crowley and *The Fatherland* on his list of usual suspects, and had discussed him with A. J. Balfour (the Foreign Secretary) and Basil Thomson (the Secret Service's liaison at Special Branch, Scotland Yard) advising them both not to worry about the Great Beast, that Gaunt had everything under control.[16] Unfortunately, owing to the Official Secrets Act and the strange, twilight landscape of the secret services, we shall probably never know Gaunt's real take on Crowley.

Fleming and Knight pondered the problem for a while. Crowley's personality was such that the two spies were unsure how far they could control him in the field. Even more importantly, Crowley's intelligence contacts were probably well known to the Germans since his early Berlin days spying on Communists for the British; thus, Crowley's cover was probably already "blown" in spook parlance, although the well-publicized raid on OTO headquarters in London in reprisal for Crowley's ostensibly pro-German activities during World War I might have been used to convince the Nazis that Crowley was really their man.

However, they turned to astrology. Via a Swiss astrologer known to Fleming, astrological advice was passed on to Hess (again, via the Haushofers and by Dr. Ernst Schulte-Strathaus, an astrological adviser and occultist on Hess's staff since 1935) advocating a peace mission to England; further, the Duke of Hamilton was persuaded to let it be known that he would entertain a visit from Hess for just that purpose. May 10, 1941, was selected as the appropriate date since an unusual conjunction of six planets in Taurus (that had the soothsayers humming for months previous) would take place at that time.[17] The aspect would signal important and long-lasting developments in the mundane world. It was a most auspicious time for an undertaking of global ramifications, and this was precisely the day Hess chose to fly, solo, to Great Britain to meet with the Duke of Hamilton to discuss a peace treaty between England and Germany that would allow the Nazis free rein on the Continent and particularly against the Soviet Union. (It is for this reason that the Soviets steadfastly refused to allow Hess to leave Spandau Prison after the Nuremberg Tribunals; Hess's mission—had it been successful—would have permitted the destruction of the Soviet Union and the probable massacre of most of its population by the SS.)

Indeed, to Hitler both the astrologers *and* the Haushofers were guilty of some kind of conspiracy. In what was eventually known as the *Aktion Hess,* the astrologers were rounded up and sent to the camps while Albrecht Haushofer was picked up for questioning by the Gestapo.

The rest, as they say, is history. On that day, coincidentally the date of the last major air raid on Great Britain, Hess made the flight, landed in Scotland, and was promptly arrested. Oddly, however, the British government did not make the use they could have of this outstanding intelligence coup and Hess languished in prison. Fleming tried to obtain permission for Crowley to debrief Hess in order to develop intelligence on the occult scene in the Third Reich and particularly among the Nazi leadership, but suddenly the "secret chiefs" turned cold toward the idea.[18] For reasons which were never made clear—and which probably had more to do with internal British politics and the danger of exposing a genuine pro-German cabal of traitors high up in the British government—Hess was treated as a pariah almost from the moment he landed and a chance to learn once and for all about the genuine extent of an Occult Reich was lost forever. The idea that Hess had been lured to Scotland by British Intelligence—and possibly with the help of the American OSS—was suspected by many in Germany. When Hess's Messerschmidt was inspected by aeronautical engineers, for example, they found numerous examples of American-made parts, including the tires and the gas tank, which gave rise to rumors that the Allies had been more than cooperative in the effort to ensure the Reichsleiter made it safely to Scotland.[19] What is more mysterious is why, once Hess had arrived safe and sound on British soil, he was then totally ignored and the incident shrugged off as the act of a madman, much to Hitler's relief as it was identical to the way *he* was handling it in Germany. What could have been a major propaganda coup against the Nazis went utterly wasted, as if by tacit agreement on both sides.

Crowley's efforts to help the British war effort did not end with Hess, however, for he plied MI5 with all sorts of plans for occult propaganda. According to published sources, these were not implemented. Yet, there was one cult countermeasure that smacks of Crowley's fine Thelemic hand. In a way, it *had* been recommended by Crowley, but its execution was left to another section of British intelligence led by Sefton Delmer of the Political Warfare Executive.

Astrological Warfare

Crowley felt that profit could be gained by dropping occult pamphlets from planes onto the German countryside.[20] While the exact nature of these proposed pamphlets has never been revealed, it seems safe to say that they would have at least contained predictions about the outcome of the war and descriptions of the Nazi leadership as "satanic," etc., and perhaps even details of the occult practices—both real and invented—of the Nazi elite. While that idea was rejected, a similar one was eventually developed on both sides of the Channel.

While the Swiss astrologer Krafft was working up his faked Nostradamus predictions (as described in Chapter Eight), there was yet another astrologer working for the spooks, this time for the Department of Psychological Warfare in London. Holding the rank of captain in the British Army, Hungarian-born Louis de Wohl made much of his connections with Nazi astrologers and managed to convince the Secret Service that he could be of inestimable value to the war effort.[21]

This was to be exploited in two ways. In the first place, de Wohl could inform British Intelligence of what the Nazi astrologers were telling Hitler, Himmler, and the rest of the leadership. In other words—since he was familiar with the methods employed by those astrologers closest to the halls of power in Berlin—he would know when Hitler was being advised to attack or retreat, negotiate or fight, declare war or sue for peace.

In the second place, he could be counted on to provide falsified astrological information that would be disseminated among the Ger-

man astrological community, causing them to counsel peaceful negotiations and to advise the Nazis of the impossibility of winning the war.

To this end, a forged version of the popular German astrological
magazine, *Zenit,* was produced by de Wohl and his collaborators—
among them the noted occult historian and wartime spook Ellic
Howe—and dropped behind enemy lines. Virtually identical to the
original *Zenit* (down to the classified ads), it nonetheless contained
subtle Allied propaganda in the form of astrological advice.

It would be the annoyingly helpful Wilhelm Wulff who would be
handed a copy of the magazine and who would identify it as a clever
British forgery to Schellenberg, all the while marveling at its authentic
appearance. Crates of it had been intercepted on the way into Germany from Sweden, and the publisher's name had been given as the
famous Dr. Korsch, an astrologer who had died in the camps years
earlier. Thus, while it would not have fooled the Nazis themselves, it
might have succeeded in alarming the general population, which was
starved for astrological advice anyway. As it is, we shall never know
the extent to which the forged *Zenit* could have been useful for, as
mentioned, crates of it were seized by the Gestapo before they could
be distributed. But another occult operation of the British intelligence
services did work admirably well.

An OBE for an OBE?

The intelligence operative known by her code-name, Anne, probably
never received the Order of the British Empire (OBE) for her amazing
work for the Secret Service during World War II, but she certainly
deserved it for she performed one of the most amazing feats of intelligence gathering of that or any war. She penetrated to the heart of the
Reichswehr in Berlin, copied classified documents, and reported on
secret conversations between military leaders . . . and all without leaving her armchair in London. She did it by utilizing her special gift of
astral travel, what New Agers today refer to as "Out of Body Experience" or . . . OBE.

This charming and intriguing story is given in only one place the
author is aware of, a book entitled *Women in Espionage* by a former

Czechoslovak government official whose book on Rudolf Hess—*Hess: The Man and His Mission*—appears in many World War II bibliographies. The official's name is J. Bernard Hutton, and he claims to have tracked down and met the mysterious "Anne" . . . who unfortunately remained loyal to the Service (and to the Official Secrets Act) and would not divulge any details of her exploits on behalf of MI5. However, he was able to determine that "Anne" had one day appeared at the office of an "Intelligence chief" with a sealed letter of recommendation from one of his friends. I like to think this "chief" was Maxwell Knight, whose tolerance for the occult was no secret, but that is pure speculation on my part.

No matter. "Anne"—a former ambulance driver whose poor health had forced her to retire—professed to be able to obtain information on Nazi military intentions by "mind-traveling": that is, she would lean back in a chair, close her eyes, and "travel" to the place desired and eavesdrop on what was being said. She could even read documents and—with her photographic memory and command of the German language (the result of some student years spent in Berlin and Zurich)—relay their contents completely and accurately upon her "return."

Anne was tested several times by the Service, and found to be quite reliable. She was then "sent" on various intelligence assignments to Germany and parts unrecorded, successfully bringing back the war-critical data as required. Mr. Hutton reports that Anne's information was treated with respect and that "British political and military strategy was influenced and helped by Anne's reports."[22]

Compared to the trance medium employed by Himmler to uncover the conspiracy behind the Beer Hall explosion, Anne wins by a landslide. One wonders if any Nazi psychics were ever aware of Anne's spiritual form wafting through the halls of the Reichswehr, the Reichstag, or perhaps even the bedrooms at Hitler's Berchtesgaden retreat, recording everything she saw with her ethereal—yet lethally photographic—second sight?

The Yonkers Connection

Lest the reader come away with the suspicion that the cult counter-strike was strictly a British affair, the author hastens to point out one particularly interesting American contribution, in the person of Samuel Untermyer.

Sam Untermyer was reportedly a member of the Golden Dawn in New York City,[23] and was well known in local legal and political circles as something of a philanthropist as well as a formidable attorney. According to investigative journalist Maury Terry, a British newspaper called Untermyer a "satanist."[24] To the British press, of course, this could have meant anything from Theosophist to cannibal. Considering Untermyer's accomplishments and sentiments, however, the author tends to agree that, if anything, he truly was a member of the Golden Dawn.

In 1903, he purchased the former estate of Samuel Tilden in Yonkers. Tilden was famous for his unsuccessful bid for the presidency against Rutherford B. Hayes in 1876. This property—known as "Greystone"—became a public park after Untermyer's death in 1940, and it would be here at Untermyer Park (within walking distance of David Berkowitz's Yonkers apartment) that the Son of Sam cult would have its earliest meetings—and where it sacrificed dogs to Satan— thirty-seven years later.

But Untermyer was also well-known for his persistent anti-Nazi crusade in New York, a crusade which began in 1933 with Hitler's accession to power in Germany and which did not end until Untermyer's death in March 1940.[25] Untermyer was tireless in promoting a boycott of German products under the aegis of his "Non-Sectarian Anti-Nazi League to Champion Human Rights" and the "World Anti-Nazi Council." The World Anti-Nazi Council was a truly global organization, with representation in Asia, Africa, and South America as well as in Europe. Untermyer even financed a touring exhibit of Nazism across the United States in the mid-1930s. More than that, however, he also threw his considerable resources behind the hunt for Nazi agents who were pouring into the country from freighters and steamship lines at New York's west-side piers. As evidence in various Congressional investigations at the time had shown, Untermyer's was a name the Third Reich had learned to fear. In May 1935 Sam Untermyer enlisted the aid of a volunteer investigator, Richard Rollins, in a campaign of counterespionage against the various Nazi and Fascist gangs who were openly and aggressively recruiting in the United States at that time, primarily under the leadership of Fritz Kuhn, the notori-

ous head of the German-American Bund, who was on the payroll of
the Third Reich and who had marched in Berlin at the head of a Bund
column during the Olympics. Rollins was named chief investigator for
a secret society, referred to only as "the Board" and under the leadership of Untermyer, composed of individuals and organizations whose
identities have never been revealed.

Rollins went on to great success against the Bund, the Silver Shirts,
the Black Legion, and the Klan, among others, always with the discreet
but powerful force of Samuel Untermyer and "the Board" behind
him. How this old Golden Dawn initiate and tireless anti-Nazi cru-
sader would have felt about his beloved Greystone estate being used
for Satan worship is left up to the reader's imagination.

In Rollins's published memoir of his anti-Nazi escapades—*I Find
Treason*—we discover a bizarre account of the fascist Black Legion
initiation ritual, whose oath is revealing, indeed:

> In the name of God and the Devil, [it begins] and by the power of light
> and darkness, Good and Evil, here under the Black arch of heaven's
> answering symbol, I pledge and consecrate my body, my limbs, my
> heart and my mind and swear by all the powers of Heaven and Hell
> that I will devote my life . . .[26]

The oath goes on to include a Masonic-type injunction that, should
the initiate break his oath, he will be torn to pieces, scattered over the
earth, and so forth, and ends with "In the name of God and the Devil,
Amen." What interests us here, however, is the invocation of both
God *and* the Devil: a peculiarity that will crop up again in the neo-
Nazi Process Church of the Final Judgment, a group that (as we shall
see in Chapter Thirteen) has been implicated in several of the twentieth century's most ghastly crimes.

Thus, as we have been at pains to prove, the cult war was not en-
tirely one-sided. The stories about Louis de Wohl, Aleister Crowley,
Jack Parsons, Dennis Wheatley, Ian Fleming, Rudolf Hess, Ellic
Howe, Maxwell Knight, and the mysterious Anne all demonstrate that
British Intelligence took the occult aspects of the conflict very seriously
and—like their Nazi counterparts—exploited whatever it could, no

matter how bizarre or "unscientific," to ensure final victory and the survival of its people. Everyone reading this book already knows who won that conflict; but perhaps they are not aware of the occult ramifications of the final *Götterdämmerung* and of its legacy to a new generation of cultists and Nazis.

III

WITCHES' SABBATH
IN AMERICA

America? You must be mad! . . . Oh, a witches' sabbath is on the way! Pity we can't be there in the midst of it. Do you suppose . . . that there is any more solid a world over there, across the big ditch, than among us here?

—GAULEITER KOCH

⚡ **10** ⚡

Walpurgisnacht, 1945

I'm positive there's going to be the maddest of Witches' Sabbaths. The Americans have all those characteristics of ours which up to now have made us the disturbers of the world. But they have a country with almost inexhaustible resources. . . . Over there radicalism can sweep away literally into infinity. Up to now America has still remained an old-world country, only reupholstered a bit. The real world has still to come into existence. Depend upon it, it will come.[1]

—Gauleiter Koch

Hitler came to power in Germany on a day sacred to the pagan calendar, and would die by his own hand on another sacred day. As there are only eight days of major pagan importance—called Sabbaths in modern parlance—the odds against this must be pretty high.

For those interested in such coincidences—perhaps what Swiss psychologist (and sometime Nazi admirer) Carl Jung would have called "synchronicity"—I submit the following in addition to the November 9 coincidences mentioned in Chapter Four:

April 30, 1919. The seven Thulists are murdered by the Red Army in Munich.

April 30, 1945. Adolf Hitler commits suicide in Berlin as the Red Army advances on the city.

Also:

April 30, 1975. Saigon falls to the North Vietnamese Communists.

Thus April 30 had grim associations for not only was it the famous Witches' Sabbath of German folklore but the day on which the seven Thulists—the Ur-Nazis—were murdered by the Reds. While it provided the spark that ignited the popular revolt against the Bavarian Soviet, it also served to oust Baron Sebottendorff from the Thule Society and thus to rob the cult of its most charismatic and powerful leader. If we were to take only the above three dates as a guide, we might be forgiven for thinking that April 30—the Witches' Sabbath—is an auspicious day for Communism as well, and that their celebration of May Day is perhaps but another indication that, on some level, they realize this. But what about the Witches' Sabbath that *Gauleiter* Koch speaks about in the quotation above? Is America—North *and* South America—ripe for conflagration?

We have focused on the Nazi Party as a cult, and the Third Reich as a government of dark initiates. Black magicians, if you will. This is not a traditional perspective on German history, but the author believes it is vitally important that we come to terms with this aspect of the Third Reich if we are to understand its current manifestations around the world. From the Skinheads of Germany and America to Colonia Dignidad in Chile and from the underground SS organization in South America, Asia, and Africa, to the domestic racial violence of the United States, this phenomenon is not comprehensible in purely economic, political, or social terms but as a virtual religious movement with its ikons, its litanies, its satanic rituals. Its bloody sacrifices. But didn't the Nazi cult effectively die in Berlin on April 30, 1945 with Hitler's suicide?

Of course not; if nothing else, his death can be seen as a martyrdom to the Luciferian cause he represented and is, even now, being viewed that way by those of his followers who keep the black candle of their unholy faith brightly lit.

The Final Days

Since the disastrous defeat of German forces at Stalingrad in 1943, Hitler's much-vaunted powers of intuition began to fade, and fade quickly. This was something that was noticed by many of his associates, and remarked upon in their memoirs.[2] Stalingrad seemed to rob the Occult Messiah of his strength, and he began to withdraw more and more from his inner circle of friends and acquaintances. He grew even more short-tempered than usual, and started to make serious strategical mistakes. Ignoring the advice of his generals, he demanded victory after victory, refusing to retreat or to listen to appeals to negotiate with the Allies. The idea of negotiation, to Hitler, was tantamount to treason. Offenders would be sent to the camps.

Then, of course, came the D-Day invasion of June 1944 and suddenly Europe was swarming with well-armed and well-fed British and American forces. A month later, and a cabal of patriotic but terrified German officers and civilians planned and carried out the assassination attempt on Hitler by placing a bomb in a briefcase beneath a conference table where Hitler was discussing military strategy with his staff. The bomb went off, but the Fuhrer (once again) miraculously survived.

As in the Röhm purge ten years earlier, Hitler demanded the death of the traitors who had conspired against not only himself but Germany. Guilty and innocent alike were either executed or offered suicide as a way out. The unfortunate victims of "Operation Thunderstorm" included Professor Karl Haushofer and his eldest son, Albrecht. As we saw previously, Professor Haushofer was sent to Dachau, where he survived the war. Albrecht was imprisoned in Berlin and later taken out—ostensibly to be moved to a safer location as Russian shells were falling on the city—and shot against a wall on a side street. Albrecht's connections with the Resistance movement had become known; what is not known is the extent to which the Gestapo ever discovered his putative involvement in the disastrous Hess affair.

The search for traitors and would-be assassins involved in the July plot continued right up to the last days of the war: to April 1945.

Himmler's final days are ably recorded by his favorite astrologer, Wilhelm Wulff, in *Zodiac and Swastika,* and in the memoir of the man who hired Wulff, Foreign Intelligence chief Walter Schellenberg, as well as in Felix Kersten's memoirs. What is remarkable about all of these is the picture they give us of the terrified head of the most dreaded police force and secret society in modern history—second, perhaps, only to the Office of the Holy Inquisition itself—asking Wulff for astrological updates on the political and military situation as the war was rapidly coming to an end. Kersten and Schellenberg were trying to get Himmler to commit to a deal with the Allies through the mediation of the Swedish government and the World Jewish Congress, but Himmler's constant indecision from day to day and hour to hour made it impossible to reach any kind of settlement. Himmler would keep referring to the oath of loyalty he took to the Führer as being sacred; this enabled him to feel he had a moral reason for what was really moral cowardice. Himmler was continually being advised to have Hitler either arrested or shot, and to take over the country and negotiate with the Allies; but his fear that the plan might possibly fail (after all, Hitler had already survived several assassination attempts) made him choose to do nothing and bear those ills he had, rather than fly to others he knew not of. Further, Wulff had advised Himmler that Hitler would not die from an assassination, although his aspects for the end of April looked particularly bleak. A prognostication like that only seemed to confirm Himmler's worst fears.

In the final days of the conflict, Wulff was by Himmler's side day and night, ready at a moment's notice to cast a chart . . . even going so far as to accurately predict Allied air raids; a talent the Nazi High Command might have made better use of much earlier in the war.

Wulff was summoned to Himmler's quarters at Harzwalde on the day Germany learned of the death of U.S. President Franklin Roosevelt—Friday, April 13, 1945—and told to bring all his charts with him, including those of Martin Bormann, Albert Speer, Seyss-Inquardt, Count Schwerin von Krosigk and Field Marshal Schörner to see who among them might be appropriate for the formation of a new German government. He also brought the charts of Churchill, Eisenhower, and Montgomery to determine the outcome of peace negotiations with them through Count Bernadotte of Sweden. To understand how desperate Himmler was for this type of astrological advice, it must be remembered that transportation and communication services were all but nonexistent at that late date in the war. Wulff was at his home in Hamburg, and the fact that a phone call got through to him at all is amazing in itself. Hamburg was being heavily bombed at the time, and the phone and electrical lines were severely damaged.

Wulff was then expected to negotiate his way—with the car and driver reserved for him by Himmler—along the shell craters, bombed-out vehicles, wounded soldiers and civilians, and the corpses of the less fortunate along the road, meanwhile dodging lethal strafing runs by Allied planes, just to be able to arrive at Himmler's hideout to (in effect) read him his daily horoscope.

Alas for the Reichsführer, he had waited too long. Events were running along faster than anyone had thought possible. Wulff spent Hitler's fifty-sixth birthday at Harzwalde with Himmler, Schellenberg, Kersten, and a representative of the World Jewish Congress, pondering the gloomy situation and trying to negotiate—unsuccessfully—for the release of ten thousand more Jews.

In the last days of April, Wulff finally managed to extricate himself from the deadly scene at Harzwalde and made his way home to Hamburg. A few weeks later, and his most famous astrological client—Heinrich Himmler—would be dead by his own hand after chewing a cyanide capsule while a prisoner of the American forces.

Thousands of miles away, Rudolf von Sebottendorff—the man who started it all in rented rooms of the Four Seasons Hotel with a "literary-cultural" society, an occult society known as the Thule Gesellschaft—ended his own life by drowning himself in the Bosporus, grieving for the end of the Third Reich he had helped to create in those heady days on the streets of Munich when the swastika banner was the symbol of all that was good and right in the world, the last best defense against the horrors of Communism and the Jewish-Bolshevik-Masonic conspiracy to rule the globe.

But not all the Nazi cultists were dead by war's end, not by any means. Some of the most notorious would remain alive to stand trial at Nuremberg, while still others would go into hiding aided and abetted by one of their sworn enemies, the Roman Catholic Church.

The Vatican Rag

The mass destruction of files that took place at the end of the war is one indication of how aware the Nazis were of their culpability for acts that would be considered heinous by the rest of the world. Most of the *Lebensborn* records were destroyed, for instance, rendering the tracing and identification of babies born out of wedlock or stolen from their homes in the Occupied Territories virtually impossible. Thousands of people now alive today in Germany and in the rest of Europe as well as in North and South America do not know who their parents—and particularly their fathers—were. Many are the descendants of high-ranking officials of the SS who were encouraged to "breed" with the racially pure maidens of the *Lebensborn* communities.

The records of many of the concentration camps were also destroyed as the relentless advance of Allied troops brought them closer and closer to the murderous estates. The results of medical experimentation on prisoners were particularly sensitive and haste was made to destroy both the documentary evidence and, where possible, the physical evidence as bodies—and body parts—that had been experimented upon were burned in the crematoria.

But another indication of Nazi guilt lies in the fact that many of the SS dived underground immediately it became apparent that they had lost the war, and that the Allies were condemning the *Schutzstaffel* as a criminal organization; this was certainly a precedent in modern history, for the armies of the vanquished are generally disarmed and the divisions dissolved, but rarely have all the members of an entire military and police apparatus been declared criminals *prima facie.* This was not so of the regular German Army, the Wehrmacht, which was immune from such treatment. The horror and outrage of the Allies was reserved solely for Himmler's secretly occult and openly pagan Black Order, and for the doctors who helped carry out sadistic medical experimentation under the aegis of the Ahnenerbe-SS.

This resulted in an underground movement of SS personnel across Europe and out to North and South America and North Africa. The Order functioned, even in defeat, as solidly as it had during the days of victory. Safe houses and secret transportation were arranged for the SS, who were being hunted all over the world. Some SS officers, confident that their identity was successfully concealed, remained behind in Germany to help organize this "underground railroad" and are still there today, as numerous reports and published research have shown. The secret and often lethal ODESSA was not merely a fantasy of fiction writer Frederick Forsythe; it existed then (in various forms, from the fiendishly effective *Die Spinne* to Hans Ulrich Rudel's *Kamaraden-werk*) and still does as I write these lines.

What does seem fantastic, however, is the assistance given to many of these men by what was always believed to be their sworn enemy: the Roman Catholic Church. While Ladislas Farago—mentioned in the Introduction to this book—must be credited with bringing this story to worldwide attention,[3] it is useful to know that, since then, it has been corroborated many times over by other authors.[4]

Why would the Catholic Church help the very men who had vowed to eradicate it, who had participated in pagan rituals designed to re-place those of Christianity, who worshipped Baldur and Thor and Freya in candlelit ceremonies in the forests and castles of Bavaria, Thuringia, Westphalia, and the other German *Länder?* Men who had caught and imprisoned thousands of Catholic and Protestant clergy-men, sent them to the camps, and executed them in cold blood?

Was it simply that the Church found common cause with Nazi anti-Semitism, and figured it would help them now and deal with Nazi paganism at a later date? Or was it more practical than that? Did the Church hope to negotiate a separate peace with the Nazis so that they both could concentrate on "the real enemy": international Com-munism?

There is certainly enough evidence to suggest that both of the above rationales played parts in the Church's unofficial policy toward the SS. In the early days of the Party, few German Christians of any denomi-nation would have been upset by the blatant anti-Semitism shown by Hitler, Streicher, Darré, Rosenberg, et al. Hitler very carefully sought to cultivate Christian (and especially Catholic) support for the Party as they remained a substantial voting bloc within the country. Indeed, the Catholic Center Party played a pivotal role in Reichstag elections that catapulted Hitler to power. And just as he wooed the financial support of leading industrialists in contradiction to his personal beliefs concerning the evils of that "Jewish invention," Capitalism, he also courted the powerful Catholic and other Christian lobbies in the country. He knew he could not afford to alienate them entirely from his program, at least not until after he had won the war; for this reason he occasionally found it valuable to attack occultism and *völkisch* pa-ganism in his speeches, even while encouraging it among his entourage and condoning its manifestation in the SS.

On its side, the Roman Catholic Church played a similar game of *realpolitik* with the Nazi Party, while at the same time many Catholic priests performed heroic service underground in rescuing Jewish and other potential victims from the camps. But there were those Catholic officials who found themselves in secret agreement with much of the Nazi platform, particularly where the potential threat of Russian Communism was concerned. Pope Pius XII, for example, was notoriously silent regarding the fate of the Jews and was eager to avoid any confrontation with the Nazis. He jumped to praise the Führer, however, when the latter moved against the "godless Communists" in the East. Like many of his contemporaries, he figured the Allies were shooting in the wrong direction.

It should be remembered that this was not an unusual position to take. Many otherwise respectable Allied leaders felt quite similarly. Even General Patton was known to have growled on occasion that they had fought the wrong enemy, and lobbied for permission to take his famous spearhead right into the Soviet Union.[5] It was this attitude that—directly or indirectly—permitted many war criminals who had committed ghastly crimes against humanity to escape forever the long reach of the Nuremberg Tribunal and even, in some cases, to find themselves working in official capacities for the Allied intelligence services in their Cold War against the Soviet Union.

While Patton may represent the peculiar stance of a United States Army four-star general, it would be Bishop Alois Hudal who would carry the fascist flag for the Vatican.[6]

Born—probably in Austria—on May 31, 1885, he was ordained a Catholic priest in 1908. The parallels between his career and that of Lanz von Liebenfels are striking. In the first place, both were Austrians, born within eleven years of each other (von Liebenfels was born on July 19, 1874, in Vienna-Penzing). Both entered the Catholic priesthood, with von Liebenfels entering the Cistercian novitiate in July of 1893 and taking his solemn vows in September 1897, eleven years before Alois Hudal.

Hudal became a professor of Old Testament and Oriental languages; von Liebenfels, under the direction of the anti-Semitic novice-master Nivard Schlögl, also studied precisely Old Testament and Oriental languages and would later (in 1905) become such an acknowledged expert in this field that he was chosen to be one of the editors of the *Monumenta Judaica,* a collection of early Hebrew and Aramaic sources for the books of the Old Testament, along with a panel of Jewish and Protestant scholars. Von Liebenfels was selected as the Catholic editor because of his unequaled knowledge of these ancient texts. The first five volumes of this series had appeared by 1908, so it is certain that Hudal would have been quite aware of his *Landsman,* Lanz von Liebenfels.

What is even more certain is that, as the years went by, Hudal would have become an admirer of von Liebenfels's work in the Pan-German community for Fr. Alois Hudal himself became something of an Armanist and fellow traveler. Just as von Liebenfels became the head of his own order of knights, the Order of the New Templars, Hudal became Procurator General of the Order of German Knights, a Catholic institution.

And, on May 1, 1933—in honor of the pagan holiday approved by the Nazis and known as Walpurgis or Beltane to the Celts, celebrated with the famous Witches' Sabbath at midnight—Father (now Bishop) Hudal presided over a meeting in Rome attended by over seven hundred members of the German expatriate colony there, including many Church officials, Nazis, and Nazi leaders such as local SA and Hitler Youth officials. On that occasion, he made a fiery speech defending the Nazi Party and its program in a blend of Catholic and Teutonic slogans, ending with the battle cry of Arminius (the hero of the Pan-Germans, *völkisch* cultists, and Aryan mystics) in the Teutoburg Forest: "German unity is my strength, my strength is German might." It was Arminius who was the inspiration for Guido von List's *Armanen-schaft,* the cult that List formed to worship Wotan and to instigate a return to the old, pagan, ways of the ancient Teutons. For Alois Hudal to invoke Arminius at this gathering in Rome was tantamount to aligning himself with the neo-pagan, Pan-German, *völkisch* movement represented by List, Liebenfels, and Sebottendorff.

This strange little man then went on to publish *The Foundations of National Socialism* in which he outlined and defended the Nazi Party programs, including the exclusion of the Jews, in no uncertain terms. Soon, his efforts in combating Marxism—a legacy of his friendship with the future Pope Pius XII, Eugenio Pacelli, which dated from 1924—became widely known as the *Aktion Hudal* in Nazi circles. Like many anti-Communist and pro-Nazi Catholic leaders such as

Archbishop Ivan Buchko of the Ukraine (who managed the incredible escape of the entire Ukrainian Waffen-SS division of eleven thousand men plus their families to North and South America and Australia),[7] Monsignor Krunoslov Draganovic (who helped the Croatian Fascists escape justice, many to Argentina),[8] and lay Catholic Gustav Celmins of the Nazi Latvian organization Perkonkrusts and leader of the Latvian SS (who became an important member of the notoriously anti-Communist Intermarium Society[9] of the Roman Catholic Church which, in addition to helping Nazi war criminals escape justice, also served as an arm of German intelligence), Hudal was greatly admired in Nazi circles and every effort was made to cooperate with his underground network of spies and collaborators even as official Nazi policy remained stridently anticlerical.

Intermarium itself is interesting, not least because one of its goals was the establishment of a new Holy Roman Empire of Eastern European nations encircling the atheistic Soviet Union.[10] Intermarium developed a close working relationship with Alfred Rosenberg,[11] who was not only the Nazis' chief pagan ideologue but also a Baltic native who was tremendously sympathetic to anti-Soviet causes of any kind. After the war, many Intermarium notables became involved with the CIA and other Western intelligence services. On Intermarium's agenda was the formation of an exile army of anti-Communists, many of whom would be former Nazis, to defend Europe's borders against the Soviet Union and eventually to partition the USSR into small, separate ethnic enclaves á la the Alfred Rosenberg and Heinrich Himmler plans.[12] This involved dividing and conquering the Soviet state and thus eradicating the "cancer" of Communism forever while ensuring that the Russians could never again consolidate their power and threaten the world. Intermarium, like Hudal's Caritas Internationalis, was to provide escape routes and "ratlines" for fleeing Nazis for many years, supplying the necessary passports and travel documents as well as steamship fare to ports all over the world. One wonders how today's Roman Catholics would feel about their Sunday donations, Widow's Mites, Peter's Pence, and other charitable contributions being used to help finance the survival of Heinrich Himmler's Black Order.

Some of the beneficiaries of Hudal's operation—which was being run by Cardinal Montini (the future Pope Paul VI) in his capacity as Vatican Secretary of State—include Heinrich Müller, the Gestapo chief who once debriefed astrologer Wilhelm Wulff, Walter Rauff, who was in charge of the mobile gas vans in which thousands of Jews were murdered, and (alleges Farago and many other European officials) Hitler's second-in-command, Martin Bormann himself. Müller disappeared at war's end and followed the ratline to Argentina along with Eichmann, Mengele, and so many others, comforted in exile with a suitcase full of American dollars. Rauff turned up in Chile. Bormann—according to Farago—did them all one better, and arrived in Buenos Aires dressed as a Catholic priest, a Jesuit.

In what must be one of the most sickening scenes to any believing Catholic is that of Bormann—as "Father Augustin"—*celebrating Mass* at the Cathedral of San Juan de Dios in La Paz, Bolivia, where he escaped when Argentina became too hot. (Klaus Barbie would find a safe house with another Nazi "priest" living in Bolivia, in this case a Croat war criminal—see Chapter Eleven.) He also performed weddings, baptisms, and other sacraments while serving in the role of "auxiliary priest." This, of course, is the ultimate blasphemy. The most-wanted war criminal in the world, a devoted Nazi since the 1920s, special assistant to pagan mystic Rudolf Hess and third in line for leadership of the Reich after Hitler and Göring, a man whose womanizing was excused by his wife because by fathering children out of wedlock he was only doing his sacred duty by the Fatherland to produce as many Aryan citizens as possible . . . this man with the blood of millions on his hands, celebrating Mass and dispensing Holy Communion to the faithful in the fiercely Catholic country of Bolivia . . . what Black Mass could ever be Blacker?

And they call Aleister Crowley a Satanist!

We will return to the exiled Nazi leaders in the next chapter for they are the springboard to today's problem of neo-Nazism, neo-Fascism, and racism around the world. As recent discoveries have made clear, many hundreds (if not thousands) of Himmler's Black Order managed to escape capture and set up shop in South America where they still wield tremendous influence.

Nuremberg

Not all the SS men managed to flee, however. Some of the worst names in German history were captured alive. Alfred Rosenberg, the

Baltic-born architect and rabid anti-Semitic, anti-Christian ideologue from Hitler's early days in Munich with Dietrich Eckart was captured and made to stand trial. Rosenberg was sentenced to death, and alone of all the condemned Nazis nearly collapsed from fright on the way to his execution.

Hermann Göring, defiant to the end, took his own life in his prison cell rather than permit his captors to do the honors.

Hess—whose story has occupied so many of these pages for it highlights the extent to which occultism was employed on both sides of the conflict—was spared execution but was sentenced to life imprisonment at Spandau; *real* life imprisonment, for the Russian vote made it certain that he would never be paroled even after many attempts by British and American authorities to have him released on humanitarian grounds. The Soviets felt that Hess had gone to Britain to arrange a separate peace so that Germany could invade Russia with impunity. World Jewish leaders wanted Hess to stay in Spandau since he had been a signatory to the infamous Nuremberg Laws, laws which robbed Jews of their rights as German citizens and as human beings, and which paved the way for the atrocities of the camps. They felt, and quite rightly, that life imprisonment was better than Hess deserved since his policies had helped exterminate many millions of innocent human beings.

When Hess died the *New York Times* ran a cover story on his life,[13] and tried to explain why the British did not exploit the Nazi's flight to Scotland as well as they might. To the British psychiatrists, Hess was a borderline madman. As proof, they cited his interest in astrology, his paranoia, and his lapses of memory. (One wonders what they would have made of Ronald Reagan. Where was British psychiatry when we needed it?)

But an interesting sidelight to the Hess story concerns one of the *Allied* inheritors of Nazi medicine, particularly in the area of mind control.[14]

The above news story notwithstanding, British psychiatrists had already examined Hess and decided he was sane enough to stand trial, but the Americans wanted to perform their own examination. For this purpose, the Scotland-born Dr. Ewen Cameron was sent to Germany to interrogate Hess and draw up a psychological profile of the Reichs Deputy. Before he was able to do so, he was approached by Allen

Dulles, the man who was so successful running spies for the OSS (America's precursor to the CIA). Dulles asked Cameron to perform a small service for him during the course of his examination.

There was reason to believe—said Dulles—that the man in custody was not Rudolf Hess at all, but a double! He asked the astonished Dr. Cameron to find some way of getting Hess to show Cameron a scar he should have received from an accident he had long before the war. If the scar was there, it was probable that the prisoner really was Hess. If it wasn't, then the man was an impostor and perhaps a plant by British Intelligence to disguise the fact that they had executed the real Hess soon after his arrival in Scotland.

Needless to say, Dr. Cameron agreed to Dulles's request and—during the course of many hours of intense psychiatric examination—attempted to get the prisoner to remove his shirt for a routine physical. The guard, however, refused to allow Hess to remove his handcuffs to enable the examination, saying that he had no such authorization. Cameron had to return to Dulles with the sad report that he was not able to verify whether the man in the prison cell was the infamous mystic Rudolf Hess.

Cameron's failure did nothing to cool Dulles's appreciation of his talents, however, for the psychiatrist soon became the architect of the CIA's notorious Montréal-based mind-control project at the Mount Royal clinic in the late 1950s and early 1960s, a project whose goal was to discover a means of countering the effects of Russian and Chinese brainwashing and to develop an American version for use as an offensive weapon. The experiments were nearly the equal of anything the Nazis themselves had come up with under the aegis of the all-powerful Ahnenerbe-SS and were, indeed, based at least partly on the results of those concentration camp experiments, the records of which had been confiscated by American intelligence, becoming part of CIA and Pentagon files shortly after the Nuremberg Tribunals. As CIA investigator John Marks points out,[15] the records of Ahnenerbe-SS experimenters Dr. Kurt Plötner and Walter Neff regarding mescaline and hypnosis research at Dachau were sent back to the States and never revealed. Thus, the files of Nazi brainwashing, interrogation, and mind-control experiments using drugs, hypnosis, and torture—techniques associated today with the worst of America's religious cults and secret societies—are still classified if indeed they survived at all the famous shredding of MK/ULTRA documents ordered by Richard Helms in the 1970s.

In a related development, Hess's final statement before the Nuremberg Tribunal on August 31, 1946 was never finished. As it seemed he was in danger of rambling on forever, the president of the Tribunal ordered him to cut it short and history was cheated out of a bizarre tale of mystical phenomena (or saved the dreary task of recording the paranoid fantasies of a mass murderer, depending on your point of view). But there are elements within Hess's statement that bear repeating here for they either cast doubt on the pronouncement of his sanity (and thus question his fitness to stand trial) or they are evidence that *some* form of mind-control was being tested on Hess while he remained a prisoner in the Tower.

> Some of my comrades here can confirm the fact that at the beginning of the proceedings I predicted the following:
> . . . That witnesses would appear who, under oath, would make untrue statements while, at the same time, these witnesses could create an absolutely reliable impression and enjoy the best possible reputation. . . . That some of the defendants would act rather strangely: they would make shameless utterances about the Führer; they would incriminate their own people; they would partially incriminate each other, and falsely at that. Perhaps they would even incriminate themselves, and also wrongly. . . . All of these predictions have come true. . . . I made these predictions, however, not only here at the beginning of the Trial, but had already made them months before the beginning of the Trial in England to, among others, Dr. Johnston, the physician who was with me . . .[16]

At this point, one would imagine that Hess was simply being realistic. It was not unusual for the Nazi defendants and witnesses to invent all sorts of stories and alibis to excuse away their crimes (Sievers is just one possible example); Hess may have tried to insinuate that the prosecution witnesses were all lying. The Nuremberg jurors were certainly in no mood to entertain such a notion, and that might have been the end of it except that Hess went on to say:

> In the years 1936 to 1938 political trials were taking place in one of these countries. These were characterized by the fact that the defendants

accused themselves in an astonishing way. For example, they cited great numbers of crimes which they had committed or which they claimed to have committed. At the end, when death sentences were passed upon them, they clapped in frenzied approval to the astonishment of the world.

But some foreign press correspondents reported that one had the impression that these defendants through some means hitherto unknown, had been put into an abnormal state of mind, as a result of which they acted as they did.[17]

Here Hess is obviously referring to the infamous show trials which had taken place in Stalinist Russia. It should be remembered that the Soviet Union formed one-fourth of the Nuremberg Tribunal, along with France, Great Britain, and the United States. Later on in his statement he specifically mentions the "Moscow trial." One imagines that this is a decidedly unwelcome tactic on the part of the defendant.

Hess goes on to link the method used to mentally condition these Russian defendants to the acts of otherwise sane Germans carrying out atrocities in the camps. His implication is that mind-control was used in a massive way to robotize the German population. He wisely drops that rather pathetic line of approach, but then his statement takes on a strange angle all its own:

I said before that a certain incident in England caused me to think of the reports of the earlier trials. The reason is that the people around me during my imprisonment acted towards me in a peculiar and incomprehensible way, in a way which led me to conclude that these people somehow were acting in an abnormal state of mind. Some of them— these persons and people around me were changed from time to time. Some of the new ones who came to me in place of those who had been changed had strange eyes. They were glassy and like eyes in dream. . . . Not only I alone noticed these strange eyes, but also the physician who attended me at the time, Dr. Johnston, a British Army doctor, a Scotsman.

In the spring of 1942 I had a visitor who quite obviously tried to provoke me and acted towards me in a strange way. This visitor also had these strange eyes. Afterwards, Dr. Johnston asked me what I thought of this visitor. He told me—I told him I had the impression that for some reason or other he was not completely normal mentally, whereupon Dr. Johnston did not protest as I had expected, but agreed with me and asked me whether I had not noticed those strange eyes, these eyes with a dreamy look. Dr. Johnston did not suspect that he himself had exactly the same eyes when he came to me.

The essential point, however, is that in one of the reports of the time, which must still be in the press files on the proceedings—this was in Paris, about the Moscow trial—it said that the defendants had had strange eyes. They had had glazed and dreamy eyes![18]

This Kafkaesque monologue goes on to cover British concentration camps (implying that the Nazi camps were no worse, and that concentration camps in general must be an internationally recognized means of solving what Hess calls "incomprehensible riddles"), and then winds up with a speech in which Hess is clearly leading up to an exposition of just what exactly happened to him in the spring of 1942, prefaced by oaths to God that he will tell the truth and calling God as his witness.

"In the spring of 1942" he begins, then is cut short. The president of the Tribunal tells him he has already used up his twenty minutes. Hess demurs, then agrees to end his statement by simply saying, "I am happy to know that I have done my duty to my people, my duty as a German, as a National Socialist, as a loyal follower of my Führer. I do not regret anything. If I were to begin all over again, I would act just as I have acted, even if I knew that in the end I should meet a fiery death at the stake . . ."[19] A fiery death at the stake. Hess imagining himself as heretic, or witch?

Was Hess insane? What *had* happened to him while he remained a prisoner of Great Britain? *Why* was his flight to Scotland not exploited in a more obvious manner? What was the relationship between the mysterious, Scottish-born Dr. Johnston and the Scottish-born Dr. Cameron, the mind-control expert? The author feels certain that, owing to the Official Secrets Act, we shall never know the whole story about the Nazi's most famous mystic, Rudolf Hess.

As for Hess himself, who practiced yoga conscientiously while imprisoned in Spandau, he never abandoned his occult beliefs and was said by his wife to be in constant telepathic communication with her until the day he died.

And what about Martin Bormann? Did he really die in Berlin in the final days as has been reported? Or was Farago right? Did Martin Bormann escape to South America?

Ironically enough, as I write these lines in the early days of 1994, new evidence has come to light to suggest that the much-maligned Ladislas Farago may have been correct after all. Hundreds of files newly released by the Argentine government of President Menem show that many more Nazis managed to flee to South America than had ever been previously imagined, not even in the wildest dreams of veteran Nazi hunters.[20] Included in these records—which consist of official files of the Argentine police and intelligence services—are the faint traces of *el gran fugitivo.* As the files reveal, the American Ambassador to Argentina had come into possession of intelligence that neatly confirmed Farago's claim that Bormann had managed to make his way into Italy through a series of safe houses and then shipped out to Buenos Aires. Due to a typographical error in transcription, the province to which Bormann had subsequently fled was incorrectly identified and the Argentine officials—at that time, working for the administration of pro-Nazi and pro-Fascist Juan Perón—shrugged their shoulders and replied that they could not help the American authorities as no such town existed in that province!

These newly released reports will, hopefully, help vindicate the late Mr. Farago's efforts to track down the most famous Nazi war criminal of all, and rehabilitate his most controversial work, *Aftermath.*

The Interrogation of Wolfram Sievers

The Ahnenerbe, for all its reputation for horror, is mentioned only rarely in the forty-two-volume set of the published Nuremberg Trial transcripts. The interrogation of Wolfram Sievers covers less than fifty pages in total,[21] and most of the evidence at the time was in the form of his Ahnenerbe *Tagebuch* or diary and which contained references to the camps and to the hideous experiments that took place under his stewardship. It is from his diary that we learn, for instance, of former SS-Tibet Expedition member Dr. Bruno Beger's involvement in the "anthropological research" being undertaken at Auschwitz. We learn of the Ahnenerbe's medical experimentation involving cancer cures, coagulating agents, and low- and high-pressure research using human guinea pigs, freezing research using prostitutes to "thaw out" frozen concentration camp prisoners, etc. In the coagulation experiments, for instance, living human beings were shot with live ammunition to create wounds to which would be applied various experimental styptic formulas to see which could be used in the field as an interim measure to stop bleeding until proper medical attention could be obtained.

Before the Tribunal, Sievers did his best to extricate himself from the medical experimentation taking place at Dachau and Auschwitz under his jurisdiction, and even went so far as to claim he was actually a member of the Resistance—calling on his old friend Dr. Friedrich Hielscher (who was imprisoned by the Gestapo for his role in the July 20, 1944, assassination plot against Hitler) as a corroborating witness[22]—but the Nuremberg jurors weren't having any. Sievers admitted to being present at some of the above-mentioned experiments, and other witnesses put him on the scene of many more. Sievers, who claimed to be little more than the business manager for the Ahnenerbe and a relay center for reports, "one of these distinguished Nazi post offices" in the words of one Nuremberg attorney,[23] was eventually prosecuted himself during that series of trials (the Doctors' Trials) which took place after the celebrated Nuremberg Trials of Hess, Göring, et. al., at which he testified.

Wolfram Sievers—Himmler's aide and chief of the Ahnenerbe—was given the death sentence and executed in 1947.

The records of the Ahnenerbe, however—some ninety microfilm rolls at the National Archives alone—remain a treasure trove for the historian of the bizarre. It is an enlightening task to wade through the thousands of documents detailing research in astronomy, anthropology, ethnology, archaeology, Icelandic lore, Celtic studies, rune symbolism, Tibetan religion, the World Ice Theory, and Norse paganism and to realize that this massive undertaking by hundreds of university professors and serious academics was pointed directly at world conquest and genocide. These Nazi academics and "mythologians"—the Joseph Campbells and Mircea Eliades of their country in some cases—were as at home in the foul abbatoirs of the death camps as they were in the lecture halls of the great German universities. To them, Auschwitz and Dachau were simply other forms of laboratory and schoolroom; higher education in the lower depths . . . a continuation of scholarship by other means.

Many of these men escaped justice. The former Catholics and Protestants who had become converts to Nazi paganism—and there is truly no fanatic like a convert—made their way to freedom and, as numerous interviews by a wide range of journalists has shown, they remained (and remain) unrepentant: true believers in the Cult of the Black Order, Himmler's *Schwarze Orden.* And, as they grow old and die, they leave behind a new generation of believers who carry on the rites of a new faith—sometimes in secret, sometimes openly—in their adopted lands.

⚡ **11** ⚡

Aftermath

This year, think twice about Germany.

—LUFTHANSA AIRLINES
Advertising slogan, circa 1970

With the dispersal of Nazi war criminals throughout the world—aided and abetted by elements within the Catholic Church and the Central Intelligence Agency—the cult of the Nazi Party was preserved. It would have been in any case, for—like Satanism, the cult with which it is popularly associated—its symbols and rhetoric have survived in the documentary films, newsreels, histories, novels, and in popular movies and television shows.

The Nazi underground has been glamorized to a large extent, particularly by Hollywood. Such films as *The Boys from Brazil* and *The Odessa File*—both based on best-selling novels—help perpetuate the idea of a secret society of evil geniuses bent on world domination through mad science and single-minded politics; in other words, a typical cult (if a bit more successful and affluent than most). The Nazi image is a coherent one, much more comprehensible and identifiable than that of the armies and nations that opposed it during the war. It had a single symbol, the swastika, and a single leader, Hitler. It had an elite priesthood of murder and ritual, the elegantly black-clad SS with its silver death's head emblem. Nazi fashion and regalia have even survived today in the erotic fantasies of many sadomasochists and other fetishists, and it shares this peculiarity in common with satanism and "black magic."

By comparison, American propaganda films made during the war show a casual, wise-cracking, gum-chewing, sloppy, unshaven, and generally disheveled GI as the epitome of Allied resistance to the Nazi threat. That was supposed to make Americans feel better. The enemy was impeccably dressed, spoke fluent English with an exotic accent (our boys knew about four words in German, two of them being "mach schnell"), never had a hair out of place, and had Continental manners even when torturing spies. And, of course, scenes of the concentration camps and the mass murder of Jews virtually never appear in these films as it took years before the Allies would officially admit that the death factories even existed. The anti-intellectual, deliberately unsophisticated pose of the typical American GI—as depicted by Hollywood—was supposed to be somehow equivalent to moral superiority: a troubling perspective that exists to this day in our entertainment media and even among our politicians and religious leaders. Brilliant students are portrayed in television sit-coms as hopeless, socially maladjusted "nerds" in vain competition with the handsome but brain-dead jocks who have become teen idols. Former vice president and convicted felon Spiro Agnew was famous for his attacks on what he called "pseudo-intellectuals," and a glance at former President George Bush's bedside reading would make a high school English teacher blush. Nixon himself, besieged on all sides by protesting college kids, had an abhorrence of the intelligentsia as revealed in his famous Watergate tapes. As the author once had occasion to remark to some survivors of China's Cultural Revolution in Beijing, intellectuals are treated as the enemy in every country: in China as Capitalists, in America as Communists. They agreed.

Somewhere along the line, somewhere between Joe Goebbels and Joe McCarthy, Americans began believing—and embracing—their own propaganda.

And those Americans for whom intellectual and cultural sophistication held certain attractions that could not be matched by Iowa corn-country square dances or homespun Bible Belt homilies found them-

selves having more in common with the Hollywood image of the typical SS officer than with the type of American GI portrayed by, say,
Frank Sinatra, John Wayne, or Henry Fonda. As a certain, subtextual
cultural identification with the SS began to take place among our basically intelligent but incompetently educated American youth it would
not be long before *political* identification would occur . . . with unfortunate consequences.

As they filtered into South America, the escaping Nazi refugees
brought with them their brotherhood, their talent for organization,
and all their old loyalties. They had also become a criminal organization, one that was—at least on paper—being hunted down by the
nations of the world. Branded as international criminals, it was no
great moral leap from the name to the game. They became involved in
the drug trade, arms dealing, and international terrorism. The unholy
alliance between Nazi war criminal Klaus Barbie and fascist Italian
terrorist Stefano delle Chiaie in Bolivia is just one example among
many.

Unlike other "patriotic" organizations that, forced underground,
became criminal societies—the Sicilian Mafia and the Chinese Tongs
come readily to mind—the Nazis did not abandon their core beliefs.
They retained their religion of anti-Semitism and Teutonic superiority, and the rest of the world continued to identify Nazis this way. In
Argentina, they began to reissue their primary tracts. Everything from
Mein Kampf to the *Protocols of the Elders of Zion* was republished in
Spanish-language versions for the edification of the masses. Moreover,
such men as Wilfried von Owen—a senior aide to Propaganda Minister Joseph Goebbels—would retire peacefully to Buenos Aires to write
neo-Nazi tracts for publication in Europe.[1] The Nazis came to realize
that not all South Americans were "subhumans"; many were the children of German, Swiss, and Italian immigrants who had come to
South America over a hundred years ago during various migrations,
just as they had to the United States. Although they were now the
Spanish-speaking citizens of Colombia, Bolivia, Argentina, Chile,
Uruguay, and Paraguay (for instance), their blood was still "racially
pure."

South America had been a magnet for Nazi personalities even before
the war began. Ernst Röhm, the SA commander who was murdered

in the famous purge of 1934, spent several years training troops in Bolivia after the Beer Hall Putsch. Max Sollmann, one of the youngest participants in the Putsch and the future *Lebensborn* leader, lived for many years in Colombia after 1923, returning to Germany only in 1934.[2] Richard Walther Darré, the pagan high priest of the Third Reich, was born in Argentina. And, of course, Baron Sebottendorff himself traveled throughout Latin America in his incarnation as a Mexican consul.

For those who find this odd it should be recognized that in Latin America generally, and in Argentina, Bolivia, and Chile in particular, there is an element of the population that still considers itself "European" as distinct from the local "Indian" peoples. Europe is worshiped from afar as the natural homeland of these second-, third-, and fourth-generation Italians, Germans, and others. European fashion, literature, music, and cuisine are preserved—as if in a time capsule—in major cities like Buenos Aires in Argentina; in Bolivia, the German population forms the cultural and economic elite of La Paz; and in Chile there is an entire region of the country—centered in Valdivia—where the local newspaper and even the street signs are in German; and where, during the war, the Nazi Party was firmly entrenched.

This was the environment in which the fleeing Nazis suddenly found themselves. It was congenial, familiar, and in many cases all too anxious to accommodate men the rest of the world considered monsters but who were greeted as if they were a European government-in-exile. All this, coupled with the fact that many Nazis were cooperating with the American intelligence services and had the protection of the Church, ensured that even the local national governments would go out of their way to see to it that they were not inconvenienced by extradition requests, arrest warrants, and the other annoying demands of international law. Also, many Nazis came with their own funds: enormous sums of money that had been embezzled from the Party treasury or stolen from their Jewish victims.

But South America was not the only place Nazis found refuge. Nazis—particularly Nazi scientists—were welcomed in certain Arab countries in North Africa and the Middle East (Otto Skorzeny's assistance to the Nasser regime in Egypt is well known, for instance) and, of course, we had our own Nazi elite serving in the American space program including, but not limited to, Dr. Wernher von Braun. Many

Nazis, including former SS officers, worked for American intelligence services in Europe after the war. And future President Richard Nixon himself assisted in the protection of known Nazis both in his home state of California and as vice president under Eisenhower.[3]

And in Switzerland, perhaps one of the more outlandish Nazi survivals yet: admirers of *Ostara* publisher and Hitler mentor, Lanz von Liebenfels, who survived the war he midwifed and who died on April 22, 1954.

The Abbey of Thelema

Before we follow the ratlines of the Nazi Cult to North and South America, a glance at its European survivals will do us well. As I write these lines [1994], a neo-Fascist has just won a tremendous victory in the first-ever democratic election on Russian soil. Vladimir W. Zhirinovsky—whose ultra-nationalist Liberal Democratic Party won heavily—has already met with right-wing political leaders (including a former SS officer) during a tour of Germany and Austria. He has even gone so far as to recommend that Bulgaria should annex Macedonia (shades of *Anschluss!*), a now-sovereign nation that was once part of Yugoslavia.[4]

There are those who play down Zhirinovsky's potential for harm by citing his electoral victory as nothing more than a protest vote by the newly democratized Russian people who are fed up with a variety of other political leaders, including current President Boris Yeltsin. But then, they said similar things about Hitler.

An entire book could be written about Russian occultism and its effect on the political life of Europe, from Blavatsky to Yuliana Glinka and Sergey Nilus to Rasputin, and to the most recent emergence of a millennial cult in the Ukraine that predicted the world would end in November, 1993. But it might be better at the present time to keep our eyes on the more blatant of the Nazi survivals, and what better place to begin our study than with a modern-day Abbey of Thelema in the German-speaking district of Appenzell, Switzerland.

The Swiss OTO is noteworthy for several things. In the first place, they are probably the best-organized and most profitably run Thelemic (i.e., Crowleyan) enterprise on earth. From all accounts, including but not limited to Mr. King's,[5] they perform the most perfect of all Gnostic Masses (an occult version of the Catholic Mass) to be found. Although, as someone who has witnessed many a Gnostic Mass in the States, the author must offer the proviso that virtually anything would be an improvement. Further, they run a guesthouse, a printing press, and operate their own apothecary specializing in "Paracelsian" remedies: an industry for which the Nazis would have given them high marks indeed.

What calls our attention to the Swiss OTO, however, is an item recorded by Francis King in his *Satan and Swastika*,[6] in which he mentioned that—in the first issue of its newsletter *E.O.L. Mitteilungsblatt,* dated June 9, 1954—the Abbey published a Memorial notice for Lanz von Liebenfels, calling him a "shining example of unswerving faith and the very highest virtue"![7] That the best-run example of a Thelemic community should have openly praised one of the spiritual fathers of the Third Reich is a phenomenon that is troubling, to say the least. That they are serious Thelemites and devotees of Aleister Crowley cannot be denied. How, then, do they manage to reconcile these two conflicting philosophies?

This is a problem that vexes the student of modern occultism, because admiration of Crowley and his philosophy has emerged in organized Satanism, neo-Nazi political parties, racist hooliganism, alienated teenagers, and jaded rock-and-rollers alike. Crowley once wrote—in an attack on Arthur Edward Waite, a former colleague in the Golden Dawn and the author of many books on occultism—"Magick is a mirror, wherein who sees muck is muck."[8] One could perhaps also say, "Crowley is a mirror in which one who sees a Nazi, is a Nazi." As Crowley was certainly an anti-establishment sort of fellow, and as Nazism is about as anti-establishment as you can get in most countries, it would follow that Nazis might find a kindred soul in Aleister Crowley. Yet, one would think that the OTO of Switzerland—an organization that is arguably the oldest continuous Thelemic Lodge in the world—would know better.

The implications are distressing.

We may remember that the Ordo Templi Orientis (OTO)—the German occult Order to which Crowley belonged and of which he became its somewhat disputed OHO (Outer Head of the Order)—

had splintered into various factions around 1925. One group went with Crowley. Another remained independent of Crowley and his religion of Thelema. Still another became the Brotherhood of Saturn, an organization that survived the war and also exists to this day.

Recourse to a useful flowchart provided on electronic bulletin boards by something calling itself the "Boleskine Chapter of the Thelema Grand Lodge OTO"[9] indicates that the Swiss OTO has direct lineage to both Karl Germer and Theodor Reuss via Frater Paragranus (Josephus Metzger) declaring the latter to be OHO although whom it recognizes as OHO at this time is not clear. What is clear is that this Swiss lodge was once the private domain of Theodor Reuss himself, presumably when he went to Ascona in the waning years of his life and founded the same "Mysteria Maxima Veritas" Lodge. The Lodge continued under the leadership of Karl Germer as OHO even after Germer left for the United States, but after Germer's death it seems to dangle off the edge of the flowchart as the Order itself went through several sea changes with Kenneth Grant's Nu-Isis Lodge in England, Grady McMurtry's operation in the States, and various other offshoots such as Brazilian Marcelo Ramos Motta's version of the Order, which was successfully sued by the McMurtry gang in a United States court.[10] Germer had died without leaving a Templar heir, and the resulting fracas has served only to splinter this already heartily splintered organization still further.

In conversations with the author, Grady McMurtry—several years before his death in 1985—related that in 1941, before Jack Parsons totally lost control of his life, he initiated McMurtry—then an army lieutenant—into the OTO. McMurtry later served in the European Theater in some capacity and made Crowley's personal acquaintance in London at about the time Crowley was strategizing with the likes of Fleming, Wheatley, and Knight. Crowley elevated McMurtry to the IX° in the OTO hierarchical scheme—the highest rank attainable save by those ruling as OHOs—and McMurtry then returned to the United States after the war, still under Germer's leadership there. Once Germer died, however, several individuals calling themselves OHO began running their own OTO organizations. As recently as the 1980s, the American outfit now legally recognized as the OTO in the States claimed adherence to a set of vile regulations published in what is known as the *Blue Equinox,* i.e., Crowley's hardbound periodical that was usually published in white covers and which was, only once, bound in blue covers; hence its informal title. These archaic strictures are a legacy of Crowley's early German period, mixed with elements of a monarchical Victorian hangover, which have become incomprehensibly precious to those otherwise antiestablishment hippie types who constitute the leadership of the Order. That Crowley later repudiated the "Blue laws" and adopted the stridently libertarian views of the more succinct *Liber OZ*[11]—which was published in London and California in 1939 as the world was being plunged into the Second World War—seems clear to this author, who finds himself in general agreement with what has been written on the subject of Kenneth Grant,[12] who more than anyone seems best qualified to serve as OHO of the Order . . . the cosmic wisdom of the American legal system notwithstanding.

It was McMurtry and his adherents, however, who—on the basis of some rather thin evidence and the loose interpretation of some Crowley correspondence—managed to convince a US District Court judge that his claim to rulership of the OTO was genuine. Thelema never had that much luck with worldly courts, and there is no reason to suppose that this case was an exception. McMurtry continued to work for the US government in various capacities before retiring to run the OTO in 1969 after the disastrous theft of vital documents and irreplaceable books from Germer's widow, Sascha (who was also beaten up in the process), in 1967. It seems that the perpetrator of this crime was believed to be yet another organization calling itself OTO, this time the "Solar Lodge of the OTO," implicated in the Charles Manson case which exploded with the Tate/La Bianca murders in August of 1969. As the above chronology makes clear, McMurtry remained so out of touch with the OTO that it would be two years before he learned of the attack on Sascha Germer and the theft of the OTO "family jewels."

One cannot help but form scenarios in one's mind with such an embarrassment of paranoid riches at one's disposal. We have shown how Crowley was involved to some extent with the spymasters of MI5, including those famous personalities Dennis Wheatley, Ian Fleming, and Maxwell Knight, during World War II and particularly during the Hess affair. McMurtry, an Army officer, was initiated by Parsons at Cal-Tech in 1941 before going overseas to obtain greater initiations from Crowley himself during the war. McMurtry, who mustered out of the army with the rank of captain, went on to work as an analyst for the government while simultaneously teaching a course in poli sci at George Washington University in Washington, DC in the sixties. The scenario that presents itself is intriguing. One wonders if—as the US federal government has been known to do with many other suspect organizations, including the Ku Klux Klan and the Black Panthers—they had not infiltrated an agent into the American OTO who eventually became one of its leaders? After all, L. Ron Hubbard himself once claimed to have infiltrated the OTO for either LAPD, Naval Intelligence, or the FBI, depending on the source.[13] Was McMurtry on a similar mission, this time for the army or for some secret, frantic faction thereof? After all, Hess had flown to Scotland in 1941—the same year McMurtry joined Parsons's Agapé Lodge in California. McMurtry then shipped out for Great Britain, where he met Crowley who was being considered at that time for a role in the debriefing of Hess. Did the fledgling American intelligence services want to know what the rather more professional British services were up to with Hess and Crowley? Was McMurtry then "reactivated" at the time of the Manson killings to investigate the possible involvement of the group calling itself the "Solar Lodge of the OTO"?

Alas, there is absolutely no evidence at all to support what has been imagined in the preceding paragraph. None whatsoever. Not a shred.

And, as there has been much litigation over the history, reputations, and legitimacy of the various OTO lodges, the author must demur at this point and instead refer interested readers to such sources as the first edition of Ed Sanders's *The Family*[14] for more detail on the so-called Solar Lodge of the OTO and other ancillary information. Chapter Ten in that edition is the relevant material; it has been deleted entire from later editions, including the recently released paperback update that boasts a photo of Charlie Manson on the cover . . . replete with swastika tattoo. The litigious McMurtry gang at work? Also, please note that Chapter Five of the original is also missing. That was the material on the Process Church of the Final Judgment, a Scientology offshoot that was implicated in various crimes of a heinous nature in the late sixties and whose nefarious reputation has been resurrected by investigative journalist Maury Terry in *The Ultimate Evil,* a study of the links that may exist between the Son of Sam cult and the Manson Family via the Process Church. It should be remembered that the Process is in the line of descent—should we say, apostolic succession?—from Jack Parsons and hence of the OTO. (The wife of the founder of the Process even claims to be a reincarnation of Nazi propagandist Joseph Goebbels!)[15] If any of the rumors, half-truths, and innuendo concerning the Process are ever proven, then it may be that Parsons actually succeeded in incarnating his Antichrist in California.

To Live and Die in LA

We must at once employ investigators in England to follow and check the reports of trials and police announcements concerning missing children, so that we can include short announcements in our broadcasts, that a child has disappeared in such-and-such a place, and that this is probably the result of a Jewish ritual murder . . .[16]

—HEINRICH HIMMLER

During the height of the Satanic Cult Survivor hysteria in the late eighties and early nineties, an otherwise respectable doctor and professor—a published author on psychotherapeutic technique and on the uses of hypnotism in psychotherapy—D. Corydon Hammond was quoted in a two-part series of articles on the phenomenon (published in the *New Yorker*)[17] as saying that he believed the prevalence of satanic cults in America today was due to the influence of Nazis who had become initiated into satanism and black magic by a mysterious rabbi during the war. These Nazis then emigrated to the United States where they set up shop and organized the underground satanic movement that has been accused of the kidnapping and murder of children and young adults.

While this may seem like another case of the blood libel in fin de siècle America instead of fin de siècle Europe or Russia, we should pause for a moment to digest what is being stated and who is stating it:

1. Mysterious rabbi initiates *Nazis* into black magic and satanism. (This complies with most anti-Semitic literature of the past

thousand years or so, except for the Nazi part, which is a new twist. During the Middle Ages Jews were believed to be sorcerers and demonolators and most grimoires of the period contain Hebrew prayers and writing as part of their rituals.)

2. These Nazis then disappear into the fabric of American life after the war, presumably along the same ratlines that served so many other war criminals.
3. They form underground cells of satanic composition.
4. They begin to prey on unsuspecting Christian children, abusing them sexually and murdering them in horrible, unspeakable ways. (The blood libel, in all its pristine ugliness.)
5. They even *breed* children for use as human sacrifices in their rituals. A nice twist on the *Lebensborn* concept and one even the Nazis didn't think of.
6. This theory is put forth by a respected psychotherapist who teaches at the Utah School of Medicine.

The "blood libel" was a technique used to instigate pogroms against the Jews in Europe, in modern times used effectively in pre-Revolutionary Russia and, of course, by Julius Streicher in the pages of his anti-Semitic rag *Der Stürmer*. Simply stated, the blood libel accused the Jews of murdering Christian children in horrible ways as human sacrifices during secret ceremonies in the temples. Whether the children had, in reality, been murdered by anyone even vaguely Jewish was not important. Whether the children had been murdered at all was irrelevant. Whether there were any missing children or not was not the issue. The blood libel—or the ritual murder charge, as it was also known—was an invention of yellow journalists who, working for the government or for some right-wing faction, published these unfounded, inflammatory stories in a deliberate attempt to instigate pogroms against the local Jewish population. The attempts usually worked. Thousands of Jews were murdered by angry mobs many times over many years before the Holocaust began by using this technique.

In the present-day version of the blood libel, however, we seem to lack a readily identifiable social or ethnic group as a convenient target. Satanists are few and far between and relatively invisible. So, comparatively speaking, are Nazis. What, then, is the value of the blood libel if there are no social outcasts to destroy?

Well, perhaps there are.

One of the world's most famous—positively archetypal—social out-casts is the aforementioned Charles Manson. Manson has perhaps concretized evil for an entire generation. Accused, tried, and convicted of ordering the Tate/La Bianca murders of 1969, Manson remains in prison at the time of this writing, consistently denied parole year after year as he serves a life sentence for the murders.

Although much about Manson remains a mystery, there is enough evidence to show that he borrowed at least some of his act from Scien-tologists during one of his previous prison terms, and even wrote an article for the official Process magazine. Manson told his followers that he wanted to instigate a race war between blacks and whites in America, believing that he and his Family would survive the holocaust by hiding out in the desert. After the smoke cleared and the blood dried, they would then come roaring out of the desert to take charge of what was left of the planet Earth. Noting Manson's anti-Semitism and his hatred of blacks, it's easy to see how he figured the race war would end.

Mason has claimed to be both Jesus Christ and the Devil, a claim that seems ludicrous at first glance but is easy to understand once one knows that the Process believed that Jesus, Satan, and Lucifer were equal members of a triune power of the universe. This quasi-Gnostic belief is nothing new—it is, after all, warmed-over Manichaeism—but in modern dress it can seem scandalous and fantastic.

As he spent more and more time in prison after the Tate killings, he became infected with Nazi ideology, probably via the Aryan Broth-erhood, which serves as a violent, all-white "gang" both within the prison system and without. As is well known, he eventually carved a swastika into his forehead, and formed a relationship with James N. Mason of the Universal Order,[18] an offshoot of the American Nazi Party of George Lincoln Rockwell. Mason eventually realized that Manson was the latest incarnation of Adolf Hitler, and began to de-vote all his time to promoting Charlie's philosophy among his neo-Nazi brethren.

It is no exaggeration to say that the Manson killings stupefied the entire nation. A lovely, pregnant, blond actress who starred in B-mov-ies but who had never harmed anyone was hideously mutilated and slain in her own home by a band of men and women who also slashed and killed her houseguests. Ironically, although all the perpetrators were white Gentiles—"racially, they are all tops" according to Mason—the image of the short, long-haired, bearded Manson ordering the death and mutilation of Sharon Tate could have come from the pages of *Der Stürmer* or *Ostara* as an example of a subhuman species violating the pure Aryan Woman. Manson as *agent provocateur?* Indeed, his idea was to frame the blacks for the murders. Thus, the blood libel at work.

But link Manson with Nazis and the Process, and you have a perfect formula for a different sort of blood libel. In middle-America's confused understanding of world history and current events, what image could be more potent than a Charles Manson/Nazi/Satanist conspiracy to destroy American youth? Add that little extra fillip of anti-Semitism in Dr. Hammond's analysis (that the Satanic Nazis learned their occultism from a rabbi) and you have it all. Mysterious Men In Black with vast occult powers, rampaging sexual urges, and demonic bloodlust corrupting and murdering America's children with reckless abandon. Who can be trusted? Obviously, only mainstream fundamentalist religious groups; only patriotic, right-wing political groups. The more conservative, the better. These individuals have no fear of the man waving a large cross and shouting the name of Jesus, of God and Country. They fear . . . the Others.

Streams of Satanic Abuse Survivors have gone running to therapists with newly retrieved "memories" of these ritual murders, contributing to a growing national hysteria (at least on the talk shows). While none of these "victims" remembers the names or addresses of the actual persons involved in the killings and the abuse, or can in any other way identify the perpetrators, the horror these "victims" feel is still palpable. They want justice. They want to punish *someone.* But in these politically correct times, at whom can one point a finger? Certainly not at the Jews. Nor at any other ethnic or religious group (unless one considers these mysterious satanists members of a religious group; they are *not* to be confused with members of Anton LaVey's Church of Satan). Alas, one must be content to be a victim without an identifiable—and hence punishable—victimizer. The whole point about these alleged satanic organizations is that they are well organized, highly secretive, perform their rituals in remote settings, and breed their own children for sacrifice so that there are no birth records and certainly no death records, either. In other words, they commit the perfect crimes, and if it wasn't for this suddenly vast array of "survivors," we would never even know the cult existed.

Unfortunately, all the hype concerning Satanic Cult Survivor Syndrome has obscured the fact that neo-Nazi cults, embracing some form of occultism inherited from their SS forebears, *do* exist and *do* intend harm—violent harm—for most members of the human race. In fact, it is almost a mistake in some cases to speak of *neo*-Nazi cults, for the Nazi era is still very much with us and has been lovingly preserved by unrepentant war criminals in safe havens in Argentina, Brazil, Chile . . . and the United States.

While Dr. Hammond's thesis may be a bit extreme, there can be no doubt that Nazis escaped to America, and that they brought their cult of race mysticism and swastika worship with them. Combined with the legendary Nazi hatred for Judaism and Christianity, this cult is still blatantly pagan although it would be an exercise in hyperbole to consider it "satanic" in any strict, ideological sense. Nazis do not worship the Devil as such; for them, as for other pagans of various persuasions—including the benign Wicca movement—the Devil is purely a Judeo-Christian concept. Only someone still in the thralls of some form of Judeo-Christianity would consider going to all the trouble to worship Satan.

Yet, the various gods and goddesses that compose traditional Nordic paganism *are* viewed as demons by the Catholic Church. They were certainly "false gods," and to worship them would have been enough to send anyone to the stake during the Inquisition. Witches' Sabbaths are not Black Masses, but participation in them was reason enough for execution. Hence, Himmler's sympathy for the witches who were destroyed by the Church during the Middle Ages; they were, after all, fellow travelers to the Nordic *Armanen* brothers and the Celtic Druids. Thus, the difficulty in drawing lines of demarcation where the Church sees none. To the conventional Catholic point of view, witches and Druids and Nordic pagans are of a piece with satanists: in the Church's eyes they all worship the Devil.

The writings and speeches of Nazi apologists like Walther Darré, Alfred Rosenberg, Heinrich Himmler, Baldur von Schirach, and Hitler himself make it clear just what the Nazi platform was on organized religion and the future of Aryan spirituality. They understood the concept of "spirit" to be racially determined. Thus, there was a "Jewish spirit" as distinct from an "Aryan spirit." The spirit was, therefore, a function of the blood. Previous authors, such as Houston Stewart Chamberlain, had written that one could somehow "become Jewish" simply by associating with Jews long enough; for Chamberlain and others, race was not the determining factor in what the later Chinese ideologues would term "spiritual pollution"; rather, the environment itself was the critical element. Although Hitler greatly admired Chamberlain, he insisted that the German spirit was a vastly different creature than the Semitic spirit, and that racial purity determined spiritual purity. In this way, all possibility of individual, personal spiritual advancement was denied. One was either born perfect, or one's soul was doomed from the outset. And there was no mystery about who was who: your birth certificate told the story. There was no such thing as a "human spirit": there was only a racial spirit. And should a German woman have sexual intercourse with a Jew only once, her soul would become polluted forever and her children—even if engendered by an Aryan male—would always contain a taint of Jewish corruption; hence the racial Nuremberg Laws which forbade sexual intercourse (let alone marriage) between Jews and non-Jews in Hitler's Germany.

When the Nazis escaped along the ratlines to the Americas, they brought these beliefs with them. They remained as indispensable a part of their spiritual repertoire as *Mein Kampf* or the *Protocols*. And they functioned as silent masters behind a legion of front men in the host countries, financing the publication of what most of the world would consider "hate literature" but which to the Nazis remain their sacred scriptures. These men were in urgent need of something similar to what the Chinese call "reeducation" or what the cult fighters call "deprogramming," but the world did not understand the Nazi Party (and particularly the SS) as a cult and was not equipped to deal with the problem; and the continued threat of Communism and the need for an overwhelming solution to the Communist "problem" made these veteran anti-Communists valuable men to have as intelligence agents, saboteurs, and military advisers wherever the Communist threat was present.

That is why we witness a resurgence in Latin America, for instance, of every form of Nazism, from political parties that parade the swastika and other runic designs as official emblems to pogroms against various

ethnic minorities—usually the Native American populations—to totalitarian forms of government that were established to defeat the
greatest enemy of Nazism after the Jews, International Communism.

A casual observer might decide that these political coruscations are
isolated incidents, the black-leather fantasies of a handful of crazed
and chronic underachievers trying to get our attention. Unfortunately,
this is not the case. The flashy neo-Nazi groups of Latin America perform a valuable service for the old war criminals in hiding. They take
the public's political temperature, so to speak, while at the same time
taking the heat off the *Kamaradenwerk*. And a major player in that
underground Nazi network—the ratline *par excellence*—was Otto
Skorzeny.

Hitler's Commando

Skorzeny's career as the creator of Hitler's elite commando force—
trained in foreign languages, sophisticated weapons, and demolition
devices, various forms of aircraft including experimental planes, and
combat and assassination techniques—is celebrated all over the world.
It was Skorzeny, after all, who performed the impossible rescue of
Benito Mussolini from under the nose of his captors. It was Skorzeny
who dressed members of his force in American uniforms in one of the
last battles of the war and thus contributed to many American deaths
by means of the artful deception.

And it was Skorzeny who inherited the responsibility for maneuver-
ing the stolen Nazi art treasures out of Germany and occupation hands
into Spain, Portugal, and eventually to South America. These art treasures formed the capital with which Skorzeny financed *Die Spinne
(The Spider)*, his version of ODESSA (the Organization of former SS
Officers), and with which he aided the escape and survival of many of
his former colleagues, including (but not limited to) Eichmann and
Mengele. Skorzeny never stood trial at Nuremberg when he was easily
one of the most important war criminals ever to survive the Occupation. Instead, he made himself useful to American intelligence and,
later, to West German industrialists and reconstituted Nazis enjoying
the protection of Adenauer. He figured prominently in the Perón re-

gime in Argentina and was even entrusted with bringing Evita's body from Italy to Argentina after the death of her husband.

Skorzeny was a fanatic Nazi who kept the pagan faith throughout his career until his death from cancer in 1975. His involvement with the regimes of Farouk and Nasser in Egypt went so far as to include creating an Egyptian Gestapo staffed almost completely with former SS officers, a measure that received wholehearted support from CIA Director Allen Dulles, who was at that time involved with Reinhard Gehlen in developing an anti-Communist espionage service within the ranks of the CIA. It is evidence of this kind of collusion between the CIA and former SS officers, Nazi financiers, and concentration camp doctors that has given rise to speculation about Nazi mind-control methods being developed under CIA auspices in the decades after the war (with a nod to Dr. Hammond).

The commando unit Skorzeny created under Hitler remained largely intact after the war and formed the network of SS men around the world—financed by Nazi money hidden in various European and South American treasuries—that contributes to the survival of Nazi ideology today, more than fifty years after the end of World War II. With so much support being given to these men by various governments—including America's—is it any wonder that Nazism is enjoying a kind of spiritual rebirth all over the world? Estimates range as high as seventy thousand former SS officers—members of Himmler's elite Black Order, initiated with pagan ritual into his version of the Masons and Jesuits rolled into one—remained at large after the war. As such, it constitutes one of the largest—and best-funded, best-trained, best-equipped, and best-connected—cults in the world today. And the second generation is being trained and indoctrinated in the streets of London, Berlin, New York, Buenos Aires . . . and in secret, heavily armed estates like Colonia Dignidad.

The Ratlines

An undeclared war is being waged in Latin America today against the democratic institutions and the independence of the New World republics. This war is being conducted with fearful efficiency by the

*soldiers of the Third German Empire, who have been distributed by
thousands throughout the political underground of this continent.
They are the agents of Adolf Hitler . . .*[19]

—HUGO FERNANDEZ ARTUCIO, WRITING IN 1942

To appreciate the ease with which lines of communication and
transportation were set up between the Nazis in Europe and their
support groups in South America, one only has to look at the history
of South America in the twentieth century, particularly during the war
years. Beginning in the 1930s, there were waves of German immigration coming to the continent. At first, these were German Jews fleeing
the newly established Aryan state. Then, Nazi diplomats began replacing their Weimar counterparts in embassies from Bogotá to Buenos
Aires, and forming relationships with local Nazi parties in these countries. Of all the South American nations, those most likely to welcome
Nazi influence were Argentina, Chile, Ecuador, and Bolivia. All of
these countries had high concentrations of German-speaking people
in influential areas of government and commerce. Bolivia, for example, had a relatively open immigration policy and visas could simply
be purchased. The Bolivian airline, LAB, was owned and operated by
Germans, a situation that Allen Dulles would fight hard to change as
it posed a strategic threat to US interests. Of course, Ernst Röhm had
worked in Bolivia in the 1920s as a military adviser.

Bolivia also had—and probably still has—a homegrown Nazi Party:
the *Organización Nacional Socialista Americana* (American National
Socialist Organization) or ONSA.[20]

Chile, by comparison, had no less than *three* Nazi Parties when the
war broke out,[21] plus was host to an exiled Bolivian Nazi Party; this is
one of the reasons why Chile remained the only country in South
America that did *not* declare war on Germany. One of these parties,
the National Socialist Movement (*Movimiento Nacional Socialista* or
MNS), founded by Jorge Gonzalez von Mareés in 1932, was an attempt to build Nazism with Chilean characteristics (to paraphrase an
old Maoist slogan). The members of this party were actually referred
to as *Nacis,* but by 1937 the movement became disaffected with Hitler
and, although still remaining basically anti-Semitic and nationalistic,
it severed its relations with other Nazi and Fascist organizations in

Chile. It attempted a coup against the administration of President Alessandri, but was brutally suppressed when fifty of its members were murdered without a trial. Eventually, the Nacis threw in with presidential candidate Aguirre Cerda and helped him win by a narrow margin, so their influence was not altogether imaginary. We will look at more modern—and more lethal—Nazi movements in Chile in the next chapter.

But by far the most blatantly pro-Nazi and pro-Fascist government in South America was that of Argentina's Juan Perón. A critical link in the Nazi ratline, Perón's government bent over backwards to accommodate fleeing Nazis and, as recent revelations have shown, more than one thousand such war criminals managed to find safe haven in Perón's Argentina.[22]

Prior to Perón's accession to power in 1946, however, Argentina had become a focal point for Nazi strategy in the region. The Party Leader *(Parteileiter)* for South America was headquartered in Buenos Aires.[23] The Party Leader was at least nominally in charge of all SS, SA, Arbeitfront, Hitler Youth, and Gestapo activities in the entire region. In Berlin, the Nazi Party had a separate section and a secretary-general for the Nazi Party of South and Central America. To better appreciate this policy, one merely has to imagine—for instance—the sheer audacity of having a United States Republican Party of Pakistan, for instance, or an American Democratic Party of Rumania. We who tend to think of our political parties as purely domestic affairs have to rearrange our thinking when it comes to understanding the Nazis, who saw themselves as eventually ruling over the entire globe. In this, they were not too different from their mortal enemies, the Communists, who organized in foreign countries but who owed their allegiance to Moscow. The essential point of departure, however, is that the Communists were consciously *international* while the Nazis were *national.* The Nazi Parties in South America were not independently operated affairs, not even on paper. They were simply divisions of the greater Nazi Party in Germany, and all the same rules applied (i.e., as regards race, religion, etc.). A full-blooded Native American Peruvian, for example, would have no more chance of joining the Nazi Party in La Paz or Sucre than would someone one-quarter Jewish in Berlin.

Argentina had a Nazi-style party in power for a while in 1943 when the *Grupo de Oficiales Unidos* or GOU executed a neat coup that resulted in a short-lived, pro-Fascist military dictatorship.[24] Previously, the Uriburu government of 1930–32 had attempted to create a self-consciously Italian Fascist government there, with mixed results that ended in failure. While Argentina remained passively pro-Nazi and pro-Fascist during the war (and only declared war on Germany at the last possible moment), it did not succeed in becoming the Nazi dream state until 1946.

Juan Domingo Perón had served as a military attaché to Mussolini's Italy before the war broke out and liked what he saw. Like so many other Latin American generals, he found the totalitarian power structure of Fascist Italy and Nazi Germany appealing. Even more, the swaggering machismo of Il Duce and the flashy black uniforms and jackboots of the SS helped to form a persistent idea among Latin military leaders of what a real army and a real government should look like. That is, they admired the surface manifestations of the movement and the brutally simple approach to administrative problems favored by the right-wing totalitarian regimes. No one could accuse the platforms of either Fascism or Nazism of being hard to understand; Communism, by comparison, was largely intended to be a "scientific" approach to government and economics and required learning a whole new vocabulary and doing at least *some* reading. There wasn't much reading required of the aspiring Fascist or Nazi. Even Hitler, it is said, did not read most of the books he owned but scanned pamphlets which contained brief quotations from the literary and philosophical giants of German history. He could thus quote these dead white gentlemen as if he had read their entire works.[25] This was the approach favored by the right-wing extremists who saw themselves as men of action rather than as political philosophers.

Many who write on the Nazi scene in South America have disparaged the movement. They claim that Nazism could never gain a real foothold in South America because the history and culture of that society is so different from that of Germany or Italy.[26] For one thing, because the population is so diverse, a racial program could never succeed. For another, long exposure to North American forms of democracy would mitigate against the creation of a purely nationalistic political force.

Unfortunately, this perception of South American politics is only partially correct. It is true that the populations of many Latin countries are racially diverse; that does not stop those of white skin from looking down on those with dark skin. It also does not stop those of largely European ancestry from discriminating against those of Native American blood. The vast destruction of indigenous peoples taking place in the Amazonian rain forests is but one example of this callous disregard for those of different race. South America is as class-conscious as any other region; at times, even more so. Family connections are everything, from Colombia in the north to Chile and Argentina in the south. One's last name can prove an entrée to the country club, or a permanent ban from the seats of power and influence.

As for North American democracy, the people of Latin America know all too well how it has been used against them; the overthrow of Salvador Allende in 1973 was only one example. One could cite Guatemala, Nicaragua, the Dominican Republic, and El Salvador as others, not to mention the repeated attempts to assassinate or overthrow Fidel Castro of Cuba.

Thus, Nazi sensibilities became popular among the vested interests in Bolivia, Argentina, Chile, and Ecuador, and virtually everywhere in South America that boasted an elite ruling class that was almost invariably white and non-Indian. While it was difficult in some countries to organize an anti-Semitic party due to the tiny and relatively uninfluential Jewish populations there, the emphasis was switched to anti-Communism. And, as Communists began to organize among the lowly and dispossessed (usually Native American) peoples of Bolivia, Chile, Argentina, and the rest of South America, anti-Communism took on some racist characteristics.

Christianity—particularly Roman Catholicism—is a strong force in Latin America, perhaps less so now than during the 1940s and 1950s, when religious laws in many countries were virtually indistinguishable from federal laws (legislation pertaining to marriage, divorce, and abortion come readily to mind); but nonetheless, the Church still wields moral power and its "liberationist" priests and nuns are well loved by the poor. Thus, in Latin America, the Nazis faced some of the same philosophical and cultural hurdles that they encountered in Christian Germany. Yet, while pious Catholicism is the norm among the poorer and middle-class populations of Latin America, occultism was popular among the elite and the educated classes. They indulged in everything from spiritualism to Gnosticism to ritual magic and Rosi-crucianism, particularly in the urban areas. This, coupled with some native occult beliefs such as Santería, Macumba, and a host of other practices that are the product of African and Native American religions mixing with imported Roman Catholicism, produced an atmosphere that was conducive to cults and nontraditional religious sects. Further, many otherwise intelligent Latinos of the author's acquaintance express surprise at the vehemence which the name of Hitler or the subject of Nazis arouses in many a *norteamericano*. While many Latins would not automatically embrace *der Führer*, they do tend to see him as a brilliant, if flawed, statesman who could not have been the demon the "northern" press makes him out to be. While most of the population would resist Nazism as a foreign import, if nothing else, and a not very useful alternative to democracy or Communism, the oligarchies of these countries tend to admire Nazism as a philosophy dear to their hearts: an ideology where might is right, and will power (plus automatic weapons) is everything. And, since members of the Church—including individual priests, nuns, and bishops—have recently become involved in anti-government protests and conspiracies from Central to South America, at times even siding with Communist and Socialist extremists against right-wing dictatorships . . . well, then, who needs the Church?

For these reasons the Nazi Party remains as antagonistic as ever to Christianity. While some Christian prelates may see in the Nazi Party a useful bulwark against the greater evil, Communism, by far the most popular priests and bishops in Latin America are the antigovernment preachers and martyrs. And now, with the collapse of Communism in Russia and Eastern Europe, the Party must reevaluate its usefulness to a host of military regimes. The ongoing struggle of *Sendero Luminoso* (Shining Path) guerrillas in Peru, for instance, is a boon to those aging Nazi antiterrorism consultants who still ply their trade in the South. While the antigovernment forces in South America may eventually change their program from doctrinaire Communism or Maoism due to lack of support abroad, they will persist in their policy of overthrowing the relative handful of powerful families in charge of the Latin American economies.

And then, of course, there is the drug trade.

Imagine

Nazis and their sympathizers are rarely boring. At the very least, they are revolting and perhaps even ridiculous. At best, they are surreal. One such case is that of Carlos Lehder Rivas,[27] a former kingpin of the Medellin drug cartel of Colombia: neo-Nazi, multimillionaire drug lord, convicted felon, prosecution witness against former Panamanian President and Santería practitioner Manuel Noriega, and *huge* John Lennon fan.

Lehder's father was a German engineer who managed to emigrate to Colombia before the end of the war. Carlos Lehder himself was born in 1947, the product of a union between his German-born father and Colombian mother. His parents divorced shortly after Carlos was born, and his mother took him to New York City, where he eventually wound up selling pot in the Bronx as a teenager before getting arrested for grand-theft auto at the age of twenty-six. He had been stealing cars since he was eighteen.

By 1975, he was out of jail and back in Bogotá. Three years later, and Carlos Lehder was one of the richest men in the world. He had understood that the key element in any narcotics operation was transportation, and—with his newly acquired pilot's license—he set up a marijuana transport system that was the marvel of South American criminal enterprises.

Not content with being a mere drug trafficker, however, Carlos Lehder decided he wanted to run the country. By 1983 he had formed a political party—the *Movimiento Civico Latino Nacional* (MCLN)—a rabidly nationalist, anti-American, anti-Communist, and neo-Nazi party in which Hitler was extolled as "the greatest warrior in history,"[28] and Lehder's own open involvement in the drug trade was nothing less than a means of toppling the imperialist forces (the United States) and destroying their influence in Latin America. He opened a resort hotel, the *Posada Alemana (German Inn),* a pastiche of Bavarian-style architecture, with a statue of Lehder's idol, John Lennon, as centerpiece of the hotel's disco: a club which blared a constant stream of Beatles music at all hours of the day and night. The statue itself is worthy of attention for here Lennon is depicted in the nude, wearing only a Nazi helmet, holding a guitar, and with a bullet hole in his heart! How the peaceful, antiestablishment and pro-love pop singer and composer was linked with Nazism in Lehder's mind is anyone's guess; perhaps Mr. Lennon's marriage to a Japanese woman was enough to convince the drug dealer that Lennon's sympathies were with the Axis powers?

In any event, Lehder's many speeches to the press and to crowds of curiosity-seekers in his hometown of Armenia consistently invoke this theme of Nazism and the drug trade, equating cocaine with the atomic bomb: the secret weapon of the Nazis in their ongoing struggle against capitalism and American imperialism. Most DEA agents regarded these speeches as the ravings of a coked-up *narcotraficante* . . . but then there was that little matter of a military coup in Bolivia, a coup masterminded by drug-runner and former Gestapo chief Klaus Barbie with the assistance of a secret Masonic organization based in Italy.

The Butcher of Lyon

Barbie—like so many other rabid Nazis—had been a devout Catholic in his youth, joining several Catholic youth groups in and around his childhood home of Trier, close to the borders of France and Luxembourg on the Mosel River. Trier was the scene of many violent clashes between the French and the Germans during and after the First World War, and later between the Nazis and those who opposed them during the chaotic thirties. At some point, Barbie experienced a kind of spiritual crisis and—on April 1, 1933—he joined the Hitler Youth at the age of nineteen.

The previous month, Hitler had offered to compromise with the Church, calling it an essential part of German folk *(volk)* heritage. While previously the Church was certain that it would suffer severely under the Third Reich because of the latter's aggressive neo-paganism, this new attitude was welcomed with relief and many clergymen jumped on the bandwagon. This might have been the reason young Barbie decided to throw in with the Nazis, but his real motivations are unknown.

Several months later, after the signing of the German-Vatican Concordat on July 20, 1933, the bishop of Trier scheduled a rare public showing of that cathedral's famous Robe.

The Robe is supposedly that which was worn by Christ on his journey up Golgotha to be crucified.

> One of the most famous relics in Catholic Europe, the robe was only exhibited at supreme moments in history, and its showing involved the organisation of an international pilgrimage. The bishop could not have invented a more perfect stroke of international propaganda for the new Nazi authorities.[29]

Nazi dignitaries attended the showing, along with contingents of uniformed SA (Storm Troopers). The showing lasted for several months, during which pilgrims from all over Europe made their way to the cathedral for this once-in-a-lifetime glimpse of one of the Church's most holy relics. It is one of those scenes one rarely sees in the movies: an ancient Catholic cathedral, files of altar boys swinging censers, red-robed prelates chanting in Latin before a sacred relic . . . and columns of Storm Troopers in swastika armbands as the honor guard!

While there is evidence that Barbie may have secretly joined the Nazis even before 1933,[30] it is certain that by 1934 he had already attained a position with the SD, the *Sicherheitsdienst* or Secret Service, a division of Himmler's SS.

Eventually, his work for the SD progressed to the point that Obersturmführer Barbie became Gestapo chief of the French city of Lyon in November 1942. It is from that point on that his record of barbarity and cruelty—a record that earned him the nickname "Butcher of Lyon"—was begun.

Barbie was responsible for sadistic, horrific crimes against the Jews, Communists, and the French Resistance. He took a particular delight in interrogations, and eyewitness accounts of his participation in the torture of men and women in the basement cells of Montluc Prison are enough to turn anyone's stomach. In the case of Maquis leader André Devigny, for example, Barbie ordered his pet Alsatian to attack the defenseless prisoner, a man who had already been subjected to "savage beatings, the cold-water treatment of the baignoire, injections, and red-hot irons placed on the soles of his feet."[31] The dog began by ripping Devigny's clothing from his body with his fangs and then continued by tearing the man's flesh from his bones.

Miraculously, Devigny survived this encounter with Barbie and went down in French Resistance history as the only prisoner ever to escape from Montluc Prison. Unfortunately, the use of trained, vicious dogs as interrogation and torture tools also survived and was implemented with gusto in the Nazi fortress and cult center in Chile known as Colonia Dignidad. (See Chapter Twelve.)

At the end of the war, and with a price on his head and a warrant for his arrest, Barbie managed to find employment with American intelligence in Germany, specifically for the US Counter Intelligence Corps, or CIC.[32] As a Nazi turned informer and spy, Barbie entered into such illustrious company as Reinhard Gehlen, Otto Skorzeny, and SS Colonel Freddy Schwend. Barbie soon proved very useful to his American handlers, developing an intelligence network that extended from penetrations within French intelligence all the way to Eastern European emigré groups and intelligence services there.

But Europe got too hot for Barbie. Wanted by the French for war crimes committed in Lyon, Barbie knew his days of enjoying the patronage of his American superiors were drawing to a close. The Americans could not afford to let Barbie fall into French hands, for fear that he would reveal American intelligence operations against them. (To the Americans, the French intelligence service was riddled through with Communists and could not be trusted. They spent almost as much time spying on their Allies as they did keeping tabs on the Soviet Union.) So, they arranged his escape along the ratline to South America; and for this purpose they used the offices of a Croatian priest, Dr. Krunoslav Draganovic, himself a war criminal and Fascist (a member of the dread pro-Nazi *Ustase*) wanted by the Yugoslav authorities but who enjoyed the protection of the Vatican nonetheless.[33]

Like Barbie, Fr. Draganovic was also in good company. He was not the only Catholic priest in Yugoslavia accused of war crimes. The atrocities committed under the aegis of the Fascist State of Croatia—formed in 1941 under Ante Pavelic—outdid even the Nazis for sheer brutality. While the Jews were certainly on the list, so were the approximately two million Eastern Orthodox Serbs, who were forced either to convert to Roman Catholicism . . . or be put to death. Even conversion was no guarantee of safety, as many new converts (men, women, children) were dragged from their first Mass and executed on the streets outside the churches. One Franciscan priest was even the commandant of a Croatian concentration camp.[34] Actions such as these mitigate against Vatican protestations of innocence, or the equally disingenuous argument that an accommodation had to be reached with the Nazis to prevent further bloodshed or the murder of innocent Catholics.

These were the people Draganovic represented and for which an arrest warrant was issued, although he never served any time in prison and was never even tried in a court of law. This is the man who arranged Barbie's escape for the CIC.

After a series of adventures, Barbie found himself (and his entire family) a new home in Bolivia in 1951 with a visa made out in the name of Father Roque Romac (the pseudonym of yet *another* Croat war-criminal priest, a Franciscan who ministered to his newfound flock in the area of Cochabamba) and for a while Barbie was the perfect bourgeois businessman. Then, forming and cementing relationships with the underground Nazi cult in South America—and among men such as Skorzeny, Freddy Schwend, Eichmann, and many others—Barbie, as "Klaus Altmann," began to carve out a position of influence in the various shifting military regimes in La Paz. It will be remembered that Bolivia had been host to German immigrants for years before the war began, and was a target of US intelligence efforts (notably under Dulles) to neutralize their influence on Bolivia's political life.[35] Barbie fell in with the German emigré community, and—linking up with wheeler-dealer Freddy Schwend and, eventually, Italian pro-Fascist terrorist Stefano delle Chiaie—found himself a lucrative position as a *lieutenant colonel in Bolivian Intelligence!*[36]

Schwend and Barbie began running guns between Bolivia, Peru, and Chile using their contacts in the *Kamaradenwerk* (the informal association of ex-SS officers organized by Luftwaffe ace and Hitler pet Colonel Hans Ulrich Rudel) and among the more fascist of the various Latin American governments who became their clients and, occasionally, their suppliers as well. The gun trade eventually led them into the drug trade, where the abilities of Barbie as a military organizer were enhanced by the arrival of Stefano delle Chiaie. Delle Chiaie enjoyed a serious reputation abroad as a master terrorist who had been responsible for a series of lethal bombings throughout Italy in the late sixties. He had also been involved in an aborted military takeover of the country in 1970, and had to flee Italy for the relative safety of

Franco's Spain. It was in Spain that he met—and cultivated—"El Brujo," Argentina's own version of Rudolf Hess: José Lopez Rega, self-professed Rosicrucian, Perónista, mystical advisor to Isabel Perón, founder of the notorious AAA death squads . . . and member of *Propaganda Due,* P-2, the supersecret Masonic society dedicated to the overthrow of the Italian government and its replacement by a Fascist regime.[37] Lopez Rega was an intimate of such men as P-2 founder Licio Gelli who spent many of the postwar years in exile in Argentina, plotting to restore pro-Fascist, anti-Communist governments in South America as well as in Europe and using his own version of Hitler's "dangerous element," the initiatory secret society P-2, as his vehicle for bank manipulations and the subversion of governments.

As we shall see in the next chapter, delle Chiaie would also become involved with Michael Vernon Townley, the American terrorist and spy who planned and organized the assassination of former Allende minister Orlando Letelier in Washington, D.C. on behalf of Chile's secret police, DINA. Townley, of course, was a frequent visitor (and adviser) to Colonia Dignidad.

With all this talent cropping up in Bolivia, it was inevitable that the phenomenon known as "narco-terrorism" would be born. Elements of Italian, Argentine, and Bolivian mercenaries—trained and led by former SS officers—formed the security detail (known as the melodramatically nomenclatured *Fiancés of Death*) for Bolivia's drug smugglers and even warded off violent attacks from Colombia's rival Medellin cartel. For some time it seemed that Barbie and his friends could not reach any higher and then came July 1980 and the Garcia Meza military coup, masterminded in part by Klaus Barbie and Stefano delle Chiaie and funded by Argentine intelligence and the shadowy P-2.

The coup ushered in a new period of severe and brutal military repression in the country, as perhaps could be expected of a government created and managed by drug smugglers, terrorists, Fascist cultists, and Nazi war criminals. Carlos Lehder's inspiration had obviously been the Meza/Barbie coup, and Nazi gatherings took place rather openly in La Paz complete with swastika banners and raucous singing of the "Horst Wessel Song" in Bolivian clubs and bars. Barbie continued as chief of "internal intelligence" and delle Chiaie went abroad to forge links between the government of Bolivia and such legendary homicidal madmen as Major Roberto D'Aubuisson of El Salvador, the man who ordered the assassination of Bishop Romero. At home, Barbie concentrated on removing all opposition to his growing narcotics trade . . . with the approval and assistance of the government.

Eventually, though, the sadistic dream had to end. Delle Chiaie was fingered in the bombing, in August 1980, of the railway station in Bologna, Italy, in which eighty-four passengers died. He dropped from view, narrowly escaping capture. The foreign press had already identified Barbie as the "Butcher of Lyon" wanted by the French government. And, slowly, Barbie's spiderweb world began to unravel. A civilian government was elected in Bolivia by a population finally driven to outrage by the excesses of the Cocaine Army and in February 1983, Barbie was extradited to France to stand trial almost forty years after the end of World War II.

Barbie's story is instructive for two reasons. In the first place, it demonstrates the danger and continuing threat of the Nazi underground against political regimes all over the world. In the second place, Barbie remained a committed Nazi: a man who bought into the cult of Nazism with his whole heart and soul and who never, ever, lost faith with the religion of Hitler, Himmler, Hess, and Rosenberg. The racial conceits; the anti-Christian, pro-pagan ideology; the anti-Communist crusade . . . it was all present in Barbie's reign of terror in Bolivia and included the other organizers of neo-Nazi intrigue, Skorzeny and Rudel.

Drugs, guns, murder-for-hire, military coups, instruction in Nazi torture and interrogation techniques, Nazi nightclubs and the "Horst Wessel Song" . . . these are all the hallmarks of what is often mistakenly referred to as "neo-Nazism." There was nothing "neo-" about Klaus Barbie. He was the genuine article. And there was nothing "neo-" about Colonia Dignidad, the latest in a long line of concentration camps and cult centers courtesy of the Third Reich.

⚡ **12** ⚡

Is Chile Burning? The Overthrow of Allende, the Murder of Letelier, and the Role of Colonia Dignidad

The demon of world domination has spoken. He has proclaimed the great secret: the world can be dominated. Bowed with weariness, the peoples demand subjection. And those who resist will be tamed by terrible blows and sufferings. Modern society is charged with a magical current which in all men creates the same thoughts . . .[1]

—KONRAD HEIDEN
(Emphasis mine—P.L.)

The followers of Crowley also speak of a magical current. In their worldview, the operative wave of energy for the New Age is something called the "93 current"; and, like the current described in Heiden's biography of Hitler, this current "in all men creates the same thoughts." To the Thelemite, these thoughts are of personal freedom: a freedom that is not bestowed, like a favor, by some benevolent authority but inherited as a birthright; in other words, the 93 current is akin to what most people think of as the New Age or the Age of Aquarius . . . except, perhaps, with a bit more of a bite. To Hitler, however, these "thoughts" were instead of the master/slave complex: a mutual need for subjugation within the heavily ritualized context of the necromantic cult. As we shall demonstrate, his necromancers are hard at work restoring the current to life in Latin America today.

As we saw in the previous chapter, the Nazi underground in South America—established long before the war began—was in full swing in the fifties, sixties, and seventies. Yet, after the death of Juan Perón—probably their strongest supporter among the South American dictators—the Nazis knew they had to find another venue for protecting their lives and their interests. Isabel Perón (Juan Perón's third wife) was sympathetic to the Nazi cause, but a trifle insane. She surrounded herself with occultists, Rosicrucians, and other psychic sycophants (such as José Lopez Rega, the right-wing fanatic and occultist, and P-2 initiate, known as *El Brujo,* "the Witch") in a style that would have made Rudolf Hess blush. She was eventually eased out of power and placed in an asylum.

So, the natural destination for refugee Nazis thus became Chile. Sharing a long border with Argentina striated with hidden mountain passes across the Andes through which the Nazis could secretly come and go as they pleased, Chile also boasted a large German-speaking population that had been in place for nearly a hundred years. These descendants of Chile's first German immigrants were now in positions of power and influence in the country, so much so that when I returned from my visit to Colonia Dignidad my seatmates on the plane—business people from Florida—solemnly affirmed that no commerce of any kind was possible in Chile unless you went through "the Germans": lawyers, bankers, industrialists, manufacturers of every type . . . like an anti-Semitic stereotype in reverse, all these (they said) were Germans. This means not merely Chilenos with German-sounding last names, but people who steadfastly hold onto their language, their culture, and their German heritage in the midst of what used to be the longest-running democracy on the continent.

Certainly, the capital city of Santiago boasts many fine German restaurants—a disproportionate share, one might think. One evening during my stay, I happened to be dining in the downtown Sheraton Hotel. Pages carrying signs with small bells paraded through the lobby and dining rooms, looking for "Sr. Schwarz" or "Sr. Müller" or "Sr. Schulz," rarely a Gonzalez or Rodriguez. Never a Smith.

And Santiago's version of Central Park boasts an enormous sculpture—replete with busty Valkyries and heroic Nordic workingmen—dedicated to the German Immigrant. This, across the street from one of Santiago's finest German restaurants, an establishment that shares the same building with the Israeli legation!

And all was just fine until 1970, when the unthinkable happened.

A professed Socialist and longtime political celebrity in Chile, Salvador Allende Gossens was elected president of the Republic in a three-way vote. During the height of the Vietnam War, the drug-and-peace culture of the sixties, and worldwide student revolt against the establishment, there was suddenly a democratically elected Marxist president in America. This was cause for rejoicing everywhere there was even a hint of liberal or left-wing sympathy, even though quite a few of those who applauded Allende's election were not Marxists. For many people, Allende's success at the polls was simply an indication of the strength of the democratic process. A Socialist had become the leader of his country without firing a shot, in a free and open election, and in the Western Hemisphere besides.

Allende became the toast of the revolutionary elite. He is seen chatting now with Fidel Castro, now with Pablo Neruda, now with Gabriel García Márquez. A kind of Latin Camelot was taking place in Chile as artists, writers, musicians, philosophers, and academics crowded around the new president, talking of human rights, emancipation of the working class, and the extrication of Chile's economy from the death grip of the *norteamericanos.* For years in the streets of New York City one had become familiar with posters showing the bearded-and-bereted Che Guevara—the martyred Argentine hero of the Cuban revolution—and one grew accustomed to the various Socialist and Communist splinter groups who marched in the streets of Greenwich Village shouting ¡*Venceremos*! But here, in Chile, it had actually happened. Legally. In the fine old democratic tradition that the United States was supposedly sworn to uphold throughout the world and particularly in the sphere of influence covered by the Monroe Doctrine: Latin America.

But Richard Nixon was president of the United States, and Henry Kissinger was his Torquemada. Democratic or not, freely elected or not, chief executive of a sovereign nation or not, Salvador Allende Gossens had to go.

And nowhere was that sentiment more strongly shared than among the members of the Nazi underground.

The Mountains of Madness

Is it the Andes Mountains, perhaps, that give Chile its unique spiritual character? One of the most literate nations on earth (at the time of Allende, anyway), it surpassed the United States in the proportion of its people who could read and write. And this relatively tiny country had given the world not one but two Nobel Prize–winning poets.

To the metaphysical Chilean author Miguel Serrano,[2] the Andes are the West's equivalent of the Himalayas. Where a North American might expect llamas instead of lamas, he sees these venerable peaks as the spiritual domain of ancient supernatural forces; he believes a secret priesthood resides somewhere within the Andes chain, possessing the secrets of immortality, and of communion with the gods. Serrano— whose books on Jungian-type themes are familiar to North American readers—also wrote on the metaphysical aspects of Hitler's Germany in a volume which has not been translated into English nor made available in the United States, even in the original Spanish. While I was in Chile, I bought a copy and was startled by the fact that this author of the charming little alchemical love story, *El/Ella,* would have written so extensively on the initiatic aspects of the Third Reich in such terms of open admiration, insisting—thirty years after the war— that National Socialism would be the salvation of Chile!

I purchased the tome in an enormous bookstore, the size of one of our superstores except that this was in Chile in 1979. At the same table browsed a tall, thin, well-dressed man in a full-length, grey beard.

I had seen this man at least once before, in New York. At the moment, I could not place the connection but thought it strange that I would run into him here, so far from the streets of Jackson Heights.

This man would dog my steps during my stay in Chile. It seemed wherever I went in Santiago, he would be there; sometimes even ahead of me. And he would be one of the last people I would see before I had to leave the country in an expeditious manner two weeks later. In Chile, it was suddenly becoming difficult to tell the mystic from the Fascist.

Colony of Righteousness

Those who follow those stories of ritual child abuse we read about in the tabloids and hear about on such talk shows as "Maury Povich," "Oprah," "Donahue," "Geraldo," et. al., know that the thread that runs through all of them involves a satanic cult in a remote area that kidnaps or breeds children for sexual abuse, torture, and human sacrifice. To those who scoff at these outrageous claims, we have only to point to Colonia Dignidad as a prime example of all the "survivors'" worst nightmares.

Paul Schäfer was one of the founders of the Colony of Righteousness and was, and is, its only leader. Schäfer jumped bail in Germany in 1961 on charges of child sexual abuse,[3] but that did not stop him from taking a group of families with him when he fled to Chile, arriving there in 1962 at the age of forty with around sixty "blond, blue-eyed settlers"[4] . . . including some children who were brought there under false pretenses, taken from their families back in Germany. His flock came from the town of Siegburg, across the Rhine from Bonn, where Schäfer claimed to be a psychologist, and where he ran a youth home where the sexual-abuse charges originated. Schäfer, also the leader of a Baptist sect (a sect which evidently condones sexual intercourse between adults and children among other peculiarities), bought an old ranch called *El Lavadero* about 250 miles south of Santiago in the Parral region and quickly converted it into a self-sufficient, model community known as Colonia Dignidad, the "Colony of Righteousness" or "Dignity Colony."

The population of the Colony eventually grew to about 350, composed of 250 adults and 100 children.[5] According to reports in the Chilean and German press, the sexes are rigorously separated and sexual intercourse is forbidden[6] (except, one gathers, at the discretion of Schäfer). And, since sex is prohibited, the only way the Colony has been able to increase its population has been by "importing" children from Germany.[7] German authorities have been investigating charges that from thirty to forty children reported missing from the Bonn and Cologne areas have wound up at the Colony.[8] Thus, charges of both child abuse and international child abduction have been leveled at this remote cult community by eyewitnesses, escapees, and responsible members of the West German and Chilean governments. The parallels between Colonia Dignidad and the stories told by "satanic cult survivors," however, are even stronger.

Spanish is not spoken; instead only German, and, oddly, English are used.[9] Old-fashioned, 1940s-era clothing is worn and fourteen-hour workdays are the norm. No television, radio, or newspapers are allowed in the Colony. There is, however, a shortwave unit on the premises which is used to communicate with an office the Colony maintains in Santiago and which was probably the radio I heard being used during my visit.

The Colony established a free clinic on its premises: free, that is, on specific days of the week to members of the local population. They also have their own factory for processing meat, a sixty-five bed hospital, a bakery, dairy, flour mill, machine shop, power plant . . . and their own airfield. By 1985, they had even opened their own roadside restaurant on the Pan American Highway.

Accounts of the size of the Colony vary from news report to news report. Everything from 12,000 acres[10] to 37,000 acres[11] has been offered, and accounts of its operations also include a mine, a lumber mill, and a gravel factory. The author believes it is safe to say that the Colony has grown considerably over the years and that estimates of a 37,000-acre settlement might not be far from the mark, considering the other purposes to which the Colony was put both during and after the Allende regime.

In 1963, a year after the Colony first established itself in Chile, the *Partido Nacional Socialista Obrero de Chile* (the National Socialist Chilean Workers Party) was formed under the leadership of Franz

Pfeiffer.[12] Taking more than its name from the National Socialist German Workers' Party, it became famous for its swastika banners, armbands, Fascist salute, and *Heil Hitlers* as it attracted approximately ten thousand members its first year. And Pfeiffer's was only one of many neo-Nazi organizations in Chile—including the lethal, swastika-brandishing *Patria y Libertad* (*Fatherland and Liberty*) Party founded by Pablo Rodriguez Grez,[13] a member of Jorge Alessandri's unsuccessful 1970 presidential campaign—but it was the only one to host a "Miss Nazi" contest, to which Nazi organizations throughout South America sent their dewy, swastika-eyed contestants. For those who like to keep track of such things, the winner in 1968 was the rather chubby brunette Señorita Porteña, obviously selected more for her value as a sturdy breeder of future Storm Troopers than for any traditional, chauvinistic, petit-bourgeois esthetic considerations.[14]

It was in this climate that, in 1966, the first of many accusations against Schäfer and the Colony surfaced when Wolfgang Müller escaped the "watchdogs, electronic alarms and six-foot barbed wire fences"[15] to describe life inside the Colony. Müller—who had been brought over from Germany as a member of the original Siegburg group when he was sixteen—claimed that he had been forced into slave labor at the Colony, was beaten, and had been sexually abused by Schäfer in Germany when he was twelve years old. One of Müller's more interesting claims—especially in light of later events—is his insistence that Schäfer had given him "memory-altering drugs"[16] when Müller attempted to rebel or to reveal the details of his abuse at Schäfer's hands. He also complained of electroshock treatments being administered by camp doctors (shades of Barbie at Montluc Prison). After his third escape, he wound up at the West German embassy in Santiago and now lives in that country under an assumed name, still afraid for his life.[17]

Müller also revealed the existence of several former Nazis who lived at the Colony but denied that Nazism was part of the Colony's ideology. Later that same year, another escapee—Wilhelmine Lindeman—appeared with the same story of mind-altering drugs. This time, there was medical proof of her story: doctors discovered evidence of injections on her body.[18]

The author has been unable to obtain Schäfer's war record, but it is clear that—born in 1922—he was of draft age when the war was in its early stages. As virtually every able-bodied man was eventually pressed into Hitler's "total war," Schäfer must have spent at least a few years in uniform. But whose? The Wehrmacht's, or the black-and-silver uniform of the SS? His open friendship with anti-democratic, pro-Nazi regimes and his hosting of several former Nazis indicates that he did not spend the war years in the camps as a persecuted Baptist minister. His self-professed background—however flimsy or fraudulent—in psychology, his knowledge of mind-altering drugs, and (as we shall see) of specific forms of torture seem to indicate a somewhat more sinister education than Baptist Sunday school or Wehrmacht close-order drill. Indeed, when I "met" Paul Schäfer in 1979, he was the epitome of the "Hogan's Heroes" stereotype of the SS officer, although he wore a brown uniform with a Sam Browne belt and a campaign cap, an outfit that was more Storm Trooper than *Schutzstaffel*. One imagines that the SA commander Ernst Röhm was more his idol than Heinrich Himmler . . . but who can say?

The charges against Colonia Dignidad in the sixties came to nothing. Authorities tended to disbelieve Wolfgang Müller's more outrageous claims, and Wilhelmine Lindeman later recanted her story when the Colony informed her that her husband had arrived from Germany and was living at the Colony. She disappeared back into the sadistic embrace of Schäfer and his cohorts, and was never heard from again. The Chilean Senate, to its credit, began an official investigation . . . but "amid charges of bribery, the inquiry was dropped."[19]

Then, came the election of Salvador Allende, and the Colony took on a more active role in the political life of Chile and within the criminal milieu of the United States of America.

The attempt to deprive Allende of his electoral victory began immediately after his election, and the telexes flew like curses between Santiago and Washington. The Chilean generals conferred day and night on the feasibility of staging a military coup that would prevent Allende from taking the oath of office, and this plan almost succeeded except that incumbent President Eduardo Frei finally refused to support anti-democratic measures; a heroic move considering the amount of pressure being put on him by ITT, the CIA, and the generals. While this is not the place to go into a deep discussion of the Allende regime and its aftermath, a little of the background is necessary to appreciate the extent to which Nazi organizations—and specifically the Nazi cult centered at Colonia Dignidad—maneuvered to overthrow yet another South American government.

Eventually, Allende was sworn in as president and the generals began a series of conspiracies aimed at destabilizing the new regime with the connivance of Chilean business interests, the US Ambassador to Chile Edward Korry, and ITT. (It should be remembered that ITT had a history of supporting Nazi regimes. Walter Schellenberg, head of the Foreign Intelligence section of the SD, was named to ITT's German Board of Directors and remained on the Board for the *duration of the war,* and was paid a director's salary by the home office in New York.)[20] Funds were routed through to the truckers' union, for example, to enable it to go on a protracted strike. Anyone who has been to Chile knows that the country needs the truckers to survive: it is one, two-thousand-mile-long highway from the desert in the north to the snowy wastes of the south.

On December 2, 1971—after a year's worth of destabilization attempts by Chile's agricultural, industrial, and mining oligarchies—a tightly orchestrated demonstration of roughly fifty thousand housewives marched on the Presidential Palace, La Moneda, to protest Allende's economic policies. It is worthwhile to mention that these fifty thousand women were the wives, mothers, and mistresses of Santiago's wealthiest citizens and that the march originated in the exclusive Providencia section of the city that the upper class calls home. They marched on the palace carrying pots and pans which they banged together, creating a cacophonous din, and were accompanied in their procession by members of *Patria y Libertad* acting as a kind of bodyguard.[21] The "Empty Pots" demonstration—in which some women actually clashed with police—was carried on most major wire services and scenes were shown on the nightly news in the United States with the implicit suggestion that these women represented the poor people of Chile who were starving due to Allende's mismanagement of the economy. It was an artful piece of disinformation, and it certainly worked to great effect outside Chile.

By the spring of 1973, however, rumors of an impending military coup were rampant in the capital. Among the conspirators creating discord both in the city and in the countryside was a young American, Michael Vernon Townley. Townley was a member of *Patria y Libertad* and an associate of other right-wing terror groups. A right-wing fanatic himself who carried out assignments for a variety of masters, Townley also contributed to the development of the interrogation program at Colonia Dignidad.[22]

Working directly for, and reporting to, the generals, Townley was given the rank of major in the Chilean Army and together with Colonel Pedro Espinosa and the Chilean Secret Police (DINA), liaised with *Patria y Libertad* to create a climate of terror in the country conducive to a military coup. *Patria y Libertad* had already planned one coup attempt earlier in the Allende regime and was ripe for another. When the time finally came—in September 1973 with the military invasion of Santiago, the bombing of La Moneda, and the assassination of Allende—the roving, Freikorps-like bands of *Patria y Libertad* and the Chilean Nazi Party were cleaning up the streets and rounding up the usual suspects: intellectuals, students, artists, Communists, outspoken opponents of the army, and outspoken defenders of the president.[23]

Most of these prisoners were taken to the National Stadium, including two young American men who were subsequently murdered.[24] Many were tortured and then executed. Many others were simply "disappeared," their bodies found later—sometimes years later—in shallow graves and in roadside ditches.

A few others—the most unfortunate of all—found themselves at the Colony.

Concentration Camp Chile

One of Townley's tasks in the immediate aftermath of the coup was to establish a state-of-the-black-art detention center at Colonia Dignidad.[25] The following story would seem fantastic were it not supported by eyewitness accounts, statements of DINA defectors, and later United Nations, US, German, and Chilean government and Amnesty International reports.

If we were to believe Paul Schäfer, Colonia Dignidad is nothing more than a Christian religious commune organized around somewhat Calvinist lines of hard work and prayer. If we are to believe virtually everyone else, Colonia Dignidad is an after-hours club on a side street in Hell. Colony leaders had already established firm ties with the military long before the coup. According to Farago, it was a favorite hangout of Chilean Air Force officers (and, of course, Martin Bormann and Josef Mengele). Schäfer cultivated government connections through both his Santiago-based office and his Colony, where he also maintained a radio link with various DINA (secret police) operatives abroad in Colombia, Venezuela, and Europe.[26] Inquiries into the Colony's operations were effectively hushed with the strategic placement of bribes, all the way up to the Senate. And somehow the Colony had bribes to spare.

According to the soldiers I spoke with that night in Parral, the mail arrives virtually every day with envelopes full of money for the Colony. As it turns out, some of this money comes from pensions being paid to Colony residents from the (formerly) West German government[27] (one of the reasons all the Colony residents are German citizens?) But the soldiers I spoke with insisted that money came in from all over the world, including the United States. Its source can only be a cause for speculation, and concern.

With the coup, however, the Colony got a chance to put its electro-shock and narcotics "therapies" to the test. Townley and DINA agents had the run of the Colony, both at Parral and at the Colony office in Santiago.[28] While DINA maintained contact with its agents all over the world through the Colony's radio link, Townley helped design the specially equipped interrogation cells. These were tiny, soundproofed rooms built underground where "political prisoners" were taken not only for actual interrogation of a political or military nature, but also for the purpose of developing new methods of torture.

At first, each prisoner was questioned closely to obtain sufficient information concerning his or her personality in order to develop an appropriate torture and interrogation scheme. This individualized approach is already well known to the intelligence professionals the author has come into contact with over the years. The ostensible goal is to enable the interrogator to so finely tune the torture procedure that the victim surrenders his or her will more completely, more expeditiously. In practice, however, and with such a "scientifically" adjusted scheme of programmed sadism, there is tremendous room for an interrogator who is so inclined to subject the victim to unimaginable suffering over a long and sustained period of time. That this is what, in fact, took place at the Colony is beyond doubt for, certainly, there was nothing "scientific" about the dogs.

> In Colonia Dignidad prisoners have allegedly been subjected to different "experiments" without any interrogation: to dogs trained to commit sexual aggressions and destroy sexual organs of both sexes.[29]

I have used the exact words of the United Nations report of October 1976 to avoid being charged with unnecessarily embellishing my account with sensationalistic hype.

According to the same UN report:

> The detainees' heads are covered with leather hoods which are stuck to their faces with substances that are supposedly chemicals. In these [underground] cells, interrogations are carried out through electronic equipment, including loudspeakers and microphones, while detainees are tied naked to metal frames to receive electric shocks.[30]

(When the Colony was finally visited in 1986 by a group that included Chilean, West German, and Amnesty International officials, the underground rooms where prisoners had been held and tortured were discovered and identified.)[31]

What has been described, therefore, is a scene that not even the Nazi death camp commandants were able to invent: torture and interrogation by remote control! Individual prisoners in hermetically sealed, soundproofed cells underground, tied to metal frames, being asked questions by invisible interrogators over a loudspeaker and being jolted with electricity from a remote control panel when slow in answering. And the man who helped design this infamy was the electronics expert and radio freak, the American Michael Townley.

A Death in Washington

Townley would probably have remained unknown to most Americans had it not been for the assassination of Orlando Letelier and Ronnie Moffit in downtown Washington, D.C. Letelier had been Allende's ambassador to the United States and his minister of defense in the last days of the president's administration, and had been one of the first to be arrested once the generals took over. Letelier had then been transferred, first to the prison ship *Esmeralda* and then to Dawson's Island, a frozen wasteland at the far south of Chile, where he was tortured and starved for months before pressure from the world's governments forced General Pinochet—who had named himself dictator-for-life of the country—to release him and send him into exile.

Letelier was not one to turn his back on his country. He waged what can only be called a tireless, global campaign to destroy Pinochet's government by peaceful means. He spoke eloquently before trade unions, longshoremen's unions, and whoever else would listen, urging them not to cooperate with the Chilean regime. The result was the refusal of these unions to unload Chilean vessels, to transport Chilean goods, and a general consciousness-raising among world governments concerning the severe human rights abuses that were taking place under the openly pro-Nazi Pinochet and his Nazi-trained secret police, the DINA. That is when Pinochet ordered Letelier killed and—through his henchman Colonel Contreras of DINA—selected Michael Townley to carry out the assassination.[32]

Townley had already met Pinochet in the company of Stefano delle Chiaie, the Italian terrorist and *compadre* of Nazi conspirators Klaus Barbie, Freddy Schwend, and others.[33] Delle Chiaie had brought his friend, Prince Valerio Borghese, with him. The prince had been the main organizer of the aborted coup against the Italian government, and was a member of Licio Gelli's Masonic P-2 society.[34] Between them, they were able to provide professional advice, logistical support, and commandos sufficient to carry out the program of hunting down all of Pinochet's enemies including, but not limited to, Orlando Letelier.

By August of 1975, Townley was in Europe on an assignment from DINA to murder Carlos Altamirano, a Chilean Socialist leader. Delle Chiaie had intervened, saying that Altamirano was too difficult a target, and recommended another enemy of the Chilean junta, Bernardo Leighton. Receiving the green light from Santiago, Townley arranged for the hit to be carried out. Leighton survived the attack, however, even though he had been seriously wounded.[35]

Pinochet, Townley, and delle Chiaie would meet again, this time in Madrid, where Pinochet was attending the funeral of colleague and fellow traveler Generalissimo Francisco Franco, the Fascist dictator of Spain since the days of the Spanish Civil War.[36] Then, in 1976, Townley—with the aid of a group of the ubiquitous anti-Castro Cubans—set the bomb which blew up the car carrying Orlando Letelier and his assistant, Ronnie Moffit. The car exploded by radio remote control just outside the Chilean Embassy in Washington, D.C., in full view of Letelier's mortal enemies. Eventually, Townley would be apprehended and would plea bargain his sentence by giving details of his escapades to the US government and turning in the Cubans who helped him carry out the assassination. The resulting revelations enabled the US government to issue an arrest warrant for Townley's longtime boss, Colonel Manuel Contreras of DINA; a warrant that, predictably, was never honored by the Chilean government.[37]

The Colony Under Siege

This century has seen its Waco, its Jonestown. It has survived, limping, its Auschwitz, its Cambodia. It stares with a kind of numb horror at its Bosnia and Somalia. But there may be yet another conflagration awaiting its last years in Colonia Dignidad.

Shortly after Letelier's murder, a DINA informant—Juan Rene Muñoz Alarcon, a former member of the Socialist Party—made a deposition to a human rights group in Santiago run by the Catholic Church.[38] In that taped statement, he identified Colonia Dignidad as one of the sites where the "disappeared" had been sent in the years following the Pinochet coup.

Juan Muñoz was stabbed to death shortly after making his deposition.

That same year, 1977, reports were published concerning testimony by one Samuel Fuenzalida—a former DINA agent—who admitted transporting political prisoners to Colonia Dignidad in 1974 and turning them over into the personal custody of *Lagerkommandant* Schäfer.[39]

In 1984, Georg Pakmor and his wife Lotti managed to escape the Colony. Tragically, their adopted son was left behind. They confirmed reports of beatings, drug injections, and other brainwashing techniques by Schäfer and his medical staff to the West German government.[40] According to reports published in the *Washington Post* on Christmas Day 1987, the West German government at that time was sending anywhere from $48,000 to $80,000 in pensions to Colony members *each month*.[41]

That same year, an American citizen mysteriously "disappeared" while hiking near the Colony. Boris Weisfeiler was an American who was born in Moscow. Although his body was never found, the Chilean government officially concluded that the hiker had drowned in a river near the Colony.[42]

In 1988, the Pakmors appeared before a Bonn government subcommittee and gave detailed testimony about the conditions at the Colony. They testified that young boys were being given injections in their testicles, and that Schäfer was observed by them viciously beating a young girl bloody.[43] Testimony from another witness—Hugo Baar, a cofounder of the Colony who escaped in 1984—referred to the famous Mercedes-Benz limousine, the one that blocked my escape in June of 1979. According to Baar, the limo is bulletproof and heavily armed. Occasionally, Schäfer is known to loan it to his good friend, General Pinochet.[44]

Obviously, in spite of the rising storm of publicity, nothing was being done to stop Schäfer or to close his hideous Colony. Yet, all that began to change in 1990 with the establishment of the civilian government of Patricio Aylwin (a former Allende opponent). On February 1, 1991, President Aylwin ordered the revocation of the Colony's nonprofit charter after an investigation that began shortly after his inauguration.[45] Unfortunately, Paul Schäfer's right-wing friends in Chilean Congress have been running interference in the courts and thereby prolonging the ugly situation in Parral.[46]

Germany's former ambassador to Chile, Horst Kullak-Ublick, who was one of the few people allowed inside the Colony, was interviewed in a Chilean newspaper about his visit.

The people inside the Colony [he said] are simple, industrious people, most of them farmers from Bavaria . . . My impression was that they were all hypnotized, under the command of one person, Paul Schäfer . . . The answers we received were completely monotone, always the same.[47]

And, in case there was any doubt, President Aylwin's own commission reported that, indeed, the Colony had been used as a DINA torture and detention center. More importantly, the report revealed that the Colony had loaned its own doctors to the secret police. These doctors spoke only German, and—in a sickening replay of the selection ramps at Auschwitz—listened to recordings of Wagner and Mozart in the torture cells while they "treated" the prisoners.[48]

The government report also revealed that the Colony had served as a conduit for gun-running, the weapons having been smuggled in from Argentina . . . and Germany. This was, of course, during the same period of time that Klaus Barbie was running guns into Chile from Argentina, Bolivia, and Germany: a circumstance that is highly suggestive. Put together Barbie, delle Chiaie, the Italo-Argentine P-2 Society, Schwend, Rudel, and Skorzeny, the overthrow of Allende with the connivance of neo-Nazi groups like *Patria y Libertad* and the Chilean Nazi Party (not to mention the CIA and ITT) and Wolfgang Müller's sworn testimony concerning Nazis at the Colony, and you can easily come away believing that Farago was right, after all. In fact, Farago didn't know the half of it.

Perhaps the most sobering evaluation of all was given by former Colony leader Hugo Baar who said—in an interview published in *Time* magazine—"I fear for the lives of the Dignidad people if it comes to conflict there. I am certain that shootings cannot be avoided, and I say that out of deep conviction."[49]

Waco in the Andes? A Nazi Jonestown?

With the exception of Farago's statement concerning "voodooism," the news reports are all suspiciously silent about the religious practices conducted at the Colony. Although Schäfer is represented as a schismatic Baptist, nothing is said of what—if any—religious services were being held there. That the Colony leadership is fanatically German and devotedly anti-Communist is a given; but, then, so are many upstanding German citizens. That the Colony leadership proudly supported a right-wing military coup against the constitutionally elected Socialist president is also now beyond doubt. That the military junta itself was blatantly pro-Nazi—as was virtually the entire nation during the Second World War—is also proven. Why would Schäfer have picked Chile as a place to run to once things got hot in Germany, if not because he knew it was—and largely still is—a Nazi refuge? Why would he allow his premises to host Nazi war criminals—as has been testified by Wolfgang Müller, for instance—unless he were in sympathy with the Third Reich? And what services did he perform for the Reich as a young man during the war? From the foregoing, the author feels it is safe to assume that Schäfer was not hiding in the Andes Mountains to practice a particularly devout form of Baptist Christianity.

The only other evidence the author has to offer is what he was told by soldiers of the Chilean Army the night before his visit to the Colony. "They have their own religion," they assured me. "They celebrate festivals that are not on the Christian calendar." Accepting for a moment that Chile is largely a Catholic country and that the practices of a traditional German Baptist might seem strange or unusual to a soldier of rural background and upbringing, the celebration of holidays "not on the Christian calendar" gives one pause. Christmas, after all, is still December 25 whether or not one is a Catholic or a Baptist. The only possible deviation from that date for a Christian would be Russian Christmas, celebrated by members of the Russian Orthodox Church who still employ the Julian Calendar. There was nothing remotely Russian Orthodox about the Colony, except perhaps for its anti-Communism. (Elements of the Russian Orthodox Church during the war were notoriously pro-Nazi, but that is another story.)

So, we are left with a bit of a mystery.

The soldiers went on to reveal that these celebrations took place at night and involved candlelit processions and chanting. At times, great bonfires were burned. These could either be harmless religious processions such as those the author himself was a participant in as a child, or something a bit more sinister. With the Colony's activities over the last thirty years being relentlessly revealed in all their revolting glory, one must assume that its religious practices were more in keeping with the pagan cult activities of the Third Reich than with the holy day festivities of Sts. Peter and Paul Catholic Church of Commercial Avenue, South Chicago. Although the author did what he could to get out of candlelit processions as a boy, he was never able to concoct a story about injections in the testicles or demonic dogs.

If the author's informants were correct, the only reasonable assumption to make is that the sect practices a form of Teutonic paganism, observing the traditional sabbaths of April 30, August 1, October 31, and January 31 in addition to the solstices and equinoxes. These, of course, are the same festivals celebrated by the child-snatching, baby-breeding satanic cults currently the object of so much attention in the American press; they are also the holy days of many other, much more benign, pagan sects including the embarrassingly folksy Wicca phenomenon. As the Colony is known for child-snatching, child sexual abuse, and weird religious observances, it gets the author's vote as the only real, verifiable, satanic cult fitting the profile, a cult from which "satanic cult survivor syndrome" is more than today's psychological fad. Further, it goes some length to represent the fears of Dr. D. Corydon Hammond, who posited the existence of a satanic cult run by former Nazi brainwashers.

In other words, Colonia Dignidad has it all.

The Colony has since changed its name from Colonia Dignidad to Villa Baviera (Bavarian Village),[50] an innocuous-sounding title that nevertheless emphasizes its sinister heritage, for we have now come full circle in our study of Nazi occultism: from the elegant Four Seasons Hotel in Munich, Bavaria's capitol, in 1919 in the days of the Thule Gesellschaft and their successful overthrow of the Communist regime to the "Bavarian Village," a concentration camp in modern Chile, and its involvement in the successful overthrow of a Socialist president . . . and the fiendish torture and murder of its opponents and the brainwashing of its residents.

The murder of Letelier and Moffit; the assassination of President Allende; the military coup in Chile; the detention and "remote control" torture of political prisoners; the training of sadists; the Western Hemisphere's own concentration camp; missing children; sexual abuse; more murder; Nazis in the Andes, running guns, drugs, and escaping justice, keeping their twisted faith alive for Fatherland and Race; a monomaniacal cult leader, prepared to take his people down with him; brainwashed slave-laborers; soundproofed rooms for rape and torture; bizarre religious rituals far from the prying eyes of society; doctors torturing and killing in the service of the State.

The many separate strands that make up the fabric of the late twentieth century are snarled in a tight little knot known as Colonia Dignidad.

⚡ **13** ⚡

Nazi Occultism Today

Myths do not necessarily disappear with the circumstances that first produced them. They sometimes acquire an autonomy, a vitality of their own, that carries them across the continents and down the centuries.[1]

—NORMAN COHN

Anyone who interprets National Socialism merely as a political movement knows almost nothing about it. It is more than religion; it is the determination to create a new man.[2]

—ADOLF HITLER

We may think that what we have been discussing so far is a mere curiosity of the past. No one—save for a few crazies, Skinheads, or white supremacists—believes in the authenticity of the *Protocols of the Elders of Zion* anymore, do they? No one believes in the superiority of a supposedly "Aryan" race. There is no more Holocaust. World War II is over.

If only that were so.

The world is still in the grip of World War II; in fact, it is still in the grip of World War I. With the collapse of Russian Communism,

the map of Eastern Europe is slowly coalescing into the old boundaries. What used to be Yugoslavia has now reverted into a mélange
of independent republics that despise each other and still cling to a
pre–World War II mind-set. Croatia is beset with rumors of the old,
anti-Semitic Ustase coming back to power as old Nazis are rehabili-
tated for new government posts.[3] And the myth—incredible as it may
seem today—of a Jewish-Masonic conspiracy to rule the world is being
used as a rationale for that region's despicable program of "ethnic
cleansing," another euphemism (like "final solution") for genocide.[4]

Israel—a creature of World War I—is still not at peace. The Nazis
who orchestrated a continual campaign of warfare and terror after
World War II (from bases in Egypt, Syria, and Europe) have given
way to Muslim fundamentalists who have become, if anything, more
racist and more superstitious in regard to the Jews than the Nazis
could have ever hoped for. The Nazis, who had no love for the Muslims, are now sitting back and hoping that the Arabs and the Jews
(Semites all) finish each other off.

And what about America?

Nazi occultism in America goes back as far as Nazism in America,
which is to say, from the beginning. Its origins and early development
are, if anything, more secret and obscure than those of its German
manifestation because the Nazi Party was considered a subversive
movement in the United States and its more flamboyant leaders (such
as Fritz Kuhn) were often hauled in front of Congressional commit-
tees—such as the Dies Committee or the House Un-American Activities Committee—or subject to the resources of individuals and
organizations which were expended in uncovering criminal wrongdo-
ing by members of the various Nazi and Fascist organizations operating on American soil. In Germany, Nazism was homegrown. In
America, it was an imported threat, a foreign power operating on
American soil.

Initially, if we look at such organizations as the German-American
Bund, we find that American Nazism was fueled by propaganda smuggled in from Germany via any one of a dozen sea and land routes. The
texts of Nazism became more important than the physical presence of
Hitler et al. since there was no television and air travel between the
two countries was not what it is today (even allowing for the fact that

Hitler was the first national leader to use aircraft during an election campaign to visit several cities on the same day). American Nazis had to rely upon the printed word for virtually all of their information concerning National Socialism, and the printed word in this case was everything from *Mein Kampf* and the *Protocols* to Alfred Rosenberg's *Myth of the Twentieth Century*. George Viereck—Crowley's former boss—was a natural source for much of this propaganda, secure as he was in the paid employ of the Third Reich. Father Coughlin, the infamous anti-Semitic Catholic priest and rabble-rouser from Detroit, was another source. In fact, in Coughlin we have the somewhat bizarre example of a Catholic priest promoting Rosenberg's pagan ideology by selling *Myth of the Twentieth Century* from his own concession stand in front of his Shrine of the Little Flower, along with a nice selection of swastikas.[5]

Naturally, the predicament of American Nazism escalated when the United States entered the war in December 1941. From that moment on until about the early fifties, the activities of American Nazis—when revealed—were the stuff of espionage stories and spy fiction. But in the fifties, the *neo*-Nazi movement was born (largely as a result of virulent anti-Communism) and several groups took to the streets. Eventually some of them, such as the American Nazi Party of George Lincoln Rockwell, would become well known. Others, such as the National Renaissance Party, would not attain quite the same heights of publicity as the American Nazi Party, but that wasn't for lack of trying.

Aside from the purely political, however, many of these organizations either formed an inner, occult circle of their own (such as in the National Renaissance Party) or formed ties to secret cults and weird religions (such as those between the Ku Klux Klan and the NRP, or between Pelley's neo-Nazi Silver Shirts organization in the 1930s and the UFO-contactee I AM cult).[6]

From the other direction, that of the cults themselves, some took on openly Nazi characteristics. The Church of Satan (founded on Walpurgisnacht 1966) published rituals which were said to be genuine Nazi ceremonies;[7] and the leader of Church of Satan offshoot Temple of Set made a special pilgrimage to Himmler's occult center, Wewelsburg, to cop some astral rays. The Process Church of the Final Judgment—which sported a swastika-style emblem and glowing tributes to

Nazism in issues of its official magazine—boasted a leader who claimed to be the reincarnation of Nazi propaganda chief Joseph Goebbels.[8] In this chapter, we will examine these movements, many of which the author himself has observed from close range. If nothing else, they provide evidence that the link between Nazism and the occult is ubiquitous and remains strong after all these years. They also tell us something important about this "political" phenomenon known as Nazism, for why do many cults openly admire and/or emulate Nazism rather than, for instance, Communism or the Christian Democrats? In the first place, *a propos* the famous dictum of Marx, "religion is the opiate of the people" and has no place in a scientifically ordered society such as Socialism or Communism attempts to be. Indeed, the occultism in Russia was all on the side of the "White" or anti-Communist forces, a phenomenon of which Rasputin was but a single example.

But in the second place cult members understand the link between the essentially occult aspects of the Third Reich and their own magical practices. The following examples go a long way toward proving that—even if mainstream historians and political science majors don't agree or understand why—the occultists themselves recognize that the Nazi Party in general, and the SS in particular, was a cult . . . just as Hitler and Himmler had intended. Further, it was one of the best run and most efficient cults in the history of the world. Its modern-day devotees can hardly be blamed for admiring its effectiveness, if nothing else.

Modern Thulists

We have all seen each other somewhere before, and in the same way we will see each other again in the next world.[9]

HIMMLER TO HIS GRUPPENFÜHRERS
DACHAU, NOVEMBER 1936

Today, the ideals of the *Germanenorden,* Thule Society, List Society, and the Order of the New Templars are alive and well, at home and abroad. One modern neo-Nazi party—founded in America—based its entire ideology not only on the writings of List, Liebenfels, and Sebottendorff but also on Blavatsky and even, to an extent, Aleister Crowley and Anton LaVey (the founder of the Church of Satan). This was the National Renaissance Party of James Madole. His tracts were cleaned-up, modern-day versions of *Ostara,* replete with theosophical and occult references which supposedly bolstered Madole's anti-Semitic philosophy. His members wore runic armbands and quasi-Nazi uniforms to rallies, and had extensive links with the Ku Klux Klan, as the author can attest from personal acquaintance with both Madole and certain prominent Klansmen, notably Roy Frankhouser (who at one time also acted as an FBI informant). James Madole, until the day he died, lived in his mother's apartment in New York City—an apartment he had decorated as a combination of satanic chapel, Hindu ashram, and Nazi Party headquarters. Fascinated with snakes and panthers, there were large brass representations of the former with red glass eyes, and a heavy golden pendant of the latter, which he hung around his neck in lieu, I suppose, of the Iron Cross, First Class.

Madole was a relatively congenial human being in polite company. Completely bald, he bore a scar that he claimed was the result of a brick thrown at him by a demonstrator many years ago, and he had an entourage of young men in a motley assortment of uniforms who acted as his personal bodyguard, his SA. He possessed a thorough knowledge of the war and was fascinated by stories of the heroism shown by German troops in combat, particularly against the Russian Army. He had a serious junk food habit, downing enormous quantities of ice cream and milk shakes, and grinned (or grimaced?) at inappropriate times.

He also brushed away any consideration of the death camps as being irrelevant to the big picture. While acknowledging that the Jews were murdered in the millions—he was not, at least as I knew him, a Holocaust revisionist—he found justification for genocide in his theosophical worldview. "After all," he would claim to his shocked or admiring listeners, "if the Jews have souls, they will all be reincarnated anyway, and this time not in Jewish bodies (since we will have exterminated them all) but in Aryan bodies, as members of the Master Race. If they don't have souls, then they aren't human anyway. So, what's the problem?" This, of course, is a slight deviation from the "Jewish soul" idea of some earlier Nazi theorists.

His vision of the ideal society was a combination of his reading of Plato and Blavatsky. He saw society structured along the lines of the Indian caste system in a "pyramid of power" as he called it, with the common laborers at the bottom holding up the merchants, warriors, and Brahmins in various levels to the top, at which he placed the All-Seeing Eye that is to be found in Masonic designs and on the back of the dollar bill. This was a concept borrowed from Blavatsky by way of Himmler, who found the caste system equally compelling and who identified with the Kshatriya caste, the Warrior Elite.

One could say with some justification that the National Renaissance Party was quite small and hardly a military or a political threat to America or anywhere else. But the point to be made is that this Party—with its extensive philosophical framework—exerted an influence over other racist organizations which lacked the pseudo-intellectual underpinnings of the NRP. Forging links with the Ku Klux Klan, the NRP went on to attempt to bring the Church of Satan into the fold, an approach that Anton LaVey wisely rebuffed.[10] Madole was attracted to LaVey's Nietzschean philosophy and crypto-Nazi rituals; but La-Vey's organization promotes fierce independence as a way of life. The slavish obedience required of a Nazi organization would be repugnant to a genuine, LaVey-style satanist. Madole would die without having made this—to him—important connection, and the National Renaissance Party would die with him.

In the interim, however, his close association with the Klan enabled him to influence those Klan members who were literate enough to appreciate his lengthy printed discussions on the esoteric background of the Nazi Party and his "theosophical" take on racism. When I visited Klansman Roy Frankhouser's "church" in Reading, Pennsylvania, the occult influence (on the decor if nothing else) was striking. A flag-draped altar with a row of human skulls wearing Kaiser-era spiked helmets was the least of it. The upstairs room where I sat with Frankhouser, waiting for a contingent of Madole's Nazis to arrive as the Klansman melodramatically placed a Luger on the table between us as if expecting violence from your bantamweight correspondent, was further evidence of the influence of occultism on the American supremacist movement. Portraits of Nazis and Klan cross-burning photos were cheek by jowl with framed Nordic pagan emblems and runes, and volumes by Blavatsky were sandwiched in between the obligatory *Mein*

Kampf, biographies of Hitler, Himmler, et. al., and histories of the war.

The Ku Klux Klan itself was formally organized around occult principles. Albert Pike, a former general in Robert E. Lee's Confederate Army and chief of intelligence, was responsible for writing up the constitution of the new organization at a meeting of Klan leaders in Nashville in 1867. Pike was a Mason of the Scottish Rite and head of its Southern Jurisdiction at the time. He was also a disciple of the French occultist Eliphas Lévi, who had so much influence over Blavatsky's German patron, Marie Gebhard (Chapter One), and whose writings inspired generations of occultists in America and Europe, including Aleister Crowley, who claimed to be a reincarnation of the French magician. Thus, even this the most celebrated of homegrown, American racist societies had its origins among Freemasons and European ceremonial magicians, and was organized by yet another spy-turned-mystic.

As if to reinforce that link Robert Shelton—as is well known by now—attempted to form an alliance between his United Klans of America organization and LaVey's Church of Satan. LaVey refused the compliment, as he did with the National Renaissance Party and other neo-Nazi and white supremacist groups. This has not stopped the Klan from forming links with other Satanic groups in America and abroad, however, including occult-oriented biker gangs and, of course, Skinhead clubs.

Frankhouser himself was nothing if not a joiner. In his career, he has belonged to the American Nazi Party, the National States Rights Party, the Minutemen, and the above-mentioned United Klans of America, as well as Madole's National Renaissance Party. With over sixty arrests for everything from inciting to riot to disorderly conduct, he was nicknamed "Riot Roy" by his fellow Klansmen, but that didn't stand in the way of his gradual assumption of leadership positions within the Klan. In 1965, he was appointed Grand Dragon in charge of the Pennsylvania "realm" and extended his recruiting program into neighboring New Jersey, New York, Maryland, and Delaware.

In 1974, he was indicted on explosives charges. He blew his cover as a federal snitch at that time, claiming that he had infiltrated the Black September organization and had thereby prevented the assassinations of Zionist leaders in America; certainly a strange accomplishment for an avowed Nazi and anti-Semite. Yet—bloodied but unbowed—by 1987 he was serving as an "aide" to convicted felon, presidential hopeful, and occult conspiracy theorist Lyndon LaRouche and was convicted himself of obstruction of justice in regard to a La-Rouche credit card fraud scheme.[11]

Another modern Thulist is the notorious leader of the White Aryan Resistance movement, Tom Metzger, whose newsletter stumped for Nordic, neo-Odinist paganism for years before he was effectively silenced by criminal indictments and lawsuits brought in the wake of the murder of an Ethiopian immigrant in Portland by Skinheads he had indoctrinated and trained.[12] His syndicated talk show was a forum for all sorts of wild-eyed racist and religious theories, but the lawsuits have severely hampered his ability to attract new members. The Christian Identity movement—which is large now and which continues to grow at an alarming rate—has picked up the baton. It has abandoned Metzger's *overt* paganism for a fanatical type of "white" Christianity founded on anti-Semitism and racism, and acts as a unifying medium for otherwise disparate Klan, neo-Nazi, and Skinhead factions throughout the Americas and Europe. Given the support enjoyed by the Third Reich among German Lutherans both in America and in Europe, and the sometimes tacit, sometimes overt assistance given to the Nazis by the Catholic Church and in the person of such sick individuals as Father Coughlin of Detroit and his followers, it is perhaps inevitable that the next phase of Nazi occultism will be an "initiated" interpretation of the Old and New Testaments, à la that of Otto Rahn and Karl Wiligut, in which the Jews become descendants and worshipers of a Satanic Jehovah and the mythical, misnomered Aryan Race becomes the true inheritor of divine right, the "real" Chosen People.[13]

A New Protocol?

To those historians and sociologists who feel that the paranoid vision of reality presented as truth in the pages of the *Protocols of the Elders of Zion* would never find a home on modern American soil, one merely has to shift one's perspective for a moment and review what is taking place among the African-American population today. While

many might disagree with the extreme views expressed by Louis Farrakhan and his aides,[14] there is still a strong element of suspicion
among African-Americans with regard to white conspiracies against
their lives, suspicions that—of course—have some basis in reality.
With recent revelations concerning the Tuskegee Syphilis Project as
well as what we already know about the race eugenics programs that
were in place in over twenty American states in the twenties and thirties—combined with the long history of slavery, bigotry, and racial
brutality in the United States—it is no wonder that rumors concerning a white conspiracy to kill off the African-American population are
commonplace. As Patricia A. Turner points out in her important
study, *I Heard It through the Grapevine: Rumor in African-American
Culture,* these rumors take the form of beliefs that various edible com-
modities—such as Church's Fried Chicken or Tropical Fantasy fruit
punch—marketed in black communities contain chemicals designed
to make black men sterile; or that the FBI (or the KKK, or both) was
responsible for the Atlanta Child Murders; or that AIDS was created
by American scientists as a chemical-biological weapon being tested
on African and Haitian populations; or that whites have been responsible for the drug epidemic among American blacks as part of a well-
planned genocide program that also includes the above elements.
These fears of a widespread conspiracy by the government—a government owned and operated by a white majority bent on the destruction
of the black race—or by the Ku Klux Klan (a secret society) in cooperation with elements of the government, are so similar in essence to the
fears promulgated by the *Protocols* that one can't help but marvel at
this little-understood social phenomenon, and worry about its implications for the future of American race relations. In America, anti-
Semitism among the black population is an extension of several hundred years of general white oppression, oppression that *can be proven.*
There never existed any proof of a worldwide Jewish conspiracy
against anyone, much less a worldwide conspiracy of Freemasons;
by contrast, the enslavement and murder of blacks (and Native Americans) by American and European Whites is thoroughly documented.
Thus, these "rumors" among the African-American population have
some basis in reality; and a "Black" *Protocols* would be a bit more
difficult to refute. Natural expressions of outrage, therefore, can be
exploited more easily by those vicious elements within American soci-

ety that desire a violent end to the race conflicts that exist in our
culture. White America would never be able to promote the idea of a
black conspiracy equivalent to the "Jewish-Masonic" conspiracy since
the African-American community has so obviously been an underclass
in this country for centuries; but it *could* use the perfectly understandable anxieties of the black population toward the intentions of their
white neighbors as a means to instigate a race war from which it believes only the whites would benefit. This was Charles Manson's intent
in 1969, and it is a mission that has been adopted by a new generation
of neo-Nazis (including the occult-oriented Universal Order of former
American Nazi Party member James Mason) today.

    The occult aspect of the American right is usually ignored (as it is in
most histories of the Third Reich) since white supremacy is considered
largely a law enforcement or human rights issue here in the States. In
telephone conversation with researchers over at Klanwatch I learned
that the cultic aspects of the Skinhead, Klan, and neo-Nazi movements here were not the focus of any particular study or concentration
by them or by their patrons at the Southern Poverty Law Center in
Montgomery, Alabama. While they acknowledge that initiation rites
of various types are employed, this element of the "white underground" is usually glossed over. Such Skinhead initiation ceremonies
as the bringing back of the severed ear of a victim (as related to me
taking place among Skinhead groups in and around Port Arthur,
Texas) are treated as footnotes to the larger, social and criminal, file
that is gradually developing around life in the radical right.

Nazis and Satanism

That indefatigable chronicler of serial killers, Dr. Joel Norris, once
revealed in an article for *Penthouse* cowritten by Jerry Allen Potter
entitled *The Devil Made Me Do It*[15] that convicted murderer, cannibal,
and self-professed satanist Stanley Dean Baker had a swastika tattoo
carved on his left arm and that his girlfriend had a swastika tattoo
carved between her breasts, and that Baker had himself carved swastikas into the bodies of his ritual victims. He told investigating officers
about his membership in a cult operating in the Santa Cruz Moun-

tains near Los Angeles that combined elements of satanism with Nazi iconography. This was during the time of the Manson trial, and elements within the Baker investigation believed that the Santa Cruz cult was a sister organization of the Manson cult, and that both were "splinters" of some larger, older society in which ritualistic murder with Nazi overtones is a central feature. This concept—that there exists in the land a Nazi-oriented satanic cult—was given further impetus when Charles Manson himself carved a swastika into his own forehead. Many of his gnomic proclamations include a defense of the Third Reich, and he has blamed America for starting the Second World War (a point of view in line with that of such Nazi apologists as Father Coughlin).

Convicted of murder, Stanley Baker served only fourteen years in prison even though he had stabbed a man, dismembered him, and devoured his heart. While in prison, Baker began his own satanic cult and also managed to construct a total of eleven weapons, which were eventually confiscated by prison authorities. None of this activity, however, stood in the way of his obtaining parole after only fourteen years of incarceration. What is interesting about the Baker case is the early manifestation of a Nazi/Satanic *Weltanschauung* in California, and the existence of a cult—sometimes linked, perhaps erroneously, with the Process Church of the Final Judgment—that practiced human sacrifice and various other atrocities on kidnapped victims. It has been revelations such as those in the Baker case that have fueled the fears of those who believe in the Satanic Cult Survivor phenomenon.

To get a clearer picture of the twilight world where Nazism and Occultism meet in the twentieth century, however, we would do much better to begin with the Temple of Set.

The Temple of Set

As mentioned, the Church of Satan was founded on Walpurgisnacht—that is, April 30—1966, the twenty-first anniversary of Hitler's suicide and nine years before the fall of Saigon. Much has already been written about the Church and its flamboyant founder and leader,

Anton Szandor LaVey. The basic elements that comprise the Church of Satan may be gleaned from any of LaVey's works most of which are still in print, such as *The Satanic Bible* and *Satanic Rituals*. These books, together with the *Necronomicon,* are often found at cult sites in the United States and have been—rightly or wrongly—featured on various radio and television talk shows on the dangers of modern-day satanism.

LaVey, however, is hardly your fiendish, blood-sucking, baby-killing satanist. If nothing else, he has been far too public a person. A serious look at what he has written will illustrate the point that the Church of Satan is basically a hedonistic cult; a kind of *Playboy* fantasy with horror sound track. That's not to say that some fairly strange activity did not take place at the Church's headquarters in San Francisco. It is well known by now that Manson Family member Susan Atkins was a member of the cult,[16] and that actress Jayne Mansfield performed the cult's rituals in her own home the year preceding her tragic death.[17] It is also known that LaVey acted as technical consultant for Polanski's film, *Rosemary's Baby,* a story of modern-day satanism in New York City,[18] in which he also played the part of Satan. One can only stand back, slightly dizzy, as the coincidences pile up: for Polanski's wife was, of course, Sharon Tate, who was murdered by the Manson Family of which Susan Atkins (a Church of Satan member) was a prominent figure. Thus we have, for those interested in Zen semiotics, the wife of the director of this satanic film being killed by a minion of Satan who was (however briefly) in the director's own employ! Further, Witch high priest Alex Sanders claimed that Ms. Tate had been initiated into his version of witchcraft while she was in England on location for another film. It is such tight, incestuous little knots in the warp and woof of the American experience that make it easy to see elements of an occult conspiracy taking place in the culture. That this "conspiracy" may be largely unconscious and unpremeditated in nature does not necessarily comfort the researcher; rather, such a theory can imply a more pervasive, more insidious evil.

Nazism does figure to some extent in LaVey's philosophy, however, and *The Satanic Bible* honors such figures as Karl Haushofer while *Satanic Rituals* contains German occult ceremonies. LaVey's feelings toward Nazi political parties, though, are typified by his scorn of a possible satanic concordat with the National Renaissance Party mentioned above.

But when it comes to former Church of Satan member Michael Aquino and his espousal of Nazi occultism we are on solid ground.

Michael Aquino first encountered satanism on a visit to LaVey's Church of Satan after watching LaVey and his satanic entourage attend the premiere of *Rosemary's Baby* in 1968. Aquino became fascinated by LaVey's philosophy and began to correspond with him . . . from his post as a US Army intelligence officer and psychological warfare expert in Vietnam.

In 1970, Aquino found himself stationed in Kentucky, where he began a Church of Satan grotto and corresponded heavily with members and prospective members of the Church. LaVey authorized him to write the Lovecraftian "Call to Cthulhu" ritual for use by the Church and, indeed, Lovecraft's idiosyncratic metaphysics has been exploited more than once by Aquino over the years, which is another indication of how the *Necronomicon* has managed to enjoy cult status among both satanists and "white light" cultists alike.

Aquino eventually obtained a master's degree in political science from the University of California (at Santa Barbara) and ultimately a doctorate from the same university. Thereafter, he began to report directly to the Joint Chiefs of Staff as a lieutenant colonel with top-secret clearance. In the meantime, Aquino—tired of LaVey's grandstanding and what he perceived to be the founder's anti-intellectual bias—had split off from the Church of Satan to form his own organization based on a personal revelation, the Temple of Set.

To Aquino, *Set* is representative of a certain force in nature that is not necessarily identical to the Satan with which most Christians believe they are familiar. That is, Set is not the personification of *evil* but of ideas in opposition to those of Christianity: a separate, personal theology that transcends Judeo-Christian metaphysics to include this "Dark Lord." Thus, while Christians may view Set as evil owing to its opposition to their own religion, Set (according to Aquino) is not evil in any objective sense.

Aquino took a decidedly intellectual approach to satanism, and issued a fifty-page "required reading" list. He reorganized what was essentially a Church of Satan command structure and staffed his Circle of Nine with former COS members. His wife, Lilith Sinclair of the

Church of Satan's New York grotto, was known to the author during her days running an occult bookstore on West Fourth Street in Manhattan, down the block from his favorite Chinese boutique. Lilith had appeared in various magazine pieces every time *Newsweek* or *Time* wanted to run an underresearched story on witches or devil worship. Tall, with strikingly beautiful ebony black hair and chiseled, fashion-model features, she makes the perfect complement to Aquino's rather more studied Prince of Darkness–in–mufti appearance. Together they have appeared on television talk shows—such as Oprah Winfrey's—eloquently defending their brand of satanism and excoriating cult murders, ritual child abuse, et cetera with calm reason and studied, logical argument.

But then there was that Wewelsburg episode . . .

Consistent with Aquino's decision thoroughly to explore the Dark Side of human experience is a fascination with Nazi occultism. Aquino believes that he can divorce the occult aspects of the Third Reich from its political, social, and criminal aspects. To that end he performed the *Wewelsburg Working,* a magical operation in which the occult essence of Wewelsburg—and thus of Himmler's SS cult center with all its mystical resonances—is distilled into an engine of power that can be used by Aquino to effect a satanic renaissance.

He visited Wewelsburg in the early eighties and was duly impressed by Himmler's occult fantasy, some of which was still intact. On one of his visits he performed a magical ritual in the North Tower of the castle, a ritual designed to unleash the power of Wewelsburg on the rest of the world: to jump-start the next phase of human evolution. As Hitler says in the beginning of this chapter, the National Socialist mission was just that, to create a new man; certainly this theme is to be found all through Nazi writings and speeches from the very earliest days. But what is wrong with this approach to evolution?

Human evolution is Darwin's engine, one Blavatsky would ride to the end of the line. In a sense, *Origin of Species* and *The Descent of Man* launched the craziness of the twentieth century. Among Christians, you're either "fur it or agin it," as if evolution were a political platform. Among certain Nazis (and certain Satanists, like Aquino) evolution has to be helped along, directed, pushed in the right direction. If the author may be permitted a personal observation, the mistake the Nazis make in this regard is probably quite similar to the ones the Communists have made with respect to dialectical materialism and history: Communism, according to Marx, is the result of a natural process. It is a force of history. If Marx is correct, then we will all one day find ourselves living in Communist societies because Capitalism will inevitably give way to Socialism, which will then give birth to Communism. From this point of view, the downfall of the Soviet Union is due more to the *premature* creation of a Communist state in a feudal land in the midst of a Capitalist world than it is to any inherent flaw in Communism itself. Russia went from an agriculturally based society directly into a Communist society, which was a violation of pure Marxist theory. The same problem is evident in the People's Republic of China today, which has to make accommodations with a free-market economy in order to survive.

The same may be true for evolution. Darwin saw evolution as a force of nature and, in a sense, it is therefore also a force of history. We may be living in an age where the very essence of a human being is undergoing a subtle—perhaps psychic—change. It is said that humans are the only creatures who are conscious of their own inevitable death; that what differentiates us from the rest of the animal kingdom is the certain knowledge that we will one day die. Perhaps now, after Darwin, we have also become the only creatures who know that they are a *process,* creatures constantly in the state of becoming. There will inevitably be those of us who, anxious for the next phase and worried that it won't come out the way we want it, will try to engineer evolution along certain lines that seem sensible to us *today* but which might spell disaster for us tomorrow. (It has become a staple of recent stand-up comedy routines, for instance, that if global warming proceeds apace only the dark-skinned races will survive, a lack of pigment being no protection against the sun's deadly ultraviolet rays.)

Thus, from a purely pragmatic point of view, the Nazi occultists were blind to the enormous damage they were doing to the human race by limiting its racial—and thus its genetic—options so drastically. Along with the enormous numbers of Jews that were killed, virtually the entire Gypsy population of Europe was also destroyed. This loss can never be replaced. Of course, it is to the credit of some contemporary occultists like Aquino that they distance themselves and their philosophies as far as possible from a defense of genocide or mass murder;

the evolution they seek is a purely spiritual one, with no element of Nazi eugenics. The author agrees with Aquino's observation that the Third Reich was a state governed on magical principles; that is, after all, the thesis of this book. But the author cautions that—worthy as the Nazi phenomenon is of investigation and exegesis—not every magical state merits the emulation of other magicians. At the risk of sounding preachy, the Third Reich was an occult device that blew up in the faces of its creators because of its inherent design flaws; rather than try to build a better bomb, today's magicians might be better served by understanding its power source and diverting it toward more peaceful (and productive) uses. Aquino's approach to Nazi occultism is an intellectual one. As a lieutenant colonel in the army and someone schooled in psychological warfare, who served in that capacity in Vietnam, Aquino's professional reactions to the similarities between psychological operations and the techniques both of high magic and Nazi occultism are understandable. While Aquino does not advocate mass murder, it is simply too easy to identify his interest in—and use of—Nazi occult techniques with a general approval of Nazi atrocities, and this is what has hurt his reputation in the "occult community."

Unfortunately, there are more than enough Nazis in the world today who do not share Aquino's relatively benign approach to the rites of Satan and Swastika.

For instance James Mason's Universal Order—which advertises in the satanic newsletter *The Black Flame: International Forum of the Church of Satan*—sports a "backward spinning" swastika symbol superimposed on a pair of scales.[19] The reader may recall that Charles Manson carved a swastika on his forehead, but since he did so in a mirror the effect was a swastika spinning in reverse from the direction he had intended. James Mason (who boasts he joined the American Nazi Party at the age of fourteen) retained that particular form of the swastika even as he extolled Manson as the next Hitler, and the "greatest living philosopher of revolution in the world today." The collected writings of Mason—as well as his thoughts on George Lincoln Rockwell and the National Socialist Liberation Front (an even more fanatic version of the American Nazi Party)—is entitled *Siege*. Advertising blurbs in *The Black Flame* hail it as the "*Mein Kampf* of the 90's"; a dubious distinction to be sure.

In the same issue of *The Black Flame* can be seen another full-page advertisement for something called the Abraxas Foundation (which can be reached at the same post office box as Storm Productions, which markets *Siege*).[20] The logo of Abraxas is yet another rune, one used in SS-Oberführer Wiligut's own signature, and its official journal is called *Wake.* Presented as a publication devoted to "Social Darwinism, Primal Law, Resurgent Atavism, Blood Mysticism" and more, it promises that the reader will be instructed on how to integrate the "darkest aspects of man and nature" in his or her life. The premier issue contained articles on "Nature's Eternal Fascism" and "Long Live Death." Although publication in the Satanic *The Black Flame* does not imply total acceptance by the editors of the content of these ads, it is safe to assume that the advertisers know where their market is.

In the same issue, an article by Jeffrey Deboo entitled "Naziism [*sic*], Racism and Satanism"[21] gives the Church of Satan's party line on why Nazism and LaVey-style satanism are basically incompatible. "Naziism is not Satanic. Racism is not Satanic," writes Deboo. "Anti-Semitism is not Satanic." And from a strictly Church of Satan standpoint, this is true. But individuals such as James Mason and organizations such as the Abraxas Foundation do not follow Anton LaVey's philosophy as much as they may admire that forerunner of modern, "mainstream" satanism. And their thoughts, their ideals, are being perpetrated on another generation that can neither remember World War II nor identify its principle players. The new scriptures of international racism and resurgent Nazism are being written today not by politicians but by occultists. Not by the inward-looking, Golden Dawn–type of ceremonial magician bent on acquiring Knowledge and Conversation with his/her Holy Guardian Angel, and not by the folksy, back-to-the Earth, Wicca-style worshiper dancing naked in the forests, kissing trees; but by a peculiar breed of dark magician: occultists who are little more than frustrated SS officers yearning for the day when a magically oriented totalitarian regime takes the field once more and settles the world's problems by the oldest and simplest expedient available, the two-step formula of exclusion and annihilation. These individuals understand the secret source of Nazism's power, even if academia does not.

Death's Head, Skinhead

The leader of a New York OTO lodge once told me, almost in passing, that Caliph Grady McMurtry had initiated several "skinheads" he had met in a bar into the OTO. At the time the word meant nothing to me. I assumed "skinhead" was the colloquial term for a young military recruit who typically has been shorn of all his hair. Therefore, the fact that the biker-jacketed, former army captain McMurtry would have initiated a bunch of buck privates into the Order in a moment of drunken hubris made perfect sense to me.

It was only later that this episode took on a whole new meaning.

There is a tremendous amount of ignorance in the United States concerning the facts of World War II, particularly among the young. In fact, as recent screenings of Spielberg's Holocaust film, *Schindler's List,* before minority audiences in America's inner cities have shown, there is very little sympathy for Jews. Black and Latino high-school students from Oakland, California, for instance, have expressed the opinion that since they grew up with gruesome, technicolor violence all their lives, the type of violence depicted in the black-and-white *Schindler's List* seems almost comical by comparison. Indeed, they laughed out loud in the theater (which caused a minor sort of *cause célèbre* for a while). Experts on the scene, surprisingly, did not condemn this behavior as racist; instead, they saw it as a lamentable result of the general ignorance among America's youth concerning anything having to do with Hitler, the Third Reich, and the Holocaust.[22]

Certainly, as the author was growing up in the Bronx in the mid-sixties and attending high school there as a history honors student, there was virtually no discussion of the Second World War in class. The history texts carried the story, but it was toward "the end of the book" and we never—even in honors history—managed to reach that section of the text before the year's end. What I knew about Hitler in those days was whatever I saw in the movies or on television, plus whatever I happened to pick up from relatives who had served in the armed services or from neighbors who were survivors.

This continuing lack of education at the secondary-school level contributes in its own way to the rise of the Skinhead phenomenon here in the United States (and probably in Germany as well, where open and frank discussion of the Third Reich is understandably an uncomfortable experience, coupled with the fact that many parents and grandparents had somehow participated in the Third Reich in some capacity and are either loath to discuss it with their children and grandchildren or speak about it in somewhat different terms than we do here; certainly there are very few Jews left in Germany to set the record straight). After all, young men are quite probably getting the story of the Third Reich from those very individuals who have the most to gain by painting Hitler as a misunderstood genius, and his eugenics programs as models of scientific objectivity.

A survey by the American Jewish Committee in 1993, for example, revealed that an astounding number of Americans do not believe that mass killings of Jews had taken place during the war. The same percentage of Americans could not identify Auschwitz, Dachau, and Treblinka as concentration camps.[23]

Another survey, this time by the Anti-Defamation League of B'nai B'rith in 1992, shows that twenty percent of Americans are still prejudiced against Jews, and that thirty-one percent of Americans think that Jews have too much power. But these percentages decrease sharply in direct relation to the amount of education received, the lowest percentage of anti-Semitism being found among the college-educated.[24]

The Skinhead phenomenon itself was born among the poorly educated, economically stressed lower-income classes of Great Britain. At first, it was only a social organization that had no overt racist ideology or character. It was little more than a club for adolescent sons of white, English workingmen to gather together, drink beer, and listen to a particular, angry form of rock music (called Oi) that was being born in the row-house and public-housing districts of London and Liverpool. The members—in addition to the shaved heads from which they take their name—wore heavy, steel-tipped work boots, knit shirts, and suspenders. Some sported tattoos on their hands, arms, or heads. Like many youthful fads, it attracted the disaffected young who were simply looking for acceptance and a surrogate family to replace what was often a miserable home life in the English slums.

However, as Great Britain's unemployment rates began to climb there was a gradual move among the Skinhead groups to blame the economic situation on immigrant workers (particularly the Pakistanis) who, they believed, were taking their jobs away from them. A punk-rock group calling itself White Power became popular among the Skinheads with its overtly racist and anti-Semitic lyrics. The British National Party—a neo-Nazi, ultra-right-wing, ultra-racist political party in England—began recruiting Skinhead clubs as the shock troops for its own interpretation of civil disobedience and eventually much of the Skinhead movement was transformed from an apolitical street gang to a kind of British *Freikorps*.

In case the point is missed, in a local 1993 election in East London the British National Party managed to elect Derek Beackon—an unemployed truck driver and self-proclaimed racist—to a council seat there, garnering 1480 votes even though experts had put the membership of the National Party at no more than a thousand in the whole country. It was the first time the Party had won any kind of election anywhere, and their success was met by a wave of protest and racist violence throughout East London as police officers and civilians alike were wounded in some of the worst fighting since the Poll Tax riots of 1990. A speech by Conservative MP Winston Churchill—the grandson of the famous wartime prime minister—did not help matters when it included a plea for the cessation of immigration to Great Britain in order to preserve the "traditions of English life."[25]

Racial attacks have jumped seventy-six percent in Great Britain since 1988, accounting for nearly eight thousand such incidents in 1992 and about the same in 1991.[26] Although England is largely recognized as the birthplace of the Skinhead movement, it has taken much stronger root in Germany, where Skinhead violence is more dramatic and widespread. In 1992, over two thousand neo-Nazi attacks there resulted in seventeen deaths, including the famous firebomb attack on a Turkish apartment in Mölln that claimed the lives of one woman and two young girls.[27] And, to make matters worse, there is an international network of racists using the Skinhead groups as recruiting platforms all through Europe and America.

For instance in 1991, in the wake of more than two hundred arson attacks against foreigners in a single two-month period in Germany, American Klansman Dennis Mahon paid a visit to that country to form links with racist groups there. In October of that year he arranged a typical Klan cross-burning in a forest outside Berlin, attended by local neo-Nazi Skinheads.[28] That same year, a march honoring Rudolf Hess was attended by representatives of seven European countries,[29] and local police investigators have evidence pointing to the existence of a Canadian neo-Nazi Skinhead group operating in Germany.[30] Further, the *Independent* newspaper of Great Britain reported that a training ground outside Vienna was being used for paramilitary exercises by British neo-Nazis.[31]

Certainly, the number of former Nazis who wound up serving in Adenauer's postwar government was a scandal, and gives the lie to those historians who denigrate the charges that there exists in Germany a Nazi conspiracy on the governmental level. Even if we do not count such outspoken neo-Nazis as Franz Schönhuber, for instance (a former commander of the Waffen-SS who runs the Republican Party of Bavaria), the number of covert Nazis-in-place in Germany and other world governments represents a serious threat to national—and global—peace; perhaps not today, or even tomorrow, but soon the lack of concern on the part of citizens and politicians alike will be shown to have permitted the rebirth of a particularly virulent form of cult behavior.

For instance, as recently as 1993 roughly a hundred German neo-Nazis went on a rampage in Aurich armed with clubs and tear gas guns, which they used to attack a leftist youth club there. (The attack was successfully repulsed by police.)[32] But the Nazis finally crossed the line when they mailed a letter bomb to the mayor of Vienna, who was wounded in the attack which took place on December 5, 1993. The mayor, Helmut Zilk, was a Socialist and an outspoken advocate of minority rights. He was one of six individuals targeted by the same group, and one of five who were injured. The sixth bomb—addressed to a member of the Austrian Green Party—was intercepted by police and defused before it could explode.[33]

A police investigation of the affair revealed the existence of a neo-Nazi hit list of some 250 intended victims, ranging from journalists to priests, politicians to social workers.[34] As the German and Austrian governments become more zealous in pursuing neo-Nazi hate groups and prosecuting them for their crimes, research has revealed that the groups are becoming more sophisticated in the use of forged identification papers, high-tech explosives, and underground guerrilla-type operations including running safe houses all over the Continent. They are supported by well-wishers who perceive a definite threat to their jobs and income levels from the influx of foreign immigrants to Western Europe after the collapse of Communism. Afraid that their way of life is under attack from refugees from the civil war taking place in former Yugoslavia as well as from Rumania and other former Eastern Bloc nations, and including imported Turkish and Asian labor, they offer clandestine support to those willing to carry out acts of terrorism that, they hope, will scare the newcomers back East.

(A similar movement in South Africa—the Afrikaner Resistance Movement—is an openly neo-Nazi group agitating for the creation of a "volkstaat," or "People's State," an all-white enclave in the predominantly black republic.)[35]

In the United States, the neo-Nazi movement has also attracted attention because of its potential for violence. The Silent Brotherhood, for example, is run by a neo-Nazi who gives the official name of his organization in German as *Brüder Schweigen*. Groups such as the Silent Brotherhood, the Aryan Brotherhood, the Aryan Nation, the Aryan Resistance Movement, the White American Revolutionary Army, the White Aryan Resistance, Robert Miles's Mountain Church of Jesus Christ, and something called the Church of Jesus Christ Christian have all been implicated in various felonies throughout the South and West, including armored car robberies, counterfeiting, and assassinations. The murder of Denver radio talk show host Alan Berg on June 18, 1984, by The Order is one example of the lengths to which these groups will go.[36]

The Order is perhaps one of the most secretive, and yet most violent, of these groups. Patterning itself on an identically named organization in the famous racist novel, *The Turner Diaries,* The Order was also responsible for the largest armored-car robbery in US history. Taking place in Ukiah, California on July 18, 1984 (exactly a month after the murder of Berg), the heist netted The Order a staggering $3.6 million. The Order's founder and leader, Bob Mathews, intended to use some of that money to purchase sophisticated laser weapons that would allow him to knock out the Los Angeles power grid (once again, this was a plot element in *The Turner Diaries).* Eventually The Order was routed and its members either killed in firefights or serving time in federal prisons; but not before some of the money they managed to steal wound up spread around in the coffers of various other right-wing hate groups.[37]

According to one informant who told the story to former Order member Thomas Martinez, The Order was receiving contributions from German "families" living in South America.³⁸ This German Nazi–South American Nazi–North American Nazi link is reinforced by stories that German neo-Nazi terrorist Manfred Roeder, for instance, met with Dr. Mengele in Brazil as late as 1978 before coming to the States and meeting with American neo-Nazi groups. Roeder was eventually convicted of the 1980 firebombing of a Vietnamese shelter in Hamburg, Germany, which killed two of the boat people.³⁹

The fact that Mathews's organization is called The Order is very revealing. The only other "Orders" in contemporary racist history are, of course, von Liebenfels's Order of the New Templars and Himmler's own *Schwarze Orden,* the Black Order or SS. It should come as no surprise that Hitler himself saw the value in such homegrown American racist cults, for he once sent Kurt Lüdecke—a prominent businessman and member of the intimate circle around Hitler before winding up in Oranienberg concentration camp—on a special mission to America to visit the Imperial Wizard of the Invisible Empire of the Ku Klux Klan, Hiram Evans, to form an alliance between the Nazi Party and the Klan.⁴⁰

Many of these groups have informal links with each other and through something called the Christian Identity movement, which claims that the US Government is being run by Jews, and that Jews are the sons of Satan and must be exterminated; in this tortuous theory (eerily familiar to students of Nazi ideology), the "real" Lost Tribes of Israel are the Aryans and the Jews are merely descendants of Cain. Like such SS theorists before them as Rahn, Wiligut, Darré, Rosenberg et al., they have reinterpreted Christianity to the extent that up is down, white is black, and good is evil. The Lord of the Jews thus becomes Satan, even though they may secretly believe that their own god is a white warrior-demon, a light-bearing spirit known as Lucifer. Cynically, these "ministers" of the anti-Semitic "churches" preach an unrecognizable Christianity with one voice and instigate pogroms and assassinations with another. In the absence of a real grass-roots pagan movement in America, they have adopted the trappings of fundamentalist Christianity as their mythic vehicle. But it is a secret, occult Christianity that they represent, for they are only the modern manifestations of the original Ku Klux Klan which met at night in the woods, dressed in hooded white robes, burning crosses, and swearing oaths in Masonic-style initiation ceremonies. One cannot imagine the same rituals taking place between Fidel Castro and Che Guevara; it is a typically right-wing phenomenon, and its political overtones are almost universally racist, supremacist, and totalitarian. The Christian Identity movement is itself probably an attempt to create a "white" fundamentalist Christianity as distinct from the "black" Southern Baptist and Pentecostal denominations. By putting a different spin on the Old Testament and the Chosen People, the Christian Identity "ministers" hope to exclude not only Jews from the New World Order, but also all other races, with their unevolved, "polluted" form of Christianity.

The occult—if only in its outward trappings of elaborate, candlelit ceremonies in the night accompanied by terrifying oaths sworn on the skull and bones—is an integral part of these organizations; it's the glue that holds them together and which helps to create the sense of family, of a union based on blood, that is so essential to the functioning of these groups.

The ranks of these fledgling Nazi organizations are filled with young men looking for surrogate families in a social pattern that is very similar to the one that can be found among those who join cults and secret societies. Jim Jones and David Koresh (leaders of similarly Christian cults which are far more popular here among the right-wing than openly pagan cults, which are usually seen as representative of hippie-style countercultural revolt) both operated on the basis of what was known in the Third Reich as the *Führerprinzip* or "Führer principle": that the leader must be obeyed blindly in all things. Although one is accustomed to hearing the term *Führer* applied to Adolf Hitler, the word was actually used in a wide variety of titles and ranks of social and military responsibility within the Reich. The SS ranks, for instance, all had the word "Führer" attached to them, such as *Oberstürmführer* or *Standartenführer* or *Gruppenführer*. Thus, a pyramid of power was developed whereby each rank owed absolute allegiance and obedience to the rank above, culminating (of course) in the supreme leader and Führer of all Germany, Hitler himself. Since this system meant that individuals had no real independence of thought or action, it also implied that individuals were not separately culpable for any acts they might commit. "I was only following orders" became the clichéd response of the war criminal when confronted with the hideousness of his crimes and, indeed, within the context of the Führer principle it was a perfectly logical (if morally reprehensible) response. In German, it was called *befehlnotstand,* and as such was an integral part of the *Führerprinzip.*

Once individual action is proscribed, individual responsibility (within the context of the cult) also ceases to exist. That is why any such group is to be feared, from neo-Nazi Skinhead gangs to David Koresh–style religious cults. They are virtually identical in social function. Their members are isolated from society in a tight circle of fellow "true believers"; thus paranoia becomes an instrument of the Führer, who uses it to instill a sharp sense of camaraderie among his followers and a deep suspicion of anything coming from the outside world. This leads inevitably to the stockpiling of weapons and to preparations for a "day of judgment," a Holocaust that will cleanse the earth of the nonbeliever, the Semite, the subhuman. The conspiracy theory of world government is a necessary element of both the neo-Nazi organization (which sees the world as being run by a Zionist cabal, called ZOG or "Zionist Occupation Government" à la the *Protocols*) and the fanatic religious cult (which understands the world to be in the grip of Satan and his followers). Like James Jesus Angleton of the CIA, hunting for the Soviet mole he could not see but "knew" was there all along, these cult leaders insist that the invisible conspiracy—an invisible government—is very real, and very dangerous. And matters are only made worse when our governments are caught in the act of concealment and conspiracy themselves, thus giving weight to the arguments of the cults that the whole world—governments, schools, churches, social institutions, the arts, the sciences, *even reality itself*—is the result of a spiritual/political conspiracy to destroy humanity in the course of some satanic mission to rule the globe and populate it with demons.

Cheap air travel and the information superhighway (elements of which are already in place) are making it easier for these cults to communicate with each other and to influence each other. German Skinheads are training in Croatia; Canadian Skinheads are training in Germany; American Klansmen are burning crosses in Berlin; Tom Metzger had his own cable television show; and white supremacists routinely advertise and recruit through computer bulletin-board systems that are accessible by anyone in the world with a telephone and a modem.

One of the nations with the largest OTO affiliation anywhere was, at least until a few years ago, Yugoslavia. The author does not have reliable data on the present status of these lodges. Either the Thelemites have taken up arms to contribute to the genocidal free-for-all . . . or, more likely, they are now running for their lives while being hunted by a new incarnation of Himmler's SS. That would be ironic, of course, for Dr. Rudolf Steiner—the founder of Anthroposophy and a former OTO leader himself—was born in the town of Kraljevec just outside Zagreb in what is now Croatia.

Summary

If, after all the arguments given in the preceding pages, we still have a problem regarding Hitler as a cult leader (and the Nazi Party as a cult) that is probably because he was more successful than most. Shrewder, more pragmatic, and more charismatic than most other cult leaders, he also came along at the right time for a Germany that was suffering humiliation after its military defeat in World War I, a severe economic depression, and the annexation of its territories by neighboring countries. In a sense, the siege mentality so indicative of cult life was already in place by the time Hitler arrived on the scene promising a heaven on earth to those willing to die for the cause. In the end, the only troops he trusted (particularly after the July 1944 assassination attempt) were the black-clad officers of Himmler's SS, the elite Order that had been designed along purely pagan—and anti-Christian, anti-Jewish—lines, a cult priesthood whose headquarters at Wewelsburg was outfitted like a Nietzschean Camelot to receive the Aryan Holy Grail.

Should the West lose complete faith in its politicians, and in its political and judicial processes, and should the economy slide backward toward collapse, then this pathetic handful of cults abroad in the land will surely give birth to a new Messiah and Americans—many of whom don't believe the Holocaust ever took place even if they *do* know what it was—will embrace a cult leader the likes of which we have never seen. The coming chiliastic panic that is almost sure to set in with the turn of the century will give rise to apocalyptic cults promising salvation at the expense of the rest of humanity: a self-selection process involving the Chosen and the Not-Chosen. Racial hatreds will be manipulated and exploited by all sides in this conflict because, in the end, it will be easier to discriminate against someone on the basis of something obvious, like skin color, than it will be on the basis of one's personal philosophy, political affiliation, or religious denomination. In this war, one's skin becomes one's uniform, and defection is not possible. There will be no more open discussion of ideas, because ideas will be suspect. Reading will become the privileged occupation of a handful of cult leaders who, like the priests and bishops of the Middle Ages, will edit and interpret the meanings of texts for the benefit of a functionally illiterate congregation. Signs and omens will foretell the coming of a New Man, a Divine Leader, a Messiah who must be obeyed if destruction on a massive scale is to be averted. And the people—confused, embittered, hungry, fearful—will bow their heads and accept the inevitable. They will trade in their freedoms forever for the promise of security today.

And Hell will be full of secret delight once more.

Epilogue:
Hasta La Vista, Baby

My driver squeezed shut his eyes. His knuckles were white as he gripped the steering wheel like a life preserver. He faced forward, even when being questioned by the men who crowded around his side of the car, peering through the windows into the backseat looking for an Israeli kidnap team à la Eichmann.

"How many of them are there?" they asked.

"When did they arrive?"

"Where are they staying?"

To all of these questions my driver could barely open his mouth to reply.

They tried a more soothing tone next.

"Listen, we have to be careful, you know. These Israelis have diabolic intentions towards us." That was the word they used: "diabolic."

In the meantime a youngish man in an old-fashioned blue lab coat knocked on the window on my side of the car. I rolled it down.

And he spoke that phrase that every true aficionado of the war movie and the spy flick longs to hear in real life, but knows he never will. There, in the foothills of the Andes Mountains, with a white Mercedes-Benz limousine blocking my escape through a remote-controlled gate and with burly security men—old men, with the mark of war and brutality on their faces like the sign of Cain—covering every angle of escape, I heard it in a thick, German accent.

"Your papers, please."

I handed my passport through the open car window, knowing full well it was a dangerous thing to do but not knowing how to avoid it. If they wanted to, they could certainly have managed to drag me from

354

the car, and that would have been the end of it. My passport was passed back to some people in the reception building—if that is what it was—and I didn't see it again for about a half-hour. At the time, I had no idea what they were doing with it and assumed they might have been making a photocopy or were examining it to see if it was genuine.

The young doctor, if that is what *he* was, began to ask me questions. First in German, then in Spanish. I decided I did not want to dicker for my life in a foreign tongue, so pretended no knowledge of either language. Finally, the man began to speak to me in fairly good English but with that accent that, to Americans, sounds so comical in war movies. But before he began questioning, Paul Schäfer arrived and positioned himself at the rear of my car, where I could not, at first, see him. He asked the questions, in German, and the doctor translated them into English—and my answers into German.

"Why are you here?"

I used the story I had come up with on the bus ride down. It wasn't very good.

"I am studying German emigration to South America."

The high-pitched bark of a laugh Schäfer gave that admittedly lame excuse was straight out of the same war movie as "Your papers, please."

Then they demanded the film from my camera.

I was loath to give that up, but again there was little I could do. I removed it from the camera, handing it through the window of the still-locked car door to the young doctor. It had photographs of the reception area, the gate, and the town of Parral.

As I fumbled with the camera I managed to turn to the side and glance out the rear window. There I saw a man dressed in a brown uniform with no flashes or other identification that I could see. He was portly, and appeared to be bald with a head shaped like an artillery shell. He wore a soft campaign-style cap and a Sam Browne belt that diagonally crossed his ample frame. Basically, he looked like a militarized Easter egg. I tried to get a glimpse of a holster, but Schäfer kept strutting back and forth, pacing behind the car as his security men were inspecting it from all angles and even going so far as kicking the tires.

It was a standoff, and I didn't know why. Certainly my driver thought I was done for, as I discovered later. On the way up to the place I had asked him quite bluntly if the Colony was in any way a "Nazi" community, or if Nazis were known to live or visit there. As the guardians of Colonia Dignidad descended on the beat-up Chevrolet, I wished I had kept my mouth shut. The driver had volunteered that, indeed, everyone knew it was an *estancia nacista*. I replayed our conversation back in my mind at fast-forward and almost winced when I remembered I had asked him about Bormann.

And about Mengele.

Few people knew it at the time—and I certainly wasn't one of them—but Mengele had died earlier that year in Brazil. Everyone in Parral knew Mengele's name, of course, but my driver could not confirm any rumors that he had been there. But "many, many Nazis" had visited the Colony over the years and Bormann was one name that few men dared to whisper, even on the pitch-dark evenings of a Chilean winter. Even to their friends.

Finally, my passport was handed back to me. For some mysterious reason, they had suddenly decided to let us go. We had been held there for about three-quarters of an hour or longer.

The gate swung open electronically and the white Mercedes vanished. Schäfer disappeared. Many of the other men blended back into the landscape, and I was warned to return to Santiago immediately and to leave the country at once. I was not welcome in Parral, and Chile could easily become a hostile environment.

It had taken us about an hour to make the twenty-five-mile drive up the dirt road to the Colony from the Pan American Highway that morning.

It took us twenty minutes to make it back.

We swerved around oxen in the road, children playing, *huasos* on horseback . . . all at an alarming speed. My driver was so relieved we had gotten out alive he was laughing and sobbing. "*¡Que milagro*" he yelled, and banged on the dashboard for emphasis. What a miracle. The gringo was still alive.

When we arrived at the town, the driver dropped me at the square from where we had left less than three hours earlier. I paid him, and tipped him heavily. It was only another hour or so until my bus would arrive and take me back to Santiago, so I decided to wait around the central square still shaken by what had happened and angry as hell that I had lost my film containing the only known shots of Colonia Dignidad "in captivity."

A moment later, two more soldiers walked up to me. This was a different pair from the two I had met with Señor Molinas that morning.

"*¿Señor Levenda?*"

I swallowed. *They knew my name.*

They asked to see my passport. They passed it between themselves, stared at my photo, then at me, then carefully wrote down my name and passport number in colored ink in their notebooks. Then they started to ask me about my trip.

"You are the one who went to visit La Colonia."

I nodded, my mouth dry. I could only imagine I was being arrested.

It seemed the whole town knew where I had gone and what had happened. The soldiers certainly knew all about it and, from the direction they had come and the amount of time elapsed, I knew they hadn't yet had a chance to talk to my driver. They must have been reached by radio from the Colony. That meant that the Colony had its own communications procedures with the army. The implications were unnerving.

"What happened?"

"Were they armed?"

"Did they take you inside?"

"How did you get out?"

I answered them as best I could. Were they armed? Yes, sure they were armed, but they didn't brandish their weapons openly. They didn't have to. And the hefty bulges in their jackets and coats along with suggestive pattings after the artless fashion of hoods everywhere told the story quite eloquently.

Once I had answered their questions to their satisfaction, they gave me much the same advice as had the Germans.

"Leave Parral on the next bus."

No problem.

"And you had better leave Chile, too. You are a very lucky man."

Sometime later my bus arrived, and I boarded it gratefully. It was a bit crowded, but I found an aisle seat toward the rear and settled in for the roughly 250-mile return trip to Santiago.

Then, every fifty miles or so, the bus could come to a stop in the middle of the highway. The doors would open, and soldiers would come on board. These were not the same, dusty, down-home troops I had chatted with, and drunk moonshine with, in Parral. These men were smartly turned out with cold stares and automatic weapons. They would confer briefly with the driver, who would gesture toward my seat. One of the soldiers would walk down the aisle toward me and ask to see my passport. I would get a long, hard look, and then they would leave and the bus would be allowed to continue along its way.

This happened about four times. On the last two occasions it was enough for the soldiers to stop the bus, talk to the driver, give me the "look," and nod.

But every one of them, at every stop, knew my name.

When I arrived back at the Grand Palace Hotel I found a note waiting for me. I was confirmed on the next flight out of Santiago for the United States, leaving the following day. The message could not have been clearer. I was unofficially being declared *persona non grata* by the Pinochet regime because I had had the temerity to stand in the parking lot of Colonia Dignidad and take pictures of the reception building. For this, I was graced with military roadblocks all the way back to the capital and a seat on the next flight out of the country. And it wouldn't stop there.

For the next eighteen hours until my flight I could not shake the bearded man. He seemed to be everywhere I was, and was frequently there ahead of me. He was standing nonchalantly outside the Grand Palace Hotel when I went downstairs for a last, long look at Santiago. He was in the German restaurant that evening where I brazenly went to order my last meal, sitting at a long table when I went in, surrounded by what appeared to be students from the University. When I walked to my table, they stopped speaking and were silent until I had placed my order. I could feel their stares like cold raindrops on my skin.

A few hours later, as I walked along Huerfanos on my way back to the hotel, the bearded man was once again ahead of me. Just standing there.

And when my taxi arrived to pick me up the next morning, he was standing across the street. This time, he was openly staring at me from eyes that glowed like two brass cartridges.

He was such a conspicuous figure that I can only assume that I was meant to notice him and to take his presence as a kind of warning. But I had seen him several times before my trip to Colonia Dignidad. How had he known what I was up to? So few people back in New York knew where I was going, or when. I went over a mental list of people who would have been in a position to notify elements of the Chilean security police—DINA—as to my itinerary. I could count them on the fingers of one hand, and still have spares.

One was a Chileno who was a victim of Pinochet's regime. Conceivably he could have betrayed me to DINA, but only if they had something to hold over him. Family, maybe a wife, back in Chile whose life would be in danger unless he cooperated with them. But I knew—or, at any rate, thought I knew—that this was not the case.

And then there was an occultist.

Suddenly the pieces began to fall into place. The occultist was a member of a "satanic" cult in New York with ties to Brazil and Argentina. It was entirely possible that this person secretly disapproved of my venture to Chile, and took the opportunity to notify cult members of my trip. My opposition to Fascism and totalitarianism was well known in occult circles in the United States, and I had appeared on radio and television talk shows debating Nazis, Klansmen, and Satanists (of the Church of Satan variety). The bearded man, therefore, was quite possibly not connected with DINA at all but with this cult that boasted so many South American connections. They had even produced a Spanish-language version of Crowley's *Book of the Law* although they were not part of Grady McMurtry's O.T.O.

On the plane back, the seriousness of my predicament finally hit me. All the anxiety that I had not allowed myself to feel during my capture by the Nazis of Parral, the army roadblocks, and the conspicuous tail by the bearded man, descended upon me like an anvil. I spent most of the trip to Miami in the plane's rest room, vomiting.

When I arrived in Miami and passed through Customs and Immigration procedures, the last installment of my adventure then took place. As I came through the line with my luggage, preparing to re-check it for a flight to New York, three men in suits left their position by the opposite wall and approached me. One of the men flipped open an identification wallet and closed it again rapidly, too rapidly for me to make out what agency he represented. But he was from my own government.

"May I see your passport, please?"

Once again, I proferred my very popular documents to yet another government representative. At least, I thought, this time it was United States officials. Certainly, I had nothing to fear from them?

They stood around me for a moment, framing me in a kind of mis-en-scène. I thought I detected a smile, but it could have been a sneer. Without explanation they returned my passport to me, thanked me, and allowed me to pass on my way.

When I looked back, they were no longer there.

Sitting in the lounge, waiting for my flight to be called, and finally wondering why I had been stopped by those three men, I picked up a copy of the Miami newspaper. And nearly dropped it.

There, as a banner headline, was the reason I had been allowed to leave Colonia Dignidad alive: GERMANS EXTEND STATUTE OF LIMITATIONS ON WAR CRIMES.

I scanned the article quickly as if it were a telegram addressed directly to me. It said that the West German government, meeting in Bonn, had voted to extend the statute of limitations on Nazi war crimes. The statute had been due to expire that month. What the vote meant was that the German government could continue to hunt down the monsters who created, aided, and abetted the atrocities of the Third Reich . . . forever. It meant that whoever was hiding out at Colonia Dignidad would never be safe.

I had probably stumbled into their domain as the vote was being counted. They perceived my presence there as a device intended to provoke them into some kind of action that would swing the vote against them. Either that, or they assumed that I was there to register their reaction in some way; or as the advance guard of a new contingent of Israeli commandos (which was, indeed, what they had suggested to my driver). In any of these cases, it would not have been prudent to drag me from the car and shoot me. Instead, they allowed me to escape unharmed. It was a tactical decision, and it saved my life. Had I turned up a day later—after the outcome of the vote was made public—I have no doubt I would have been enlisted in the ranks of the "disappeared," tortured and murdered by the men of Colonia Dignidad.

A month later, in August of 1979, Jack Anderson's column published a story about Colonia Dignidad. It included references to secret CIA testimony before Congress and to Amnesty International reports on human-rights abuses taking place there. It spoke a little of the torture that was a main feature of the Colony; it mentioned that the Colony had been used as an interrogation center for DINA, the Chilean secret police, where technocrats were trained in the black arts of torture and for the first time I realized just what I had escaped from.

Two weeks later I was fired from my job with a large, multinational corporation that did a lot of business with the Chilean military (and the armies of virtually every free-world dictatorship).

A week after that, and I was followed down a Brooklyn street at six in the morning by a taxi full of bald-headed, beefy thugs—perfect strangers—shouting anti-Semitic epithets at me.

A few days later, and I was approached by a strange man in the Astoria section of Queens. Sporting a straw hat and dressed in a white suit with an impossible red carnation in his lapel (he reminded me somehow of the Peter Lorre character in *Casablanca*), he tugged at my arm and whispered to me in an accent I could not place:

"Don't worry. You are among friends here."

Before I could ask him what he meant, he walked away with a smile and dissolved into the streetscape.

In the months immediately following my return, I made several overtures to various agencies and media in an attempt to tell not only my personal story but to warn interested parties that there was more at stake in pursuing Nazis in hiding than revenge for what happened at the death camps. It was my contention that the Nazi underground posed a serious threat to peace, particularly in South America, and that world governments should ardently hunt these war criminals, sadists, and butchers to the ends of the earth for national-security reasons if nothing else. I told my story to Jack Anderson's people by phone, and to Simon Wiesenthal's people, and to members of various Jewish groups of my acquaintance. I was met with polite attention . . . and reluctance to become involved in that particular spin on the Nazi war-criminal story. The involvement of Colonia Dignidad in the Pinochet regime was well known; the CIA had reported as much to Congress. Amnesty International was compiling horror stories of torture and sexual abuse. But the full details of Klaus Barbie's reign of terror in Bolivia were not yet revealed; and Farago's book was still being laughed off the shelves. There was simply no interest in the story of a single man (possessing no journalistic credentials whatsoever) who had visited Colonia Dignidad in search of a story about "Nazi voodooism."

And then the fall of Communism, the rise of the Skinhead phenomenon, elevated levels of racial violence in American streets, revelations concerning the rites of human sacrifice at Matamoros, the Branch-Davidian massacre at Waco, and "ethnic cleansing" in Bosnia, all contributed to a growing sense that something is terribly wrong out there; that perhaps the ghoulish specter of the Third Reich had not been put to rest after all, and that it takes more than bullets and B-movies to exorcise a demon.

And I hauled out my notes, and refreshed my memories, and decided to write this book.

We have seen how some occultists—what Aleister Crowley would have called "Brothers of the Left Hand Path"—were responsible for creating a peculiar moral environment from which the bizarre religious, racial, and political theories of the Third Reich germinated. We have also seen how the notorious *Protocols of the Elders of Zion* was introduced to the Western world by a Theosophist when it was already on the verge of being discredited in Russia. Indeed, both directly and indirectly, that fabulous creation of Madame Blavatsky—her Theosophical Society—can be found at the root of virtually all of the occult societies that gave rise to the Thule Gesellschaft and, eventually, to the Third Reich itself. This influence was preserved among those contem-

porary neo-Nazi cults—such as the National Renaissance Party—
whose leaders understood the tremendous impact Theosophical
thought exerted on the List Society, the Order of the New Templars,
the Golden Dawn, and (eventually) on the political platforms of the
Nazi Party. Racial theory including the superiority of the Aryan
"race," the supreme significance of the swastika and other runic emblems, the universal application of an initiated interpretation of world
myths, and a "scientific" approach to religion . . . all of this can be
traced back to Theosophy. Certainly, eugenics programs were in place
in the United States that proved to be the model for the German
variety; *Lebensraum* tactics had been used by the United States against
the Native American population for centuries; and racial laws forbidding marriage between blacks and whites were in place all through the
American South. But in Nazi Germany, these programs were given a
certain, moral foundation in the writings of the Nazi "Church
fathers": List, von Liebenfels, Darré, Rosenberg, and in the speeches
of Hess, Himmler, and Hitler himself. What were vicious little social
programs of dubious scientific value in the United States became elevated to the level of literally *cosmic* importance in Nazi Germany. No
dissent was permitted; no discussion or argument tolerated. And those
who did disagree were exiled, tortured, murdered by the State.

This was not simply totalitarianism at work. The wholesale slaughter of the Jews and other "subhuman races" was of virtually no political or economic value to the Third Reich. On the contrary, the
Holocaust was an expensive and extremely problematic program. Vital
resources were diverted from the war effort to the pursuit and execution of isolated, powerless groups of people who posed no real threat
to the State. Human resources as well as valuable raw materials were
wasted in the design, creation, and maintenance of the death camps.
There was no *earthly* reason for all this. It was *not* logical, *not* pragmatic. The Holocaust could only be considered of value in a strictly
metaphysical sense to the Nazis: they actually believed they were engaged in a spiritual struggle of truly divine proportions, that the Jews
were the children of Satan—a subhuman species that, through its demonic collaboration with Freemasons and Communists, was intent on
destroying the world and delivering its ashes to their Lord and Master,
the Father of Lies.

To fight these insidious demoniacs, the Nazis created a secret society of their own. Borrowing the "skull and crossbones" motif from the Freemasons and dressing in black uniforms, initiated in candlelit ceremonies in awesome arenas, wearing a ring inscribed with magical runes, these sorcerers of the Right prepared themselves for battle with the Eternal Enemy of the Left. This was not politics. This was not economics. The SS was a cult, and its high priest was a man who believed himself to be in telepathic communication with the spirit of a Saxon king; a man who destroyed the lives of over a thousand concentration camp prisoners in the creation of his Grail center at Wewelsburg; the same man who created the Einsatzgruppen, the roving bands of SS men who hunted down Jews and commissars with equal ferocity and fed them to the crematoria; the same man who gleefully ordered "scientific" experimentation on living human subjects in the death camps.

This enormity was too great to simply disappear at war's end. He had indoctrinated his people all too well. They were the initiates of an elite secret society and would not trade in their beliefs, their cherished ideals, for a green card or a farm in Bolivia. They possessed "secret knowledge" incomprehensible to the profane, to the noninitiate, and jealously guarded this knowledge to their dying days, passing it on to select members of the Aryan Race so that the flame would never be extinguished.

The flame, that is, of a particular Hell.

From a purely philosophical point of view the Nazis' reluctance to simply jettison Christianity altogether is compelling. They could not just ignore the Church and go on about their pagan business. They had to *demonize* the Church to a large extent: they had to identify it as the Enemy. One cannot help but wonder if this was not due to a deep sense of betrayal; that in their hour of need the German people looked to the Catholic Church (or to the Lutheran ministries, or to any of the other Protestant denominations) for succor and found its spiritual strength—its moral courage—wanting. The ambivalence of the Nazi "church fathers" to the Catholic Church in particular is striking: they wanted to retain something of value from their childhood idea of Christianity (for von Liebenfels, for instance, it was the extensive liturgical calendar, the pageantry, the hyperorganized and ritualized lifestyle, the myth of the Grail and the Knights Templar), but they wanted to throw out Canon Law, the Papacy, and Christian moral values. They wanted to rediscover the Cathar tradition as they understood it: a kind of proto-Christian paganism; a Gnostic, illuminated version of Christianity, perhaps, but without the strict moral code that the Cathars were known to adhere to. The Nazis sensed that there was something wrong, something dark, at the heart of Christianity—a Lie—and the reaction of the Catholic Church itself is telling for, in its silence and in its meek acquiescence to the evils being perpetrated by the Nazis, it betrayed a shocking sense of doubt in its own institutions. Catholic bishops openly assisted the Nazi hierarchy. Catholic monks took part in the Holocaust. And, when Hitler invaded the Soviet Union, Pius XII applauded.

Were the Nazis somehow blackmailing the Church with evidence of some monstrous crime that has never come to light (*did* the Nazis find the Templar treasure? *were* they in possession of the Grail?), or was the Church's notorious lack of conviction during World War II somehow evidence that the *Church itself had lost its own faith?*

When each year that passes brings more revelations of how the United States aided and abetted the escape of Nazi fugitives, how can we instruct our young people on the evil of the Third Reich? When high-ranking Roman Catholic clergymen ensured the survival of thousands of war criminals by providing them passports, safe houses, and transport out of Europe . . . when the Church has covered up the sexual abuses perpetrated by its own priests . . . when it has been revealed how the Catholic nuns of Montréal, virginal brides of Christ, tortured the orphan children under their own care as late as the fifties and sixties . . . how can we speak to our children about morality? Wouldn't it be a normal reaction to try (as did the Nazis) to rescue the idealized portrait of a gentle Jesus, God of Love, from the clutches of the Church? Worse, how can we insist that these same Nazis are the very portrait of all that is wrong with society, with civilization, with power run amok . . . when we shamelessly exploited their talents during our Cold War with Communism, both in Europe (with the Gehlen organization) and in South America?

Thus, with a growing number of white men taking part in racist attacks against Jews, blacks, and Asians and using the Nazis as their

role models, we find ourselves in a desperate moral dilemma. Since
Vietnam, and through Watergate and Iran-Contra, the American people have become cynical about their elected officials, about their lies,
their treachery, and about the abuse of power that seems endemic to
Washington. Clearly, the idea of moral political leadership seems a
quaint memory. Who, then, will tell the Skinheads and whatever new
generation of neo-Nazi ideologues and radicals that comes along in
the next few decades that Hitler was a psychopath; that the social
programs of the Third Reich were a monstrous fraud; that the racial
ideas of the Nazi Party had no basis in science; that the SS was not an
institution to be emulated, that it consisted of murderers, rapists,
junkies, and thugs?

Sadly, we must expect that when we say these things to our chil-
dren—and to our children's children—they will point to Klaus Barbie
and Reinhard Gehlen and Werner von Braun and Otto Skorzeny and
Freddy Schwend and Valerian Trifa *and* Pius XII *and* Paul VI *and*
Bishop Hudal and hundreds if not thousands of others and ask,
"Then, why?"

And if America's cults become the surrogate families for children
who have been abused, neglected, or scorned at home (or at the Boy
Scout troop, the day-care center, even in church), we may never even
have the chance to hear the question.

For, as Charles Manson—neo-Nazi mystic *par excellence*—once
prophesied at his trial with regard to his own Family:

"What about *your* children? These are just a few. There is many,
many more coming right at you."

Notes

NA: National Archives
CDS: Captured Documents Section

From Thomas Mann, *Doctor Faustus,* p. 244.

Introduction: At the Mountains of Madness

My defense of Farago is probably idiosyncratic since such is not a popular attitude to take toward *Aftermath.* For instance, in a footnote to his *The Occult Roots of Nazism,* Goodrick-Clarke lumps *Aftermath* together with such pop novels as *The Holcroft Covenant,* which is either an oversight from that otherwise cautious author or a deliberate underestimation of Farago's work.

One of the shrillest critics of Farago's work is Gerald L. Posner, whose latest offering, *Case Closed,* purports to "prove" the Warren Commission's findings that Lee Harvey Oswald acted alone in the assassination of President Kennedy. Posner attacked Farago in a book, coauthored with BBC television producer John Ware, entitled *Mengele: The Complete Story.* In this work, safely begun two years after Mengele's death in Brazil, Farago is needlessly and brutally characterized as an incompetent, venal swindler who was duped at every turn in his quest for Mengele, a quest which resulted—says Posner—in the murder of an innocent man wrongly assumed to be Mengele (pages 268–274). Incredibly, Posner lays this crime at Farago's door; an ironic leap for someone who criticizes the JFK conspiracy theorists for similar "leaps." We may be certain that Mr. Posner will provide the

367

reading public with more such proofs in the future in his zealous defense of government-approved cover stories and socially acceptable mythology. Perhaps a book that will prove Senator Joe McCarthy's famous list of suspected Communists in the U.S. government was genuine or a study proving that George Bush had nothing at all to do with Iran-Contra?

1. *Table Talk*, p. 61.
2. Farago, 1974, p. 385.
3. Webb, p. 308 and pp. 489–515.
4. Richard A. Schweder in "'Why Do Men Barbecue?' and Other Postmodern Ironies and Growing Up in the Decade of Ethnicity," quoted in *Harpers*, Vol. 286, No. 1717, June 1983, p. 22.

Part One

Quotation from Friedrich Nietzsche, *Beyond Good and Evil* in *The Philosophy of Nietzsche*, p. 554.

CHAPTER ONE: OF BLOOD, SEX, AND THE RUNE MAGICIANS

My primary sources for this chapter were Nicholas Goodrick-Clarke, *The Occult Roots of Nazism*, and Norman Cohn, *Warrant for Genocide*, in addition to the works of Madame Blavatsky cited in the text and my own research among study groups and associations in the United States devoted to epigraphy and runes, such as the Epigraphic Society and the Midwestern Epigraphic Society, a chapter of the former whose journal is an extremely valuable resource.

1. *See* Rehse collection: Thule Obituary Notice.
2. *See* for instance Heiden, p. 243.
3. Foucault in *The History of Sexuality*, Vol. 1, quoted in *The Foucault Reader*, pp. 258–272, "Right of Death and Power Over Life."
4. Lifton, pp. 383–385.
5. Goodrick-Clarke, pp. 17–22.
6. For instance Blavatsky, *Secret Doctrine*, Vol. II, pp. 103–104.

7. Cohn, 1967, pp. 77–107, in chapter titled "Secret Police and Occultists."
8. Wolpert, pp. 263 and 290.
9. Wolpert, pp. 304–341, on Subhas Chandra Bose (1897–1945) and Durga Das, pp. 129, 256 257, and also NA, CDS, T82, R90, frames 0246901–05 for Nazi approval of Bose's resistance movement and recognition of his "administration" in India.
10. Howe, *Urania's Children,* p. 78.
11. Ibid., p. 78; Goodrick-Clarke, p. 23.
12. Published in English by various houses as *Tarot of the Bohemians.*
13. Howe, op. cit., p. 85.
14. Such as *Magic, White and Black* and *The Life of Philippus Theophrastus Bombast* (a biography of Paracelsus).
15. King, 1976, p. 75.
16. *See* Francis King, *Sexuality, Magic and Perversion,* for more detail on these colorful characters.
17. Waite, *The Psychopathic God,* p. 75.
18. Cohn, 1967, pp. 77–107.
19. Holand, *Norse Discoveries and Explorations in America,* 982–1362.
20. Ibid., pp. 264–286.
21. Fell, *America B.C.*
22. For example Blavatsky, op. cit., p. 106, pp. 586–593, etc.

Chapter Two: Volk Magic

As for Chapter One, Goodrick-Clarke was helpful here as was Francis King, *Satan and Swastika* (which anticipated much of the former's scholarship), and John Toland's *Adolf Hitler.*

1. Claude Lévi-Strauss, p. 221.
2. Refer to Colquhoun, *The Sword of Wisdom,* and Howe, *The Magicians of the Golden Dawn.*
3. Howe, op. cit., p. 177.
4. Colquhoun, pp. 84–87.
5. Guido von List, *Die Ursprache der Ario-Germanen und Ihre Mysteriensprache* (Leipzig, 1914).
6. For instance "Das Geheimnis der Runen" in *Neue Metaphysische Rundschau* [9] 13 [1906] cited in Goodrick-Clarke, p. 71.
7. Howe, *Urania's Children,* p. 46.
8. Langer, p. 186.

9. NA, CDS, T580, R202, Ord. 627.
10. Rahn, pp. 245–261.
11. See for instance Ashley Montague, *Man's Most Dangerous Myth: The Fallacy of Race.*
12. Toland, p. 802.
13. Payne, 1973, p. 98 re Theodor Fritsch and his *Handbuch der Judenfrage.*
14. *See* for instance NA, CDS, T580, R202 *Germanenkunde* file.
15. Goodrick-Clarke, p. 65.
16. Kersten, p. 31.
17. *Holy Blood, Holy Grail,* New York, Delacorte, 1982.
18. *See* for instance Cohn, 1967, p. 184f., quoting from *Der Bolschewismus von Moses bis Lenin—Zweigespräch zwischen Adolf Hitler und mir,* Munich, 1924.
19. Not in the printed stage play version of *The Man in the Glass Booth* but would have appeared at Act I, Scene 1, p. 21.
20. Waite, pp. 92–93.
21. Goodrick-Clarke, p. 97.
22. Charpentier, *The Mysteries of Chartres Cathedral.*
23. For instance in *Holy Blood, Holy Grail* and *The Messianic Legacy.*
24. Charpentier, pp. 54–67.
25. Cohn, 1967, pp. 132–133.
26. Goodrick-Clarke, p. 126.
27. Of course, many prominent *völkisch* occultists were also members and combined membership in the Thule with membership in similar societies, such as the List Society or the Order of New Templars. Goodrick-Clarke has done yeoman's work in uncovering the links between many of these individuals, and his work has been aided, in part, by sources such as Ellic Howe, Reginald Phelps, and Helmut Möller, who have published much of this information in historical "trade" journals not easily accessible to the nonacademic.
28. Goodrick-Clarke, p. 133.
29. Hering's diary is an unpublished manuscript, cited by Goodrick-Clarke, p. 127 and passim.
30. Toland, pp. 90–93.

Chapter Three: The Occult Messiah

Sources on Hitler's life and interest in occultism included Toland's *Adolf Hitler,* Konrad Heiden's *Der Fuehrer,* Joachim Fest's *Hitler,* Waite's *The Psychopathic God,* and Langer's *The Mind of Adolf Hitler.* Otto Friedrich's *Before the Deluge* was also valuable. Many details on Eckart's philosophy and influence came from the Rehse Collection at the Library of Congress.

1. Schellenberg, p. 112.
2. Library of Congress collection and Waite, p. 62.
3. Toland, p. 49.
4. Ibid., p. 52.
5. Bullock, p. 35, probably based on Greiner, pp. 86–94.
6. Many popular histories of the Nazi occultism phenomenon unfortunately suggest that Hitler was everything from ritual-practicing satanist to trance medium and associate the Thule Gesellschaft with all sorts of demonolatry, or what Golden Dawn member and Nobel Prize–winning poet William Butler Yeats used to call "Dhyabolism." Trevor Ravenscroft's best-selling *Spear of Destiny* spins a wild tale of Hitler attending séances with Dietrich Eckart and of the Golden Dawn, the Thule, and all sorts of Far Eastern cults being part of some giant satanic web: essentially turning the *Protocols* idea around on its defenders by implying that there *is* a worldwide conspiracy of Freemasons and that they are all Nazis! A saner approach—and the one the author hopes is being adequately defended here—is that Hitler's worldview was the product of influences from such occult legends as Guido von List and Lanz von Liebenfels, and that he derived much of his cosmology (including his platform concerning race) not from politicians but from occultists, such as those in the Thule and including such men as Eckart and Rosenberg, who were fellow travelers. In this sense, then, Hitler was a tool of other occultists: men who were intelligent, well read, well traveled, and insightful into the workings of the human psyche. Lanz von Liebenfels saw his dreams realized in Hitler, and said as much during his lifetime. Hitler devoured Liebenfels's writings and even met the Master. For an impoverished nobody with his own delusions of grandeur, that meeting alone was more important than most historians realize.

   As for the Thule being somehow linked to foreign occult societies: although there is very little, if any, hard evidence for this, anyone who studies occultism (particularly those forms of the last century or so) knows that occultists keep track of each other; they read each other's books, incorporate elements of each other's rituals and philosophies, and meet for drinks hoping the other will pick up the tab. Thus, while Guido von List would never admit to borrowing heavily from the Golden Dawn, for instance—since occultists never acknowledge their sources unless they are appropriately ancient and thereby long dead—such an influence can be traced by the acute researcher. This does not imply that

List would have been sympathetic to the Golden Dawn's teachings, only that he saw something bright and shiny there and picked it up for his own tiara.

7. Sklar, p. 55.
8. Ibid.
9. *See* for instance *Witness to the Holocaust,* pp. 38–43.
10. In fact, there were so many Catholics in the Nazi hierarchy that I had once toyed with calling this book *Lapsed Catholics' Revenge!* but thought better of it.
11. As discussed in *The Messianic Legacy,* p. 2, and Bultmann, *Jesus and the Word,* p. 8.
12. *Kabbalah Unveiled,* London, Routledge & Kegan Paul, 1970.
13. Rollins, p. 270. See letter dated Aug. 24, 1936, on *Vehmgericht* stationery as part of a hoax involving one von Reitzenstein, a probable Nazi agent provocateur.
14. Langer, pp. 263–265.
15. Schellenberg, p. 112.
16. Goodrick-Clarke, pp. 194–197.
17. Toland, p. 52.
18. Greiner, pp. 86–94.
19. Toland, p. 139.
20. Ibid., p. 68.
21. Ibid., pp. 93–94. Captain Mayr, Hitler's case officer when the latter was a V-Man working for the army, was one of those rounded up after the Blood Purge and sent to a concentration camp. He perished at Buchenwald in 1945.
22. For example in Pauwels, Bergier, p. 345: *"Suivez Hitler. Il dansera, mais c'est moi qui ai écrit la musique. Nous lui avons donné les moyens de communiquer avec Eux . . . Ne me regrettez pas: j'aurai influencé l'histoire plus q'un autre Allemand . . ."*
23. Trevor Ravenscroft, *The Spear of Destiny,* whose most shocking claims have been shown to be largely the result of channeling, although Hitler *did* remove the Spear and bring it back to Germany.
24. Webb, pp. 286–290.
25. Library of Congress, Rehse Collection, microfilm file on Dietrich Eckart.
26. Friedrich, p. 133.
27. Ibid., p. 119.
28. Cohn, 1967, p. 169.
29. Friedrich, p. 132.
30. NA, CDS, T84, Sr. 17, R6, Frames 5245–48.
31. Howe, *Urania's Children,* p. 93.

32. Pool and Pool, p. 91.
33. Toland, p. 296.
34. Toland, p. 569, and Friedrich, p. 376.
35. Heiden, p. 767.
36. Friedrich, p. 376.
37. Schellenberg, p. 113.

CHAPTER FOUR: THE ORDER OF THE TEMPLE OF THE EAST

Information on the sex-magic lodges of Germany came from a wide variety of sources, primary among them being Francis King's *Modern Ritual Magic, The Magical World of Aleister Crowley,* and *Tantra: The Way of Action.* John Symonds's biography of Crowley, *The Great Beast,* was consulted as well as Ellic Howe's *The Magicians of the Golden Dawn.*

1. Schellenberg, p. 112.
2. Pauwels and Bergier, pp. 347–353.
3. Richard Cavendish, *The Black Arts,* New York, Putnam, 1967.
4. King, *Magical World of Aleister Crowley,* p. 42 and p. 192, n. 1.
5. Howe, *Golden Dawn,* p. 262.
6. Goodrick-Clarke, pp. 61–65.
7. Deacon, pp. 25–37.
8. Crowley, *Equinox* Vol. III, No. 3, [1936]: *The Equinox of the Gods,* Chapter VIII.
9. *Liber AL vel Legis,* III/46.
10. Schellenberg, p. 112.
11. These pamphlets—*De Arte Magica, De Nuptis Secretis Deorum cum Hominibus,* and *De Homunculus*—were translated into German by Theodor Reuss circa 1913 and have been available the past few years in a variety of imprints, including that of Sure Fire Press in Edmonds, Washington. For their original German titles, please refer to the Bibliography.
12. *Moonchild,* London, Mandrake Press, 1929.
13. Rahn, p. 252.
14. *Science* magazine, 1967; see also Berry, *Sex, Economy, Freedom and Community,* New York, Pantheon, 1993.
15. Hillel and Henry, *In Pure Blood.*
16. Marx and Engels, pp. 87–90.
17. Symonds, pp. 126–130; Regardie-Stephenson, pp. 24–26.
18. Symonds, p. 128.

19. Regardie-Stephenson, pp. 113–116.
20. Ibid., pp. 111–113.
21. Peter Gay, pp. 383–384, footnote.
22. Ibid., p. 448.
23. Higham, pp. 37–50.
24. Crowley, quoted in Regardie-Stephenson, pp. 105–110, "The Last Straw."
25. Symonds, p. 129.
26. Ibid., p. 130.
27. King, *Magical World of Aleister Crowley,* p. 153.
28. Ibid., pp. 78–79.
29. NA, CDS, T175, R415.
30. King, op. cit., p. 144.
31. Ibid., p. 149.
32. Goodrick-Clarke, p. 27.
33. Symonds, pp. 258–259.
34. King, op. cit., pp. 161–162.
35. *See* for instance King, pp. 151–152.
36. Sontag, p. 93.
37. Ibid., p. 93.

Chapter Five: Cult War 1934–1939

Many of the same sources were consulted here as for Chapter Four; in addition the National Archives was an important source of information, as was the Library of Congress, Rehse Collection.

1. Mary Shelley, p. 42.
2. Berenbaum, p. 25.
3. Library of Congress, Rehse Collection, Thule Society file.
4. Waite, p. 238; Heidin, pp. 385–386.
5. Heiden, p. 389.
6. NA, CDS, T175, R415, no frame number: "Betr.: Freimaurer.-Wehrmacht-Für die Wehrmacht gelten nachstehende Befehle betr. Zugehörigkeit zu Freimaurerlogen und logenähnlichen Organisationen. I. Befehl des Herrn Reichskriegsministers vom 26.Mai 1934. (1 p. 90 J (I a) Nr. 2066/34). 'Ich verbiete jedem Angehörigen der Wehrmacht, auch Arbeitern, Angestellten und Beamten, die Zugehörigkeit zu Freimaurerlogen und ähnlichen Organisationen. Wo eine derartige Bindung besteht,

ist sie umgehend zu lösen. Eine Übertretung dieses Verbots ist als Grund
für fristlose Entlassung anzusehen.'"

7. NA, CDS, T175, R415, no frame number: "Betr.: Verfahren in Freimaurer und Rassesachen."
8. Cohn, 1967, pp. 135–136.
9. Von Lang, pp. 22–23; Padfield, pp. 198–199.
10. NA, CDS, T175, R415, Frame 2940297.
11. NA, CDS, T175, R415, Frame 2940296.
12. NA, CDS, T175, R415.
13. NA, CDS, T175, R415.
14. NA, CDS, T175, R415.
15. NA, CDS, T175, R415.
16. *The American Heritage Dictionary of Indo-European Roots,* p. 67, entry
under *s(w)e-*.
17. Padfield, p. 44 and p. 90.
18. Cohn, 1967, p. 132.
19. Ibid., p. 195.
20. King, *Magical World of Aleister Crowley,* pp. 156–157; Symonds, pp.
282–284.
21. Symonds, p. 283.
22. Ibid., p. 284. For more details see Deacon, pp. 310–311; Masters, p.
128.
23. King, op. cit., p. 161.
24. Ibid., pp. 155–156; Symonds, p. 278.
25. King, op. cit., p. 161.
26. Gilbert, p. 36.
27. Wulff, *Zodiac And Swastika,* New York, 1973.
28. Trevor-Roper, *The Last Days of Hitler,* New York, 1962.
29. Wulff, p. 112.
30. Goodrick-Clarke, pp. 164–168.
31. Trevor-Roper, op. cit.
32. Howe, *Urania's Children,* p. 110.

Part Two

Quotation is from Peter Gay, p. 628. At the risk of stating the obvious,
Freud intended this in a somewhat ironic fashion. He was asked by the
Gestapo to sign a statement that he had not been maltreated by them, which
he did (in order to leave Nazi territory) and appended the cited remark.

CHAPTER SIX: THE DANGEROUS ELEMENT

The memoir of Walter Schellenberg was helpful here, as well as the Captured German Documents section of the National Archives, individual items as cited below. But a word must also be said for Michael Kater's definitive 1974 study of the Ahnenerbe, which has so far not been available in English. During one of my first visits to the National Archives in 1977, Kater's name came up invariably whenever the Ahnenerbe was mentioned. His sometimes witty, sometimes justifiably contemptuous, but always insightful rendering of the activities of this organization made for a congenial traveling companion during the final days of writing this book.

1. Rauschning, 1939, p. 237.
2. Hillel, p. 80.
3. Goodrick-Clarke, p. 178.
4. Kater, 1974, pp. 7–8.
5. Ibid.
6. Ibid., p. 455.
7. NA, CDS, T580, R202, Ord. 633, *Keltische Studien,* letter dated Sept. 24, 1937 to Sievers at Ahnenerbe from Dr. Helmut Bauernfeld in Munich regarding an issue of *Germanien,* the official Ahnenerbe publication.
8. Kater, op. cit., p. 455.
9. Toland, p. 139.
10. Hedin, p. 330.
11. *Nuremberg Tribunals,* Vol. XX, p. 541, Interrogation of Sievers on 9 August 1946.
12. NA, CDS, T175, R665, Frames 702–730, Sievers *Tagebuch* 1943, Ahnenerbe organizational chart showing a Sven Hedin Institute. As Schäfer was eventually to command all of the "scientific" departments of the Ahnenerbe, it is educational to see just how much of this organization was composed of "wissenschaftlich" offices. It is obvious that, at least on paper, Schäfer's administration was the lion's share of the Ahnenerbe and that included the scientific "experiments" at Dachau, Auschwitz, Natzweiler, etc.
13. NA, CDS, T81, R128, Frame 150982.
14. Kater, op. cit., p. 213.
15. NA, CDS, T82, R21, Frame 0211045, article in *Völkischer Beobachter* dated August 11, 1941.
16. NA, CDS, T82, R21, Frames 0211013 and 0211172–73: *Deutsche Akademie* list of members attending visit to *Konzentrationslager Dachau;* for Ahnenerbe involvement in Dachau, see (for instance) Sievers testimony

in *Nuremberg Tribunal,* Vol. XX, pp. 515–561, and, of course, Kater, op. cit.

17. Schellenberg, p. 33.
18. Padfield, p. 248.
19. Ibid., Höhne, p. 152.
20. Höhne, pp. 152–153.
21. Schellenberg, p. 32.
22. Hillel, p. 38 and illustration number 14.
23. Brennecke and Gierlichs, *Handbüch für die Schulungsarbeit in der Hitler Jugend.*
24. NA, CDS, T580, R202, Ord. 627 file marked *Die Externsteine;* typescript headed: *Abschrift aus: Monatsschrift "Niedersachsen" 9. Jahrgang 1903/04, S-323.*
25. NA, CDS, T580, R202, Ord. 627 file marked *Die Externsteine;* letter dated 29.1.1937 Detmold, addressed to *Generalsekretär d. "Deutschen Ahnenerbes e.V." Herrn SS. Unterst. Führer Wolfram Sievers.* (This is also another indication that the Ahnenerbe was under SS control long before Sievers's stated claim—in front of the Nuremberg Tribunal—that it only became part of the SS in 1940. While there is some mystery as to where all of its funding came from before 1940 when the Ahnenerbe became part and parcel of Himmler's Personal Staff, there can be no doubt that SS officers filled its upper ranks. Thus it was managed and run by SS men regardless of where the money came from initially. As Kater has pointed out, p. 80, Schäfer was quite successful in raising funds from various sources for his SS-Tibet expedition.)
26. Schellenberg, p. 347.
27. Ibid., pp. 32–33.
28. For the guidance of those willing to wade through mountains of microfilm records in Washington, there is a collection of Ahnenerbe documents on microfilm rolls 121–211 of publication T580. Some of the rolls may prove more interesting to readers than others, and the following is a small selection of choice topics:

Roll	Order Number	Topic
121		Sievers Diary for 1944
128		Sievers Diary for 1943
144	170	Wüst on the Rig-Veda
	171	Wüst on Indo-Germanic beliefs
147	199	Astronomical works
148	199	Astronomical works (continued)
	200	Weather Science (the above two rolls con-

		cern applications of Hörbiger's World Ice Theory)
193	434	Records of the Kafiristan Expedition (shades of Rudyard Kipling and *The Man Who Would Be King*)
195	469	World Ice Theory
202	627	Externsteine; Icelandic Research; Runic Research; *Germanenkunde* (Teutonic Science)
	633	Celtic Studies
	637	Tibet Expedition
210	97a	Bayeux Tapestry
211		Bayeux Tapestry
999		Ahnenerbe personnel files

Also *see* T175, Rolls 664–665 for Sievers Diaries from 1939–1945 inclusive, which contain some duplication of Rolls 121 and 128 above, and T175 Roll 99 for some interesting Rahn/Wiligut correspondence.

29. Rahn, p. 111.
30. Goodrick-Clarke, pp. 155–160.
31. NA, CDS, T580, R202, Ord. 627 in file *Germanenkunde,* 35 pages entitled *Nordland Und Unser Deutsches Ahnenerbe.*
32. NA, CDS, T580, R202, *Völkischer Beobachter,* dated 22.8.38.
33. NA, CDS, T580, R202, *Völkischer Beobachter,* dated 26.10.38.
34. NA, CDS, T580, R202, Ord. 627, typescript entitled *Das Ahnenerbe Forschungsstätte für Germanenkunde, Detmold. Plan Einer Island-Forschungsfahrt (Sommer 1938).*
35. Schellenberg, p. 347.
36. NA, CDS, T81, Rolls 127–132.
37. NA, CDS, T580, R202, Ord. 637, *Tibetexpedition.*
38. NA, CDS, T81, R128, Frame 151284, *Personalfragebogen für "Das Ahnenerbe"* and Frame 151258.
39. NA, CDS, T81, R128, Frame 150982.
40. NA, CDS, T81, R128, Frame 151284.
41. Kater, op. cit., pp. 79–80.
42. NA, CDS, T81, R128, Frame 151254. I should also mention that—unknown to me previously—Tibet House also has in its possession a curious film made of the 1942 American Brook Dolan expedition to Tibet. This was shown to me first, in error, when I requested the SS film. The Brook Dolan footage was an official OSS film, in sound and

color, made during the height of the war and essentially following in the footsteps of Schäfer et al.

43. NA, CDS, T81, R128, Frames 151622–630.
44. NA, CDS, T81, R128, Frame 151625.
45. NA, CDS, T580, R202, Ord. 637 file *Tibetexpedition.*
46. NA, CDS, T580, R202, Ord. 637 file *Tibetexpedition.*
47. Müller-Hill, pp. 51–52.
48. Ibid., p. 52.
49. Ibid., p. 135–36 and NA, CDS, T81, R128 Frame 150726, letter dated 16.8.43 to Fräulein Kjellberg from Dr. Volkmar Vareschi on Sven Hedin Institute letterhead.
50. NA, CDS, T580, R195, Ord. 469 and R147, Ord. 199.
51. Hinted at in Serrano's *El/Ella* and more blatantly in his *Adolf Hitler, el último avatara.*
52. NA, CDS, T580, R195, Ord. 469, *Welteislehre.*
53. NA, CDS, T580, R195, Ord. 469, *Welteislehre* typescript entitled *Die Welteislehre und Ihr Erster Bearbeiter Philipp Fauth.* Fauth was an astronomer and the coauthor of Hörbiger's core document, *Glazialkosmogonie.*
54. Lifton, pp. 418–429.
55. King, 1989, p. 50.
56. Hüser, p. 384

CHAPTER SEVEN: LUCIFER'S QUEST FOR THE HOLY GRAIL

My primary source was my translation of Rahn's own work, as cited below, collated with Goodrick-Clarke's brief synopsis of Rahn's life and Paul Ladame's introduction to *La Cour de Lucifer,* as well as documents from the National Archives. As Rahn does not turn up in Kater's encyclopedic work, one can only surmise that his was not an official program of the Ahnenerbe but was directly answerable only to Wiligut and the Reichsführer-SS himself.

1. Rahn, p. 86 (my translation).
2. Schellenberg, p. 347.
3. For example in Rahn, p. 66.
4. Adams, p. 92.
5. Fulcanelli, *The Mystery of the Cathedrals,* London, Spearman, 1971.
6. Birks and Gilbert, *The Treasure of Montségur.*
7. Ibid., p. 39.
8. Ibid., p. 48.

9. Ibid., p. 150.
10. Ibid., p. 38.
11. Ibid., pp. 18–19.
12. Ladame in Rahn, p. 14; implied in Hüser, p. 207.
13. Goodrick-Clarke, pp. 188–189; documented in Hüser, p. 206.
14. NA, CDR, T175, Roll 99.
15. Ladame in Rahn, p. 13.
16. Ladame in Rahn, p. 23.
17. Goodrick-Clarke, p. 189.
18. The difficulty in obtaining the German edition, of *Luzifers Hofgesind* has resulted in my reliance on the French translation by Nelli, *La Cour de Lucifer,* and all page numbers refer to this otherwise invaluable edition, which contains a foreword by Paul Ladame and a Translator's Preface by René Nelli.
19. Rahn, p. 93.
20. Rahn, pp. 94–95.
21. Rahn, p. 57.
22. Rahn, p. 48.
23. Ladame in Rahn, pp. 28–29.
24. Ladame in Rahn, pp. 24ff.
25. Hüser, p. 208.
26. Ibid., p. 207.
27. Cocks, pp. 202–211.
28. Birks and Gilbert, p. 40.
29. Baring-Gould, p. 258.

Chapter Eight: The Psychics Search

Schellenberg's memoir was helpful, as was Wilhelm Wulff's memoir, *Zodiac and Swastika.*

1. *The Schellenberg Memoirs,* London, 1956.
2. Schellenberg, p. 386.
3. Ibid.
4. Wulff, pp. 84–89.
5. Ibid., p. 88.
6. Ibid., pp. 75–78.
7. Ibid., p. 75.
8. Ibid.
9. Ibid., p. 74.

10. Ibid., p. 77.
11. *See* Marks, *The Search for the "Manchurian Candidate."*
12. For instance NA, CDS, T175, R665, Sievers *Tagebuch* 1944 regarding freezing experiments at Dachau; Nuremberg Tribunals, Vol. XX, pp. 515–561, Sievers testimony regarding medical experimentation at Dachau and other camps, including that of Sigmund Rascher.
13. Marks, pp. 4–5.
14. NA, CDS, T175, R665, Sievers *Tagebuch* 1945, entry number 14 on Feb. 2, page 37, which reads as follows: *Drogen für bestimmte Zwecke / für Zusammenarbeit mit RSHA, Amt VI, SS-Stubaf. Lassig verweiss Hirt in Zusammenhag mit von Sowjets verwendeter Steppenraute auf Mescalin (synthetisch herstellbar) und Canabinol.*
15. NA, CDS, T175, R665, Frames 1–309 and Padfield, pp. 436–438.
16. NA, CDS, T175, R665, Frames 702–730.
17. Marks, p. 6.
18. Marks, p. 18.
19. Marks, p. 11.
20. Schellenberg, pp. 108–110.
21. Simpson, pp. 46–49.
22. Ibid., p. 47.
23. Ibid.
24. Howe, 1967, p. 120ff.

CHAPTER NINE: CULT COUNTERSTRIKE

Richard Deacon's *History of the British Secret Service* was an important source, as was Anthony Masters's biography of Maxwell Knight.

1. Deacon, pp. 310–311.
2. Masters, p. 108.
3. Wheatley, p. 273.
4. Ibid., p. 282.
5. Howe, 1967, p. 196; Deacon, p. 315; Masters, p. 128.
6. Koppes, p. 3.
7. Ibid., p. 12.
8. Ibid., p. 13.
9. Masters, p. 68.
10. Masters, p. 67.
11. Symonds, p. 8.
12. Masters, p. 75.

13. Masters, p. 68.
14. Masters, p. 127; Deacon, p. 320.
15. Symonds, p. 129.
16. Symonds p. 129; Deacon p. 224.
17. Howe, *Urania's Children,* p. 195.
18. Masters, p. 129.
19. Deacon, p. 319.
20. Deacon, p. 311.
21. Howe, 1967, p. 204ff.
22. Hutton, p. 130.
23. Terry, p. 192.
24. Ibid.
25. Rollins, p. 62ff.
26. Rollins, p. 73.

Part Three

Quotation from Rauschning, 1942, p. 81.

CHAPTER TEN: *WALPURGISNACHT,* 1945

Christopher Simpson's *Blowback* was a valuable resource, in addition to the published records of the Nuremberg Tribunals.

1. Rauschning, 1942, pp. 84–85.
2. Schellenberg, p. 112.
3. Farago, *Aftermath: Martin Bormann and the Fourth Reich.*
4. Simpson, *Blowback;* Linklater et al., *The Nazi Legacy.*
5. Farago, 1982, pp. 4, 90–91, and pp. 131–132.
6. Farago, 1982, pp. 182–96; Higham p. 299.
7. Simpson, pp. 180–181, fn.
8. Simpson, pp. 185–187; Linklater et al., pp. 185–196.
9. Simpson, pp. 177–185.
10. Ibid., p. 181.
11. Ibid.
12. Hillel, p. 143.
13. *New York Times,* Aug. 18, 1987, pp. A1, B8–9, "Rudolf Hess Is Dead in Berlin, Last of Hitler Inner Circle."

14. Thomas, pp. 153–154.
15. Marks, p. 11.
16. *Nuremberg Tribunals,* Vol. XX, Hess Testimony on 31 August 1946, pp. 368–369.
17. Ibid., p. 369.
18. Ibid., pp. 370–371.
19. Ibid., p. 373.
20. *New York Times,* Dec. 14, 1993, "Argentine Files Show Huge Effort to Harbor Nazis" by Nathaniel C. Nash.
21. *Nuremberg Tribunals,* Vol. XX, Sievers Testimony, pp. 516–561.
22. Ibid., p. 541.
23. Ibid., p. 521.

CHAPTER ELEVEN: AFTERMATH

Higham's *American Swastika* is a valuable and much-neglected work on this important subject. *Nazi Legacy* by Linklater, Hilton, and Ascherson is the definitive Klaus Barbie story, with emphasis on his Nazi and criminal activities in South America and, therefore, quite valuable as a source.

1. *New York Times,* Feb. 16, 1992, p. 4E.
2. Hillel, p. 12.
3. Higham, pp. 216–220, 231–232.
4. *New York Times,* Dec. 27, 1993, p. A6, "On Tour, Russian Nationalist Challenges Bulgarian Leader."
5. Francis King, in conversation with the author in New York City, circa 1975.
6. Francis King, *Satan and Swastika,* p. 64.
7. Ibid., p. 65.
8. Crowley, *The Book of the Goetia of Solomon the King,* p. 4.
9. Downloaded from an EBBS at Bapho-Net By The Sea, one of many Thelemic BBS, which was being run by Tony Iannotti, SYSOP, in Park Slope, Brooklyn (and may still be).
10. *Equinox* Vol. III, Number 10, p. 101ff.
11. See *Liber OZ* as produced in Kenneth Grant.
12. Refers to Kenneth Grant books: *Magical Revival,* etc.
13. Parker, p. 195–197.
14. Sanders.
15. Schreck, p. 127.
16. Quoted in Cohn, 1967, p. 206.

17. *New Yorker,* May 24, 1993, pp. 72–73, "Remembering Satan—Part II" by Lawrence Wright.
18. Schreck, pp. 141–147.
19. Fernandez Artucio, p. 12.
20. Gunther, p. 403.
21. Ibid., p. 267.
22. *New York Times,* Dec. 14, 1993, "Argentine Files Show Huge Effort to Harbor Nazis" by Nathaniel C. Nash.
23. Fernandez Artucio, p. 84ff.
24. Payne, 1980, pp. 172–175.
25. Fest, p. 211.
26. Payne, 1980, pp. 175–176.
27. Shannon, pp. 112–117; Mills, pp. 1127–1128.
28. Shannon, p. 116.
29. Linklater, p. 31.
30. Ibid., pp. 33–35.
31. Ibid., p. 76.
32. Ibid., p. 132ff.
33. Ibid., p. 185ff.; Simpson, op. cit.
34. Linklater et al., pp. 187–188.
35. Gunther, p. 400.
36. Linklater, p. 266.
37. Ibid., p. 278; Marshall et al., pp. 70, 76.

Chapter Twelve: Is Chile Burning?

Most of this chapter was taken from the headlines as the story broke and as they are cited below. Some additional information was kindly supplied by Amnesty International.

1. Heiden, p. 5.
2. Refer to Serrano, *El/Ella,* and *Adolf Hitler, el último avatara,* passim.
3. *Times of the Americas,* May 15, 1991, "German Settlers Accused of Torture and Sexual Abuse" (TOA).
4. *Time,* May 16, 1988, p. 58, "Colony of the Damned."
5. TOA, op. cit.
6. *Washington Post,* Dec. 25, 1987, "German Settlement Stirs Controversy in Chile."
7. TOA, op. cit.
8. *Washington Post,* op. cit.; TOA, op. cit.

9. Freed, p. 114.
10. *Washington Post,* op. cit.
11. TOA, op. cit.
12. Farago, p. 385.
13. Rojas Sandford, p. 112.
14. Farago, p. 385.
15. TOA, op. cit.
16. *Washington Post,* op. cit.
17. *Time,* op. cit.
18. *Washington Post,* op. cit.
19. Ibid.
20. Higham, pp. 201–202.
21. Rojas Sandford, pp. 101–102.
22. Freed, pp. 114–116.
23. Ibid., p. 114.
24. *See The Execution of Charles Horman: An American Sacrifice,* Thomas Hauser, New York, Harcourt Brace Jovanovich, 1979, for more detail on the murdered Americans. This story was subsequently made into a film by Costa-Gavras entitled *Missing,* starring Jack Lemmon and Sissy Spacek.
25. Freed, p. 114.
26. Ibid., p. 116.
27. *Washington Post,* op. cit.
28. Freed, pp. 114–116.
29. Ibid., p. 115.
30. *Washington Post,* op. cit.
31. *Time,* op. cit.
32. Linklater et al., p. 278.
33. Ibid., pp. 212–213.
34. Marshall et al., pp. 68–75, 253 n. 80, 254 n. 97.
35. Linklater et al., p. 213.
36. Ibid.
37. For further details on the assassination of Orlando Letelier, master-minded by Michael Vernon Townley under orders from Manuel Contreras of DINA, see *A Death in Washington* (Freed) and *Assassination on Embassy Row* (Dinges and Landau).
38. *Washington Post,* op. cit.
39. Ibid.
40. Ibid.; *Time,* op. cit.
41. *Washington Post,* op. cit.
42. *Time,* op. cit.

43. Ibid.
44. TOA, op. cit.
45. *New York Times,* Feb. 3, 1991, p. 6, "Chile Orders an End to a Mysterious Colony."
46. *TOA,* op. cit.
47. Ibid.
48. Ibid.
49. *Time,* op. cit.
50. *Washington Post,* op. cit.

CHAPTER THIRTEEN: NAZI OCCULTISM TODAY

Much of this chapter is the result of my own personal interviews and research undertaken under sometimes unpleasant circumstances.

1. Cohn, 1967, p. 254.
2. Fest, p. 555.
3. *New York Times,* Oct. 31, 1993, p. 10, "Pro-Nazi Legacy Lingers for Croatia."
4. *New York Times,* June 6, 1993, p. 44, "Freemasons Begin to Lift the Veil of Arcana" by Iver Peterson.
5. Higham, p. 69.
6. Lyons, p. 118.
7. LaVey, *Satanic Rituals,* Avon, 1980.
8. Schreck, p. 127.
9. Ackermann, p. 245.
10. Lyons, pp. 117–118.
11. *Ku Klux Klan Encyclopedia* p. 210.
12. ADL Report, *Young Nazi Killers: The Rising Skinhead Danger,* 1993, p. 31, and *Klanwatch Intelligence Report,* February, 1993, #65, p. 8.
13. Klanwatch Special Report, *The Ku Klux Klan: A History of Racism and Violence,* Fourth Edition, 1991, p. 46.
14. Speech of Khalid Abdul Mohammad, Nation of Islam National Spokesman, at Kean College, N.J., Nov. 29, 1993, included the following remarks: "You see everybody always talk about Hitler exterminating 6 million Jews. That's right. But don't nobody ever ask what did they do to Hitler? What did they do to them folks? They went in there, in Germany, the way they do everywhere they go, and they supplanted, they usurped, they turned around and a German, in his own country, would almost have to go to a Jew to get money. They had undermined

the very fabric of the society. . . . I don't care who sits in the seat at the White House. You can believe that the Jews control that seat that they sit in from behind the scenes. They control the finance, and not only that, they influence the policy making. . . . You're not the chosen people of God. Stop telling that lie. . . ," (Reprinted in *New York Times,* January 16, 1994, p. 27 by ADL) It's interesting and ironic to note that the above is in total agreement with both Nazi propaganda and neo-Nazi propaganda; the Nation of Islam, of course, would be the first on the Nazi hit list (after the ADL) if ever a white supremacist organization took power in the United States. Further remarks detailed a desire to murder white babies, women, old people, and the mentally and physically infirm in South Africa: essentially a program of racial eugenics identical to Hitler's except, of course, that only those of racially inferior—i.e., white—blood would be subject to these measures whereas in Nazi Germany the mentally and physically infirm and the aged were destroyed regardless of race.

15. *Penthouse,* Jan. 1986, Vol. 17, No. 5, p. 48ff.
16. Lyons, p. 88.
17. Ibid., pp. 108–109.
18. Sanders, 1971, p. 77.
19. *Black Flame: International Forum of the Church of Satan,* Vol. 3, Nos. 1 and 2, p. 12.
20. Ibid., p. 6.
21. Ibid., p. 15.
22. *New York Times,* Feb. 6, 1994, p. 17, "'Schindler's Dissed" by Frank Rich.
23. *New York Times,* Dec. 5, 1993, p. 14, "A Survey on Holocaust Finds Many in U.S. Ignorant of It" by Alan Riding.
24. *New York Times,* Nov. 22, 1992, p. 34, "20% In U.S. Hold Bias Against Jews."
25. *New York Times,* Sept. 19, 1993, "East London Torn by Racial Tensions" by Richard W. Stevenson.
26. Ibid.
27. *New York Times,* Dec. 9, 1993, p. A9, "Germans Sentence 2 in Firebombing" by Stephen Kinzer.
28. *New York Times,* Nov. 3, 1991, p. 16, "Klan Seizes on Germany's Wave of Racist Violence" by Stephen Kinzer.
29. Ibid.
30. Ibid.
31. Ibid.
32. *New York Times,* May 10, 1993, p. A10, "Neo-Nazi Brawls Hit Several German Cities."

33. *New York Times,* Dec. 6, 1993, p. A3, "Mayor of Vienna Wounded by Bomb."
34. *New York Times,* Dec. 12, 1993, p. 6, "In Retreat, Europe's Neo-Nazis May Become More Perilous" by Stephen Kinzer.
35. *New York Times,* Dec. 21, 1993, p. A3, "Talks on New South African Constitution at Impasse" by Kenneth B. Noble.
36. *New York Times,* Dec. 27, 1984, p. B7, "Links of Anti-Semitic Band Provoke 6-State Parley" by Wayne King.
37. Martinez, pp. 269–272.
38. Ibid., p. 273.
39. Ibid.
40. Webb, p. 312.

Bibliography

Ackermann, Josef. *Himmler.* New York: Doubleday, 1968.

Adams, Henry. *Mont-Saint-Michel and Chartres.* New York: Houghton Mifflin Company, 1933.

Anti-Defamation League. "Young Nazi Killers: The Rising Skinhead Danger," New York: ADL, 1993.

Arendt, Hannah. *Eichmann in Jerusalem.* New York: Viking, 1963. Library of Congress 63-12361.

Artucio, Hugo Fernandez. *The Nazi Underground in South America.* New York: Farrar & Rinehart, 1942.

Baigent, Michael and Leigh, Richard and Lincoln, Henry. *Holy Blood, Holy Grail.* New York: Delacorte. 1982.

———. *The Messianic Legacy.* New York: Dell Publishing. 1989. ISBN 0-440-20319-8.

Baigent, Michael and Leigh, Richard. *The Temple and the Lodge.* New York: Little, Brown & Co. 1989. ISBN 1-55970-021-1.

Baring-Gould, Sabine. *A Book of the Pyrenees.* London: Methuen & Co. 1907.

Barzun, Jacques. *Race: A Study in Superstition.* New York: Harper & Row. 1965. Library of Congress 64-25106.

Benedict, Ruth. *Race: Science and Politics.* New York: Modern Age Books. 1940.

Berenbaum, Michael. *The World Must Know: The History of the Holocaust as Told in the United States Holocaust Memorial Museum.* Boston: Little, Brown & Co. 1993. ISBN 0-316-09135-9.

Bernard, Dr. Raymond. *The Hollow Earth.* New York: University Books, Inc., 1969.

Birks, Walter and Gilbert, R. A. *The Treasure of Montségur.* Great Britain: Crucible. 1987. ISBN 0-85030-424-5.

Black Flame: International Forum of the Church of Satan, Vol. 3, Nos. 1 and 2, p. 12.

Blum, Howard. *Wanted! The Search for Nazis in America.* New York: Quadrangle. 1977. ISBN 0-8129-0607-1.

Brennecke, Fritz and Gierlichs, Paul. *Handbuch für die Schlungsarbeit in der HJ: Vom Deutschen Volk und seinem Lebensraum.* Munich: Zentralverlag der NSDAP, Franz Eher Verlag. 1937.

Bullard, Sara, ed. *The Ku Klux Klan: A History of Racism and Violence.* Montgomery, Alabama: Klanwatch, 1991.

Bullock, Sir Allan. *Hitler, A Study in Tyranny.* New York: Harper Torchbook, 1964.

Bultmann, Rudolf. *Jesus and the Word.* New York. 1934.

Cavendish, Richard. *The Black Arts.* New York. Putnam. 1967.

Charpentier, Louis. *The Mysteries of Chartres Cathedral.* London: Research into Lost Knowledge Organization. 1972.

Cocks, Geoffrey. *Psychotherapy in the Third Reich: The Göring Institute.* New York: Oxford University Press. 1985. ISBN 0-19-503461-9.

Cohn, Norman. *The Pursuit of the Millenium.* New York: Oxford University Press. 1972. ISBN 0-19-500456-6.

———. *Warrant for Genocide.* New York: Harper & Row. 1967. Library of Congress 67-11324.

Colquhoun, Ithell. *Sword of Wisdom: MacGregor Mathers and the Golden Dawn.* New York: G.P. Putnam's Sons. 1975. SBN 399-11534-8. Library of Congress 75-21919.

Conot, Robert E. *Justice at Nuremberg.* New York: Harper & Row. 1983. ISBN 0-06-015117-X.

Cookridge, E.H. *Gehlen: Spy of the Century.* New York: Random House. 1972. ISBN 0-394-47313-2. Library of Congress 71-159385.

Crowley, Aleister. *Magick in Theory and Practice.* New York: Magickal Childe Publishing. 1990.

———. *The Book of the Goetia of Solomon the King.* New York: Magickal Childe Publishing. 1989.

———. *Die Magie des Hochalters* ("The Art of Magic"). Schmiedeberg: Die Oriflamme. 1913.

———. *Von den geheimen Hochzeiten der Götter mit dem Menschen* ("Of the Secret Wedding of Gods and Men"). Schmiedeberg: Die Oriflamme. 1913.

———. *Von der Bereitung des Homunkulus* ("The Homonculus"). Schmiedeberg: Die Oriflamme. 1913.

———. *The Equinox of the Gods.* London: OTO. 1936. Published as *Equinox* Volume III, Number 3.

Das, Durga. *India from Curzon to Nehru and After.* New York: John Day Company. 1970.

De Santillana, Giorgio and Von Dechend, Hertha. *Hamlet's Mill.* Boston: Gambit, Inc. 1969.

Deacon, Richard. *A History of the British Secret Service.* New York: Taplinger Publishing Co. 1969. Library of Congress 72-107017.

Denomy, Alexander J., CSB, Ph.D. *The Heresy of Courtly Love.* New York: The Declan X. McMullen Co. 1947.

Dinges, John and Landau, Saul. *Assassination on Embassy Row.* New York: Pantheon Books. 1980. ISBN 0-394-50802-5.

Donner, Frank J. *The Age of Surveillance.* New York: Vintage Books. 1981. ISBN 0-394-74771-2.

Eisenberg, Azriel. *Witness to the Holocaust.* New York: Pilgrim Press. 1981. ISBN 0-8298-0432-3.

Ellis, Havelock. *The Task of Social Hygiene.* New York: Houghton Mifflin Co. 1915.

Epstein, Benjamin R. and Forster, Arnold. *The Radical Right.* New York: Random House. 1967. Library of Congress 67-20361.

Farago, Ladislas. *Aftermath: Martin Bormann and the Fourth Reich.* New York: Simon and Schuster. 1974.

———. *The Last Days of Patton.* New York: Berkley Books. 1982. ISBN 0-425-05388-1.

Feig, Konnilyn G. *Hitler's Death Camps: The Sanity of Madness.* New York: Holmes & Meier. 1979. ISBN 0-8419-0675-0.

Fell, Barry. *America B.C.: Ancient Settlers in the New World.* New York: Pocket Books. 1989. ISBN 0-671-67974-0. Library of Congress 75-36269.

Fernandez Artucio, Hugo. *The Nazi Underground in South America.* New York: Farrar & Rinehart. 1942.

Fest, Joachim C. *Hitler.* New York: Harcourt Brace Jovanovich. 1974.

Freed, Donald with Landis, Fred. *Death in Washington: The Murder of Orlando Letelier.* Connecticut: Lawrence Hill & Co. 1980. ISBN 0-88208-123-3. Library of Congress 80-52434.

Friedlander, Henry and Milton, Sybil, eds. *The Holocaust: Ideology, Bureaucracy, and Genocide.* The San José Papers. Milwood, NY: Kraus International Publications. 1980. ISBN 0-527-63807-2.

Friedrich, Otto. *Before the Deluge: A Portrait of Berlin in the 1920's.* New York: Harper & Row. 1972. ISBN 06-011372-3. Library of Congress 70-156522.

Gay, Peter. *Freud: A Life of Our Time.* New York: Doubleday. 1989. ISBN 0-385-26256-6.

Gilbert, Martin. *The Holocaust: A History of the Jews of Europe During the Second World War.* New York: Holt, Rinehart & Winston. 1985. ISBN 0-03-062416-9.

Godwin, Joscelyn. *Arktos: The Polar Myth in Science, Symbolism, and Nazi Survival.* Grand Rapids: Phanes Press. 1993. ISBN 0-933999-46-1.

Goodrick-Clarke, Nicholas. *The Occult Roots of Nazism.* New York: New York University Press. 1992. ISBN 0-8147-3054-X.

Grant, Kenneth. *The Magical Revival.* London: Frederick Muller, Ltd. 1972. SBN 584-10175-9.

Greiner, Joseph. *Das Ende der Hitler-Mythos.* Zurich: 1947.

Gunther, John. *Inside South America.*

Hammond, D. Corydon. *Handbook of Hypnotic Suggestions and Metaphors.* New York: Norton. 1990.

———. *Improving Therapeutic Communications,* San Francisco: Jossey-Bass. 1977.

Hauser, Thomas. *The Execution of Charles Horman: An American Sacrifice.* New York: Harcourt Brace Jovanovich. 1978.

Hedin, Sven. *My Life as an Explorer.* New York: Boni & Liveright. 1925.

Heiden, Konrad. *Der Fuehrer: Hitler's Rise to Power.* Boston: Houghton Mifflin. 1944.

Hitler, Adolf. *Mein Kampf.* Boston: Houghton Mifflin. 1943.

Hillel, Marc and Henry, Clarissa. *Of Pure Blood.* New York: McGraw Hill Book Company. 1976. ISBN 0-07-028895-X.

Higham, Charles. *American Swastika.* New York: Doubleday & Co. 1985. ISBN 0-385-17874-3. Library of Congress 82-45528.

Höhne, Heinz. *The Order of the Death's Head.* New York: Coward-McCann, Inc. 1970. Library of Congress 69-19032.

Holand, Hjalmar R. *Norse Discoveries and Explorations in America, 982–1362.* New York: Dover. 1969.

Howe, Ellic. *The Magicians of the Golden Dawn.* New York: Samuel Weiser, Inc. 1978. ISBN 0-87728-369-9.

———. *Urania's Children.* London: William Kimber. 1967.

Howe, Ellic and Möller, Helmut. *Merlin Peregrinus: Vom Untergrund des Abedlandes.* Würzburg: Köingshausen & Neumann. 1986. ISBN 3-84479-185-0.

Hüser, Dr. Karl. *Wewelsburg 1933–1945: Kult- und Terrorstätte der SS. Eine Dokumentation.* Paderborn: Verlag Bonifatius-Druckerei. 1982. ISBN 3-87088-305-7.

Hutton, J. Bernard. *Women in Espionage.* New York: The MacMillan Company. 1972. Library of Congress 79-183407.

Joffroy, Pierre. *A Spy for God: The Ordeal of Kurt Gerstein.* New York: Harcourt Brace Jovanovich. 1971.

Kater, Michael H. *Das "Ahnenerbe" der SS 1935–1945: Ein Beitrag zur Kulturpolitik des Dritten Reiches.* Stuttgart: Deutsches Verlags-Anstalt. 1974. ISBN 3-421-01623-2.

Kersten, Felix. *The Kersten Memoirs: 1940–1945.* New York: The MacMillan Company. 1957. Library of Congress 57-7888.

King, Francis. *The Magical World of Aleister Crowley.* London: Arrow Books. 1987. ISBN 0-09-951570-9.

———. *Modern Ritual Magic: The Rise of Western Occultism.* Dorset: Prism Press. 1989.

———. *Satan and Swastika.* St. Albans: Mayflower. 1976.

———. *Tantra: The Way of Action.* Rochester, VT: Destiny Books. 1986. ISBN 0-89281-274-5.

Klanwatch Intelligence Report, No. 65, Feb. 1993.

Kogon, Eugen. *The Theory and Practice of Hell.* New York: Berkley Publishing Corp. 1960.

Koppes, Clayton R. *JPL and the American Space Program: A History of the Jet Propulsion Laboratory.* New Haven: Yale University Press, 1982. ISBN 0-300-02408-8.

Landon, H. C. Robbins. *Mozart and the Masons.* New York: Thames & Hudson. 1983. Library of Congress 82-60140.

Von Lang, Jochen and Sibyll, Claus, eds. *Eichmann Interrogated: Transcripts from the Archives of the Israeli Police.* New York: Vintage Books. 1984.

Langer, Walter C. *The Mind of Adolf Hitler: The Secret Wartime Report.* New York: Basic Books. 1972.

Lifton, Robert Jay. *The Nazi Doctors.* New York: Basic Books. 1986. ISBN 0-465-04904-4.

Linklater, Magnus and Hilton, Isabel and Ascherson, Neal. *The Nazi Legacy: Klaus Barbie and the International Fascist Connection.* New York: Holt, Rinehart and Winston. 1984. ISBN 0-03-069303-9.

Loftus, John. *The Belarus Secret.* New York: Alfred A. Knopf. 1987. ISBN 0-394-52292-3.

Lyons, Arthur. *Satan Wants You: The Cult of Devil Worship in America.* New York: The Mysterious Press. 1988.

Mann, Thomas. *Doctor Faustus.* New York: Knopf. 1948.

Marks, John. *The Search for the "Manchurian Candidate": The CIA and Mind Control.* New York: Times Books. 1979.

Marshall, Jonathan and Scott, Peter Dale and Hunter, Jane. *The Iran-Contra Connection.* Boston: South End Press. 1987. ISBN 0-89608-291-1.

Martinez, Thomas. *Brotherhood of Murder.* New York: Pocket Books. 1990. ISBN 0-671-67858-2.

Masters, Anthony. *The Man Who Was M: The Life of Maxwell Knight.* New York: Basil Blackwell, Inc. 1985. ISBN 0-631-13392-5.

Marx, Karl and Engels, Friedrich. *The Communist Manifesto.* New York: Washington Square Press. 1964.

Miale, Florence R. and Selzer, Michael. *The Nuremberg Mind: The Psychology of the Nazi Leaders.* New York: Quadrangle Books. 1977. ISBN 0-8129-6280-X.

Montagu, Ashley. *Man's Most Dangerous Myth: The Fallacy of Race.* New York: Oxford University Press. 1974. Library of Congress 73-92869.

Mosse, George L. *Nazi Culture.* New York: Schocken Books. 1981. ISBN 0-8052-0668-X.

Müller-Hill, Benno. *Murderous Science: Elimination by Scientific Selection of Jews, Gypsies, and Others. Germany 1933–1945.* New York: Oxford University Press. 1988. ISBN 0-19-261555-6.

Murray, Margaret. *The Witch-Cult in Western Europe.* Oxford: Oxford University Press, 1921.

———. *The God of the Witches.* London; Sampson, Low, Marston & Co., 1933.

New Yorker, "Remembering Satan—Part II" by Lawrence Wright, May 24, 1993, Vol. LXIX, No. 14, pp. 72–73.

New York Times, "Links of Anti-Semitic Band Provoke 6-State Parley" by Wayne King, Dec. 27, 1984, p. B7.

———. "Rudolf Hess Is Dead in Berlin, Last of Hitler Inner Circle," Aug. 18, 1987, p. A1, B8–9.

———. "Nazi Victims Seek Argentine Justice" by Shirley Christian, July 10, 1988, p. 9.

———. "Chile Orders an End to a Mysterious Colony," Feb. 3, 1991, p. 6.

———. "Klan Seizes on Germany's Wave of Racist Violence" by Stephen Kinzer, Nov. 3, 1991, p. 16.

———. "Duke: The Ex-Nazi Who Would Be Governor" by Peter Applebome, November 10, 1991, p. A1.

———. "Argentina Faces Some Evil History, But Not All" by Nathanial C. Nash, February 16, 1992, p. E4.

———. "20% in U.S. Hold Bias Against Jews," Nov. 22, 1992, p. 34.

———. "Neo-Nazi Brawls Hit Several German Cities," May 10, 1993, p. A10.

———. "Freemasons Begin to Lift the Veil of Arcana" by Iver Peterson, June 6, 1993, p. 44.

———. "East London Torn by Racial Tensions" by Richard W. Stevenson, Sept. 19, 1993.

———. "London Police Battle Anti-Fascist Protestors," Oct. 17, 1993, p. A6.

———. "Pro-Nazi Legacy Lingers for Croatia," Oct. 31, 1993, p. 10.

———. "A Survey on Holocaust Finds Many in U.S. Ignorant of It" by Alan Riding, Dec. 5, 1993, p. 14.

———. "Mayor of Vienna Wounded by Bomb," Dec. 6, 1993, p. A3.

———. "Germans Sentence 2 in Firebombing" by Stephen Kinzer, Dec. 9, 1993, p. A9.

———. "In Retreat, Europe's Neo-Nazis May Become More Perilous" by Stephen Kinzer, Dec. 12, 1993, p. 6.

———. "Argentine Files Show Huge Effort to Harbor Nazis" by Nathaniel C. Nash, Dec. 14, 1993.

———. "Talks on New South African Constitution at Impasse" by Kenneth B. Noble, Dec. 21, 1993, p. A3.

———. "On Tour, Russian Nationalist Challenges Bulgarian Leader," Dec. 27, 1993, p. A6.

———. "'Schindler's' Dissed" by Frank Rich, Feb. 6, 1994, p. 17.

Newton, Michael and Judy Ann, *The Ku Klux Klan: An Encyclopedia* New York: Garland Pub., 1991.

Niel, Fernand. *Les Cathares de Montségur.* France: Robert Laffont. 1973.

Nietzsche, Friedrich. *The Philosophy of Nietzsche* (collection). New York: Modern Library. 1954.

Padfield, Peter. *Himmler: Reischführer-SS.* New York: Henry Holt & Co. 1990. ISBN 0-8050-1476-4.

Painter, Sidney. *French Chivalry.* Ithaca: Cornell University Press. 1965.

Parker, John. *At the Heart of Darkness.* New York: Citadel, 1993. ISBN 0-8065-1428-0.

Pauwels, Louis and Bergier, Jacques. *Le matin des magiciens.* Paris: Gallimard, 1960.

Payne, Robert. *The Life and Death of Adolf Hitler.* New York: Praeger. 1973. Library of Congress 72-92891.

Payne, Stanley G. *Fascism: Comparison and Definition.* Madison: University of Wisconsin Press. 1980. ISBN 0-299-08060-9.

Penthouse, "The Devil Made Me Do It" by Dr. Joel Norris and Jerry Allen Potter, Jan. 1986, Vol. 17, No. 5, p. 48ff.

Pool, James and Pool, Suzanne. *Who Financed Hitler.* New York: Dial Press. 1978. ISBN 0-8037-9039-2.

Posner, Gerald L. and Ware, John. *Mengele: The Complete Story.* New York: Dell Publishing Co. 1986. ISBN 0-440-15579-7.

Rahn, Otto. *La Cour de Lucifer: Les cathares gardiens du Graal.* Paris: Claude Tchou. 1974.

Rauschning, Hermann. *Men of Chaos.* New York: G.P. Putnam's Sons. 1942.

———. *Hitler Speaks.* London: 1939.

Ravenscroft, Trevor. *The Spear of Destiny.* New York: Putnam's Sons. 1973.

Regardie, Israel and Stephensen, P.R. *The Legend of Aleister Crowley.* Phoenix: Falcon Press. 1983. ISBN 0-941404-20-X. Library of Congress 83-81836.

Reitlinger, Gerald. *The SS: Alibi of a Nation, 1922–1945.* New York: Viking Press. 1957. Library of Congress 57-7862.

Rojas Sandford, Robinson. *The Murder of Allende.* New York: Harper & Row. 1976. ISBN 0-06-013748-7.

Rollins, Richard. *I Find Treason: The Story of an American Anti-Nazi Agent.* New York: William Morrow and Co. 1941.

Sanders, Ed. *The Family: The Story of Charles Manson's Dune Buggy Attack Battalion.* New York: E. P. Dutton & Co. 1971. ISBN 0-525-10300-7. Library of Congress 77-125906.

———. *The Family* (Revised and Updated). New York: Signet. 1990. ISBN 0-451-16563-2.

Schellenberg, Walter. *The Schellenberg Memoirs.* London: Andre Deutsch. 1956.

Schreck, Nikolas, ed. *The Manson File.* New York: Amok Press. 1988. ISBN 0-941693-04-X.

Schrötter, R. and Wüst, Walther. *Tod und Unsterblichkeit im Weltbild Indo-germanischer Denker.* Deutsches Ahnenerbe, Reihe C: Volkstümliche Schriften. Berlin: Nordland-Verlag. 1938.

Serrano, Miguel. *El/Ella: A Book of Magic Love.* New York: Harper & Row. 1972.

———. *Jung & Hesse: A Record of Two Friendships.* (Published in Spanish as "El Circulo Hermetico"). New York: Schocken Books, 1968.

———. *Adolf Hitler: el último avatara.* Santiago de Chile: La Nueva Edad. 1984.

Shannon, Elaine. *Desperados.* New York: Penguin Books. 1989. ISBN 0-451-82207-2.

Shelley, Mary. *Frankenstein.* New York: Bantam Books. 1981. ISBN 0-553-21044-0.

Simon, ed. *Necronomicon.* New York: Avon Books. 1980.

Simpson, Christopher. *Blowback: America's Recruitment of Nazis and Its Effects on the Cold War.* New York: Weidenfeld & Nicolson. 1988. ISBN 1-555-84106-6.

Von Simson, Otto. *The Gothic Cathedral.* New York: Harper Torchbooks. 1962. Library of Congress 55-11599.

Sklar, Dusty. *Gods and Beasts.* New York: Thomas Y. Crowell. 1977. ISBN 0-690-01232-2.

Sontag, Susan. *Under the Sign of Saturn.* New York: Farrar Straus Giroux. 1980.

Stefansson, Vilhjalmur. *Ultima Thule.* New York: The MacMillan Company. 1940.

Suster, Gerald. *John Dee: Essential Readings.* Great Britain: Aquarian Press. 1986. ISBN 0-85030-417-2.

Symonds, John. *The Great Beast: The Life of Aleister Crowley.* London: Rider & Co. 1951.

Taylor, Telford. *The Anatomy of the Nuremberg Trials: A Personal Memoir.* Boston: Little, Brown, 1992. ISBN 0-316-83400-9.

Terry, Maury. *The Ultimate Evil.* New York: Doubleday, 1987. ISBN 0-553-27601-8.

Thomas, Gordon. *Journey into Madness: The True Story of Secret CIA Mind Control and Medical Abuse.* New York: Bantam Books. 1990. ISBN 0-553-28413-4.

Time, "Colony of the Damned," May 16, 1988, p. 58.

Times of the Americas, "German Settlers Accused of Torture and Sexual Abuse," May 15, 1991.

Toland, John. *Adolf Hitler.* Garden City: Doubleday & Co. 1976.

Trevor-Roper, Hugh. *The Last Days of Hitler.* New York: 1962.

Trial of the Major War Criminals Before the International Military Tribunal. Vol. XX. Nuremberg: 1948.

Tusa, Ann and Tusa, John. *The Nuremberg Trial.* New York: Atheneum. 1984. ISBN 0-689-11496-6.

Waite, Robert G.L. *The Psychopathic God: Adolf Hitler.* New York: Basic Books. 1977. ISBN 0-465-06743-3.

Washington Post, "German Settlement Stirs Controversy in Chile," Dec. 25, 1987.

Webb, James. *The Occult Establishment.* La Salle, IL: Open Court. 1976. ISBN 0-912050-56-X.

West, Nigel. *Molehunt: Searching for Soviet Spies in MI5.* New York: William Morrow and Co. 1989. ISBN 0-688-07653-X.

Wheatley, Dennis. *The Devil and All His Works.* New York: American Heritage Press. 1971. Library of Congress 79-145620.

Wilson, Colin. *Aleister Crowley: The Nature of the Beast.* Great Britain: The Aquarian Press. 1987. ISBN 0-85030-541-1.

Wolpert, Stanley. *A New History of India.* New York: Oxford University Press. 1977. ISBN 0-19-502153-3.

Wulff, Wilhelm. *Zodiac and Swastika.* New York: Coward, McCann & Geoghegan. 1973. SBN 698-10547-8.

Acknowledgments

This became a very different book from the one I set out to write fifteen yeas ago. In fact, this became a very different book from the one I set out to write a *year* ago.

In the last twenty years I have been on familiar terms with several of the occult lodges and political parties described in these pages; I am not certain if one should *acknowledge* organizations such as the Ku Klux Klan or the National Renaissance Party, or the dark lords of Colonia Dignidad. I don't know if the years I have spent on the periphery (or in the middle) of such groups as the Church of Satan, Scientology, the various OTOs, the Craft, StarGroup One, and the many, many schismatic churches, sects, and underground temples of North America, South America, Europe, and Asia—years that have certainly been enlightening—merit a comprehensive rundown of all the personalities that have helped shape my . . . well, my *Weltanschauung,* if you will.

Instead, I will confine myself to thanking a few key people who made my life—and this project—easier.

A really decent study of Nazi occultism would have to be many thousands of pages longer than this one and would probably lose the general reader in a morass of footnotes and citations in German, Icelandic, Russian, Latin, Hebrew, Arabic, Greek, Sanskrit, French, Spanish, and God knows what else. What I had to content myself with in the interim, however, was this study—this exposé if you will—of the general outlines of occult theory and practice among elements of the Third Reich with a particular emphasis on the Thule Society, the SS, and the Ahnenerbe-SS. In order to help me accomplish this, I was fortunate enough to have the help of many devoted individuals who may not have believed in my story but who supported my efforts to tell it.

Ingrid Celms—once herself a victim of the Third Reich—helped with many of the translations from German into English of core Thule documents from the early (pre-WWII) period. She performed this in her spare time and with great (and perhaps distasteful) labor, and for this she has my heartfelt thanks. It should be pointed out, though, that I performed other translations and am ultimately responsible for any errors that may have crept in.

I should thank the resources and staff of the New York Public Library, Main Branch at Forty-second Street and Fifth Avenue, always my second home no matter where my first one happens to be.

The staff at the Westerly Public Library performed admirably in helping obtain hard-to-locate items from outside the state library system; they and the interlibrary loan program are to be commended.

The people at the Southern Poverty Law Center and its creature, Klanwatch—and particularly Klanwatch researcher David Webb—provided tremendous assistance in locating examples of contemporary racist activities in the United States that had a bearing on my thesis. These courageous individuals under the leadership of Morris Dees stand up to the Klan and the neo-Nazis every day of their lives—sometimes under dire threat—and are to be warmly applauded.

The Anti-Defamation League of B'nai B'rith was a source of information on Skinhead activities and statistics that were informative and vital to my work. Many thanks.

The Religious Movement Resource Center at Fort Collins, Colorado, was very helpful in helping to assess the cult aspects of the Skinhead movement and in suggesting other lines of inquiry.

Ms. Amy Schmidt of the Center for Captured Records at the National Archives was particularly generous with her time, for which I will always be grateful. And earlier, in the seventies, I had several fruitful conversations with Dr. Robert Wolfe at the National Archives, which led me onto the right path with regard to locating Ahnenerbe documentation and introducing me to the work of Michael Kater.

Amnesty International—in particular Ms. Betsy Ross—provided valuable assistance in locating documents and testimony concerning the operation of Colonia Dignidad.

Tibet House was the unexpected source of an actual *film* of the Ernst Schäfer SS-Tibet expedition, something which I previously had no idea existed, as well as an *official OSS* film of the 1942–43 Brook Dolan expedition. My thanks to Ms. Erin Gould and to Mr. Norbu Chophel for their help in locating and interpreting this valuable resource material, and in providing me with a list of other individuals and organizations specializing in Tibetan studies from the point of view of foreign expeditions.

As always, Judith McNally provided her excellent critique of the manuscript in early stages and suggested revisions. I have taken most, if not all, of her advice and any shortcomings in the finished product are the result of my stubbornness rather than her judgment.

My thanks also to my agent, Jack Scovil, for his endless patience while I struggled to provide him with a marketable property once and for all.

John Douglas, my editor at Avon, deserves recognition as a fellow conspiracy gourmet for whom paranoia is an essential condiment. Nazi occultism . . . what more paranoid a combination is there?

And, as usual, my thanks and love to Rose and Alex (excuse me, "Vivica") who suffered through endless monologues on Nazism, satanism, and the Decline of the West.

Peter Levenda
Shanghai, 1994

Index

A∴-A∴ (*Argentum Astrum*), 43, 157–159, 246
Abbey of Thelma, 284–289
Achmeteli, Dr. Michael, 237
Adolf Hitler (Toland), 46
Aftermath (Farago), 15–17, 20
Agartha legend, 66
Ahnenerbe (Ancestral Heritage Research and Teaching Society)
    application of work of, 225–226
    archaeological sites and, 178, 225
    background information, 168–169
    description of, 171–175
    Deutsche Akademie and, 174–175
    Hedin and, 173–174
    Himmler and, 172, 182
    history of, 172–174
    Hörbiger Doctrine and, 197–200
    Iceland Project and, 187–191
    legacy of, 278
    Nazi Party's image and, 169–171
Nuremberg Trials and, 277
Paderborn and, 179
pagan library of, 181
researching, 169
rune scholars and, 183–187
SS and, 167, 182–183
Tibet Expedition and, 191–197, 200
Aktion Hess, 251
Aktion Hudal (Hudal), 15, 269–270
Albigensians, 204–209
Alessandri, Jorge, 298, 315
Allende Gossens, Salvador, 14, 17, 21, 311 312, 316 318, 326
Altamirano, Carlos, 321
Anderson, Jack, 361–362
Angleton, James Jesus, 351
Anthroposophical Society, 43, 84
Anti-Semitism
    Christianity and, 349–350
    current, 345
    Ford and, 100–101
    List and, 78
    Lovecraft's, 91
    Nazi Party and, 63–64

Anti-Semitism (*continued*)
  Protocols of the Elders of Zion
    and, 47–49, 148
  "rational," 78–79
  in United States, 345
  von Liebenfels and, 78
Aquino, Michael, 339–340, 342
Arab countries, Nazis escape to,
  283
Archduke Ferdinand's assassination, 89
Argentina, 15–16, 298–299
Ark of the Covenant, 71
Armanenschaft, 56, 118
Artucio, Hugo Fernandez,
  296–297
Aryan race
  brothel for propagation of,
    127–128
  as Chosen People, 53
  flame passed on to select mem-
    bers of, 364
  Himmler and, 214–215
  as Master Race, 53, 331
  psychic powers and, 69
  racial supremacy and, 48–49,
    60, 65–66, 225
  scientific view of, 61–63
Astrologische Rundschau (Vollrath), 46
Astrology
  ban on, 161
  British intelligence services
    and, 252–253
  cult counterstrike and,
    252–253

  Hess and, 244, 250
  internal consistency in,
    240–241
  Nazi Party and, 161–164
  origins of, 161–162
  Sidereal, 162
  Third Reich history and,
    160–161
Augsburg, Dr. Emil, 237
Aylwin, Patricio, 323–324

Baar, Hugo, 323–324
Baigent, Michael, 67, 208–209,
  222–224
Baker, Stanley Dean, 336–337
Balfour, A. J., 250
Baltzli, Johannes, 46
Barbie, Klaus ("Butcher of
  Lyon"), 282, 303–308, 362
Bavaria, 33, 74
Beer Cellar Explosion (November
  1939), 235–239, 254
Beer Hall Putsch (November
  1923), 76, 92, 98, 102, 142,
  144, 168, 236
Before Hitler Came (*Bevor Hitler
  Kamm*) (Sebottendorff), 77,
  143
Beger, Dr. Bruno, 196, 277
Berg, Alan, 348
Bergier, Jacques, 110, 191
Bergson, Henry, 133
Berkowitz, David, 255
Besant, Annie, 41, 46
Birks, Walter, 208–209

Black Flame, The (Mason), 342–343

Black Order (*Schwarze Orden*), 50, 279, 349

Blavatsky, Madame Helena Petrovna, 38–41, 52, 61, 362

Bloch, Peter, 20

Blood ideology, 37–38, 112

Blood libel, 289–290

Blood Order, 142

Blood Purge (June 1934), 144, 146–147, 168

Blood religion, 214

Blood and Soil doctrine, 115

Blue Equinox, 286–287

Blunt, Anthony, 247

Bolivia, 297, 362

Book burning (May 1933), 31, 142–143

Book of the Law, The (Crowley), 120–121, 135–136, 139, 155, 359

Borghese, Prince Valerio, 321

Bormann, Martin, 15–16, 20, 271, 277

Brainwashing, 233. *See also* Psychic powers

Branch Davidian cult, 202

Braun, Eva, 102

British intelligence services
astrology and, 252–253
Crowley and, 131–133, 156
cult counterstrike and, 240–241

British National Party, 346

Brotherhood of Saturn, 136–138

Brownshirts. *See* SA (Storm Troopers)

Broyard, Anatole, 18

Buchko, Archbishop Ivan, 269–270

Büchs, Mark, 20

Bultmann, Rudolf, 83

Bulwer-Lytton, Lord, 66, 88

Busch, Gertrude "Billy," 156

Butcher of Lyon, 282, 303–308, 362

"Call to Cthulhu" ritual, 339

Cameron, Dr. Ewen, 272–273

Carnarvon, Lord, 109

Carter, Howard, 109

Caste system, 40

Cathars, 204–209, 224, 365

Catholic Church
escape of Nazis and, 15, 267–268
Humanae Vitae and, 124–125
paganism and, 293
sex and, 124
silence of, about Nazi activities, 364–365

Celmins, Gustav, 270

Chile. *See also* Colonia Dignidad
Allende and, 317–318
arrival to, 13–17, 20–23
departure from, 358–360
"disappeared" in, 17, 318
"Empty Pots" demonstration in, 317

Chile (*continued*)
  military coup in, 317–318
  Nazi Parties in, 297–298
  Nazi refugees in, 14, 16–17, 310–312
  Santiago, 311
  secret police in, 316, 318–319, 322, 359, 361
Chosen People, 53
Christian Identity movement, 350
Christianity. *See also* Catholic Church
  anti-Semitism and, 349–350
  crucifix and, 71
  Holy Grail and, 203–204
  Nazi Party and, 301, 364–365
  in South America, 300–301
Church of Satan, 329, 337–339, 343
Clement V, Pope, 70
Coburg liberation, 97–98
Cohn, Norman, 48, 96, 327
Colonia Dignidad
  accusations against, 315–316, 324
  Anderson's article on, 361
  Chilean emigrés and, 17
  Colonia Italiana versus, 25
  detention centers at, 318–320
  extension of limitations on war crimes and, 360–362
  future of, 322–326, 360–362
  growth of, 314
  language of, 314
  location of, 21–22
  name change of, 326
  Nazis and, 19
  pagan celebrations of, 325–326
  Pfeiffer and, 314–315
  Pinochet regime and, 362
  political role of, 316–318, 362
  researching, 22–26
  rumors of, 20
  Schäfer and, 313, 315, 318–320
  torture at, 305, 319–320
  visiting, 21–26, 354–358
Colonia Italiana, 25
Colony of Righteousness. *See* Colonia Dignidad
Communism
  cults and, 294
  fall of, 362
  as force of history, 341
  in Germany, 32
  Hanussen and, 105
  putsch against (Munich), 143
  Sebottendorff and, 33
  Western society's decline and, 30
Concentration camps, 171, 242, 266
Contreras, Colonel Manuel, 322
Correspondences, occult, 118, 121–122
Croatia, 328
Crowley, Aleister
  A∴-A∴ and, 43, 157

biography of, 247
Book of the Law, The and,
 120–121, 135–136, 139,
 155, 359
British intelligence services
 and, 131–133, 156
cult counterstrike and,
 241–243
deportation of, 134–135
espionage and, 131–133, 139,
 156, 241–243
female relationships of, 146
Golden Dawn and, 116–119,
 152
Holy Books and, 159–160
marriage of, 119–120, 156
noble blood and, 58
number 555 and, 91
occultism and, 108, 120–21
Ordo Templi Orientis and, 68,
 123–125, 136, 244,
 285–286
Parsons and, 244–246
sex cults and, 115–121
sex-magic and, 121–126
Thelemic community and, 285
Viereck and, 130–132
Wheatley and, 246–248
Crucifix, 71
Crusades, 71
Cult counterstrike
 American contributions to,
 254–257
 astrology and, 252–253
 British intelligence services
 and, 240–241

Crowley and, 241–243
mind-traveling and, 254
Order of the British Empire
 and, 253–254
Rollins and, 255–256
United States and, 254–257
Cults. *See also* Cult counterstrike;
 Nazi party
 Black Order, 50, 279, 349
 Branch Davidian, 202
 Communism and, 294
 deprogramming and, 294
 I AM, 62, 329
 satanic, 54, 289–295
 sex, 115–121, 127–128
 Son of Sam, 255
 in United States, 289–295,
 366
 war inside Nazi, 147–151,
 156–157
 witch, 180

D-Day invasion (June 1944), 263
DAP (*Deutsche Arbeiterpartei*),
 77–78, 91
Darré, Richard Walther, 115,
 172, 189, 283
Darwin, Charles, 38–39,
 340–341
D'Aubuisson, Major Roberto,
 307–308
Dauthendey, Max, 57
De Santillana, Professor Giorgio,
 61–62, 212
Deacon, Richard, 119

Deboo, Jeffrey, 343
Dee, John, 118–119
Delle Chiaie, Stefano, 282, 306–308, 321
Democracy, 154–155, 300
Deprogramming, 294
Deutsche Akademie, 110–111, 174–175
Devigny, André, 304–305
Devil and All His Works, The (Wheatley), 243
Devil worship, 293
Die Sphinx, 42
Die Spinne (The Spider), 295
Dietrich Eckart Society, 220
DINA, 316, 318–319, 322, 359, 361
"Disappeared" in Chile, 17, 318
Doctor Faustus, 31
Doubling phenomenon, 200–202
Draganovic, Monsignor/Dr. Krunoslov, 270, 305–306
Drexler, Anton, 36, 77
Dreyfus Affair, 48
Driberg, Tom, 246–247
Drug trade, neo-Nazi, 307
Dulles, Allen, 272–273, 297

Ebertin, Frau Elsbeth, 98–100
Eckart, Dietrich
    Ford (Henry) and, 100–102
    Hitler and, 92–95, 100
    mystical concepts and, 93
    occultism and, 92–95
    Rosenberg and, 114
    Thule Gesellschaft and, 78
Edda, 61–62, 64, 187
Edelweiss Society, 134
Ehrhardt Free Corps Brigade, 35–36, 95–96
Eichmann, Adolf, 148–149, 237
Eisner, Kurt, 32–34, 75
Elser, Georg, 236
"Empty Pots" demonstration, 317
Encausse, Gerard, 43
Engles, Friedrich, 30
Enochian (occult correspondences), 118
Ernst, Karl, 105
Espionage. See also British Intelligence
    Anne (code name) and, 253–254
    Barbie and, 305
    Crowley and, 131–133, 139, 156, 241–243
    German Intelligence and, 133
    occultism and, 132–134
    Reuss and, 133
    Rollins and, 255–256
    Viereck and, 130–132
Evolution, 29–30, 38–39, 340–341
Externsteine monument, 175

Family, The (Sanders), 288
Farago, Ladislas, 15–16, 267, 319, 324

Farrakhan, Louis, 335
Fascism, 62, 109, 226, 228
Fatherland, The, 129, 132, 241
Felkin, Dr. R. W., 117–118
Fell, Barry, 52
Feminism, 68
Fest, Joachim, 46
Fleming, Ian, 241, 243, 248–250
Ford, Henry, 100–102, 201
Forsythe, Frederick, 266–267
Foucault, Michel, 37–38, 112
*Foundations of National Socialism,
    The* (Hudal), 269
France, 35
Franco, Generalissimo Francisco,
    322
Frankenstein, Victor, 141
Frankhouser, Roy, 19, 332–334
"Frater H," 245–246
Frater Saturnus. *See* Grosche, Eu-
    gene
Frater Uranus. *See* Germer, Karl
Freemasons
    Eichmann and, 148–149
    fear about, general, 150–151
    Göring and, 150–151
    Himmler and, 153–154
    lineage of, 153
    Nazi Party and, 147–151,
        154–155, 364
    Ordo Templi Orientis and, 158
    Rosenberg and, 114
    secrecy of, 151–153
    studies of, 153–154
Frei, Eduardo, 316

Freikorps (Free Corps), 34–36,
    90, 95–97
Freud, Sigmund, 130, 165
Fritsch, Theodor, 73
Fuenzalida, Samuel, 322
Führerprinzip (Führer principle),
    202, 350–351
Fuller, Major General C.F., 116

Gadal, Antonin, 210
GALCIT (Guggenheim Aeronau-
    tical Laboratory, California
    Institute of Technology),
    245
García Márquez, Gabriel, 311
Gaunt, Sir Guy, 249–250
Gebhard, Marie, 42
Geheime Staatspolizei (Gestapo or
    Secret State Police), 169
Genocide. *See* Holocaust
German Intelligence, 133
German School Bund, 33
German Theosophical move-
    ment, 38, 45–46
German Workers' Party, 77, 91.
    See also Nazi Party
German-American Bund, 256,
    328
Germanenorden (German Order
    Walvater of the Holy Grail),
    33, 73–77, 79, 123, 154,
    185
Germany
    book burning in, 31, 142–143
    Communism in, 32

Germany (*continued*)
  post-World War I, 32–36, 89
  right wing in, 35
  Thule Gesellschaft's rise in,
    33–36
Germer, Karl, 133, 135–137,
    139, 155–157, 159–160,
    286
Germer, Sascha, 287
Gestapo (*Geheime Staatspolizei* or
    Secret State Police), 169
Gilbert, R. A., 208–209
Glauer, Adam Alfred Rudolf. *See*
    Sebottendorff, Baron Ru-
    dolf von
Glimpses of the Great (Viereck),
    130
Glinka, Yuliana, 47–48
Goebbels, Dr. Joseph, 238, 282,
    330
Golden Dawn
  Crowley and, 116–119, 152
  Hermetic Order of, 43
  List and, 118
  Mathers and, 56–57
  origin of, 84
  "Secret Chief" idea in, 65
  Tree of Life symbol and, 117
Gonzalez, Jorge, 297
Goodrick-Clarke, Nicholas, 118
Göring, Hermann, 150–151,
    243, 272
Gorsleben, Rudolf John,
    184–185
Grail. *See* Holy Grail

Great Beast, The (Symonds), 247
Greiner, Josef, 88–89
Greystone estate, 255
Grosche, Eugene, 136–139, 157
Guevara, Che, 311
Gutberlet, Wilhelm, 106–107,
    228–229

Hakenkreuz (hooked cross), 58.
    See also Swastika
Hamilton, Gerald, 156
Hamlet's Mill (de Santillana), 61
Hammond, Dr. D. Corydon,
    289, 293, 326
Hanussen, Erik Jan, 102–105,
    142
Hartman, Dr. Wilhelm, 229
Hartmann, Dr. Franz, 43–45,
    123
Hauser, Thomas, 17
Haushofer, Albrecht, 114, 242,
    244, 251, 263
Haushofer, Karl, 109–112, 114,
    133–134, 174, 242, 263,
    338
Hedin, Sven, 89, 92, 173–174,
    192
Hegal rune, 184–185
Heiden, Konrad, 309–310
Heimsoth, Dr. Karl-Günther,
    164
Heinrich, Wolf, 105
Hell, described
Helms, Richard, 273–274
Hennig, Richard, 51

Heraldry, occultists' interest in, 58

Hering, Johannes, 76

Herzl, Theodor, 48

Hess, Rudolf
astrology and, 244, 250
death of, 272
flight to England by, 112–113, 160–161, 242, 248–252
Hitler and, 92, 109–111, 113
Nuremberg Trials and, 272–276

Hidden Masters tradition, 65

Hielscher, Dr. Friederich, 173–174, 278

Himmler, Heinrich
afterlife and, 330
Ahnenerbe and, 172, 182
Aryan race and, 214–215
final days of, 263–265
Freemasons and, 153–154
Hidden Masters tradition and, 65
Holy Grail and, 203–204
ideological opponents of, 215
Lebensborn and, 69
missing children and, 289
paganism and, 67, 176, 180
Rahn and, 212–213, 216–217
Röhm's death and, 147
Schellenberg and, 176, 191, 205–206, 264
SS and, 167–168, 175

Hirsig, Alma, 132

Hirsig, Leah, 132, 137

Hitler, Adolf
ascension to power and, 141–143, 261
assassination attempts against, 114, 235, 263
blackmail plot against, 144–146
blinding injury of, 89–90
Coburg liberation and, 97–98
commando unit of, 295–296
as cult leader, 352–353
Ebertin's letter to, 98–100
Eckart and, 92–95, 100
Ford and, 101
Führerprinzip and, 350–351
Greiner and, 88–89
Gutberlet and, 106, 228–229
Hanussen and, 102–105
Haushofer and, 109–112
Hess and, 92, 109–111, 113
Mein Kampf and, 48, 102, 109, 145
mother's death and, 85
Mussolini's rescue and, 227
nadir of political career and, 102
National Socialism and, 327
Nazi Party and, 36, 90–92
number 555 and, 90–91
occultism and, 80–81, 86–87, 89, 144, 167
opera and, 87–88
popularity of, growing, 94–95
poverty of, 87
prison sentence of, 36, 109

Hitler, Adolf (*continued*)
  Rosenberg and, 114–115
  Schellenberg and, 80, 106, 108, 123
  schooling of, 59, 82–85
  synchronicity in life of, 261–262
  Twenty-Five Point program and, 94
  von Liebenfels and, 68, 87
Holand, Hjalmar R., 51
Holocaust, 142, 345, 363
Holy Blood, Holy Grail (Baigent, Leigh, and Lincoln), 67, 208–209, 222–224
Holy Books (Crowley), 159–160
Holy Grail
  Cathars and, 204–209, 224
  Christianity and, 203–204
  crusade against, 204–209, 221
  Himmler and, 203–204
  Holy Blood, Holy Grail and, 208–209, 222–224
  Lucifer's Servants and, 217–222
  Order of the Knights of Templar and, 207–208
  Parzival and, 208–214
  Protocols of the Elders of Zion and, 67
Holy Inquisition, 83–84
Hörbiger Doctrine, 197–200
Hörbiger, Hans, 197–200
Howe, Ellic, 238
Hubbard, Ron L., 246, 288

Hübber-Schleiden, Dr. Wilhelm, 42
Hudal, Bishop Alois, 268–271
Human sacrifice, 95–97, 178–179, 362
Human Vitae, 124–125
Hüser, Dr. Karl, 221–222
Hutton, J. Bernard, 254

I AM cult, 62, 329
I Find Treason (Rollins), 256
Iceland, 64
Iceland Project, 187–191
Illuminaten Orden, 153
India, 43, 93
Intermarium Society, 270
International, The, 132, 241
Isis Unveiled (Blavatsky), 38, 40
Israel, 328
ITT, 316–317

Japanese troops, 232
Jehovah, 218–219
Jews. *See also* Anti-Semitism
  blood libel and, 290
  Holocaust and, 142, 345, 363
  Masonic Society and, 48
  Star of David and, 58
Jones, Charles Stansfeld, 244
Jones, Jim, 350
Juan Rene Muñoz Alarcon, 322
Jung, Carl, 261

Kelley, Edward, 118–119, 202
Kellner, Karl, 121

Kelly, Gerald, 119, 133
Kelly, Rose, 119
Kensington Stone, 51–52
Kersten, Felix, 65, 162–163, 264
King, Francis, 285
King Tut's tomb, opening of, 109
Kissinger, Henry, 312
Knight, Maxwell, 247–248, 250
Knowledge and Conversation of
    his Holy Guardian Angel,
    157–158, 343
Koch, Gauleiter, 259, 261
Koresh, David, 202, 350
Korry, Edward, 317
Krafft, Karl Ernst, 236–239, 252
Krause, Wolfgang, 51
Kristallnacht (1938), 142
Krohn, Dr. Friedrich, 91
Ku Klux Klan, 19, 332–333, 335,
    350
Kuhn, Fritz, 142, 255–256, 328
Kullak-Ublick, Horst, 323
Küntzel, Marthe, 137, 155, 157

Ladame, Paul, 219–220
LaRouche, Lyndon, 334
Last Days of Hitler (Trevor-
    Roper), 162
LaVey, Anton Szandor, 332–333,
    337–339, 343
Lebensborn society, 127–128,
    168–169
Lebensraum ("living room"), 42,
    111–112, 128, 363

Lebensreform ("life reform"), 44, 61
Lehder Rivas, Carlos, 302–303
Lehmann, Julius, 33
Leigh, Richard, 67, 208–209,
    222–224
Leighton, Bernardo, 321
Lennon, John, 302
Letelier, Orlando, 21, 307, 320–
    322, 326
Lévi, Eliphas, 42
Lévi-Strauss, Claude, 55
Lifton, Dr. Robert J., 200
Lincoln, Henry, 67, 208–209,
    222–224
Lindeman, Whilhelmine, 315
Link, The, 249
List, Guido von
    anti-Semitism and, 78
    death of, 61
    Golden Dawn and, 118
    List Society and, 60–62
    noble blood and, 56, 60
    occultism and, 55–58, 84
    runes and, 50, 52
    thesis of, 58
    Thule Gesellschaft and, 33
    Tree of Life symbol and, 118
    Völkisch movement and, 61
List Society, 60–62
Lopez Riga, José, 307, 310
Lovecraft, H.P., 91, 170
Loveday, Raoul, 135
Lucifer's Servants (Rahn), 182–
    183, 217–222
Lüdecke, Kurt, 349

Lumen Club or Lodge, 133–134
Lundeen, Ernest, 131

MI5, 241, 247–248, 254
McMurtry, Grady, 286–288, 344
Madole, James, 19, 331–332
Magick, 120–121, 248, 285
Mahon, Dennis, 346
Malina, Frank J., 245
Mandrake ritual, 104
Mann, Thomas, 31
Manson, Charles, 64, 287–288, 291–292, 336, 338, 366
Mao, Tse-tung, 30
Marks, John, 235, 273
Marriage, sex and, 126–129
Martinez, Thomas, 349
Marx, Karl, 30, 341
Marxism, 269
Mason, James, 342–343
Masons. See Freemasons
Master Race, 53, 331
"Master of the Sidereal Pendulum," 228–229
Mathers, S. L. "MacGregor," 56–57, 113, 133
MCLN, 302
Medellin drug cartel, 302, 307
Medical experimentation, 233–235, 273
Mein Kampf (Hitler), 48, 102, 109, 145
Mengele, Dr. Josef, 16
Mescaline experiments, 233–234, 273

Metzger, Tom, 334, 351
Meza, Garcia, 307
Mind traveling, 254
Mind-control, 233. See also Psychic powers
Missing (Hauser), 17
MNS, 297
Moffit, Ronnie, 322, 326
Molay, Grandmaster Jacques de, 70
Molinas, Francisco, 23–24
Morning of the Magicians (Le matin des magiciens) (Pauwels and Bergier), 110, 191
Morte d'Arthur, Le (Malory), 208, 219, 223
Movimiento Civico Latino Nacional (MCLN), 302
Mudd, Norman, 137
Müller, A.E., 178–179
Müller, Heinrich, 270–271
Müller, Wolfgang, 315, 324–325
Münchener Beobachter, 34–35
Mussolini (Il Duce), 109, 226–229
My Life as an Explorer (Hedin), 173

Narco-terrorism, 307
National Renaissance Party, 19, 329, 331–332, 363
National Socialism, 327–329
National Socialist German Workers' Party (NSDAP). See Nazi Party

National Socialist Movement
   (*Movimiento Nacional Socialista*) (MNS), 297
Nauhaus, Walter, 76
Naval Research Institute,
   229–232
Nazi occultism
   Aquino and, 339
   modern, 328–330
   race theories and, 341–342
   study of, 31–32
Nazi Party
   Ahnenerbe and image of,
      169–171
   American view of, 169–171
   anti-Semitism and, 63–64
   in Argentina, 298
   astrology and, 161–164
   in Chile, 297–298
   Christianity and, 301,
      364–365
   cult of, 47, 155, 352–353
   cult war, 147–151, 156–157
   Darré and, 115
   democracy and, 154–155
   Ford (Henry) and, 101
   formation of, 36
   Freemasons and, 147–151,
      154–155, 364
   Hitler and, 36, 90–92
   neo-Nazism and, 46–47
   preservation of, 19, 280–284
   Protocols of the Elders of Zion
      and, 47–49
   Rosenberg and, 115

Sebottendorff and, 143
sex and marriage and,
   126–129
Skinheads and, 19
swastika and, 58–59, 91
Thule Gesellschaft and, 36
Völkisch movement and, 57
World Ice Theory and,
   197–200
Nazi/Satanist conspiracy, 291–
   293, 337
Nazis. *See also* Nazi Party; *specific
   names*
   American propaganda films
      and, 281–282
   Colonia Dignidad and, 19
   devil worship and, 293
   Edda and, 64
   escape of, from Germany, 14–
      16, 267–268, 280–284
   letter bombs of, 347
   satanism and, 336–337
Nazism
   apologists, 293–294
   LaVey and, 338–339
   paganism and, 181, 279
   Péron and, 298
   racism and, 343
   resurgence of, 18–19
   threat, continuing, 308
   underground, in South
      America, 310, 361–362
   in United States, 328–330
Nebe, Arthur, 229
Necronomicon, 91, 109, 170, 339

Neff, Walter, 273

Neo-Nazi movement, 46–47, 293, 302, 329, 348–352

Neruda, Pablo, 21

Nietzsche, Friedrich, 27, 88

Nixon, Richard, 284, 312

Nordic World-Tree, 178, 182

Norris, Dr. Joel, 336

Nostradamus prophecies, 239, 252

NRP, 332

NSDAP (National Socialist German Workers' Party). *See* Nazi Party

Nuremberg Laws, 110

Nuremberg Trials
  Ahnenerbe and, 277
  Bormann and, 277
  Haushofer (Karl) and, 114
  Hess and, 272–276
  Rosenberg and, 271–272
  Sievers and, 277–279

OBE, 253–254

Occultism. *See also* Nazi occultism
  Allies and, 240
  Blavatsky and, 362–363
  blood ideology and, 37–38, 112
  conspiracy and, 113
  correspondences and, 118, 121–122
  Crowley and, 108, 120–121
  Eckart and, 92–95

espionage and, 132–134
  Gutberlet and, 106–107
  Hanussen and, 102–105
  Hitler and, 80–81, 86–87, 89, 144, 167
  List and, 55–58, 84
  moral environment and, 362
  Nazi ban on, 113, 134
  Nazi organizations and, 350–351
  racism and, 47
  runes and, 49–54
  Russian, 284
  self and, 157–158
  sex and, 37–38, 112
  study of, 18–19, 31–32
  von Liebenfels and, 84–85, 87
  Western, 44

ODESSA (Organization of former SS Officers), 266–267, 295

O'Higgins, Bernardo, 22

Ohlendorf, Otto, 70, 115

OHO (Outer Head of the Order), 123, 135–136, 139, 285–287

ONT (Order of the New Templars), 68–72

Order of the British Empire (OBE), 253–254

Order of the Eastern Temple. *See Ordo Templi Orientis* (OTO)

Order of the Knights Templar, 207–208

Order of the New Templars
    (ONT), 68–72
Order, The, 348–349
Ordo Templi Orientis (OTO)
    ban on, 155
    Crowley and, 68, 123–125,
        136, 244, 285–286
    formation of, 43
    Freemasons and, 158
    McMurtry and, 286–287
    sex-magic and, 138–140
    splintering of, 285–286
    Swiss, 284–286
OSS, 273
Ostara, 67–68, 80, 86–87, 92
OTO. *See Ordo Templi Orientis*
Outer Head of the Order
    (OHO), 123, 135–136, 139
Overholser, Dr. Winfred, 234

P-2 Society, 307, 324
Paderborn, 179
Paganism
    Catholic Church and, 293
    Colonia Dignidad celebrations
        and, 325–326
    Himmler and, 67, 176, 180
    Nazism and, 181, 279
    Nordic, 33
    Odinic, 49
    Walpurgisnacht and, 34, 83,
        115, 337–338
Pakmor, Georg, 322–323
Pakmor, Lotti, 322–323
Palm Sunday Putsch, 34

Pan-German movement, 33–34,
    49, 63. *See also Völkisch*
    movement
Parsons, Jack, 244–246, 286
Parzifal, 87–88, 208–214, 219,
    223
Pastor, Eilert, 51
Patria y Libertad (Fatherland and
    Liberty), 317–318, 324
Patton, General George, 268
Paul VI, Pope, 15
Pauwels, Louis, 110, 191
Pelley, William Dudley, 62
Péron, Juan Domingo, 15–16,
    298–299, 310
Pervitin experiments, 235–236
Pfeiffer, Franz, 314–315
Phillipe le Bel (king of France),
    70
"Phony war," 192–193
Pike, Albert, 333
Pinochet, General Augusto, 17,
    321–322, 359, 362
Pius XII, Pope, 269
Ploetz, Dr. Alfred, 189
Plötner, Dr. Kurt, 233–234, 273
Pohl, Hermann, 33, 74
Polanski, Roman, 338
Politics of sex, 126–130
Potter, Jerry Allen, 336
Process Church of the Final Judg-
    ment, 329–330, 337
Protocols of the Elders of Zion
    anti-Semitism and, 47–49,
        148

Protocols of the Elders of Zion
  (*continued*)
  Blavatsky and, 40, 362
  dissemination of, widespread,
    94
  Holy Grail and, 67
  in modern times, 334–336
  Nazi Party and, 47–49
  Rosenberg and, 150
Psychic powers
  application of, 225–226
  Aryan race and, 69
  Beer Cellar Explosion and,
    235–239
  Mussolini's rescue and,
    226–227
  Naval Research Institute and,
    229–232
  suicidal fanaticism and,
    232–235
  "truth drug" and, 233–235
Psychopathic God, The (Waite), 47

Race eugenics programs, 69
Racial purity. *See* Aryan race
Racial supremacy, 48–49, 60,
    65–66, 225
Racism, 47, 343, 346–347, 353,
    365–366
Rahn, Otto, 126–127, 182–183,
    208–211, 213–214,
    217–222
Rascher, Sigmund, 225, 234
Rathenau, Walther, 95–97, 178
Raubal, Geli, 145–146

Rauff, Walter, 270–271
Rebozo, Bebe, 101
Rehse, J.F.M., 145–146
Reich's Security Headquarters
    (RSHA), 148, 237
Religion and science, 40
Reuss, Theodor, 123, 133, 136,
    139, 286
Rienzi, 87–88
Rites of Eleusis, 126
Rodriguez Grez, Pablo, 315
Roeder, Captain Hans A., 230
Roeder, Manfred, 349
Röhm, Ernst, 96, 144, 147, 164,
    168, 282–283, 297
Röhm Purge, 105, 137, 164, 263
Rollins, Richard, 255–256
Roman Catholic Church. *See*
    Catholic Church
Romero, Bishop, 308
Rosemary's Baby (film), 338–339
Rosenberg, Alfred, 92, 114–115,
    150, 154, 189, 271–272
Rosicrucian Order, 66, 248
RSHA (*Reichsicherheitshauptamt*
    or Reich Security Service),
    148, 237
Runes
  Blavatsky and, 52
  described, 50
  Edda, 62, 64
  finding, 50–51
  hegal, 184–185
  Kensington Stone, 51–52
  List and, 50, 52

occultism and, 49–54
scholars of, 183–187
Sebottendorff and, 50
studies of, 51–52

SA (Storm Troopers), 97, 168
Sanders, Alex, 338
Sanders, Ed, 288
Sanguinity impulse, 37
Santiago (Chile), 311
Satanic Abuse Survivors, 292
Satanic Cult Survivor hysteria, 289, 293
Satanic cults, 54, 289–295
Satanism, Nazis and, 336–337
Schäfer, Dr. Ernst, 174, 192–197, 199
Schäfer, Paul, 313, 315–316, 318–320, 323–324, 355
Schellenberg, Walter
 Elser and, 236
 Himmler and, 176, 191, 205–206, 264
 Hitler and, 80, 106, 108, 123
 ITT and, 317
 Mussolini's arrest and, 227
Schneider, Rudi, 82
Schneider, Willy, 82
Schönhuber, Franz, 347
Schrötter, R., 181
Schulte-Strathaus, Dr. Ernst, 250
Schwartz-Bostunitsch, Dr. Gregor, 134, 148
Schwarz, Franz X., 145
Schweizer, Dr. Bruno, 189–191

Schwend, Freddy, 306
Science and religion, 40
Scientology, 246
SD (*Sicherheitsdienst* or Security Service), 148–149, 304, 317
Search for the "Manchurian Candidate," The (Marks), 235
Sebottendorff, Baron Rudolf von
 Before Hitler Came and, 77, 143
 birth date of, 141
 Communism and, 33
 Freikorps and, 34
 Germanenorden and, 73–77
 Nazi Party and, 143
 post-World War I activities and, 143–144
 runes and, 50
 South American travels of, 283
 suicide of, 147, 265
 Thule Gesellschaft and, 46–47, 79
 Vollrath and, 46
Secret Doctrine, The (Blavatsky), 38–41, 61
Self, occultism and, 157–158
Serrano, Miguel, 182, 197, 312
Sesselmann, Marc, 94
Sex
 Catholic Church and, 124
 cults, 115–121, 127–128
 ideology, 37–38, 112
 marriage and, 126–129
 mystication of act of, 138
 occultism and, 37–38, 112

Sex (*continued*)
    politics of, 126–130
Sex-magic, 45, 121–126,
    138–140
Sexuality impulse, 37, 112
Shelton, Robert, 333
Sidereal astrology, 162
Sidereal pendulum, 106–107,
    228–229
Siege (Mason), 342–343
Sievers, Wolfram, 172, 174, 179,
    233–234, 277–279
Silver Shirts, 62
Six, Dr. Franz, 70, 115, 237–238
Skinheads
    economics and, 345–346
    future and, 344–352
    informing of truth and, 366
    Metzger and, 334
    Nazi Party and, 19
    origin of, 345
    rise in number of, 18–19
Skorzeny, Otto, 229, 295–296
Social Darwinism, 69–70
Sollmann, Max, 283
Son of Sam cult, 255
South America. *See also specific*
    countries
    Christianity in, 300–301
    Nazi underground in, 310,
        361–362
    Nazis' escape to, 14–16,
        282–283
    politics, 299–300
Soviet Union, 32, 90, 263, 284

Sprengel, Anna, 117–118
SS (*Schutzstaffel*)
    Ahnenerbe and, 167, 182–183
    background information,
        168–169
    cult of, 167, 183
    doubling phenomenon and,
        200–202
    headquarters, 175–178
    Himmler and, 167–168, 175
    ODESSA and, 266–267, 295
    pagan rituals of, new, 176–181
    religious ceremonies and, ban
        on, 176
    secrecy and, 175–176
    Tibet Expedition and, 191–
        197, 200
    after World War II, 266
Star of David, 58
Steiner, Dr. Rudolf, 43, 46, 84,
    93, 118, 123, 148
Steinschneider, Herschel. *See* Ha-
    nussen, Erik Jan
Stempfle, Fr. Bernhard, 34, 109,
    144–146
Storm Troopers. *See* SA
Straniak, Ludwig, 230–232
Strasser, Gregor, 164
Strasser, Otto, 236
Streicher, Julius, 63, 290
Strowigk, Hans, 149
Suicidal fanaticism, 232–235
Swastika
    design of, 58–59
    Manson and, 64

Nazi Party and, 58–59, 91
symbolism of, 58–60
Universal Order and, 342
"Swastika Circle," 163
Symonds, John, 156, 247, 250
Synchronicity, 261–262

Tantric rituals, 122–123
Tate, Sharon, 64, 291–292, 338
Tchaikovsky, Peter Ilich, 85
Temple of Set, 337–343
Terry, Maury, 255, 288–289
Teutonic Grail Order, 66–67
Teutonic legend, 49–50, 55–56,
    62–64, 197, 211
Thelema, 124
Thelemic community, 285–286,
    310
Theosophical Society
    birth of, 38
    Blavatsky and, 38–41
    German Section of, 42–47
    Hartmann and, 43
    headquarters of, 43
    impact of, 362–363
Third Reich, 37, 48, 78, 160–
    161. *See also* Hitler, Adolf;
    Nazi Party
Thomson, Basil, 250
Thule, 64–65, 182–183
Thule Gesellschaft (Thule Society)
    Blavatsky and, 362
    Eckart and, 78
    List and, 33
    meetings of, 33

modern, 330–334
Nazi Party and, 36
Palm Sunday Putsch and, 34
philosophy of, 37–38
power struggle of, in Munich,
    33–34
rise of, in Germany, 33–36
Sebottendorff and, 46–47, 79
secrecy and, 154
symbol of, 33
ultra-right groups in, 72–79
von Liebenfels and, 33
Tibet Expedition, 191–197, 200
Tilden estate in Yonkers, 255
Time Machine, The (Wells), 66
Toland, John, 46
Townley, Michael Vernon, 307,
    317–322
Tränker, Heinrich, 135–136, 155
Tree of Life symbol, 117–118
Trithemius, Johannes, 119
Trujillo, Rafael, 131
Turner Diaries, The, 348
Turner, Patricia A., 335
Tuskegee Syphilis Project, 335

Ultima Thule, 62–66, 191
Ultimate Evil, The (Terry),
    288–289
United States
    anti-Semitism in, 345
    cult counterstrike and,
        254–257
    cults in, 289–295, 366
    Klan in, 19

United States (*continued*)
  Nazism in, 328–330
  neo-Nazi movement in,
    348–352
  race eugenics programs in, 69
  satanic cults in, 289–295
Universal Order, 342
Untermyer, Sam, 255–256
Urania's Children (Howe), 238

Viereck, George Sylvester, 129–
  132, 242
Villa Bavaria (Bavarian Village).
  See Colonia Dignidad
Völkisch movement
  apologists, 54
  Aryan supremacy and, 65–66
  Hedin's writings and, 173
  List and, 61
  Nazi Party and, 57
  salvation and, 49
  translation of term of, 61
Völkischer Beobachter, 35, 92,
  106, 154, 188
Vollrath, Hugo, 44–46
Von Braun, Dr. Wernher,
  283–284
Von Bülow, Werner, 185
Von Eschenbach, Wolfram,
  208–210
Von Fritsch, General, 176
Von Karman, Theodore, 245
Von Kleist, Captain Franz Rin-
  telen, 250
Von Liebenfels, Jörg Lanz
  anti-Semitism and, 78

escape to Switzerland by, 284
Hitler and, 68, 87
Hudal and, parallels to,
  268–269
noble blood and, 56
occultism and, 84–85, 87
Order of the New Templars
  and, 68–72
satanic cults and, 54
Social Darwinism and, 69–70
Teutonic Grail Order and,
  66–67
Thule Gesellschaft and, 33
Von Oven, General, 35
Von Owen, Wilfried, 282
Vorkommando Moskau, 237

Wagner, Richard, 87–88,
  209–210
Waite, Arthur Edward, 210, 285
Waite, Robert G. L., 47
Waldensians, 205–206
Walpurgis, 269
Walpurgisnacht, 34, 83, 115,
  337–338
Walsingham, Sir Francis, 119
Warrant for Genocide (Cohn), 48
Webb, James, 18
Weisfeiler, Boris, 323
Weishaupt, Adam, 153
Wells, H. G., 66
Westcott, Dr. William Wynn, 43,
  118
Western society's decline, 30
Wewelsburg, 177–178, 340

Wewelsburg Working, 340

Wheatley, Dennis, 241, 243, 246–248

Wiesenthal, Simon, 16, 362

Wiligut, Karl Maria, 193, 211–212, 221, 224

Wirth, Hermann, 172

Witch cults, 180

Witches' Sabbath, 83, 261–262

Wohl, Louis de, 252

World Anti-Nazi Council, 255

World Ice Theory, 197–200

World War II
    final days of, 263–265
    ignorance about, 344
    impact of, 327–328
    mass destruction of files at end
      of, 265–266

science fiction image of, 170–171

SS after, 266

Wulff, Wilhelm, 161–164, 229, 232, 253, 263–265

Wüst, Dr. Walther, 174–175, 181, 192

Yarker, John, 44

Yggdrasil, 178, 182

Yugoslavia, 228, 284, 328, 348

Zenit, forged, 253

Zhirinovsky, Vladimir W., 284

Zilk, Helmut, 347

Zodiac and Swastika (Wulff), 161, 164, 229

ZOG (Zionist Occupation Government), 351